BLIND MAN'S BREXIT

LODE DESMET and
EDWARD STOURTON

BLIND MAN'S BREXIT

How the EU took control
of Brexit

SIMON &
SCHUSTER

London · New York · Sydney · Toronto · New Delhi

A CBS COMPANY

First published in Great Britain by Simon & Schuster UK Ltd, 2019
A CBS COMPANY

Copyright © Lode Desmet and Edward Stourton, 2019

The right of Lode Desmet and Edward Stourton to be identified
as the authors of this work has been asserted in accordance
with the Copyright, Designs and Patents Act, 1988.

1 3 5 7 9 10 8 6 4 2

Simon & Schuster UK Ltd
1st Floor
222 Gray's Inn Road
London WC1X 8HB

www.simonandschuster.co.uk
www.simonandschuster.com.au
www.simonandschuster.co.in

Simon & Schuster Australia, Sydney
Simon & Schuster India, New Delhi

The author and publishers have made all reasonable efforts
to contact copyright-holders for permission, and apologise
for any omissions or errors in the form of credits given.
Corrections may be made to future printings.

A CIP catalogue record for this book
is available from the British Library

Hardback ISBN: 978-1-4711-8642-4
eBook ISBN: 978-1-4711-8643-1

Typeset in Perpetua by M Rules

Printed and bound by CPI Group (UK) Ltd, Croydon, CR0 4YY

MIX
Paper from
responsible sources
FSC
www.fsc.org   FSC® C020471

CONTENTS

INTRODUCTION

Our First Colony –
How Europe Took Control of Brexit

That day was spent hanging around. The marathon negotiations to agree the terms of the United Kingdom's exit from the European Union had at last been brought to a conclusion, and on 14 November 2018 everyone in the European Parliament in Strasbourg was waiting for Theresa May to come out of her Cabinet meeting in London and say the magic words: they have agreed to my deal – the infamous Article 50 Withdrawal Agreement. But the meeting took longer than hoped for – although not really longer than expected – and Guy Verhofstadt, the Brexit coordinator of the European Parliament, got restless. He kept checking his watch and the messages crawling along the bottom of the TV screen in his office. 'Come on, statement following Cabinet meeting at Downing Street, but she's not doing it for the moment.' Everybody was expecting good news – those were the rumours than had filtered through – but the delay was going to mess up Verhofstadt's whole evening. His press team had loads of interviews lined up for him to react to the decision in London. But what was he going to say if there was no decision? 'I can't come on TV with the message: we're waiting; it's taking longer than expected.' He told them to cancel everything and they took off to their own office two floors below.

I fled the scene as well, because after two years of filming him, I had learned when to hide from Verhofstadt. I took my camera and joined Bram Delen, Verhofstadt's speechwriter, and Jeroen Reijnen, his head of media and communications, who share a small office with opposing desks, and a window that looks out on a lot of concrete.

To keep myself busy, I decided to film them one more time, because the end was obviously near now, and when I had all my shots, wide and close up, I asked, 'Any famous last quote? These might be the last images I make of you here in the office in Strasbourg.'

Bram smiled, thought for a moment, and then shouted, 'We got rid of them. We kicked them out. It took us two years. But we managed. On our terms and conditions.' And Jeroen, who had to up Bram's bravado, added, 'We finally turned them into a colony, and that was our plan from the first moment.'

We all laughed — but we weren't finished yet.

~

'A failure of British statecraft on a scale unseen since the Suez crisis' – that is the way the Brexit talks were described by the senior Tory Jo Johnson as, in November 2018, he resigned from the government in protest against the EU withdrawal deal agreed by Theresa May. This book tracks the journey to that outcome step by step; it is the story from the other side of the negotiating table, and it is unspun; a frank, freewheeling commentary from those on the EU's negotiating team, recorded as this great and consequential political drama unfolded. And at its heart is a piece of the Brexit jigsaw that Britain's politicians and its public have simply missed, a figure every bit as central to the EU's negotiating coup as 'backroom boys' like Dominic Cummings and the money man Arron Banks were to the success of the Leave campaign in Britain.

In February 2017, Lode Desmet, a Belgian documentary maker, persuaded Guy Verhofstadt, a former prime minister of

Belgium who had been appointed as the European Parliament's representative in the Brexit negotiations, to allow him regular filming access. They agreed that the resulting film would not be broadcast until after Britain's expected departure from the European Union at the end of March 2019, and in return Verhofstadt promised to allow Lode to film freely. The working title of the project was 'The Last European', because, when it started, many in Europe feared that other member states might follow the Brexit example and the European Union might implode.

For Verhofstadt, that would have been the ultimate tragedy, because he is a passionate champion of the European cause. 'It is not chocolate, or beer or Tintin, that makes us Belgian,' he declared in a recent speech. 'No, it is our love of Europe, our passion for the European project . . . our lands have for too long been the battlefield for all Europe. Everyone has come through; the French, the Germans – twice – the Spanish, the Dutch, the Austrians, even the Italians if you go back to Roman times. Wars of religion, of succession, trench warfare with millions of dead and the world's first use of gas, of chemical weapons. Only Europe can save us from the misery of the past.'

For many in Britain, EU membership has always been a transactional arrangement, a matter of money; for most EU members the European project is existential – the Union is the guarantor of peace and security on a continent that has been ravaged by war and tyranny for much of the past century. That fundamental difference goes to the heart of Britain's negotiating failures – and Verhofstadt brings it into sharp focus. With his passionate commitment to European integration, he represents everything about the EU that British Brexiteers resent most.

And he secured himself a central role in the Brexit process. The European Parliament has veto powers over any withdrawal agreement with Britain, but, in formal terms, it has been at one remove from the day-to-day negotiations, which were handled by the EU's executive branch, the European Commission, and its main representative, the EU's chief negotiator Michel Barnier. Guy Verhofstadt, however, is an extremely skilful politician – he served for nine years as prime minister in Belgium's often turbulent political waters – and he secured the close confidence of the Frenchman.

Lode in turn made himself trusted by the Verhofstadt team, and was able to film and record almost all their interactions with Barnier, who briefed Verhofstadt and the Brexit Steering Group of the European Parliament frankly and in detail at every twist and turn of the talks, debating strategies, obstacles and solutions throughout the process. So the behind-the-scenes testimony Lode has assembled is a contemporaneous record of what was really happening.

It reveals how the EU's strategies were shaped and put into action, and charts the development of the unusual and dynamic relationship between the two main European players, Barnier and Verhofstadt. The archive material Lode has amassed during twenty-five months of near continuous filming offers a unique insight into this extraordinary moment of history. It took time for him to secure the confidence of his subjects, as he notes in his record of filming in the days after Theresa May's Florence speech in the autumn of 2017.

～

On 27 September 2017, I received a WhatsApp message from Bram Delen, Guy Verhofstadt's spokesperson and speechwriter. Michel Barnier, the chief EU Brexit negotiator, had asked to talk on the phone with Verhofstadt about the ongoing round of negotiations. The phone call was scheduled for three o'clock that afternoon.

I was at home making transcriptions, but immediately dropped everything to travel to the European Parliament in Brussels. From where I live in Leuven that's a forty-minute trip by train.

I had filmed Barnier and Verhofstadt a number of times already, but always in the presence of others. This was going to be a private conversation between just the two of them. I was curious to find out whether Barnier would be as poised and cerebral as he usually was with more people around.

I knew Barnier and Verhofstadt had had a couple of head-to-head meetings in restaurants, but Barnier refused to be filmed there. This phone call was going to happen on Verhofstadt's home turf — in his own office — and Barnier wasn't going to see me. So I sensed a chance to get some unique access. If of course Verhofstadt agreed to put his phone on speakerphone. I sent Bram a message back to ask whether he could ask his boss if he'd be willing to do that. Bram replied that he would prefer if I asked myself. So I did — and Verhofstadt agreed.

The phone call itself was shorter than I'd expected. Barnier mainly needed to vent his frustration, it seemed. A week earlier, Theresa May had made her Florence speech, apparently adopting a more flexible approach to the negotiations. Immediately afterwards, Verhofstadt had remarked, 'I have asked myself, "Why in Florence?" I have the answer. In the fifteenth century, Florence was exactly like the Conservative Party today. So that's the reason. The same environment. The Medicis fighting with the other families.' Barnier had been more cautiously optimistic, marking the speech down as a moment of 'truth, of sincerity', though he continued to worry that the British government was spending more energy arguing with itself than negotiating with him. But his hopes of a fresh approach from the British had been dashed when the next round of negotiations started; instead of progress, he was faced with a return to the negotiation positions of the very beginning. As soon as Verhofstadt got him on the phone, his disappointment poured out.

Barnier: 'I can't tell you — they want to link everything, everything.

They said it again the day before yesterday. They want to mix everything up because they want to negotiate their future relationship by paying off their past debts. And for me that's completely unacceptable. It is simply non-negotiable that they should [be able to] haggle over the future relationship with the settlement of their past debts, and the divorce.'

The only real progress, Barnier reported, was that, in the negotiations over money, David Davis had stopped talking about 'moral commitments' (as if Britain would be doing a favour by meeting them) and that the EU team had managed to persuade the British team to go through the list of commitments Britain had made, line by line. And Barnier repeated to Verhofstadt his main point: 'There is absolutely no justification for debating the future of the European Union with the United Kingdom while mixing up the subject with debts.'

Verhofstadt chipped in to agree, and Barnier took off again: 'Guy, you [using the familiar tu in French] can of course see what's behind this: it's Hammond's demand . . .as chancellor of the Exchequer, he wants – and I am speaking frankly now, just between the two of us – to negotiate general equivalence for financial services, and to pay for it with past debts.'

'Equivalence' is the system that allows the City of London continued access to Europe's financial markets, and Barnier was determined that he was not going to give that card away. 'I'll never give them equivalences – if they get them some day it will be done one bit at a time, as we did with Japan and the United States, and the Commission will keep the power to take them back . . . otherwise I'll be giving away half my hand – at the moment they are one among twenty-eight, but that way they'd be one on one.' Verhofstadt listened patiently, not even trying to break in, because there was no stopping Barnier – 'It's impossible, do you see? We'd be giving them more power than they have today. It's just not possible.'

The EU's chief negotiator ended with a warning. Theresa May, he said, was after 'à la carte' access to the European market, 'cherry picking'. And he would need all the help he could get from the European Parliament, 'the guardian of the temple of the single market', as he described it.

Before hanging up Barnier urged Verhofstadt once more to keep their conversation under wraps: 'Don't say all this publicly.' I smiled to myself because I knew that I'd just filmed the opening scene of my film. With the complicity of Verhofstadt, who even made a joke about what we just did, together — telling his chief of staff not to bother with making a written debriefing of the phone conversation with Barnier for the Brexit Steering Group, because 'We have a new method of debriefing now. We can just show them the video. They will like that. Especially when Barnier says: please keep what I say between us.'

On Verhofstadt's desk stood a figurine of Tintin's colourful cursing Captain Haddock, well known for his 'lily-livered bandicoots, freshwater swabs, ectoplasmic byproduct, prattling porpoise, scoffing braggart, and rotten sand-hoppers'. The captain winked at me.

~

The characters you will meet in this book are as colourful as Haddock's curses. The Verhofstadt team are clever, bibulous, multilingual and sometimes foul-mouthed; they talked freely in front of Lode's microphone — about their European colleagues as much as their British interlocutors. There is plenty of gossip, but this story is also, and in the first place, a civics lesson — a contemporaneous account of high diplomacy in action, in one of the most intricate political playgrounds on earth.

The bodies that run the European Union are riven with intersecting rivalries — national, political, personal and institutional (between the Parliament, the Commission and the Council, where the governments of the member states meet) — and this book will illustrate how bitter they can sometimes be. British diplomacy within the EU has always thrived on these divisions, and during Britain's four and a half decades as a member state its diplomats gained a grudging respect for their ability to put together coalitions that served Britain's interests. The British government believed it could do the same during the Brexit talks.

But they fatally miscalculated the difference between being a malcontent member and a nation that is abandoning the club altogether. As this book will illustrate, the common enemy of Brexit brought the EU together. The twenty-seven remaining states agreed a strategy and gave clear negotiating instructions to a skilled and experienced negotiator in the person of Michel Barnier. This time it was the British who were undermined by political divisions at home.

The European team remained constantly curious about British political opinion. Europe's negotiators sometimes misjudged the dynamics of the British position – and in this book we will see them anxiously trying to decode British intentions – but they paid close and sophisticated heed to the way British politics were evolving.

Their British counterparts, by contrast, were obsessively focused on and hamstrung by the domestic political debate. Good diplomacy depends on empathy, an understanding of the forces driving your partners or opponents. Britain has been stubbornly tone-deaf to the mood music from the rest of Europe.

That failure of political imagination explains the explosion of anger that greeted the publication of the details of Theresa May's European deal in November 2018. Some of the most striking evidence in this book is the repeated contrast between the public statements of optimism by the British government, MPs and commentators, and the reality of negotiations as recorded by Lode's microphone. Britain's failures look especially stark because they stand against Europe's sometimes unexpected successes.

This story is often uncomfortable; before the vote to leave the EU, Euro-enthusiasts like Verhofstadt regarded the United Kingdom as an awkward but formidable player on the European scene. After the vote they feared Britain's negotiating power. By the end of the negotiations, all too often, they laughed at the UK leaders and pitied the British people.

～

When the documentary, with all the material I'd filmed behind the scenes of the Brexit negotiations, was released in May 2019, the colony scene with Bram and Jeroen caused an uproar. Their boisterous bantering was seen (or used) as evidence of what the EU had actually been up to: subduing, shackling and humiliating the UK. It was frustrating to see a two-hour detailed account of political life and how it really works, defined as it is by human beings, be reduced to that one scene. But it was also a good reason to start writing this book. What was it about Brexit that made the British lose their world-famous dry wit and united Europe in such a rarely seen way? I often wished: if only the EU could always function as harmoniously and efficiently as it did during the Brexit negotiations.

～

The lessons here for Britain's officials and politicians are painful, but they are also essential. Britain still has a long Brexit battle ahead. On 23 March 2019, amid the chaos of what should have been Britain's final week as a member of the European Union, the former British and EU diplomat Robert Cooper wrote, in the *Financial Times*, 'If the UK prime minister had a sense of humour, she would set up the committee of inquiry now, so that it could take evidence in real time, as the tragedy unfolds.' That is the kind of evidence you will find in this book.

MISTER BREXIT

June 2016–early March 2017

'Hard to think of a more anti-British figure,' tweeted *The Sun*'s political editor, Tom Newton Dunn, on the appointment of Michel Barnier as the EU's Brexit negotiator – 'declaration of war'. That was echoed by the paper's Murdoch press stablemate, the *Sunday Times*: 'Appointing Michel Barnier, one of the least popular ex-commissioners in London, is an act of war by Brussels,' wrote the paper's political editor, Tim Shipman. The tabloid *Daily Express* had him down as the 'Most DANGEROUS man in EU', and the blogger Guido Fawkes described Barnier as a 'hardline Britain basher'.

Political reaction to the news of Mr Barnier's new job – it was announced on 27 July 2016, just over a month after Britain voted to leave the EU – was not much warmer. In an interview with the BBC, Lord Myners, a former Treasury minister under Gordon Brown, revived a catty anecdote about Mr Barnier's alleged vanity, which he had once told in the House of Lords: 'I met Mr Barnier when he was a minister,' he had reported to the upper house. 'He came to see us at the Treasury. He came down the corridor and I was watching him. I am a great fan of art and I was rather impressed that he stopped to look at every painting. I thought *This is a man with whom I share a common interest* – until I realised he was actually looking at his reflection in the glass on every painting, and adjusting his hair or his toupee. This to me is a man whom we should treat with a very long spoon.' Even the Liberal Democrat Nick Clegg, a committed enthusiast for the European Union, warned that 'he is no friend of the City of London', and 'I think he's going to drive a very hard bargain indeed'.

The charge of 'Brit-bashing' related back to the years 2010–14, when Mr Barnier was the European Commissioner responsible for the single market. He had the job of tightening up regulation of the financial services sector in the aftermath of the 2008 global financial crisis, and he made himself especially unpopular in the City of London by championing a 2013 EU reform that capped bankers' bonuses. But he also sided with Britain when the European Central Bank tried to insist that only companies based in the eurozone could clear financial trades in euros, though that episode did not feature much in the press coverage of his new job.

The appointment of Guy Verhofstadt – a 'diehard Europhile', according to one British daily – as the European Parliament's Brexit point man at the beginning of September provided another tempting target. 'Mr Verhofstadt's devotion to a federal Europe and fiery oratory – his schoolmaster resorted to taping his mouth shut to stop him jabbering – have made him a *bête noire* of Brexiters,' reported the *Financial Times*.

The appointment came about as a result of the kind of horse-trading that is routine in the European Parliament (EP). Verhofstadt was the president of the ALDE group in the Parliament – the Alliance of Liberals and Democrats for Europe. The label Liberal in this context means a mixture of free-market economics – Verhofstadt was once dubbed 'Baby

Thatcher' – and social liberalism. Verhofstadt's sharp tongue and political savvy ensured that the group – which ranked fourth in size among the Parliament's alliances – often boxed above its weight. And so it was with the Brexit job. Verhofstadt was planning to challenge the German Social Democrat Martin Schulz for the presidency of the EP. Schulz was confident that he could beat Verhofstadt, but he needed ALDE's votes to secure a majority. So Schulz offered Verhofstadt the Brexit job. Verhofstadt accepted, and pulled out of the presidency race.

Syed Kamall, the leader of the British Conservatives in the European Parliament, called it a 'backroom stitch-up', and UKIP's Nigel Farage, himself an MEP, described Verhofstadt as 'a fanatical supporter of EU federalism', declaring, 'Guy Verhofstadt hates everything we stand for, which should mean a much shorter renegotiation.'

Verhofstadt, by instinct a political bruiser, told Farage from the floor of the Parliament that Brexit at least meant that 'finally we will be getting rid of the biggest waste in the EU budget – that we have paid for seventeen years of your salary'. But the *Financial Times* presented a more emollient side to the EP's Brexit point man: '[I]n an extended interview, Mr Verhofstadt kept his sharper views in check,' the paper reported, 'denying any ill will towards Britain, quoting Thatcher and Churchill and talking with pride about his vintage Aston Martin and Elva sports cars. "I like Britain," he said. "I race British cars. How [much] more a lover of Britain can you be than racing a British car?"'

Less than a month after Verhofstadt's appointment, Britain's new prime minister, Theresa May, was on her feet at the Conservative Party conference in Birmingham. She told her party, 'Today, too many people in positions of power behave as though they have more in common with international elites than with the people down the road, the people they employ, the people they pass in the street. But if you believe you're a citizen of the world, you're a citizen of nowhere. You don't understand what the very word "citizenship" means.' And she attacked what the European Union stood for: 'The referendum was not just a vote to withdraw from the EU,' she said. 'It was about something broader – something that the European Union had come to represent. It was about a sense – deep, profound and, let's face it, often justified – that many people have today; that the world works well for a privileged few, but not for them.'

The British press has a long tradition of painting relations with Europe in bellicose terms; it goes back at least as far as Margaret Thatcher's budget battles with Brussels in the 1980s. In the run-up to the 1992 Maastricht agreement, which shaped the EU we know today, almost all European summits and negotiations were presented in the British press as stories about plucky Britain standing up to an overweening European super state. Theresa May's 2016 conference speech slipped neatly into this narrative tradition; to stand up to the 'dangerous' Barnier and 'fanatic' Verhofstadt, Britain now apparently had a Churchillian prime minister.

'A truly global Britain is possible, and it is in sight,' she told the conference.

And it should be no surprise that it is. Because we are the fifth biggest economy in the world. Since 2010 we have grown faster than any economy in the G7. And we attract a fifth of all foreign investment in the EU. We are the biggest foreign investor in the United States. We have more Nobel Laureates than any country outside America. We have the best intelligence services in the world, a military that can project its power around the globe, and friendships, partnerships and alliances in every continent. We have the greatest soft power in the world, we sit in exactly the right time zone for global trade, and our language is the language of the world.

She continued:

We don't need – as I sometimes hear people say – to 'punch above our weight'. Because our weight is substantial enough already. So let's ignore the pessimists, let's have the confidence in ourselves to go out into the world, securing trade deals, winning contracts, generating wealth and creating jobs. And let's get behind the team of ministers – David Davis, Liam Fox, Priti Patel and Boris Johnson – who are working on our plan for Brexit, who know we're going to make a success of it and who will make a reality of global Britain.

Of those four ministers – David Davis, the secretary of state for exiting the European Union; Liam Fox, the secretary of state for international trade; Priti Patel, the international development secretary; and Boris Johnson, the foreign secretary – only one, Liam Fox, survived in office for the full first phase of the Brexit negotiations.

Theresa May's strategy was dictated by the demands of party management. She had become leader and prime minister almost by accident in the political turmoil that followed Britain's unexpected vote to leave the EU and the consequent resignation of her predecessor, David Cameron. She was very nearly defeated in the leadership election by one of the party's most committed Eurosceptics, Andrea Leadsom, who was forced to withdraw only after making a political gaffe (Mrs Leadsom suggested in a newspaper interview that being a mother made her a better candidate for prime minister than the childless Mrs May). As a declared, although discreet, 'Remainer' during the referendum campaign, Mrs May believed she would always be regarded with some suspicion by the Eurosceptic wing of her party, so she went out of her way to demonstrate her commitment to their agenda. It was one of the first of many ironies thrown up by the Brexit process that the Tory Party should choose someone who believed Britain was better off in the EU to lead the country out of it.

On 17 January 2017, in the opulent surroundings of Lancaster House, just across the Mall from Buckingham Palace, the political messages the prime minister had delivered at the party conference the previous autumn emerged as fully developed government policy. The ambition was sweeping: 'I want this United Kingdom to emerge from this period of change stronger, fairer, more united and more outward-looking than ever before,' the prime minister declared. 'I want us to be a secure, prosperous, tolerant country – a magnet for international talent and a home to the pioneers and innovators who will shape the world ahead. I want us to be a truly global Britain – the best friend and neighbour to our European partners, but a country that reaches beyond the borders of Europe too. A country that goes out into the world to build relationships with old friends and new allies alike.'

And there was an olive branch to the EU: 'It remains overwhelmingly and compellingly in Britain's national interest that the EU should succeed,' she said, adding:

Our vote to leave the European Union was no rejection of the values we share. The decision to leave the EU represents no desire to become more distant to you, our friends and neighbours. It was no attempt to do harm to the EU itself or to any of its remaining member states. We do not want to turn the clock back to the days when Europe was less peaceful, less secure and less able to trade freely. It was a vote to restore, as we see it, our parliamentary democracy, national self-determination, and to become even more global and internationalist in action and in spirit.

But the 'red lines' she believed necessary to, in the words of the Leave campaign, 'take back control', were drawn with clarity. The jurisdiction of the European Court of Justice would end: 'We will take back control of our laws and bring an end to the jurisdiction of the European Court of Justice in Britain. Leaving the European Union will mean that our laws will be made in Westminster, Edinburgh, Cardiff and Belfast. And those laws will be interpreted by judges not in Luxembourg but in courts across this country.'

Britain was also to 'take back control' of immigration, so: 'What I am proposing cannot mean membership of the single market. European leaders have said many times that membership means accepting the "four freedoms" of goods, capital, services and people.' And May had another reason for rejecting the single market. 'Being out of the EU but a member of the single market would mean complying with the EU's rules and regulations that implement those freedoms, without having a vote on what those rules and regulations are.'

'A global Britain must be free to strike trade agreements with countries from outside the European Union too,' the prime minister declared, and that meant an end to Britain's membership of the customs union also, although on this point she was a little more ambiguous: 'I do not want Britain to be part of the Common Commercial Policy and I do not want us to be bound by the Common External Tariff. These are the elements of the customs union that prevent us from striking our own comprehensive trade agreements with other countries. But I do want us to have a customs agreement with the EU.'

Towards the end of her speech Mrs May deployed a punchy phrase that was to be much quoted back at her: 'And while I am confident that this scenario need never arise – while I am sure a positive agreement can be reached – I am equally clear that no deal for Britain is better than a bad deal for Britain.'

The speech was a bold interpretation of the 2016 referendum result, which, while delivering a clear, if narrow, verdict on whether Britain should leave the EU, delivered no view on what that should mean for the customs union or the single market. And it went down very well indeed in the Brexit-supporting press. The *Daily Mail* headlined the 'Steel of the New Iron Lady', comparing her favourably with her immediate predecessor, who had tried to renegotiate Britain's EU relationship before the referendum; she had, the paper declared, 'put Cameron's feeble negotiations to shame with an ultimatum to Brussels: We'll walk away from a bad deal – and make EU pay.' The *Mail*'s online iteration was equally enthusiastic: 'Theresa May lays down law to EU leaders AND Merkel and Hollande [the leaders of Germany and France] as she declares we WILL quit the single market to control immigration.' *The Times* summarised her message with: 'May to EU: Give Us Fair Deal or You'll Be Crushed'. There was even praise from the politician who had come to haunt Tory nightmares; Nigel Farage tweeted, 'I can hardly believe the PM is now using the phrases and words that I've been mocked for using for years. Real progress.'

The speech included a recognition that 'as we leave, the United Kingdom will share a land border with the EU, and maintaining

that Common Travel Area with the Republic of Ireland will be
an important priority for the UK in the talks ahead', but no
indication of how the open border on the island of Ireland could
be accommodated within the prime minister's 'red lines'. She
merely pledged to find 'a practical solution that allows the main-
tenance of the Common Travel Area with the Republic, while
protecting the integrity of the United Kingdom's immigration
system', and her declaration that 'nobody wants to return to the
borders of the past' sounded almost like a dutiful afterthought.

The *Irish Times* was unconvinced. 'May's speech indicates
Border customs controls likely to return' was its headline, and
an editorial took the view that 'the Irish position for the last
six months has been to hope Brexit would be as soft as possible.
That hope had faded in recent months and was finally buried
yesterday.' The Dublin government was guarded, but the
Fianna Fáil party, then in opposition, was unambiguous: 'The
prime minister's tone may have been conciliatory,' declared
their foreign affairs spokesman, Darragh O'Brien, 'but the
content of her speech was not.' Ireland's main business lobby
group, Ibec, warned that 'the possibility of the UK leaving
both the single market and the customs union raises fundamental questions about Ireland's future trading relations with
the UK', and called May's strategy 'an aggressive move by the
UK, showing little regard for our trading relationship and for
relations with other EU member states'.

Lode Desmet became part of the story shortly after May's
Lancaster House speech.

⁓

*In January 2017, I received a phone call from the main commercial TV
station in Belgium, VTM. They wanted to know whether I would be
interested in making a film about Guy Verhofstadt's book on the future of*

the European Union: Europe's Last Chance. *It was 'a no-holds-barred report on a once ambitious European project that has degenerated into an institutional quagmire', according to its cover. 'Europe still imagines itself to be the moral centre of the world, yet its foreign policy is conspicuous for its cowardice, the Mediterranean is developing into a migrants' graveyard and Europe has yet to succeed in overcoming the economic crisis. Guy Verhofstadt sees a solution in a big leap forward in European integration. It need not result in the creation of a superstate, but it does need to produce a more efficient and democratic Europe.'*

I said I was interested, because I am a freelancer and freelancers, like working girls, never say no straightaway. But I wondered if a book full of ideas could be turned into a good film, because films work best when they show, not explain. So I suggested an alternative. What if the documentary followed Guy Verhofstadt behind the scenes of the Brexit negotiations? A film like that would be much more exciting to watch, and it would surely also show how Europe works, what its problems, and its prospects for the future, are. I asked whether they could check. Would Verhofstadt agree to be followed and filmed in his role as Brexit negotiator for the European Parliament?

Two weeks later I was invited for dinner with Verhofstadt and his spokesperson for the Belgian press, Bram Delen, who is also his speech-writer. Delen is a very clever young man, as idealistic but more cynical than his thirty years older boss.

It turned out that the idea to make a film about Verhofstadt's book came from them. What Verhofstadt had had in mind was a film like An Inconvenient Truth, *the hugely influential 2006 documentary about the efforts of the former United States vice-president Al Gore to educate people about climate change. But this would be about the European Union. The pair had even travelled to the US to find someone interested in making it. But Verhofstadt and Delen were turned down everywhere. So a new idea was welcome.*

A few days before the dinner, Delen had asked me whether I had a

*website, because his boss was a stickler for information, and if I had
a site, Verhofstadt would surely want to have a good look at it. I told
Delen to hold on, I was just refurbishing it. I wasn't, but then I did, and
during the dinner I found out that Delen had been right. Verhofstadt
had browsed the website thoroughly.*

*When I later started filming him, I would find out how Verhofstadt
does that, the browsing. It all happens on his phone, which is not even
a very big model. He takes off his glasses, brings the phone very close to
his eyes, almost touching his nose, and reads, and scrolls. And answers
emails, and sends emails. He's on his phone whenever he has a moment,
during the day, but also at night, because he is a bad sleeper. His team
members all have stories of beeps waking them up when Verhofstadt
wants something, and wants it now.*

*But that was later. First Verhofstadt had to agree to the proposal of
being followed and filmed for two years; the Brexit negotiations had not
yet started, so maybe it was going to be even longer.*

*The dinner where he said yes took place in a small but nice Italian
restaurant with a good wine list on the outskirts of Brussels — because
good wine is another thing Verhofstadt is a stickler for. The big issue
at the table was control. I explained to Verhofstadt that the quality of
the documentary he had in mind was dependent on its veracity. Nobody
wanted to see a promotion film for a politician, except his supporters.
But a film with real access to the negotiations was something a lot of
people would want to watch. Was he willing to give up control of the
end product, in return for that broader audience?*

*It was a difficult question because Verhofstadt controls the way he
communicates thoroughly. No tweet he makes is spontaneous; they're
all discussed and improved by his press team. Every speech he gives is
written, rewritten, and rehearsed several times before the final delivery.*

*To give a filmmaker access to his life and work, without command over
the end product, would require an enormous leap of faith and trust. In the
end Verhofstadt and I came to a gentlemen's agreement: Verhofstadt would*

be allowed to see the final edit, and if there were scenes he had a problem
with, we would talk about them. Verhofstadt undoubtedly believed that
in the end he would get his way, something he always believes, and often
does. I trusted my skills and my own stubbornness. Somehow, at the end
of the dinner, the politician and I decided to trust each other.

I also raised the question of how the people Verhofstadt would be
meeting might react to the presence of a camera. Verhofstadt shrugged
and smirked: 'When they come to see me they're on my turf, and I decide
what happens there.' As things turned out, he sometimes proved almost
too helpful, trying to convince people that I was just recording pictures
without sound. I always took care to correct him.

~

There was, however, one problem: at the root of the project
lay a misunderstanding; the idea was based on information on
the role of Verhofstadt in the Brexit negotiations that was not
completely correct, even if it was (and still is) widespread.

When Verhofstadt took up his Brexit role, the Belgian public
broadcaster VRT reported the news with patriotic pride:

> The European Parliament has appointed Guy Verhofstadt
> as its representative in the upcoming Brexit negotiations.
> The European Union is putting forward three negotia-
> tors: one representing the Commission, another for the
> member states and a third to represent Parliament. Two
> of the three are Belgians. The Belgians will be playing an
> important role in the Brexit talks to determine under which
> conditions Britain will have access to the European market
> after their exit process has been completed. The European
> Commission appointed Frenchman Michel Barnier for the
> task. The European Council, i.e. the different heads of state
> and government leaders, chose the Belgian diplomat Didier

Seeuws to represent the member states. Now, the European Parliament has announced that they will be represented by Guy Verhofstadt, the speaker for the liberal democratic faction ALDE. This makes two of the three EU negotiators Belgians; moreover, Seeuws used to be Verhofstadt's spokesman when he was Belgium's Premier in different governments between 1999 and 2008.

Two years later, the Getty Images website is still putting the caption *Brexit negotiator Guy Verhofstadt* under shots of the politician. But that information is not, strictly speaking, correct. The only real negotiator for the EU in the Brexit talks was to be Michel Barnier, whose official title became 'Chief Negotiator – Task Force for the Preparation and Conduct of the Negotiations with the United Kingdom under Article 50'. Barnier alone negotiated directly with the British; Verhofstadt never did. His task was to coordinate the European Parliament's views on Brexit and liaise with Barnier: to make sure, above all, that the Frenchman took on board the prerogatives of the Parliament in his talks with the UK, and to report back about Barnier's progress (or, as it turned out, very often lack of progress) to his fellow MEPs. Verhofstadt was not the Brexit negotiator for the European Parliament, but its coordinator.

Verhofstadt's press team was only too happy to allow this misunderstanding in the media to stand; because negotiator sounds more important than coordinator, and being important is . . . important for a politician. And the fact that Verhofstadt was attributed a bigger role than he actually had was also important institutionally, for the European Parliament as a whole, which had to fight hard to make itself heard in the Brexit negotiations.

The battle was an example of a constant struggle at the heart of the European Union, which is the cause of many of its problems. The EU consists of three big institutions which vie with each other for power and influence, in roles that, after half a century, are still fluctuating. The European Parliament, with 751 representatives from twenty-eight member states (before the UK's planned departure), the European Commission, which fulfils the EU's executive role and includes most of its civil service, and the European Council, where the heads of government of the member states gather.

The European Parliament is the world's only international legislative body, but it has always felt undervalued. Its role has long been the focus for debate about the charge that the European Union is flawed by a 'democratic deficit', and its powers have been steadily enhanced. Its early rights to a voice in a 'consultation procedure', which allowed it to give non-binding advice to the Council, became a 'cooperation procedure', and then, under the Maastricht Treaty which created the EU, a 'co-decision procedure'. The 2007 Lisbon Treaty gave the European Parliament the 'ordinary legislative procedure', which means that it has, in theory at least, equal law-passing powers with the EU's Council.

The role each of the three institutions was going to have in the Brexit negotiations was set out in one succinct paragraph in the Lisbon Treaty, under the infamous Article 50, that before the referendum nobody believed was ever going to be used.

It says – under No. 2 of the Article:

'A Member State which decides to withdraw shall notify the European Council of its intention. In the light of the guidelines provided by the European Council, the Union shall negotiate and conclude an agreement with that State, setting out the arrangements for its withdrawal, taking account of the framework for its future relationship with the Union. That agreement shall be negotiated in accordance with Article 218(3) of the Treaty on the Functioning of the European Union. It shall be concluded on behalf of the Union by the Council, acting by a qualified majority, after obtaining the consent of the European Parliament.'

Those last eight words – 'after obtaining the consent of the European Parliament' – are all that Article 50 has to say on the subject; that the deal at the end of the negotiations has to be approved by the Parliament. Verhofstadt exploited this vagueness to his and the Parliament's advantage, arguing that if the Parliament was to approve the deal in the end, it was only logical that it should, from the start, be able to say what it expected from the negotiations.

He had to fight hard to be heard.

His intervention on the subject from the floor of the European Parliament in December 2016 was provocative even by his own standards. He told the representative of the European Council:

'What they are proposing is, 'Oh, simply we go forward with the Brexit negotiations, but without the Parliament.' We can invite Sherpas [EU jargon for the civil servants who do the ground work for negotiations], maybe, but that's all. You're not aware that we have to approve the agreements, at the end? You're aware of it? OK, that's already an enormous step forward. I'm going to tell you; it's time that you also involve the Parliament from day one. Do you want that we open separate negotiations with the British authorities? Is that what you want? You can get it, eh? If that's what the heads of state want, we are going to do it. Parallel negotiations. I don't want it, but apparently the Council wants it. Maybe I can give you a famous phrase of Lyndon B. Johnson. He said once: "Better to have him inside the tent pissing out, than outside the tent, pissing in."'

Verhofstadt was angry that day, but in the end he got what he wanted.

~

The new role came with new chores, however, and on my first day of film-
ing, 14 March 2017, I found Verhofstadt in a blazing row with some of
his staff about the demands it made on his time. Verhofstadt was checking
his phone in his tiny office in the French city of Strasbourg, where the
Parliament moves every month for a week; although most of its work is done
in Brussels, French governments have successfully insisted that all except a
few plenary sessions are held in Strasbourg, which remains its official seat.

The office is situated on the sixth floor of the impressive oval Louise
Weiss building, which has an inner courtyard that is almost never quiet:
the building rises 60 metres around the courtyard, and functions like an
echo chamber. Through his office windows, which are very often open —
even in winter, because it is hard to regulate the heating — Verhofstadt
can hear the click clack of heels, the rolling of suitcases of MEPs and their
staff arriving or leaving, the chatter of youngsters on a school trip, and
the songs of choirs brought along by activists or regional representatives.

But on that first day of filming it was unusually quiet outside. So the
row that erupted sounded all the louder. Verhofstadt's spokesperson for
France, Yannick Laude, was trying to persuade him to go to Paris to meet
students who were organising a Brexit event, and he enlisted the support
of Edel Crosse, his head of private office, who guards Verhofstadt's agenda.

CROSSE: Yannick has an idea for Thursday.
VERHOFSTADT: What idea?
CROSSE: He wants you to go to Paris.
VERHOFSTADT: Pffff, Thursday? I don't go to Paris, no,
     no, no, no.
LAUDE: Listen, Guy. You offered your blessing . . .
VERHOFSTADT: I AM NOT GOING, that's it, OK?
LAUDE: But yes, listen.
VERHOFSTADT: But I am not going, I am just not going.

LAUDE: So what am I supposed to say to these students
who have included your name in their promotional
material?

VERHOFSTADT: But I invited them to come and see me in
my office at Parliament . . .

LAUDE: You spent two minutes with them!

VERHOFSTADT: They were all there – and they took
photos.

LAUDE: And they want you at their event. You are Mr
Brexit. Won't you listen?

VERHOFSTADT: No.

*Yannick Laude turned to me: 'Great pictures – and that's typical,' he
said. 'I hope you got sound too?' Edel Crosse interjected. 'You are in a
bad mood.' But Laude's retort came straight back: 'I am not in a bad
mood – you've got people who trusted Guy Verhofstadt, and he's telling
them to piss off.' Crosse finished the discussion with the observation: 'If
Article 50 is triggered, what's to fuck around with in Paris?'*

~

The exchange settled one question; Verhofstadt clearly was not
going to curb his occasional attacks of grumpiness for the sake
of the camera; though he is an inspired speaker, cherished by
his supporters, and used to shaking more hands and smiling at
more people than anyone of us will ever do in several lifetimes,
he prefers, really, to be left alone.

The row between Verhofstadt and Laude, with Edel Crosse
in the middle, was conducted in a quick-fire mixture of
French and English, the two working languages in his team,
with occasionally a dash of Dutch, Verhofstadt's mother
tongue, tossed in. English is – ironically – the language most
often used, but it is spoken with all kinds of national accents.

Verhofstadt has gathered a polyglot bunch of staffers around him, from the four corners of Europe. His team reflects his pan-European dreams.

Edel Crosse's accent is Irish. She grew up in a small coastal town in the Republic of Ireland, a background audible in almost every phrase she utters (and not just in the accent). Yannick Laude's is French – although the grumpy Frenchman rarely speaks English. *Il préfère son Français*, wears it with pride like the waistcoats he sports.

The way Eva Palatova, Verhofstadt's foreign policy adviser, speaks English places her firmly in Eastern Europe; she's from the Czech Republic and turned down the job of Czech foreign minister so that she could keep working for Verhofstadt. The accent of Jeroen Reijnen, Verhofstadt's head of media and communications, is distinctively Dutch. Bram Delen's English marks him out as Belgian, as does that of Erik Janda, Verhofstadt's personal secretary and accountant, who also transports his racing cars to events when the boss is competing. It is a complex relationship; they are master and servant, but friends and – sometimes – enemies too.

The only native English speakers in the team are Nick Petre and Guillaume McLaughlin. Petre, Verhofstadt's press spokesman for the UK, hails from Theresa May's own constituency of Maidenhead in Berkshire. Verhofstadt tried hard to persuade him to run against the prime minister as a Liberal Democrat candidate when Mrs May called a snap election, but in the end the rather shy Petre declined. McLaughlin, Verhofstadt's chief of staff, has a British father and a French mother. He grew up in Brussels and remembers vividly how at the age of six he was taken to the Belgian seaside to help his parents put stickers on cars owned by British tourists, urging them to vote 'Yes' in the 1975 referendum on whether the UK should stay in the

European Economic Community (as it was then called), which it had joined two years earlier.

So with Brexit, history repeated itself for Guillaume. 'Except that' – WhatsApp quote from Guillaume – 'the 1975 one was won by over 66 per cent by those who wanted to stay.' Guillaume McLaughlin still has a British passport and his sons are at school in Britain. He takes Brexit personally.

McLaughlin, Delen, Crosse, Palatova and Reijnen are the inner circle of the Verhofstadt political operation. Occupying a slightly different orbit are Petre and Laude. They all loved that their boss was seen as Mister Brexit, even if Brexit would eventually wear them out.

On that very first day of filming, 14 March 2017, in an interview with the *Financial Times*, Verhofstadt was already looking ahead to the timeline that would unfold when Britain triggered the Article 50 process. He clocked that it would bring the negotiations right up against the deadline for the next European parliamentary elections, in May 2019, and he was determined to use that to argue the case for keeping the European Parliament closely engaged in the negotiating process.

'It will be at a very difficult moment. It will be two months before the elections, you can imagine what the mood in the Parliament is at that moment,' he predicted. 'Most of them [MEPs] will look to their [electoral prospects], is my yes or no vote going to help me to get votes in my constituency? That will be the ultimate judgement that every MEP will make, so it will be a very tricky moment, so that's why we are saying, if you want that at the end, there is a smooth process of consent by the European Parliament, it will be necessary to involve the EP from day one.' He was also determined to put down a marker for the way events would unfold once Article 50 had been triggered: 'And the second thing is that the Parliament will be the first institution . . . to give its opinion and its red lines on [what] this agreement has to be about.' Verhofstadt planned to do this in the form of a resolution that the Parliament would vote on as soon as the UK triggered Article 50 and set the divorce process in motion. He didn't mention that this resolution would be written in close conjunction with both the European Council and the European Commission. The Parliament would get its moment to shine, but only in consultation with the two other big European institutions, and of course, Michel Barnier.

The EU lead negotiator, Michel Barnier, well understood the importance of creating a united front to deal with the British. A crucial element in his negotiating strategy was constant consultation and communication between the institutions, and within the institutions, between their members – the repre-sentatives of the twenty-seven remaining member states, both those in the Council, and those in the European Parliament. Another, perhaps more surprising element, was openness: the EU decided to publish, as quickly as possible, any documents that the three EU institutions had agreed on – the Parliament's resolution, and the EU negotiation directives, for example. The idea was that making the EU line a matter of public record, one that everyone signed up to, would limit the opportunity for the British to engage in the diplomatic game of divide and conquer, wheeling and dealing behind the scenes to exploit national, party and personality rivalries.

Mrs May, by contrast, saw much less room for manoeuvre because of the raw divisions within her own party; clear state-ments of her negotiating ambitions carried the risk of alienating one side or the other in the Brexit debate. From the very first, the British side of the negotiations reflected the prime min-ister's concern with party management, while the European position was based on consensus.

2

THE BAD GUY

Late March 2017

On 25 March 2017, heads of state and government of the members of the European Union gathered in the Italian capital to celebrate the sixtieth anniversary of the signing of the Treaty of Rome, which laid the foundations of today's European Union. Theresa May was invited, but she declined – logically, since the event was designed to celebrate the EU's future, and she was just days away from issuing official notice of Britain's plans to withdraw. It was, for many EU leaders, an important declaration of confidence; after the Eurozone crisis and the deeply damaging divisions over immigration and asylum seekers in 2015, and with the Brexit battle still to come, the Union was looking somewhat ragged at the edges.

Guy Verhofstadt was there, but he eschewed the official festivities to join a pro-European march with young people elsewhere in the city. Verhofstadt saw the Brexit vote as confirmation of his belief that the EU was losing its way. His anniversary speech in Rome was characteristically pugnacious, and radical in its vision of European unity:

The reason we are all here is very clear. We want to give a message to those European leaders who are now in Campidoglio [the Capitoline Hill, the heart of ancient Rome]. To tell them, that it is not enough to make new declarations. We have enough declarations in Europe . . . What we need now is action forward, action to a real European Union . . . It's a lie that people don't want Europe. What they don't want, dear friends, is the EU as it works today. Because it is not a union. It is in fact a loose confederation of nation states. Still based on the unanimity rule. It's in fact a failed state. A fake state that we have in Europe today.

Also present in Rome that day were two vice-presidents of Verhofstadt's Brexit Steering Group, or BSG. Elmar Brok is a stout German Christian Democrat who likes his food. Verhofstadt once suggested they had 'Brokfast' together instead of breakfast. Brok became a member of the European Parliament in 1980 and, as a young man, he – just like Verhofstadt's chief of staff Guillaume – helped to campaign for a 'Yes' vote in Britain's EU referendum in 1975. His command of English and forthright views have made him a familiar face and voice on the British broadcast media. Roberto Gualtieri, a balding Italian Social Democrat, has a long history of collaboration with Verhofstadt and Brok on projects to reform the EU's institutions. Gualtieri is the dossier cruncher of the BSG. Nobody reads documents and dossiers as thoroughly and as fast as him, and nobody asks lengthier questions. At the very end of one BSG meeting, Verhofstadt asked Gualtieri whether he had a question and Gualtieri said, 'We only have five minutes left, so I think I will abstain.'

The BSG – I was the one who first started using the abbreviation, with the lame joke that it sounded like BSE, or mad cow disease – was set up to help Verhofstadt in his function as watchdog for the Brexit negotiations, but also because it was thought that Verhofstadt needed a watchdog himself. Despite his background as a prime minister of Belgium, leading coalition governments, Verhofstadt can be a bit of an Einzelgänger *– or loner. Acting on your own is not something the European Parliament condones.*

Apart from the Christian Democrat Brok and the Social Democrat Gualtieri, the BSG had three other important members: Philippe Lamberts, the Belgian leader of the Greens in the European Parliament; Gabi Zimmer, from *Die Linke*, or the Left, the current incarnation of East Germany's old Communist Party, who leads the group of the European United Left–Nordic Green Left [*sic*]; and Danuta Hübner, from Poland, who presides over the EP's important Constitutional Affairs Committee, and is a member of Civic Forum, the liberal-conservative party of the EU Council president Donald Tusk.

The Conservatives and Reformists, ECR, the group supported by the United Kingdom's Tory MEPs, were excluded, as were nationalist parties, like UKIP and Marine Le Pen's *Front National*. But keeping them out took some manoeuvring. When the Reformists pressed to be included, Verhofstadt and his allies even considered managing the situation by holding secret backroom meetings without them:

VERHOFSTADT: There is a request of the ECR to send someone who is not a British [MEP] to the Brexit Steering Group.

GUALTIERI: I think we should not say no, never, because it's always good to broaden a parliament position.

BROK: The result is, if we're going to do that, then we have to find a smaller room, of 'behind discussion'.

VERHOFSTADT: Otherwise we have to organise then
    another format, that means that we have this format,
    and that after this format you have a second meeting,
    that becomes ridiculous. At the end you have so
    many—
GUALTIERI: Layers.
VERHOFSTADT [laughing]: Layers . . . that you don't
    know in what layer you are playing. You can make
    huge mistakes, saying things that were in fact meant
    for another layer.

Two days after the Rome celebrations, the BSG met in
Verhofstadt's Brussels offices to discuss a parliamentary resolution on the guidelines for the Brexit negotiations. The
triggering of Article 50 was imminent, and the group had been
working for weeks on a text they would issue in response. For
two hours they laboured through every comma in the resolution with stubborn attention to detail. As the meeting drew
to a close, Verhofstadt cheerfully noted that if Theresa May
announced something unexpected – 'We want to stay in the
single market, or something. Or we agree with the four freedoms' – their efforts would have been in vain. 'Then we have
a totally different story and we can rip up this text,' he joked
to his colleagues.

Verhofstadt and the EU knew what Mrs May and the UK
were going to propose: in her Lancaster House speech, the
prime minister had set out her ambitions for a speedy procedure, settling Britain's future relationship with the EU at the
same time as the withdrawal agreement that would sort out
their divorce, all within the two year timetable laid down by
Article 50. At Lancaster House she had acknowledged that the
new arrangements would have to be phased in, but it would be

another six months before Mrs May's government confirmed that beyond these two years it would also need a transition – or, as she preferred to call it, 'implementation' – period for the United Kingdom. The BSG already assumed there would have to be such a period of adjustment, and as they drafted Section 28 of their statement they were debating how long it should be.

> BROK: Barnier told me today two years. Two or three
> years. Three years is already the maximum for him.
> Otherwise they [the British] will use the transitional
> period as a permanent position, for the next 100 years.
> VERHOFSTADT: 'Should not exceed three years.' You
> cannot put here something else. Two is ridiculous, too
> short. If you start with four or five everybody says: are
> they crazy, yes?
> BROK: But it's a very weak formulation, 'should not
> exceed' . . .

The Italian Roberto Gualtieri chipped in with 'OK, I accept three, but let's change years to decades', provoking general laughter. The final version of Section 28 stated that the European Parliament 'Believes that transitional arrangements ensuring legal certainty and continuity can only be agreed between the European Union and the United Kingdom if they contain the right balance of rights and obligations for both parties, preserve the integrity of European Union legal order, with the European Court of Justice responsible for settling any legal challenges; they must also be strictly limited in time, and should not exceed three years, and in scope they can never be a substitute for Union membership.'

In thirty-seven separate sections, the document identified

almost all the areas that would become headline news in the course of the negotiations over the next two years. It noted Mrs May's 'red lines' with regret, and laid out what were effectively EU red lines in return; the Union would not be prepared to compromise its core principles to accommodate Britain's position: 'A continued membership by the UK of the single market, the European Economic Area and/or the Custom Union would have been the optimal solution for both the UK and the EU-27,' it stated, '[but] [t]his is not possible as long as the UK government maintains its objections to the four freedoms and the jurisdiction of the Court of Justice of the European Union, refuses to make a general contribution to the EU budget and wants to conduct its own trade policy.'

The text was drawn up with close attention to detail, and, in accordance with the principles of transparency and consultation, it was cleared with European Commission and the Council. Crucially, it laid out a timetable for negotiations which was based on the strict letter of Article 50 and made it impossible to settle everything at once in the way Mrs May's Lancaster House speech suggested; talks on the United Kingdom's withdrawal and on its future relationship would be conducted separately. Under the heading 'sequencing of the negotiations' it said:

13. Underlines that, in accordance with Article 50(2) of the Treaty on European Union, the negotiations are to concern the arrangements for the United Kingdom's withdrawal while taking account of the framework for the United Kingdom's future relationship with the European Union;

14. Agrees that should substantial progress be made towards a withdrawal agreement then talks could start

on possible transitional arrangements on the basis of the intended framework for the United Kingdom's future relationship with the European Union;

15. Notes that an agreement on a future relationship between the European Union and the United Kingdom as a third country can only be concluded once the United Kingdom has withdrawn from the European Union.

The resolution was also very clear on the three issues that should be dealt with first: 'The legal status of EU-27 citizens living or having lived in the United Kingdom and of United Kingdom citizens living or having lived in other EU member states; the settlement of financial obligations between the United Kingdom and the European Union; and the European Union's external border.'

According to FullFact, an independent UK factchecking charity, around 3.7 million (in 2018) people living in the UK are citizens of another EU country – about 6 per cent of the total UK population. Just under 1 million of these EU citizens are Poles, over 400,000 come from Romania, and Ireland, Italy, Portugal, Lithuania, France, Spain, Germany and Latvia complete the list of the ten countries with the largest number of citizens in the UK. The number of people born in the UK who live in other EU countries is estimated at 1.2 million (data collected by the United Nations in 2015). Spain hosts the largest group, 308,000. The second largest number lives in Ireland, an estimated 254,000, France is third with 185,000, Germany hosts 103,000, and 64,000 live in Italy. The European Parliament demanded that 'their respective rights and interests must be given full priority in the negotiations'. The EU citizens in the UK and the UK citizens in the

EU were quick to organise themselves into lobby groups – the 3 Million and British in Europe. They put pressure on the European Parliament with a constant stream of letters to Verhofstadt and many other MEPs.

On the settlement of financial obligations, the resolution stressed that:

> A single financial settlement with the United Kingdom on the basis of the European Union's annual accounts as audited by the European Court of Auditors must include all its legal liabilities arising from outstanding commitments as well as making provision for off-balance sheet items, contingent liabilities and other financial costs arising directly as a result of the United Kingdom's withdrawal.

The third big issue, that of the European Union's external border, was above all about the border between Northern Ireland and the Republic of Ireland, which, with Britain's departure from the EU, would become the only land border between the EU and the UK. Although the issue did not at this stage have anything like the political prominence it would later acquire, the basic dilemma was there from the first. On the one hand the border had to be kept open, to ensure continued peace and stability on the Irish island, in accordance with the Good Friday Agreement. On the other hand, it could not simply stay open as if nothing had changed, because the EU did not want a 300-plus-mile open door for goods which might not conform to their standards to be smuggled into the single market and the customs union. The problem might be solved by a future trade agreement that maintained the alignment of tariffs and regulations in the two markets, but because the European Union insisted on the 'sequencing of negotiations' a trade agreement was not something the EU wanted to talk about at this stage.

The BSG members slaved on their resolution for over two hours, and then a bottle of wine came out – a good one, from Sicily. Bram Delen, Verhofstadt's speechwriter, produced some glasses. 'OK, we are going to not drink on the Brexit, but on the resolution,' Verhofstadt declared. 'On the revocation,' Danuta Hübner suggested. But that seemed an unrealistic proposition, so Verhofstadt stuck with what was possible. 'If we make an agreement with the Brits, we are going to pour 100 of these . . .' The wine connoisseur briefly took over from the politician.

> VERHOFSTADT: A little bit too cold, eh?
> GUALTIERI: Yeah, it's cold. French way, they serve [it like] that.
> VERHOFSTADT: So 100 per cent cabernet sauvignon, Etna. I think that it's four, five hundred metres altitude that they make it . . .

The Pole Danuta Hübner teased the group's president with, 'But you used to give good dinners, and now wine only?', at which point they turned their attention to future meetings. Verhofstadt raised his glass and put an affectionate hand on Brok's arm.

> VERHOFSTADT: This is the Brexit Steering Group, for two years together . . . Yeah!! [laughs] And then the transition period also. Again three years. Yeah!!
> BROK: At least three years.
> VERHOFSTADT: At least.

That good humour had evaporated when Verhofstadt's staff gathered two days later, on 29 March 2017. Despite the apparent unity in the Brexit

Steering Group, one member, it seemed, had played outside the rules. Guillaume McLaughlin and Eva Palatova came storming into the room where Bram Delen was preparing for a press conference Verhofstadt was due to give that afternoon, once Theresa May had formalised Britain's decision to trigger Article 50. The text the BSG had agreed was all over the pages of a British newspaper.

MCLAUGHLIN: It's in *The* fucking *Guardian*, have you seen it?

DELEN: Yeah, are you surprised, honestly? Guillaume?

MCLAUGHLIN: Well, it's not bad that it is only today in *The Guardian*.

DELEN: Yeah, that surprises me – that it is only today. Are you honestly surprised?

MCLAUGHLIN: Yeah, I'm really pissed off.

DELEN: Come on. Brok, Gualtieri, Lamberts?

PALATOVA: We have to be able to trust those people. Otherwise how can you do stuff?

MCLAUGHLIN: We're going to have to negotiate with these guys over the next year and a half . . .

Delen went on with his work, declaring, 'It surprises me that you are surprised.' It fell to Verhofstadt himself to calm his enraged chief of staff. 'We're about to publish the resolution anyway, in a couple of hours. Better that it happened today than yesterday.'

~

The road to 29 March 2017 had proved unexpectedly bumpy for Theresa May. While Guy Verhofstadt had been fighting to secure the rights of the European Parliament in the forthcoming negotiations, there was a parallel struggle between Parliament and the Executive going on in Britain. Mrs May's government argued that it had the authority to initiate the process of withdrawing from the European Union under the ancient constitutional provision known as 'royal prerogative', which, by tradition, gives British governments the right to conduct foreign affairs. But Gina Miller, a pro-European activist and fund manager, challenged that in the courts, arguing that triggering Article 50 would lead to the nullification of parliamentary Acts relating to Britain's EU membership, and that it therefore required parliamentary ratification.

When the High Court supported her, the ruling prompted one of the most notorious headlines of the Brexit debate; the *Daily Mail* put photographs of the judges who took the decision on its front page, declaring them 'Enemies of the People'. The Supreme Court, Britain's highest judicial authority, confirmed on 24 January 2017, by a majority of 8–3, that Parliament must give its authority to the invocation of Article 50. It was partly because of the case that Mrs May promised a parliamentary vote on any withdrawal agreement she eventually negotiated with the European Union.

On 1 February Parliament duly gave its consent to the triggering of Article 50 – the government was backed by the leadership of the Labour Party, and the motion went through by 498 to 114. On 29 March 2017 at twenty past twelve, Sir Tim Barrow, the United Kingdom's permanent representative to the European Union, delivered Theresa May's letter to the president of the European Council, Donald Tusk, by hand. 'I am writing to give effect to the democratic decision of the people of the United Kingdom,' it read. 'I hereby notify the European Council in accordance with Article 50(2) of the Treaty on European Union of the United Kingdom's intention to withdraw from the European Union.'

The letter was also the beginning of negotiations – the

EU had refused to begin them until Article 50 was formally invoked, arguing that they did not want to negotiate 'on the basis of a speech'. In her letter Theresa May once again spelled out the British position that Britain's future relationship with the EU should be discussed alongside a withdrawal agreement: 'We believe it is necessary to agree the terms of our future partnership alongside those of our withdrawal from the EU.' And there was an implied threat, a hint that Britain might withdraw its much-valued security cooperation if it did not get the trade deal it wanted: 'If we leave the European Union without an agreement the default position is that we would have to trade on World Trade Organisation terms,' the letter stated. 'In security terms a failure to reach agreement would mean our cooperation in the fight against crime and terrorism would be weakened.'

~

In the eternal competition between the three big European institutions, Verhofstadt wanted the European Parliament to be the first to react to May's letter. At a press conference in the afternoon, he planned to read out a carefully prepared statement, in which every word was weighed. The communiqué was composed according to a fixed ritual. Bram Delen had written a first draft on the basis of a discussion with Verhofstadt the day before. That draft was then filleted in the course of the morning by the whole team — Verhofstadt, Bram, Guillaume, Edel, Eva and Jeroen — with everyone giving comments and taking notes around a big table.

Now it was up to Bram to rewrite the statement, using Verhofstadt's annotated version of his first draft as a basis — which was no sinecure, because his boss's scribbling was . . . scribbly. 'OK, you're all set there? You have the bits and pieces?' Guillaume asked Bram.

'Yes,' he said.

'Is this Hoff's version?' Edel asked. 'Do you want me to sit here and hold your hand and help you with Hoff's writing?'

Bram nodded thankfully: 'Oh yes.'

Verhofstadt had left the room by then, to go to another meeting — only to return half an hour later with more thoughts about the statement, which he had jotted down on the sides of a document that he still needed. But no problem. He tore off the sides where he had scribbled down his thoughts and handed them one by one to Bram, who couldn't suppress a smile, much more aware than his boss of the camera registering the moment.

The main message that Verhofstadt wanted to convey was that in the treaty it was very clearly indicated that 'it is this house, the European Parliament, which has to approve the final deal, the final agreement.' He also wanted to issue a number of clear warnings, and the fact that he would have to word them carefully made him itchy. At a certain point during the morning brainstorm he'd said to his chief of staff Guillaume McLaughlin, who was reining him in, 'You're really cautious, eh? You cannot talk about this, you cannot talk about that. Blablabla. You have to be under the waterline. Maybe', he suggested sarcastically, 'we have not to appear today in the press conference, that would be the best thing.'

Delen, his hand held by Crosse, now had to find the right words for the warnings, which, notwithstanding McLaughlin's concerns, were to be clear and stark. One important point was that, between the UK and the twenty-seven remaining EU member states, there should be only one negotiator: Michel Barnier.

DELEN: We'll not accept parallel negotiations, behind our back.

CROSSE: No, because it's the principle, he wants to name it, so we can say: I don't accept what I call 'behind our back' negotiations.

DELEN: The EU will make all national concerns, no, will

take all national concerns on board – he didn't really
mention this, eh? Is it OK? – will take all national
concerns on board as its own.

*In the press conference this eventually emerged as: 'We hope for fair
and constructive negotiations. That means 'not behind our back': individual member states of the EU could be tempted to negotiate separate
agreements with the UK. For us, the EP, the unity of the twenty-seven
is vital.'*

*Another warning concerned the attempt that May had made in her
letter to bargain with security. 'What we shall never accept is that there
is a trade-off . . . saying, "Oh we can do a good agreement on security,
internal and external, if there is also a deal that we want, on trade and
economics." I think that the security of our citizens is far too important
to start a trade-off for one for the other.'*

*Then there was the delicate question of whether the United Kingdom
should be punished for having the temerity to leave the Union:*

DELEN: The point is, do we add the punitive expedition?
CROSSE: No.
DELEN: In the end it will be clear that it can never be
    better outside the Union than inside.
CROSSE: It will never be better. 'Can' never be better
    means we're gonna make an effort for it not to be
    better. 'Will' means, we believe genuinely that they
    will be worse off. There's the difference.
DELEN: And perhaps you can say . . . this is not about
    punishment, it's the iron logic of the treaties. [smiles]
    It's a bit dramatic, but yeah, no?

At 12.35 p.m., Theresa May announced the triggering of
Article 50 in Parliament. 'A few minutes ago in Brussels,' she

said from the despatch box, 'the United Kingdom's permanent representative to the EU handed a letter to the president of the European Council on my behalf, confirming the government's decision to invoke Article 50 of the Treaty on European Union. The Article 50 process is now underway. And, in accordance with the wishes of the British people, the United Kingdom is leaving the European Union.'

In Guy Verhofstadt's Brussels offices, Bram Delen gave a running commentary. 'This is an historic moment from which there can be no turning back. Britain is leaving the European Union,' Mrs May said, to the appreciative muttering of her backbenchers. Bram remarked: 'The supportive mumbling goes a bit . . .' and with his hands he showed 'down'. To which Edel said smilingly: 'They're not sure whether to be too supportive or not.' May continued, 'We will strengthen the Union of the four nations that comprise our United Kingdom. We will negotiate as one United Kingdom, taking account of the specific interests of every nation and region of the UK.' From Bram: 'The problem, either she's contradicting herself within the same speech, or she's saying things that everybody knows are completely untrue. "More than ever united" – it's the opposite.'

An hour later, Verhofstadt gave his press conference – at the side of Antonio Tajani, the Italian president of the European Parliament, with whom he had to share the spotlight. There was no way around that on such an important day. Tajani said a few words, Verhofstadt made his statement, and at the end journalists were allowed to ask questions:

JOURNALIST FROM *LE SOIR* [a Belgian newspaper]: An eminent member of the Parliament told me that the Parliament will be the bad guy in the negotiations . . . how do you see that 'bad guy' role?

TAJANI: I haven't quite got that – the bad guy is
Verhofstadt? I'm not clear whether the bad guy is the
Parliament or Verhofstadt?

LE SOIR: No, no, the question is . . .

TAJANI [laughing]: Of course I understood. But we shall
just do our job . . . We are defending the interests of
European citizens. If it's bad to defend the interests
of European citizens, we will be bad. If we need to
be bad to defend the interests of citizens, we shall be
bad. But our only objective is to defend the rights of
citizens. That's our job. We were elected to defend the
rights of citizens.

The European Parliament's Brexit coordinator followed that
with a reminder of the foundation stone of the EU's negotiating position: 'And as the president of our house, Mr Tajani
has indicated, naturally it will never be . . . outside the union
better than inside the union. And that is not a question of
revenge. That is not a question of punishment. That is the logic
of the EU.'

3

THEY'LL CHOP OFF HER HEAD

Two weeks after Article 50 was triggered, I travelled to Umbria, not far from Arezzo, where Guy Verhofstadt has restored an old villa with a small vineyard. He started making wine there seven years ago, with the help of the Sicilian viticulturist Lorenzo Landi, and it was time to bottle the result of last year's harvest — around 1,500 bottles of red wine, called Meone after the hilltop where Verhofstadt's villa is situated.

I invited myself to Meone, because as a filmmaker I thought that my audience would also want to see some scenes that had nothing to do with Brexit and its complex, technical palavers. Verhofstadt agreed without much ado, accepting my argument but requesting my help with the bottling — in return for which I asked for two bottles.

I stayed in a small hotel nearby, but on the second night I was invited to sleep at his villa, by his wife Dominique: 'Easier, no?' Verhofstadt and his wife have known each other since they were seventeen. He first saw her in an amateur film made by a household friend. Not long after they became an item and started exploring the interior dimensions of Verhofstadt's first car, a Mini Cooper — which proved to be 'quite big, certainly big enough'. And while Verhofstadt conquered the political scene in Belgium, Dominique Verkinderen became a professional classical singer.

Despite their busy careers, the couple brought two children into this world: Charlotte and Louis. As young children — while Verhofstadt was prime minister of Belgium, for almost ten years, from 1999 until 2008 – Charlotte and Louis often didn't see much of their father, nor their mother. Quite frequently they were left in the care of the house-keeper of the prime minister's official residence in Brussels. But then one evening Verhofstadt would arrive home, tell everyone to pack bags, and off they drove to Italy. Meone, the hilltop where their villa is situated, is the place where the Verhofstadts are a family. In a glass cupboard in the corridor, white bone fragments lay on display. Charlotte dug them up as a child, somewhere around the house.

What struck me most about the villa was that the guest quarters are larger than the actual family living space. There must be six or seven guest rooms, making the villa a place for encounters, not reclusion. On two occasions, I was one of the guests, and even today I wonder whether this was an act of manipulation, to keep me close, for more control or influence, or a real act of kindness and curiosity. The large guest quarters make me believe that the invitation was just that, kindness combined with a habit and desire to share meals and ideas, but I will never know. The emotional hermit Verhofstadt will certainly never tell me, that's for sure. While his wife Dominique would probably be offended by my doubts, I would be surprised if she – after forty years at the side of a husband so immersed in politics – also didn't understand them.

Verhofstadt got help with the bottling – as always – from his personal assistant Erik Janda, and his wife Marleen. They put on a steady pace, while Dominique and Charlotte were cooking. When Verhofstadt wasn't bottling, he was checking his mobile.

~

While Guy Verhofstadt was enjoying the Umbrian countryside, Theresa May's Easter break took her on a walking holiday in North Wales. In the market town of Dolgellau, Gwynedd, she was spotted buying a £32 sterling silver ring in a craft shop and attending a Palm Sunday service in St Mary's church. But most of her time was spent striding over the Snowdonian slopes with her husband, Philip. She told the *Wales Online* website that 'walking in Wales is an opportunity to get out and about and see scenery and clear your mind and your thinking . . . We stay in a hotel and try to walk every day. Walking is about relaxing, getting exercise and fresh air.'

It was during this trip that she made her momentous decision to call a general election. She had in fact already discussed the idea with a small inner circle; her influential chief of staff, Nick Timothy, had argued forcefully for an early poll, and the Brexit secretary, David Davis, was also a champion of going to the country. Davis argued that the Brexit timetable under Article 50 meant that Britain's departure from the EU would be pushed awkwardly close to 2020, the date then set for the next election under the Fixed Term Parliament Act. And the polls would have been difficult for any politician to resist; the Conservatives' lead over Labour had increased significantly since Theresa May became prime minister, and some polling in April 2017 put it at over 20 per cent.

But her announcement – made in Downing Street just after 11.00 a.m. on 18 April – came as a complete surprise. Even some senior ministers had no idea what was coming; it was reported that before the Cabinet met that morning one minister innocently remarked that the day's agenda looked thin. The decision represented a reversal of everything she had said in public on the question of an election over the previous eight months. When she launched her leadership bid, she very clearly stated her view that 'there should be no general election until 2020'. And she repeated it during her first big broadcast interview as prime minister: 'I'm not going to be calling a snap election,' she told Andrew Marr in September 2016.

May justified her change of mind on the grounds that she

needed a renewed mandate to secure the best possible outcome in the forthcoming Brexit negotiations. 'Our opponents
believe because the government's majority is so small, that
our resolve will weaken and that they can force us to change
course,' she said. 'What they are doing jeopardises the work
we must do to prepare for Brexit at home and it weakens the
government's negotiating position in Europe. If we do not
hold a general election now, their political game-playing will
continue, and the negotiations with the European Union will
reach their most difficult stage in the run-up to the next scheduled election.' That message was picked up enthusiastically
by the Brexit-supporting press; the *Daily Mail* headlined its
account of the campaign launch with the words 'CRUSH THE
SABOTEURS', reporting, 'In a stunning move, May calls bluff
of "game-playing" Remoaners.'

In her appeal to the voters, she claimed Brexit firmly as a
Conservative project, and cast the election debate in terms of
the national interest: 'Every vote for the Conservatives will
make it harder for opposition politicians who want to stop
me from getting the job done,' she said. 'Every vote for the
Conservatives will make me stronger when I negotiate for
Britain with the prime ministers, presidents and chancellors of
the European Union. Every vote for the Conservatives means
we can stick to our plan for a stronger Britain and take the right
long-term decisions for a more secure future.' And she ended
with the phrase that was to become a mantra during the campaign: 'So, tomorrow, let the House of Commons vote for an
election, let everybody put forward their proposals for Brexit
and their programmes for government, and let us remove the
risk of uncertainty and instability and continue to give the
country the strong and stable leadership it demands.'

Verhofstadt and May come from very different political

traditions. Belgium, like most continental European countries, but unlike the UK, is routinely governed by coalitions.
Verhofstadt first became the country's prime minister, in 1999,
by forming a coalition which defeated the Christian Democrats,
who had been part of almost every government since Belgium
became an independent country in 1830. As a Liberal, he led
coalitions with the Social Democrats and the Green Party,
two parties firmly on the other side of his country's political
spectrum. That kind of cross-party cooperation is alien to the
British system in which Mrs May has spent her political life.

*It takes a prime minister to know a prime minister, and Guy Verhofstadt
watched Theresa May's gambit with detached curiosity, as one professional, who knows what it takes, observes another professional. Because
there is always a lesson to learn. In the two years that I filmed him,
Verhofstadt never judged the British prime minister, nor did he com-
miserate with her. He simply watched and understood. 'She fights to
survive,' he repeatedly said. 'Because that's what you do. It's keep on
fighting or political death.'*

In his role as Mr Brexit, though, Verhofstadt was scathing
about Mrs May's decision to call for a snap election. In an
opinion piece in *The Guardian*, he wrote – or rather co-wrote
with his British spokesperson Nick Petre, 'As a Belgian, I have
a long-standing appreciation of surrealism. Having informed
European leaders that Britain is leaving the European Union
and, after laying out the UK's negotiating position in a detailed
notification letter, the prime minister is now asking the British
people how they would like their full English Brexit served. In
Brussels, we now wonder who will be joining us at the breakfast table after all.'

And he voiced the fear, widely shared within the EU, that

the prime minister was giving party management priority over the national interest: 'As with the referendum, which many European leaders saw as a Tory cat fight that got out of control, I have little doubt many on the continent see this election as again motivated by the internal machinations of the Tory party,' the piece continued. 'What has been billed as a "Brexit election" is an attempted power grab by the Tories, who wish to take advantage of a Labour party in seeming disarray to secure another five years of power before the reality of Brexit bites. Will the election of more Tory MPs give May a greater chance of securing a better Brexit deal? For those sitting around the table in Brussels, this is an irrelevance. British officials will represent the people of the UK in the negotiations, regardless of the number of Tory MPs.'

What struck some in the EU most forcefully about Theresa May's decision to hold a snap election was that it would reduce what they already considered to be a very short period in which the UK's withdrawal could be negotiated. By triggering Article 50 Mrs May had, to use another phrase which was soon to become familiar, set the clock ticking, but the general election put the Brexit process on hold, and not just for a couple of weeks, because a mixture of factors made this an unusually long campaign. Under legislation introduced in 2013 to change the system of voter registration, the government had extended the election timetable from seventeen to twenty-five working days, and the election period chosen by Theresa May included two bank holidays. In addition, the House of Lords was still in recess when she announced the election, which delayed the process of tidying up business which was going through Parliament. The campaign – from Theresa May's announcement on 18 April to polling day on 8 June – lasted for more than eight weeks, eating away at the two-year negotiating period dictated by Article 50.

It very quickly became apparent that the politics of the election and the process of the Article 50 negotiations would become entangled. On 29 April, the European Council met in Brussels to adopt its negotiating guidelines. The European Parliament had already laid out its own guidelines, and Verhofstadt met the Liberal heads of state and government over breakfast at the majestic Egmont Palace to discuss the day's agenda. All European political groups always do this before a Council meeting, with the prime ministers of their colour.

One of the most delicate aspects of the guidelines related to the possibility of what is known as a 'border poll' on whether Northern Ireland should become part of the Republic; the Good Friday Agreement, which ended Northern Ireland's Troubles in 1998, states that the British government must hold such a poll if it seems 'likely' that it would produce a vote for unification, and some Republicans and Nationalists argued that Brexit had indeed created those conditions.

Both the Parliament and the Council took the view that in the event of such a vote, Northern Ireland would become part of the EU, even if Britain left the Union ('A re-united Ireland will be automatically part of the Union,' Verhofstadt noted approvingly), and their negotiating guidelines included support for 'the goal of peace and reconciliation enshrined in the Good Friday Agreement in all its parts'. 'All parts, means exactly that,' Verhofstadt commented, again with an approving nod: 'The possible re-unification of the island.' The Dutch prime minister, Mark Rutte, sitting next to him, chipped in with, 'Theresa May, I understand, was very unhappy about this . . . She asked, "Can't you do that at the end of June, after the elections?"'

The future of Gibraltar was also raised at the breakfast meeting. There had been speculation that Spain might use the

Brexit negotiations to raise the question of Britain's sovereignty over the Rock, and Cecilia Malmström, the EU commissioner for trade and trade agreements, who is a member of the Swedish *Liberalerna*, threw in a wild card: 'I lunched with the Argentinian foreign minister,' she said. 'Maybe we could address the issue of the *Malvinas* [the Falkland Islands]?' – there was general laughter around the table – 'I said: don't think so.' From Rutte: 'Don't go there.'

While Britain turned its attention to the campaign, Verhofstadt was being lobbied in Brussels, and Irish politicians – from both north and south of the Irish border – were prominent among his visitors. The issue of the Irish border had been a sideshow during the 2016 Brexit referendum campaign – despite the warnings from the former prime ministers John Major and Tony Blair that leaving the European Union might threaten the Good Friday Agreement. All the signs were that it would be largely ignored during the 2017 election campaign too – indeed, Mark Rutte's observation suggested the Conservatives would be only too pleased to play it down.

The Conservative Party manifesto, when it was published a month into the election campaign, mentioned the issue only briefly, and the little the document did say only served to raise further concerns in Ireland. The manifesto declared that the government's commitment to the Good Friday Agreement was 'undiminished', but there was no pledge to avoid the return of a hard border on the island of Ireland. Instead, the document stated, 'We will maintain the Common Travel Area and maintain as *frictionless a border as possible* [our italics] for people, goods and services between Northern Ireland and the Republic of Ireland.'

In mid-May, Verhofstadt hosted a meeting with the Sinn Féin MEP Martina Anderson, whose life story vividly dramatises the reasons the Irish border would become such a raw issue in the Brexit talks. Anderson was born in the Bogside of Derry, a Republican stronghold, and joined the IRA in the late 1970s. At the age of eighteen, she was arrested and charged with possession of a firearm and causing an explosion. She jumped bail and escaped over the border to the Republic. In 1985 she was arrested again – this time in Glasgow, in the company of four other IRA members, including Patrick Magee, who was later convicted of blowing up the Grand Hotel in Brighton during the 1984 Conservative Party conference. She spent thirteen years in jail before she was released in 1998 following the Good Friday Agreement. Her journey from the world of violence to the world of constitutional politics was completed in 2007 when she won a seat in the Northern Ireland Assembly – she became one of the first Sinn Féin members of the Northern Ireland Policy Board the same year – and she became an MEP in 2012.

Anderson wanted to know how the European Parliament would try to exercise influence over the Brexit negotiations, and to make the argument for focusing on the issue of the Irish border. 'We're not here arguing a case of clemency for Theresa May and her government,' she told Verhofstadt. 'We know that it will be a tough negotiation and, in many ways, we accept that it has to be. But . . . we think it would be most unjust for Ireland to be the collateral damage in what was a reckless enterprise by Boris Johnson, Nigel Farage, David Cameron . . . I could name-check all of them for you.'

Verhofstadt acknowledged that the border question deserved more detailed attention. 'We're always talking about [the] financial settlement, the citizens' rights – that's very important, citizens' rights are more important than financial settlement – but . . . until now, we didn't prepare additional things . . . on the border.' He did, however, dismiss the idea of those 'technical solutions' which would feature so largely in Britain's negotiating position on how the border could be kept open. 'I don't think that technical innovation will be sufficient to solve the problem,' he said. 'Cameras, scans; not enough.'

Martina Anderson pressed home her case: 'It's not to be melodramatic, this is potentially very, very dangerous in Ireland,' she said. 'We know how robust the [peace] process is, and how hard won it has been by so many people, so we're not saying it's in jeopardy, but we're not willing to gamble on it, and we're certainly not prepared to let the Tories, and Theresa May and Boris Johnson . . . to actually gamble with it, we live there.' She took a side swipe at the British foreign secretary for good measure, accusing of Johnson of 'whinging on, saying that apparently the Europeans owe him billions, personally it seems'. And, in a comment that reflected her Republican back-ground, she declared that 'the British government will not give one curse about what happens to Ireland'.

The following day brought a visit from Dara Murphy, Fine Gael's minister of state for European affairs. Ireland's lobbying campaign around the EU to ensure that its priorities would be taken into account in the Brexit negotiations was now well underway. 'Since Brexit I've been in twenty member states, and we're doing in each one three or four days,' Murphy told Verhofstadt. 'We're talking to the media. We're talking to their opposition. Most importantly, though, we're going into their national parliaments and meeting their European and foreign affairs committees, of course their governments and their technical experts.'

Murphy flattered Verhofstadt. 'Your role will be absolutely crucial now,' he told him, and he paid tribute to Verhofstadt's greater experience by recognising that his host was 'at the very top of European politics'. He also noted the EU's impressive unity in the face of the Brexit challenge. 'I've been a minister for just three years,' he said, 'but I've never seen an issue unite the three institutions, the political families, and the twenty-seven member states.' And he delivered a crucially important message from the Irish government; there was no question of Dublin doing any kind of side deal with London over the Irish border. 'I'm interested in giving one message to you in the role you have,' Murphy told Verhofstadt. 'And it is that we in Ireland only want to engage as part of twenty-seven; we will not engage bilaterally. If you have any issues come and talk to us.'

Mr Murphy's Fine Gael is a centre-right party, and since the Good Friday Agreement relations between London and Dublin had been remarkably cordial. The two governments often found themselves acting together within the European Union. But the strains Brexit had put on the relationship between Ireland's governing party and the Conservatives were becoming more and more evident. 'I had quite a disturbing talk about Brexit with a Conservative MEP, last week,' Dara Murphy reported. 'They're using some very simplistic language. He said, "You don't keep paying your golf membership when you're leaving the club. You don't pay any more." So I said, "Well, hang on a minute. First of all, the EU is not a golf club. And secondly we're talking about golf rounds you already played."'

'Exactly, you did already all the holes,' replied Verhofstadt.

'And, if you want to continue to play golf with us in the future . . . But look, we need to work with them because they're a big European country. But the EU will be stronger, because they have been very semi-detached. They always annoyed me because they always talked about the EU in the third person. Them, those people,' Murphy ended.

That afternoon Verhofstadt held a meeting with the Brexit

Steering Group to brief them on his latest conversation with Michel Barnier. 'In a nice restaurant,' Brok teased him. 'In a restaurant where you were also, I know, Elmar. We always go to the same places,' Verhofstadt retorted. He reported that Barnier had, while the UK was gearing up for May's snap election, developed a formula for the negotiations once they got underway. 'There will be . . . a four-week cycle,' Verhofstadt explained. 'Week one will be the preparation inside the Union. Week two will be the exchange of the position papers with the UK and the finalisation of the position of the EU. Week three will be the negotiations between the chief negotiators and the technical groups. Week four will be reporting – debriefing – inside the Union.' The BSG would be briefed twice in each negotiating cycle – in weeks two and four.

～

Back in Britain the Conservative manifesto was published the following day, 18 May, and it included a policy that came as another surprise to most Conservative MPs and proved devastatingly unpopular on the doorstep. The party proposed a reform of the system of paying for social care, which meant those who were given care at home would have the same financial responsibilities as those who were cared for institutionally. At first it appeared a sensible regularisation of an anomaly, and it was designed to redress the intergenerational inequality of a system that required younger people to bear the cost of looking after older people.

But the policy was complicated and difficult to explain, and when the press understood that it would mean that people who were being cared for at home would often have to sell those homes to bear the cost of their care, there was uproar. The policy was dubbed a 'dementia tax', and it faced such a chorus of outrage that the party was forced to change tack. Four days after the publication of the manifesto, Mrs May announced there would be an 'absolute limit' on the amount anyone would have to pay for their social care.

The policy reversal inevitably provoked questions about whether her leadership really deserved the 'strong and stable' label she had claimed for it. The killer question following her statement came from a journalist on the usually sympathetic *Daily Telegraph*: 'Will anything else in the manifesto change between now and June 8th?' he asked. Mrs May's response haunted her for the rest of the campaign: 'Nothing has changed! Nothing has changed!' she barked. The dementia tax episode of course had nothing whatever to do with Britain's negotiations with the European Union, but the political fallout was to have a profound effect on the way they unfolded over the months that followed.

~

With Brexit negotiations in limbo at the British end, on Friday 5 May 2017, at his home in Ghent, Verhofstadt gave an extended and reflective interview to Lode Desmet about his ambitions and fears for the negotiations ahead. In the immediate aftermath of the British referendum, there were widespread concerns among the EU's champions that Britain's decision would begin a trend. That, at least, seemed to have receded: 'Everybody said before Brexit, and certainly after Brexit, now we are going to see a lot of exits in the European Union. A domino effect. Brexit, Dutch exit, Danish exit, Austrian exit, you name it. Even a Frexit, an exit of France,' Verhofstadt recalled:

And what we have seen is quite the opposite. People say, OK, the EU has some weaknesses, there is a lot of criticism, but we don't want to destroy it. What the public opinion is doing at the moment – and I think that will continue until 2018, 2019 – is giving a new chance to European leaders to reform the EU. And so that's a unique opportunity, but there's also a big danger. If it doesn't happen in the coming years, this reform of the Union, then the public opinion will massively be disappointed, and vote against it. And then we could lose the Union.

He was also concerned about the way Brexit was engaging so much of the EU's time and attention, a consideration that would become a significant factor when Britain asked for an extension to the Article 50 timetable two years later. 'What I see is the enormous waste of energy,' he said:

At the moment when we need to build up a strong Europe, against the Indians, the Chinese, the Americans, and the Russians who are threatening us . . . we are busy with a divorce. It's an enormous waste of energy. In Parliament, but certainly also in the Commission, not to talk about what is happening in the governments of the member states, 25, 30 per cent of our time, and energy, is going to the preparation of these negotiations, and later it will maybe be more than 30 per cent, when we start these negotiations . . . It's crazy. Enormous weakening of Europe.

Brexit is the complete opposite of what Verhofstadt stands for – indeed many Leave voters wanted to escape the European Union to avoid precisely the kind of future he envisaged. He is a European federalist. The EU's problems, according to his analysis, lay not in too much political integration, but in too little. Take the euro: 'Today you have a common currency but not instruments behind that currency,' he said. 'Like a treasury, a minister of finance, a budget, like exists behind every common currency. Behind the dollar is the USA, American budget, American treasury, treasury certificates and a whole army of civil servants. In Europe there is, besides the European Central Bank, nothing at all.'

'I don't call them dreams,' he said of his ambitions:

They are necessities. I see more and more people supporting that also. Even when a few years ago it was impossible to talk about a European army, everybody said it is a dream. But it's a necessity . . . The Americans can do four, five times more military operations than we can do. They are far more effective, because one army, one budget, and we have twenty-eight armies, twenty-eight budgets.

Europe is governed mainly by the meetings of the twenty-eight heads of government in the European Council. But they have another job. They are head of their state or their government. And that's a full-time job. I did it for nine years myself. It's more than a full-time job. So besides that they also have to govern Europe and come together six, seven times a year to fix the problems in Europe. It doesn't work like that. Governing in Europe is not a part-time job . . . I compare it always with the US. If the US were governed like Europe, it would not be Obama or Trump leading the country, but the fifty governors, all coming together and then deciding by unanimity. All this has to be reformed and maybe Brexit is a good moment to do that.

Two days later, Verhofstadt got one piece of news he was able to welcome with unalloyed enthusiasm; on Sunday 7 May 2017 Emmanuel Macron convincingly crushed the Front National's Marine Le Pen to win the French presidency. Verhofstadt watched the result coming in, live, at the news studio of the Belgian TV-station VTM, where his press team had also set up their own camera, to record a Facebook video message. 'I congratulate Emmanuel Macron on this magnificent victory,' he said in his post. 'I have supported his campaign from the first, and I am relieved, truly relieved, by the defeat he has inflicted on demagogy and populism.' But he warned that 'if populism has been defeated, it has not been conquered. Its forces remain powerful, and they flourish on the EU's failures.'

Macron would emerge as the leader whose European vision is closest to Verhofstadt's and, on 9 June 2017, Verhofstadt travelled to Paris to meet Macron's European adviser, Clément Beaune, to discuss whether an alliance could be built in the European Parliament between Macron's *En Marche* movement and Verhofstadt's group of Liberals; if he could pull it off the Liberals might become the the third, or even the second biggest parliamentary group, instead of the fourth.

Verhofstadt arrived at the train station with bleary eyes. It was the morning after Britain's general election, and he'd stayed up all night to follow the results — partly because they mattered for Brexit, but also because he is addicted to the game, his trade, politics. 'I'm dead tired. I stayed up all night to watch that stuff,' he said. 'And you know how it goes, it's a slow process, the results trickle in. Even now, eleven seats are undecided. But they [the Tories] don't have a majority, that's clear.'

A few minutes later he was joined by Guillaume McLaughlin and Yannick Laude, his spokesperson for France. The boss wanted to send out a tweet with his reaction, as quickly as possible, but like almost everyone else, they were scratching their heads for an appropriate response:

VERHOFSTADT: What do we say?
LAUDE: You are Mr Brexit, you must take time to reflect.

MCLAUGHLIN [challenging Laude]: Yes, but it's your job.

LAUDE: As for doing my job, the first thing I would say is that he [Verhofstadt] needs to say something that makes sense, and therefore he should wait until the situation is clarified.

MCLAUGHLIN: But it is clear; she's lost.

VERHOFSTADT: The situation is very clear.

MCLAUGHLIN: What could be clearer. She must resign. I don't see what else she can do.

Someone back at the office had come up with a draft tweet – but it did not pass muster with Nick Petre, the press secretary for the UK. Guillaume McLaughlin read from his phone. 'The draft tweet is awful, says Nick. Clouds over the British Isles, but in Brussels clear skies, perfect conditions to plan the future.' Verhofstadt and his chief of staff laughed. 'I agree,' said Verhofstadt, 'but give me something better.'

The tweet could have worked because Theresa May was indeed under a political cloud in London. Despite the bumps in the campaign road, her team had remained confident that her gamble would succeed right up until the moment Britain's broadcasters published the results of their exit polling when voting ended at 10 p.m. on 8 June. The poll predicted that, far from delivering the significantly higher majority the prime minister had hoped for, the election would result in a hung parliament. Initially the poll was greeted with scepticism – by the Labour opposition as much as the Conservatives. But as the night wore on and the results rolled in, it became clear that the pollsters' estimates were, broadly, right.

The Conservatives emerged as the largest party, and in fact increased their share of the vote – from 36.8 per cent in 2015 to 42.3 per cent. But Labour had managed an even more impressive leap in vote share to 40 per cent, a gain of nearly ten percentage points, yielding a net gain in seats of thirty. The Conservatives' net loss of thirteen seats meant that the slim majority David Cameron had secured two years earlier had disappeared. The prime minister made things worse for herself with a Downing Street performance which echoed her 'Nothing has changed! Nothing has changed!' comments during the campaign; she spoke as if she had secured the landslide victory that had looked within her grasp when the campaign began, made no apology to the thirty-three Tory MPs who had lost their seats, and earned herself the moniker 'Queen of Denial' on the front page of the *Evening Standard*.

In Paris, Guillaume McLaughlin's verdict was characteristically colourful. 'May may resign in two hours,' he said. 'I don't see how she cannot resign, eh? Honestly. She went in to create a bigger majority, and went out with a weaker majority. [He laughed] She didn't consult anyone about doing her election. She didn't consult very many people about her programme for the election. She ran the election programme on her own and did it very, very badly' – at this point McLaughlin pulled a face – 'They will chop off her head, *hein*! They will chop off her head. They are ruthless, the Tories. They're fucking ruthless. They'll chop off her head. She'd better jump before they chop off her head.'

Verhofstadt had spotted another aspect of the results that would have a significant impact on the Brexit negotiations.

In Northern Ireland, election night began with the Democratic Unionist Party taking a seat from the Ulster Unionist Party, which had traditionally been the more mainstream and moderate voice of Unionist opinion. By the time the full results were in, all but one constituency in Northern Ireland had fallen to the DUP or the Republican Sinn Féin

party. Sinn Féin's MPs do not take their seats in the House of
Commons, so Northern Ireland, which had voted by 55.78 per
cent to 44.22 per cent to remain in the EU, would be repre-
sented at Westminster by the ten MPs of the Brexit-supporting
DUP. Verhofstadt very quickly picked up on the implications.
'They [the Conservatives] could of course take the DUP, the
Unionists, on board. That could give them a majority of one
or two seats,' he laughed. 'Insane, no? Insane.'

And while their Thalys train trundled into Paris' Gare
du Nord, he showed Guillaume McLaughlin a tweet he had
written himself on his chief-of-staff's iPad: '. . . yet another
own goal, after Cameron now May. It will make these negotiations which were already complicated, I fear, even more
complicated.'

4

THE CHARMING BASTARD

Mid-June–late July 2017

'A year . . . after the referendum and three months after the letter of notification it is fair to say we have made no progress,' Michel Barnier told the Brexit Steering Group on 13 June. 'No more time to lose.' He reported that a 'first talk on the talks' had taken place with the British side the previous day, and that 'we are now awaiting news from London'.

Outside, Strasbourg was bathed in the first summer sun, which glittered on the glass-fronted European Parliament buildings and in the water of the River Ill, which, just behind them, joins the Rhine–Rhone Canal. The sun was not visible inside, because most meeting rooms in the Parliament are windowless. It could have been winter, autumn or spring there – with the large majority of male participants in the meeting all wearing their usual seasonless jackets, shirts and ties. Only the man behind the camera wore a T-shirt, as I always did – a conscious choice, to look the part of a rather poor, harmless passer-by.

Barnier unburdened himself of the frustration he felt about the political situation in London in the aftermath of Mrs May's botched general election:

All these words we hear, 'Great Brexit, Open Brexit, Soft Brexit, Hard Brexit, Fair Brexit', I've often said that I don't know what they mean. When I listen to the British debate over the past year, I note lots of emotion, lots of irrationality, lots of political manoeuvring. Fine, we have all that in our own political debate. But we are engaging in the un-knitting [*détricotage* was his striking French term] of forty-four years of relations, text by text. Even with goodwill we need time to resolve the problems. You've chosen to leave the EU; yes or no? For the moment, yes. So the next stage is the divorce, and all the unpleasantness that goes with a divorce.

Mr Barnier, who married his lawyer wife Isabelle Altmayer in 1982, added, 'I have no personal experience of it [divorce], but I know it is disagreeable.'

He complained that even at this late stage he was not quite sure who he would be negotiating with. 'I understand that Mr Davis is once again the secretary of state for Brexit, and I understand that in Mrs May's office her trusted aide, who I saw yesterday, is Olly Robbins. But . . .' He allowed the sentence to tail off, adding, 'The only thing I will allow myself to say as the European negotiator is that we need an interlocutor who is available, stable and accountable . . . Working with a mandate, and available.'

'And reliable,' the Italian Social Democrat Roberto Gualtieri threw in from the other side of the large conference room. Barnier smiled, and Guy Verhofstadt supplied a punchline: 'Now, come on. We can't ask for everything from the British. Let's not go overboard.' Now they all laughed.

Elmar Brok, the German Christian Democrat, had recently been in London, and had had a meeting with the British foreign secretary, Boris Johnson, which left him with 'a feeling that in the Tory Party the gambling goes on. There is a lack of seriousness to it. And therefore I am very much afraid.' He had a warning: 'We hear now all the time that because Britain is in a mess we have to move a little bit, to help them. I'm very clear that we have to do nothing. We are ready, and they have to come. It's up to them. And we have to wait while the air becomes thinner and thinner because we lose time.' It was an acute judgement; Barnier would later note that progress in the negotiations usually came in the run-up to European Council meetings, when the British side felt under political pressure to land a result.

The first round of direct negotiations between Michel Barnier and the British team took place six days later, on 19 June 2017. In his follow-up debrief with Verhofstadt and the other members of the BSG, Barnier was pleased with the way things had gone. His homework had paid off.

'We were, I mean the EU delegation, well prepared. It seems to me – we can speak frankly between us – better than the UK. Which allowed us to set the tone and the agenda.' The members of the BSG smiled. They had all seen the striking photograph of Barnier and Davis that accompanied much of the newspaper coverage of the opening session of the nego-tiations. In it, all three members of the EU team – Barnier himself; Sabine Weyand, his deputy; and Stéphanie Riso, his director for strategy, coordination and communication – have thick dossiers in front of them, while the British team, David Davis, flanked by the prime minister's adviser on Europe, Olly Robbins, and the bearded Sir Tim Barrow, the UK's perma-nent representative at the EU, had brought just one slim black notebook between them.

The second reason that, in Barnier's view, the EU team had had the edge related to that ticking clock and the political weather created by the British general election. 'The UK needed, last week,' he judged, 'for obviously internal political reasons, to get a success, and just to prove to London that they have begun the negotiations, for domestic political reasons.'

In the run-up to the first round of direct negotiations, David Davis had made some bullish comments in the British media. He promised 'a deal like no other in history' and, in mid-May, at the height of the general election campaign, he had threatened 'the row of the summer' over what the EU called 'sequencing', which described the order in which the negotiations would be conducted.

The EU negotiating guidelines – which had been agreed at the European Council meeting in April and which provided the mandate under which Barnier worked – stated unambiguously, like the parliamentary resolution, that the talks with Britain should be 'phased', and identified those three main areas the negotiations should cover first: the rights of EU and British citizens; the settlement of the United Kingdom's financial obligations to the Union; and the Northern Ireland border. The document recognised that there would also have to be discussions about the way the United Kingdom and the European Union traded and cooperated once the UK had left, but, again like the parliamentary resolution, said talks on the future could begin only when they were satisfied that 'sufficient progress' had been made on the the three divorce issues, and that, anyway, 'an agreement on a future relationship between the Union and the United Kingdom as such can only be finalised and concluded once the United Kingdom has become a third country, ' so after 29 March 2019, the UK departure date, twenty months from then.

Sequencing was a central plank of the EU's negotiating strategy; the Union's leaders were determined that Britain should not be able to use its financial obligations, the rights of EU citizens in Britain or the Irish border question, as bargaining chips to secure a better deal for the future. But Davis argued that sequencing would put the United Kingdom at a disadvantage because it meant dealing with 'the most difficult bit, the funding and Northern Ireland, before we do anything else'. He told ITV's Robert Peston that the EU's position was 'illogical', asking, 'How on earth do you resolve the issue of the border with Northern Ireland and the Republic of Ireland unless you know what our general borders policy is, what the customs agreement is, what our trade agreement is?' He duly laid out this position to the EU's chief negotiator, as Michel Barnier told the BSG on 28 June 2017.

'A word more generally perhaps on the strategy the British are facing us with,' Barnier spoke, slipping into French, 'to be more precise and concrete.' 'The strategy is to mix it all together, to have one negotiation. David Davis said to me, even before the first round of talks, "We can do everything, including a trade deal and the divorce, all that in two years." I said that is technically, politically and legally impossible. And so we will do the sequencing.'

As Barnier reported that first formal meeting, he won the argument immediately due to the political pressure on the British government in the aftermath of the general election. 'In short,' Barnier told the BSG, 'this allowed us to agree . . . to start with the most pressing uncertainty caused by Brexit. Implicitly this is an agreement on sequencing.'

At the press conference that followed that first day of negotiation, David Davis tried to scotch the idea that Britain had caved in. 'Everything is exactly the same as before,' he declared, in a phrase eerily similar to the prime minister's 'Nothing has changed'. 'We will be leaving the single market and the customs union and the timetable is exactly the one we asked for.' But Guy Verhofstadt gave a more persuasive account of what had happened to the German minister of foreign affairs, Sigmar Gabriel, during a visit to Berlin a couple of days later.

'They [the British] accepted the sequencing, because Barnier didn't use the word sequencing. He has a new wording, in French: *la première étape et la deuxième étape*, the first stage and the second stage. So he didn't use the word sequencing in the meeting. But in the press the day after: it's sequencing,' Verhofstadt laughed heartily. 'Normally in the Tour de France you only start the second stage after the first stage has been completed. You can't ride two stages at the same time.' Barnier clearly won this round, and the 'row of the summer' never really happened. But the issue of sequencing – or *étapes* – would remain a running sore in the negotiations, and the British side repeatedly found their room for manoeuvre was squeezed by the consequences. When he resigned a year later, David Davis claimed that this capitulation was No. 10's idea, and that he had resisted it.

It is evident from the Barnier debriefing to the BSG that at this stage the EU's negotiators saw money (rather than Northern Ireland) as the most contentious of the three areas under negotiation. 'The UK's objectives and tactics seem clear,' Barnier judged. 'They want to ensure we make progress on citizens and Ireland while trying to push off the issue of the financial settlement until October,' when the next phase of negotiations was due to begin, if 'sufficient progress' had been made by then. In a follow-up telephone call to David Davis, Barnier had therefore insisted that there must be progress on the financial settlement as well as the other two areas.

At this stage, the EU team still feared the British as shrewd negotiators, and so Barnier was worried. 'My opinion – if we can speak among ourselves – . . . is that they are trying to use the issue of citizens as a bargaining chip . . . I can see the British will push this issue, will push the Irish issue, and then make use of it, stating publicly, "You see, we are agreed on the rights of citizens, and these Brussels bureaucrats just want to talk about money!"'

There had been plenty of press speculation about the size of the exit bill Europe would present to Britain, but Barnier explained that the talks were a long way from a debate about figures. 'At the moment, Philippe,' and here Barnier addressed Philippe Lamberts, the Belgian MEP on the group, 'they [the British] haven't even accepted that they have obligations, legal ones. And I want them to accept that they have to enter into those discussions, that they recognise they have obligations. Afterwards we can talk about [the] scale of those obligations – but we haven't even reached that stage yet.'

Michel Barnier also noted one striking difference of approach between the two sides of the negotiations, which was reflected in the way they had prepared their respective position papers. 'It is important to read them attentively,' he said, 'because . . . the two papers are in a very different spirit, drafted in different ways. Ours is very precise, with legal foundations, while the British paper . . . expressed wishes, intentions. It doesn't have the same precision.' The charge that the British government was vague about its negotiating objectives would become another leitmotiv of the months that followed – the EU team could never quite decide whether that vagueness was tactical, or the result of political divisions and inadequate preparation.

When Philippe Lamberts noted that the negotiating process would become 'an exercise which lists all the benefits of the Union', Barnier allowed a frank insight into a broader political objective which went well beyond the details of a Brexit deal. 'I want to use this negotiating process as a whole as a teaching aid,' he said. 'Since we have got to pile up everything that's been involved in forty-four years of integration, we must explain, "This is what it means to be a member of the Union, and this is what you lose when you leave the Union." Because in each of our countries – it's too late for the UK – we need, if you will forgive me for saying so, to teach this lesson.'

~

Michel Barnier and David Davis had history; they were both Europe ministers in the mid-1990s, in the aftermath of the Maastricht Treaty, another period of Tory tension over Europe, and encountered one another during discussions on the future shape of the EU. At their first Brexit meeting they exchanged gifts – David Davis produced a rare, signed edition of the mountaineering book *Regards vers L'Annapurna*, while Michel Barnier offered a carved wooden walking stick from his home region of Savoie, in the French Alps. There was a bit of joshing about the lessons mountaineering could offer about the nego-tiating task they faced. When they appeared together at a brief press conference after the opening session, they took care to show that they were on first-name terms, and both expressed the hope that their efforts would be productive.

But in style and political tradition the two men are a study in contrasts. Davis is bluff and breezy where Barnier is suave and sophisticated. Davis's speaking style is down-to-earth common sense, while Barnier exudes intellectual poise, and he switches with fluency between French and English. Davis is a political bruiser with a long history of challenging political orthodoxy; while serving as shadow home secretary in 2008, he resigned his seat as an MP and fought a by-election to highlight what he saw as the erosion of civil rights under the then Labour govern-ment. And he came to full-time politics relatively late in life, after a career in business and, famously, a spell serving in the Territorial SAS. Barnier became active in Gaullist politics at fourteen and was elected to the French Assembly at the age of twenty-seven; he once wrote that 'very early on, politics gave sense to my life, and brought me a feeling of being useful'. It is said that some of Barnier's French colleagues looked down on him because he was educated at a business school, the *École supérieure de commerce de Paris*, rather than the *École nationale d'administration*, or *ENA*, which so many of France's leaders attended, but he has spent his career out at the heart of the French and European political establishments.

On Europe, too, Barnier and Davis are poles apart. Davis, who has expressed pride in the 'charming bastard' nickname he earned in Europe during his time as a Europe minster, is a veteran Eurosceptic and campaigned to leave the EU in Britain's 2016 referendum. Barnier, who has done two spells as a European commissioner, is, like Guy Verhofstadt and the other members of the BSG, a true believer in the European project; it was an open secret that he hoped his role as Brexit negotiator would provide a springboard for him to succeed Jean-Claude Juncker as president of the European Commission.

And Michel Barnier certainly understood the way the EU worked better than his British counterpart. In the aftermath of the British referendum – on 14 July 2016, the day after Theresa May became prime minister – Davis published a piece on the *Conservative Home* website in which he set out his vision for a post-Brexit Britain. He declared, 'So be under no doubt, we can do deals with our trading partners, and we can do them quickly. I would expect the new prime minister on September 9th to immediately trigger a large round of global trade deals with all our most favoured trade partners. I would expect that the negotiation phase of most of them to be concluded within between twelve and twenty-four months.' EU law prohibits its members from making unilateral trade agreements, but the newly appointed secretary of state for leaving the European Union ploughed on with confidence: 'So within two years, before the negotiation with the EU is likely to be complete, and therefore before anything material has changed, we can negotiate a free trade area massively larger than the EU. Trade deals with the US and China alone will give us a trade area almost twice the size of the EU, and of course we will also be seeking deals with Hong Kong, Canada, Australia, India, Japan, the UAE, Indonesia – and many others.'

Signs of strains between the two negotiators began to show when Michel Barnier came to prepare the second round of the negotiations with the Brexit Steering Group, on 13 July 2017.

As the members of the group waited for Barnier to appear, Verhofstadt remarked that Davis was rumoured to be playing a less than enthusiastic role in the Brussels talks: 'Apparently Davis doesn't want to go full-fledged in the negotiations because they are still busy with the catfight in London,' he said. 'So he doesn't want to be too long outside London.' Elmar Brok and Roberto Gualtieri also reported the gossip they had picked up.

BROK: I heard yesterday that May will leave office in
    August.
GUALTIERI: Yeah, that's one rumour. But, for Davis?
VERHOFSTADT: And that's why Davis doesn't want to
    negotiate four days here; he wants to be in London.
    While I'm here, oh-oh, what will happen there behind
    my back? And that's also why we don't receive a paper
    on the financial settlement.
GUALTIERI: And he certainly doesn't want to commit

himself to anything at all. David Davis, no. Next week he will not commit to anything.

As a prominent Christian Democrat, Elmar Brok had been invited to attend the ceremony in Stuttgart at the beginning of the month to honour the recently deceased Helmut Kohl, the chancellor who dominated German politics for sixteen years from 1982, and he reported a sighting of the British prime minister: 'She was sitting there, nobody was taking note of her,' he reported. 'She didn't talk to anybody. Nobody talked to her.'

When Barnier arrived, he confirmed that Davis's lack of attention to the negotiations was, in the view of the EU team, becoming a real problem. 'You can't imagine what it's been like,' he told Verhofstadt. 'Even the presence of David Davis . . . until yesterday . . .' He allowed the sentence to tail off. 'Because he'd rather be in London in the fight,' Verhofstadt responded.

Barnier had reached an assessment of the way the British side would organise their negotiations. 'There's a division of roles,' he said, 'between Olly Robbins, who is Mrs May's Sherpa, and who will be in the driving seat, technically, who has plenty of authority and is surrounded by senior, top-quality civil servants from the Foreign Office and the Treasury, and the British minister, who for his part sees himself more in the role of an advocate, and a commentator for the House of Commons and the House of Lords.'

Barnier repeated his view that the EU had won the battle over sequencing: 'The positive thing about this first round [of talks] is that we have constructed an operational organisation, and the British have accepted, even if not enthusiastically, sequencing,' he said. 'Because on Monday we shall begin discussions on subjects linked to an orderly withdrawal, and not on other matters, as they wanted.' But he also repeated his warning that the British would try to put off agreement on a financial settlement, so that it could be used as a future bargaining chip: 'The idea, which is both very clear and very dangerous, will be that next year, in the general negotiation they can buy pieces of the single market for the future with the debts of the past.' Barnier declared emphatically, 'No way! They have decided to divorce, to leave the Union, and we are settling the accounts.'

To my frustration as a filmmaker Michel Barnier always remained very poised, slick even. He hardly ever raised his voice. The system he and Guy Verhofstadt had agreed for keeping Parliament up to speed on the negotiations progressed in an orderly and by now predictable manner. There was a reason Elmar Brok sometimes nodded off. The BSG meetings without Barnier were livelier, especially the ones in Verhofstadt's office — there was room for a more jocular tone, although civilised manners there too prevailed. But there was an eruption of tension within the Brexit Steering Group when the German MEP Elmar Brok found out that Guy Verhofstadt had had a private meeting with Barnier.

BROK: I would like to make a remark. We should go all
    three together to Barnier, not just you. No?
VERHOFSTADT: The mandate is very clear, of the
    Conference of Presidents [the body that brings
    together the leaders of the EP's political groupings].
BROK: It's a question of cooperation. We can do it all
    individually and have three meetings with Barnier!
VERHOFSTADT: Yeah, sorry, but I follow strictly what
    was in the mandate that has been decided by the
    Conference of Presidents. I do not do more than that, I
    do not do less than that, I follow that.

BROK: Is it written there that you can see Barnier only
alone?

VERHOFSTADT: It's written that I do the normal contacts
with Barnier, so that's what I do, as coordinator.

*Roberto Gualtieri intervened to soothe the situation: 'It's of course
true that you have the duty, not only the right, to have regular contact
with Barnier, on behalf of the whole group, that's for sure. But there
are cases, where, I think it might be useful, more appropriate, specific
cases, where it would be simply more useful, if it's possible, if it's not
possible you simply go alone.'*

*Verhofstadt was seething – but biting his tongue, while he very
very quickly threw a glance at me and my camera. 'I am sure Guy will
consider [that],' Brok said. There was a long silence before Verhofstadt
picked up with the day's order of business.*

In the midst of the fraught early Brexit negotiations, Guy
Verhofstadt got caught up in an unseemly row which reminded
everyone of the institutional rivalries that bedevil the European
Union. In early July, the prime minister of Malta, Joseph Muscat,
addressed the European Parliament on his country's six-month
presidency of the EU – the presidency rotates through the EU's
member states – and the plenary meeting was extremely thinly
attended. It provoked a ferocious attack on the EP from Jean-
Claude Juncker, the European Commission president, who
was also giving a speech to Parliament that day; estimating the
number of MEPs present at about thirty, he said it proved that the
Parliament was 'not serious', and denounced the body as 'ridiculous, totally ridiculous'. Juncker pointed out that there would
surely have been a bigger attendance if Emmanuel Macron had
been there, for instance, instead of the prime minister of Malta,
which has less than half a million inhabitants.

The Parliament's president, Antonio Tajani, reacted angrily, accusing Juncker of a lack of respect. 'You can criticise the Parliament, but it's not the Commission's job to control the Parliament, it's the Parliament that has to control the Commission,' he said. Verhofstadt was among the absentees – he was having a breakfast briefing on Brexit with Czech MEPs – but decided to settle the score with Juncker in his annual speech to the ALDE barbecue, when members of the Liberal group meet each summer over grilled sausages and other marinated meats.

Bram Delen, his speechwriter, was set to work. With the help of Edel Crosse, at her desk on the sixth floor in Strasbourg, he sharpened a suitably sarcastic sally, making mischief with the fact that the biggest recent turn-outs in the EP's plenary 'hemicycle' – as it is known colloquially – had been occasioned by ceremonies to honour two giants of European politics who had died in June, the former German chancellor Helmut Kohl and the former Parliament president and Holocaust survivor Simone Veil. Crosse and Delen sat together in her office, and Edel typed.

> CROSSE: Jean-Claude, if you want a full plenary these days, you have to die!!
> DELEN: Perhaps you have to announce it a bit, because otherwise it's going to come too sudden.
> CROSSE: You want me to make it longer?
> DELEN: Yes. 'Jean-Claude, there was a full plenary for [the memorials to] Kohl and for Simone Veil, if you want a full hemicycle yourself, you know what to do.'
> CROSSE: Yeah, that's better.

On the front lawn of the Château de Pourtalès, just outside Strasbourg, Verhofstadt delivered his oration:

OK, ladies and gentlemen. As usual, and as it is now the tradition, a very short speech to welcome you here, on one of the
best and most attended . . . better attended than the plenary
I should say! So, we're all here, one year after Brexit. And I
have to tell you, if it didn't happen we should have invented it.
The Brexit. Because never in the past [have] we had so many
pro-European feelings as since this referendum in Britain.

The other side of the coin is that really for me it is hell.
Everybody who wants to see me, wants to talk about Brexit.
Every day. I have Brexit breakfasts. I have Brexit lunches.
Brexit dinners, even more awful. And I also have to skip the
plenary, because of Brexit, and I'm telling you, I'm not the
only one who's skipping the plenary. I hope that all the other
MEPs will have a good excuse, because otherwise, headmas-
ter Jean-Claude will slap you on the wrists. At midday, when
he complained to me that here were only thirty MEPs for
his speech, I said to him, 'Listen, Jean-Claude, listen very
carefully. There was a full hemicycle for Helmut Kohl. And
Simone Veil. If you want a full hemicycle for yourself, you
know what to do. It's not so difficult.'

*The attending crowd laughed, but then Verhofstadt added, to my own but
also to Bram and Edel's surprise, who'd written his speech, a serious note,
which suggested that he was really offended. 'I have to tell you really, and
that's a little bit outside my traditional speech, I was very disappointed by
him. Because he knows very well that these [absent] MEPs were not on early
holidays. That was the impression he gave when it came on television.' And
Verhofstadt pointed out, 'At the same time, I counted them myself personally, there were seventy-seven meetings going on, in the Parliament at that
time.' He repeated the figure with emphasis: 'Seventy-seven.'*

~

The second round of Michel Barnier's direct negotiations with the British team ran from 16–20 July, and left him more frustrated than ever. 'There are some subjects', he told the BSG a few days later, 'on which the UK still hasn't produced its position, and, to be frank, it seems to me that in these areas the UK still hasn't got a political mandate or the will to negotiate. Where we have documents from the UK on such and such a subject, we have been able to make progress. But where there are no positions papers we have made no progress.'

There was, however, another modest victory to report. A week before the second negotiating round began, the British foreign secretary, Boris Johnson, had dropped a characteristically headline-grabbing bombshell on the question of a financial settlement. He was given his cue by Philip Hollobone, a Eurosceptic Tory MP, who pressed him to reject any demand for an exit payment as part of a withdrawal agreement. 'Since we joined the Common Market on 1 January 1973 until the day we leave, we will have given the EU and its predecessors, in today's money, in real terms, a total of £209 billion,' Mr Hollobone told the Commons. 'Will you make it clear to the EU that if they want a penny piece more, then they can go whistle?'

Johnson replied: 'I'm sure that my honourable friend's words will have broken like a thunderclap over Brussels and they will pay attention to what he has said. He makes a very valid point and I think that the sums that I have seen that they propose to demand from this country seem to me to be extortionate, and I think "to go whistle" is an entirely appropriate expression.'

Michel Barnier's retort was elegant: 'I'm not hearing any whistling,' he said, 'just the clock ticking.' By the time the negotiators met, the British government had accepted that it would indeed have to pay something to leave the EU on good terms, though it was not clear what size of bill it would accept.

As the House of Commons' regular report on the negotiations put it, 'The UK government has acknowledged that the UK has financial obligations to the EU that will survive its withdrawal, and vice versa, and that they need to be resolved. But David Davis has not publicly said which obligations the government recognises.'

Michel Barnier's welcome for this development was qualified. 'The one positive point is that the UK has publicly recognised, for the first time, the existence of financial obligations to the Union, which will continue to exist after the date of its departure. They presented this as if it was an extraordinary and major step forward on their behalf. I tempered their enthusiasm by pointing out that it was all very well, but it was a precondition.'

And there had now been some hard pounding on the figures. 'The final round last week,' he reported to the BSG, was a monologue. 'For three, maybe four hours we presented the Commission paper – ours – on the financial settlement. They asked questions line by line, they noted this and that, and we simply answered their questions.' Michel Barnier made an offer to David Davis: his team would be ready to work through the August holidays to find a financial settlement. 'If necessary, I told David Davis . . . if they tell me tomorrow, "Here's the list of commitments," my team, our team [always the gentleman, Barnier very often made a point of telling the BSG they too were on the team], is ready to work in August, at any time, to add another session, and to work on the financial settlement.'

The picture of negotiations bogged down in trench warfare was in stark contrast to the sunny canvases being painted by Brexit-supporting politicians in London. On 17 July, just after the second round of negotiations in Brussels had begun, the prominent Eurosceptic backbencher – and former Cabinet minister – John Redwood wrote a blog entitled 'Getting out of the EU can be quick and easy – the UK holds most of the cards in any negotiation'.

Three days later, as the negotiators in Brussels drew stumps, Britain's secretary of state for international trade, Liam Fox, told the BBC that a post-Brexit free trade deal with the EU should be the 'easiest in human history'. Fox argued this because 'We are already beginning with zero tariffs, and we are already beginning at the point of maximal regulatory equivalence, as it is called. In other words, our rules and our laws are exactly the same,' and he added that, 'The only reason we wouldn't come to a free and open agreement is because politics gets in the way of economics.' For the EU negotiators, Brexit was, of course, every bit as much a political issue as an economic one.

5

HEAD IN THE FUCKING CLOUDS

Late July–mid-September 2017

Guy Verhofstadt owns several vintage cars, but the one on the back of his trailer that morning was an Aston Martin. It was the end of July 2017, and the sun was still coming up, colouring the horizon purple and orange on the motorway towards Calais. We were driving to Silverstone, where Verhofstadt was going to participate in a classic car race. The day before had been the last Brexit Steering Group meeting before the holidays.

I'd love to give you the exact model and build of the Aston Martin that was travelling with us, gently swaying on its trailer, but I'm not going to. Verhofstadt told me once, but I forgot — therefore I cannot ask him again, for he would so look down on me. And I don't want to try to look up the car on the internet either, because getting it wrong would be double the embarrassment. I believe the car was from 1959 — let's keep it at that. And it was dark green. Verhofstadt chose the colour when it was repainted.

The former prime minister of Belgium pursues his interests outside politics — classic cars, wine tasting and making, and cycling, also — with the same obstinacy and abandon as he pursues his political goals. And gathering and hoarding information is central to how he pursues them. On our way to Silverstone, he would spend hours in silence

84

checking cars on his mobile, and when he wasn't doing that he would enthusiastically rattle off names and makes of cars like a boy doing his tables, blasting me away with his knowledge, which is exactly what he also does — is capable of doing — in debates and political discussions. Bram Delen once said to me, 'It's an important asset for a politician. It's one of his strengths.' At any given time to be able to draw up the right information — name, figure, statistic — for the right occasion.

Another asset of Verhofstadt, Bram told me, is his capacity to keep on fighting for what he believes in, or wants, until the very end and beyond — against the odds and better judgement quite often, which of course sometimes really doesn't work, but sometimes also does. The trip to Silverstone showed the limits of his willpower, because an old car, however much you will it to run smoothly, is not always capable of living up to those expectations. Most participants in Silverstone had their personal mechanic with them to keep their fickle old-timers purring. But Verhofstadt was there with only his friend and personal assistant Erik Janda, whose understanding of the inner workings of a car is as limited as the technical expertise of his boss, and Marleen, Erik's wife, who knows even less — about as little as I do.

So when Verhofstadt's Aston Martin broke down, we stood — and Verhofstadt behind his steering wheel sat — all helpless. Luckily, classic car owners like to help each other out, certainly when the person to be helped is Verhofstadt, former et cetera and Brexit coordinator for the European Parliament. Aware of his own limits, Verhofstadt always keeps a couple of bottles of his Meone wine in the trunk of his car, to give away as thank yous.

Silverstone was a weird experience, because I had expected that many people would want to talk to Verhofstadt about Brexit, but in fact hardly anyone did. The only real conversation he had about the UK departure from the EU was with the UK Brexit secretary David Davis, who came to watch him race — a nice photo opportunity. But even with Davis he didn't talk much about Brexit. Just five minutes at the back of the food tent, after which Verhofstadt and Davis were joined by two of Davis's buddies, and I guess the topic changed again. I don't know for sure, because the press person who came with Davis sternly kept me away from the conversation.

Strikingly, I found out that the press guy had in fact voted to remain in the EU, but he still worked for Davis, who's been a Brexiteer of the first hour. It's how things are done in the UK, apparently. But it still surprised me. Verhofstadt wouldn't be able to bear to have people in his team who don't share his beliefs. I cannot but believe it gave him and the rest of the EU an edge in their stand-off with the UK.

~

The studious Barnier had more austere holiday habits; he once told the Brexit Steering Group that he devoted some of his downtime to swotting up on Brexit-related history. 'Since this is between ourselves,' he said, making it sound like a confession, 'I took a bit of time to listen again to General de Gaulle's press conferences in 1967.' De Gaulle, who twice (in 1963 and 1967) vetoed Britain's application to join the European Economic Community, has been a hero to Barnier since the latter's childhood. 'He explains at length, at great length,' the EU's chief negotiator continued, 'why he was opposed to the accession of Great Britain, of England, to the Common Market. He spent thirty minutes explaining it, without any notes, and he said, you see, that England wanted to join the Common Market on its own terms, and he defended the idea that we must preserve the Common Market. And here we are, I think I can say, sixty years later, in the same place; they want to leave the single market, on their own terms, and it is not possible.'

Theresa May's summer holiday again took her to the mountains – but this time in the warmer climes of Lake Garda in northern Italy. Her departure from Downing Street on 25

July was followed almost immediately by a sharp reminder of how much damage the election outcome had done to her authority over her Cabinet. On 28 July, the chancellor, Philip Hammond, gave an interview to the *Today* programme which seemed designed to put his own stamp on the Brexit process. There was a growing recognition at Westminster that there would have to be a transition period after Britain's departure from the EU, and Mr Hammond predicted that during any transition Britain would continue to operate within the EU system – 'many things will look similar', was the way he put it, so that Britons could continue with 'business as usual, life as normal'.

The chancellor suggested that such a period could last 'a year, two years, maybe three years', and he said that the free movement of people would continue beyond Britain's departure from the EU: 'We've been clear that it will be some time before we are able to introduce full migration controls between the UK and the European Union,' he told the programme. 'That's not a matter of opinion, that's a matter of fact. During the transition period that will follow our departure from the European Union, European citizens will still be able to come here, but they will have to register.' The interview fired up the rage of the Brexit-supporting press; *The Sun* declared that 'HANDBRAKE HAMMOND . . . wants to bring the Brexit process to a "standstill" until 2022', and reported that he had 'seized on the absence of Theresa May – who is on holiday in Italy – to push his agenda for a long transition after Brexit'.

Mrs May had at least been able to agree a so-called confidence and supply arrangement with the Democratic Unionists before the summer break – simply to keep her government functioning. The confidence and supply device – looser than a full-blown coalition – is a traditional way for minority governments to remain in power under the British parliamentary system; small parties agree to support the government on confidence motions and budget votes. In return they can expect to extract concessions, and the DUP extracted a very great deal, including the promise of an additional £1 billion in public spending in Northern Ireland.

The negotiations over the agreement between May and the DUP were a reminder that progress in Northern Ireland politics often comes at a snail-like pace; seventeen days elapsed between the beginning of talks, on 9 June, the day after the election, and the signing ceremony between the two party whips, with Theresa May and the DUP leader Arlene Foster in attendance. One of the commitments the DUP signed up to was that 'in line with the parties' shared priorities for negotiating a successful exit from the European Union . . . the DUP also agrees to support the government on legislation pertaining to the United Kingdom's exit from the European Union'.

Perhaps the most serious blow to Theresa May's standing as a leader was struck by the prime minister herself when, a week after the election, in the early hours of the morning of 14 June, a fire broke out at Grenfell Tower in London. It quickly spread to the cladding of the 24-storey block, and burnt on through the following day and night: it was finally declared extinguished on the evening of 16 June. It was the most serious domestic fire in Britain since the Blitz during the Second World War; it caused the deaths of seventy-two people, many of them poor immigrants, and the image of the smouldering building above one of the richest areas of the capital gave the tragedy a political edge.

On 15 June, with the fire still not entirely extinguished and the death toll far from certain, Theresa May visited the scene. The police and her civil servants had advised her that there would be a security risk if she mixed with members of the public, so the visit was restricted, and she only met members of the emergency services. She paid a very high political cost for her failure to speak to survivors or members of the victims' families. Writing about that day in the *Evening Standard* on the first anniversary of the fire, she recognised just how inadequate her reaction had been: 'What I did not do on that first visit was meet the residents and survivors who had escaped the blaze,' she confessed. 'But the residents of Grenfell Tower needed to know that those in power recognised and understood their despair. And I will always regret that by not meeting them that day, it seemed as though I didn't care.'

May's weakness that summer inevitably led to speculation about a leadership challenge against her, and the name of the Brexit secretary, David Davis, cropped up frequently in the newspaper lists of leadership runners and riders. On Sunday 9 July, both the *Sunday Times* and *The Observer* ran stories about him. 'Allies of David Davis accused of plotting Theresa May's downfall' was the headline in the *Sunday Times*, and the paper reported that 'an ally of David Davis has called on Theresa May to name the date when she will quit as prime minister as the Brexit secretary's friends were accused of running a covert operation to force a change of leader. Ministers and backbenchers said MPs close to Davis had been urging them to lobby Downing Street to get May to go, and have discussed plans to sign a letter calling on the prime minister to quit over the summer.' While *The Observer* had 'Party chiefs warn against plot to install David Davis as leader' as its headline, and recorded that 'some MPs are keen to see Davis replace Theresa May, claiming that the prime minister is so wounded that she cannot continue in office for long and that the party should act after its disastrous election result'.

The government's frailty left it vulnerable to the charge that domestic politics were hampering its ability to negotiate in Brussels. It emerged that David Davis had spent less than an hour with Michel Barnier during the July talks before returning to London to vote against an opposition motion in Parliament. Labour's Brexit spokesman, Sir Keir Starmer, declared that 'David Davis can hardly say this is the time to "get down to business" and then spend only a few minutes in Brussels before heading back to Whitehall', and claimed, 'Since the election, the government has been in disarray. There is no agreed Cabinet position on vital Brexit issues, the negotiating team is not prepared and the prime minister has lost her authority. Meanwhile the clock is ticking and the risks are increasing day by day.'

~

When Guy Verhofstadt and Michel Barnier met after the summer break, they swapped holiday stories, and Verhofstadt showed the EU's chief negotiator photos of the car he took to Silverstone. He behaved like we all sometimes do, when we can't stop ourselves and make our friends the victims of our enthusiasm — I have a couple of videos on my phone that show how at the age of fifty-three I can still score a goal in football — and Michel Barnier and his assistants smiled obligingly, as one would expect from good friends.

Verhofstadt told them he had met David Davis at Silverstone. 'Has he got a car too?' Barnier enquired. 'No,' Verhofstadt replied. 'He's fanatical about aeroplanes — so he has friends who have planes. You've got fools who drive old cars, but in Great Britain there are plenty who own planes. He knows how to fly — so that's what he talks about more than anything else, his passion for old planes.'

It was the first time that I saw Barnier so relaxed. Whether they had trouble in letting go of the summer, or the two men really liked each other, they certainly took their time before getting down to business. When Verhofstadt offered the view that restoring and driving old cars is a popular sport in Britain, Barnier replied, to general laughter: 'That's what they are trying to do with Brexit – restore an old car.'

Both well into their sixties, the two men then started trading notes on the pills they were taking; they were, they discovered, both on blood-thinning and cholesterol-lowering medication. But Verhofstadt had one extra pill that Barnier didn't have. 'It's so I can go on drinking wine,' Verhofstadt declared. 'He takes medication to correct things, and then a fourth to allow him to do everything that's forbidden,' Barnier noted. 'That's a tactic!' Verhofstadt laid out his pills on the table in front of him, for everyone to see, something Barnier would clearly never even think of doing. 'I take mine in the morning and the evening,' he teased Verhofstadt. 'I don't go for the effect, like that.' They used the familiar French 'tu' throughout the conversation.

Barnier and Verhofstadt had clearly defined their separate roles in the negotiations, and had the good sense not to tread on one another's toes. Verhofstadt explained the role he had carved out to the members of the BSG during a meeting about an opinion piece they hoped to get published in most major European newspapers. The aim of the op-ed article was to keep the European Parliament's role in the public mind, while Barnier was doing the actual talking to the UK: 'Parliament will not be heard in this whole thing if we don't say something,' Verhofstadt told the group.

The op-ed had been drafted by Bram Delen, and it had an edge to it, which the Italian Social Democrat Roberto Gualtieri questioned. 'I think that the article was very good, but it's too hard in tone. This is signed by all the people involved in the negotiations. We're not here to convince them [the British] that Brexit was a mistake . . . We're not here to make fun of them.'

He worried that 'we just put oil on the fire'. But Verhofstadt insisted, 'It needs to be printed, eh? All the newspapers need to take it. If it's not sexy as an article, they don't take it. It's not insulting saying that this [the UK's negotiating position] was for us a "cold shower", eh?' And Verhofstadt then explained how he saw the BSG's role dovetailing with Barnier's efforts as a means of putting pressure on the other side. 'Our role is different than the negotiator,' he said. 'He has to use us, in saying: you know, you have seen our Parliament, how they react? It's impossible . . . that's the idea.'

The purpose of the breakfast meeting between Barnier and Verhofstadt on 28 August 2017 was to discuss round three of the Brexit negotiations, which were due to begin later that day. With him, Barnier had Stéphanie Riso, his director for strategy, coordination and communication, and Georg Riekeles, his softly spoken but very firm Norwegian team leader for inter-institutional affairs.

Britain had submitted a series of position papers in advance of the new round, and when he launched them David Davis had returned to the issue of sequencing, arguing that the documents 'show that as we enter the third round of negotiations, it is clear that our separation from the EU and future relationship are inextricably linked'. Barnier remarked, 'So they have a tactic, to come back to our friends [the British], a tactic which it was easy to foresee, of wanting to come back to the idea of discussing everything at the same time. The more they can discuss everything at the same time, the more they can bargain, and, as I said the other day, buy the future relationship with past debts.'

Guillaume McLaughlin, Verhofstadt's chief of staff, remarked that at least 'even Boris Johnson accepts that they'll have to pay something', only to be told by Barnier that making public declarations was one thing, but that there were still no concrete documents that could serve as a basis for serious negotiations on the financial issue. Nothing new had been brought to the table since the last face-to-face talks. 'The problem is we've got nothing to talk about on that subject today. We have nothing more than we had last time, meaning nothing at all.'

The position paper that caused most comment related to the Irish border, and Stéphanie Riso took the floor. The broad objection to the British position on the border issue which she outlined was political. 'They say', she explained, 'that if there are controls at the border of Northern Ireland it's the fault of the EU 27. "We [the British] don't need controls, we can let everything through, no problem." So the problem is a European problem. And if one day we need to go back to controls or a hard border, in one way or another, that will be the fault of the Europeans.' The suggestion that finding a solution to the border question was the EU's responsibility rather than Britain's was to become a recurring source of tension, and Riso laid down a clear marker of the EU's position. She called this 'politically the most detrimental element' in the British position, and declared that there must be a 'very firm message' to reject it.

The British position paper deployed the issue of the Irish border in the service of the broader British case for moving talks on to the post-Brexit relationship between Britain and the European Union. 'Wider questions about the UK's future operation of its whole border and immigration controls for EEA [European Economic Area] nationals (other than Irish nationals) can only be addressed as part of the future relationship between the UK and the EU, and further highlights the need to move to this next phase of negotiations as quickly as possible,' it stated.

The paper on Northern Ireland was published alongside a companion paper on customs arrangements more generally. The British proposed 'a highly streamlined customs arrangement between the UK and the EU, streamlining and simplifying requirements', with 'technology-based solutions to make it easier to comply with customs procedures'. The paper also floated the possibility of 'a new customs partnership with the EU, aligning our approach to the customs border in a way that removes the need for a UK–EU customs border'. One approach, it suggested, 'would involve the UK mirroring the EU's requirements for imports from the rest of the world where their final destination is the EU', something it accepted was 'unprecedented as an approach and could be challenging to implement'.

Riso explained how this might work. 'Their idea is that the United Kingdom would act as the customs agent for Europe on its own territory. So one arrives at the border – say with a consignment of New Zealand lamb – and the United Kingdom would perform the same controls as the Union performs on its territory. The UK imposes taxes, just like the EU, and afterwards declares the money – thirty centimes for you, forty for the other . . .' Her main objection to this was extremely unflattering to the British Customs and Revenue service. 'Between these four walls,' she said, 'what's interesting to know is that, even inside the Union, even in the customs union, with the Court of Justice et cetera et cetera . . . the British have great difficulty in ensuring customs controls. And so we have very regular cases of infractions.' Georg Riekeles added, 'The United Kingdom is the main entry point for contraband coming into Europe – British ports.'

Stéphanie Riso did report one significant change in the British position. 'Today the British – and this is the most striking element in the paper on customs – realise for the first time, and we will soon be in September 2017, that we won't have time to put a new relationship into place by Brexit day. They are therefore saying . . . we need a transition period.' It had taken the British government some time to recognise this reality and, as Philip Hammond had found out when he floated the idea, it remained controversial; the Brexit Steering Group had debated the length of – not just the need for – a transition period when they drafted their response to the triggering of Article 50 nearly six months earlier.

~

When the third negotiating round ended on 31 August there was a marked difference of tone in the way the two lead negoti-ators spoke at their joint press conference. David Davis declared that 'the third round of talks have been productive and are an important stepping stone and key building block for discussions to come'. Michel Barnier, on the other hand, stated flatly, 'We made no decisive progress on the main subjects, even though – and I want to say so – the discussion on Ireland was fruitful.' A decisive negotiating deadline was fast approaching; at their October summit Europe's leaders were due to decide whether the talks on Britain's departure had made enough progress to justify opening negotiations on the post-Brexit future. 'At the current speed,' Michel Barnier told the press, 'we are far from being able to recommend to the European Council that there has been sufficient progress in order to start discussions on the future relationship.'

Barnier was as suave as ever in his public performance, and still addressed his British counterpart by his first name. In private, briefing the Brexit Steering Group four days later, the emollience had gone. 'I see in the political background, in the media sphere, that the United Kingdom has begun a kind of "blame game" on a great scale,' he said. 'Firstly when these negotiations take place, contrary to what was agreed between us, they brief the press permanently, every day and throughout the negotiating round – actually while the negotiations are happening.'

He further complained that the British were smearing his team in the press, describing them as 'bureaucrats, techno-crats, stateless and *Bruxellois*', and he accused them of trying to circumvent the Commission negotiators by talking directly to individual EU governments. 'I say that those who look for the smallest difference between what our team are doing and what the twenty-seven member states or the Parliament think are wasting their time. But they are trying all the same.'

Barnier also raised the question of trust. The picture he painted of the state of play over the financial settlement was so bleak that Philippe Lamberts asked about the possibility of international arbitration. 'If we get to that stage it will obviously compromise everything,' Barnier answered. 'All discussion of a future relationship. How do you establish a future relationship with a country that forces us go to a court of international arbitration?' He invoked the name of Winston Churchill, 'who spoke of a country's honour, its greatness, its responsibilities'.

Two days later, the European Union formally rejected the suggestion – which had so concerned Stéphanie Riso – that the EU would bear the blame if a physical border returned to Ireland. The Commission issued a statement that 'the onus to propose solutions which overcome the challenges created on the island of Ireland by the United Kingdom's withdrawal from the European Union and its decision to leave the customs union and the internal market remains on the United Kingdom.' The

Irish border was now at the heart of the Brexit negotiations, and Guy Verhofstadt set off to see it for himself.

He was pushed to do so by the Irish assistant Edel Crosse. She wanted her boss to see and hear for himself what Brexit might do to the place she came from. The trip started in Belfast where Verhofstadt, perhaps surprisingly, had never been.

The city centre looked quiet and peaceful, with lots of shoppers and strollers out in the late September sun – and street artists djembe drumming on plastic bottles, or singing Lou Reed's 'Walk on the Wild Side'. But Crosse had organised a tour that would allow Verhofstadt to also see the scars that still disfigure parts of Belfast two decades after the Troubles ended. He was accompanied by two historians from the city's Queen's University: Dr Dominic Bryan, whose early research focused on the Orange Order parades that play such a big part in the Protestant and Unionist sense of identity; and Professor David Phinnemore, who has written extensively on Brexit's impact on Ireland.

The tour did not last much longer than an hour, but it made a deep impression on Guy Verhofstadt; he couldn't stop talking about it for days.

To Antonio Tajani, the Italian president of the European Parliament, for instance, he described the so-called peace lines which still separate some of the city's communities. 'I was in Belfast and, I have to tell you, I thought the conflict had ended, but it hasn't. There are, not walls, but like fences, twelve metres high. There are in the street still gates, in iron, that are closed during the night or when it's the season of these marches – of the Protestants. Then they close the gates. So that no one can go from one neighbourhood to another.'

And what he had seen had convinced him of the need to make the Irish border a priority in the Brexit negotiations. 'If we don't take care of the problem properly,' he told Tajani, 'it will all come back – the violence. If a camera is put on one or the other side of the border, the first thing they will do, is TAK [destroy it]. I didn't follow the situation there; for twenty years there's been nothing on our television screens, but it's not over, there's like a cold war.' And he added, 'And they're also stubborn, eh?' Verhofstadt's heartfelt outburst prompted Antonio Tajani to curse the prime minister who asked Britain to vote in a Brexit referendum; he called David Cameron 'the most stupid man of the century. The most stupid man. He caused damages to England, to us, to everyone.' Verhofstadt added, 'And to Ireland.'

After touring Belfast, the next stop for Verhofstadt was the Parliament Buildings at Stormont, the seat of Northern Ireland's devolved Assembly. He met Arlene Foster, the leader of the Democratic Unionist Party, the Sinn Féin MEP Martina Anderson, who had lobbied him in Brussels, and representatives of the once-mighty Ulster Unionist Party, or UUP, the nationalist Social Democratic and Labour Party, and the non-sectarian Alliance Party. The meetings took close to three hours, with delegations filing in and out, each to have their say.

The most touching testimony I heard that morning was the one given by Captain Douglas Ricardo 'Doug' Beattie, who became a representative for the UUP after he'd been a soldier for thirty-five years in the British Army. He still called the men he fought as a soldier in the Irish conflict 'terrorists', but in a roundabout way nevertheless also admitted that even they had been victims. I found courage, solace and hope in his words. He said:

I've been a soldier for thirty-five years and part of that time spent standing on the border. At border checkpoints,

checking vehicles across. And also closing border cross-
ings . . . I lost many colleagues, killed on the border, many
families bereaved. There were many innocent women and
children killed on the border, families bereaved, there
[were] many terrorists killed, many families bereaved. If we
have a hard border in any shape or form, north or south, we
will create a flashpoint for trouble once again. So the plea is
this, no hard border doesn't need to be the starting point,
no hard border must be a finishing point, and what we must
do is come up with a solution that brings us to that finishing
point, no hard border, because if we don't, if we use this as
a bargaining chip, then we are going to create and fill more
coffins, and there will be more bereaved families if we don't
do that. My plea would be this, that the EU government and
the UK government make a clear, unambiguous statement
that there will not be a hard border.

The words still resonated in the van that took Verhofstadt and
Edel Crosse from Belfast to the border itself, a border which
would, under Brexit, become the United Kingdom's only land
border with the European Union. Verhofstadt crossed into the
Republic of Ireland near Middletown in County Armagh, in an
area with a notably violent history even by the blood-soaked
standards of the Troubles. The city of Armagh was known as
Murder Mile because it was so violent; twenty-four people
were killed in thirteen separate incidents over twenty years.
In Tynan, a couple of miles from Middletown, a 24-year-old
single mother who had joined the Ulster Defence Regiment
to help pay for her child's upbringing was shot dead in front
of her three-year-old daughter in 1977. Four years later, an
IRA hit squad crossed the border and killed 86-year-old Sir
Norman Strong, a prominent Unionist leader and veteran of

the First World War, along with his 46-year-old son. The two men were watching television in the library of their home, the eighteenth-century Gothic mansion Tynan Abbey, and their killers firebombed the building before they left. South Armagh was named 'bandit country' by a British home secretary, and the South Armagh Brigade of the IRA is thought to have been responsible for the deaths of 123 British soldiers and forty-two police officers.

Many borders run along geographical divides – sections of France's borders, for example, are marked by the Rhine and the Pyrenees – but the Irish border has no geographical logic because it was created by the partition of 1921, which divided what had been a single political entity, so it goes through farms and even houses and gardens. It runs for 310 miles and there are some 270 crossing points; during the Troubles most of the smaller ones were closed, often by blowing up the road.

Edel had arranged a visit to a farm just inside the Republic of Ireland, with a farmer whose cows graze on both sides of a divide that has today become as good as invisible. We took a right from the main road and started driving down narrow country lanes, under a grey and rainy sky – but all the rest around us was very green. I had been looking forward to this visit because for once Guy Verhofstadt was going to meet 'normal' people, and I wouldn't be filming in meeting rooms that all differ in size, but somehow never in light and atmosphere. Maybe there'd be some chatting over a cup of tea, maybe they'd feed the cows together.

Then we made our last turn and drove into the farm's courtyard. It was flooded with cars from TV crews and other media. With their camera lights on and their microphones stretched out, a group of at least twenty journalists stood waiting for Verhofstadt under the cover of the open barn. The earlier drizzle had turned into a downpour. As soon as he ran in they flocked around him and started asking questions. 'Sorry, guys,' someone tried, 'we organised this for the farmers, there will be a press conference later on.' But to no avail.

The scene made me realise how much — and why — Verhofstadt lives in a bubble, caged in. Why Edel really had to prod him to fly to Ireland and make this trip. And why Bram Delen at one point told me that his boss really preferred to go nowhere and just read reports from others who — I now understood — could still roam reality unnoticed.

Later, while typing this up, I also realised that there were similarities between what I was writing and the description of what happened with Theresa May at the Grenfell Tower. It's a good thing that I believe in the knowledge and compassion one can suck up from the written word and stories told by others — and that I saw Verhofstadt reading an awful lot. But still. Politicians, out of touch . . . the farm was a scary sight.

After the farm, Verhofstadt was driven to a hotel, not to sleep, but for more meetings, in a backroom with representatives of an organisation called Border Communities Against Brexit. It was past nine that night when he finally arrived in Dublin, where the next morning he was to meet the Taoiseach, the Irish prime minister Leo Varadkar, and address the Dáil, the Republic's Parliament.

He started, of course, with his field trip of the previous day:

Yesterday, I spent the afternoon visiting the border area in County Monaghan [the Irish Republic county immediately across the border from County Armagh] and meeting people who live and work there. At one point, I stood astride the border. One foot was in Northern Ireland, my other foot stood in the Republic. But it was completely impossible to see where one jurisdiction ended and the other started. The cows especially couldn't see it. Cows from the North, eating grass from the South, milked in the North by a farmer from the South, with their milk bottled in the South. I am Belgian, so surrealism comes naturally to me. But to reinstate a border would be more than surreal – it would be totally absurd – even for me.

Then he took a swipe at the United Kingdom's secretary of state for foreign and Commonwealth affairs. Boris Johnson had used his platform in the *Daily Telegraph* to attack the idea of multiple identities, an especially sensitive issue in the Irish context. Identity has always been at the heart of Ireland's conflicts, and people born in Northern Ireland have the right to both British and Irish passports. 'I look at so many young people with the 12 stars [of the European Union's flag] lipsticked to their faces, and I am troubled with the thought that people are beginning to have genuinely split allegiances,' Johnson wrote. 'And when people say that they feel they have more in common with others in Europe than with people who voted Leave, I want to say: but that is part of the reason people voted Leave.'

Verhofstadt's rejoinder was direct: 'Some British politicians, not to name Boris Johnson, criticise their countrymen and women for wanting to keep their European identity. He accuses them of "split allegiance". I think, this is a binary, old-fashioned and reductionist understanding of identity,' Verhofstadt declared.

I think we need to be smarter, more open and more inventive than that. It's not your origin or the fact that by accident you were born in this or that village, city or country that makes you a good citizen. No, it is the fact that you embrace the values of your community, that you cherish the fundamental rights and freedoms of the society in which you live. Values, rights and freedoms that are common in our European Union, in all nations, in every one of our member states. It's nonsense to talk about 'split allegiance'. It's perfectly possible to feel English, British and European at the same time. As it is perfectly normal to be a Dubliner, Irish and European at the same time, without being schizophrenic.

The jibe against Johnson was picked up by the British papers. Less well covered was Verhofstadt's statement of the way Brexit had changed Dublin's relationship with London. Although southern Ireland had broken with Britain a century earlier, the United Kingdom's economic, diplomatic and military clout made it the dominant partner; that was to change in the Brexit negotiations, because Ireland now had the weight of the EU behind it. 'Ireland is crucial to the Union,' Verhofstadt vowed. 'The Irish border, and all things related, are a priority in the negotiations. We will repeat this in a new resolution that we will adopt in early October. And in this we will state that Ireland must not pay the price of Brexit. Or that Ireland – or any other member – will be used as a bargaining chip in the negotiations. The interests of Ireland are part and parcel of the interests of the EU27. The Irish position *is* the European position. The European position *is* the Irish position.'

Verhofstadt also repeated the EU's determination that a solution to the issue of the Irish border must come from the United Kingdom:

The re-emergence of the border question between Northern Ireland and the Irish Republic has not been caused by you, neither by the rest of the European Union. It's the inevitable consequence of the choice of Great Britain to leave the European Union. So, the resolution of this border issue is entirely the responsibility of the United Kingdom. It is for them to come up with a workable solution. One which safeguards the Good Friday Agreement, preserves the Common Travel Area [which had allowed free travel across the Irish border since the 1920s], avoids a hardening of the border and, last but not least, doesn't compromise the Irish membership and the integrity of the single market and the customs union.

The tone was set for what was going to become the most contentious topic in two years of Brexit negotiations.

~

A couple of days later, Verhofstadt, still fired up by what he had seen on his Irish trip, had tea with the British Brexit secretary, David Davis, at the residence of Britain's permanent EU representative in Brussels, near the Royal Palace.

Guillaume McLaughlin emerged from the meeting in a rage, and described what had transpired to his Irish colleague, Edel Crosse. Leaning against the wall of Verhofstadt's office, he said, 'David Davis clearly said, "Ireland is not our problem, we'll lose a bit of money on the excise duties, but all the rest, we don't care."'

MCLAUGHLIN: Davis explained to us that Ireland is not
    a problem. They have lots of control systems. They
    know everyone going in and out, they have automatic
    crunch crunch [McLaughlin's colourful way of
    describing Britain's technology for border checks].
    They'll take a loss in excise duties, but it doesn't really

matter. So basically we don't give a fuck what goes through the border. In any case, we know who the baddies are. There might be a problem with terrorism, but OK . . .

VERHOFSTADT: We gonna find them.

MCLAUGHLIN: That was more or less what he said.

CROSSE: So, head in the fucking clouds.

Guillaume McLaughlin's anger was still boiling when he met two German visitors the following day. He started telling them, 'It was amazing to see David Davis in the Residency at the Rue Ducal. He was sitting there like that' – here Guillaume made wide, sweeping movements with his arms, sitting back – 'like he was the king of . . . yeah. This idiotic man is one of the main reasons the UK is going to collapse over the next couple of years, and he's sitting there, very happy with himself.'

'Still believing,' one of his visitors jumped in.

'Still believing', McLaughlin agreed, snapping his fingers, 'that the UK wants that, and therefore the UK should have that. But we're not really interested. It's beyond belief.'

6

IT'S WATERLOO,
IT'S AGINCOURT, IT'S CRÉCY

Late September–late October 2017

It was said – but for obvious reasons it was hard to confirm – that the office floor in the Berlaymont building in Brussels where Michel Barnier and his team had their headquarters was the most heavily secured floor in the whole of the EU, guarded by the most advanced spy technologies available. Barnier was terrified of information leaking out.

But how did information get in? The EU's chief negotiator sat down with his British counterparts every four weeks, for discussions in which they presented their papers, and he presented his papers. But what was lurking underneath this very formal ballet of exchanging official stances? What did the UK really want, really think?

Such information is crucial in any negotiation, but during the Brexit negotiations it was especially important, because it was clear – this much at least was clear – that the British government was fighting with itself over what Brexit should or could mean. During the full two years of negotiations, nobody on the European side ever claimed in my hearing they knew with even a modest degree of certainty what the UK position was. So Barnier, Guy Verhofstadt and their teams had their ears constantly attuned to even hints of insight, any useful information that might be buried in gossip, rumours or leaks – whether deliberate or accidental.

The many daily contacts between members of the European Parliament and their counterparts from the House of Commons or the House of Lords — which often follow party lines — were one source of information. Another source was civil servants from the UK and the EU, who already knew each other and, of course, got to know each other even better during the negotiations. A third way in which intelligence seeped through was the howlround world of Brussels politics and journalism, where reporters routinely pass on what they know in return for things they do not yet know — not always as a straight trade, sometimes building up a tab of favours they can call in for the future. Any meeting the Verhofstadt press team had with journalists was seen as a possibility to exchange information. 'It's about listening as much as talking,' Bram Delen confided.

One morning, one such scrap of information arrived with a beep from the mobile of Guy Verhofstadt's spokesperson for the UK — and it was judged to be valuable intelligence about the strategy of the UK Brexit secretary David Davis. Nick Petre had spoken to a journalist who had just had an off-the-record briefing with Davis, and he sent the burden of the conversation by text to another member of the team.

> UK feel treated like a banana republic
> not going to commit paying money until we know the shape
>   of the future relationship
> we will switch off access to the City of London
> need to blow up talks — in order to win a reality check from
>   the EU27 about the economic harm of no deal
> aim is to split Barnier from the EU27 — Barnier is backing
>   himself in a corner

The list was eventually forwarded to Verhofstadt, who passed it on to Barnier himself. By that time it was, of course, at many removes from the conversation on which it was based, but it made both men even more *wary than they already were, both about the intentions of the British, and the divisions that riddled them. They were aware that David Davis did not speak for everyone in the British government, but couldn't judge how far his influence stretched. Interpretation was key, and they both knew first hand, from many personal experiences, how anything declared in public could be read in (at least) two ways.*

~

Michel Barnier's sensitivity about press reporting was especially acute in September 2017 because of the interpretation – or, as he saw, misinterpretation – of a speech he had given at a conference in Italy at the beginning of the month. In the speech he had, as he told the Brexit Steering Group, expressed his often repeated view that the Brexit negotiations 'are useful because they have a value as an exercise in understanding, an education in the advantages of the single market'. He complained that 'the next day I found this on the BBC: Barnier wants to teach the British a lesson'. That gloss of course angered British Eurosceptics. The Tory MP John Redwood accused Michel Barnier of using 'disobliging language' and expressed the view that 'it's very sad that the EU does not appear to be listening to the British people since the Brexit vote'. Barnier told the BSG 'one must be careful'.

Theresa May's next move was altogether more conciliatory than the thinking reflected in Nick Petre's text on David Davis's strategy. On 22 September, she gave a speech in Florence which was designed to unblock the negotiating impasse on the three divorce issues. It was less than a month before the EU's heads of government were due to meet to judge whether 'sufficient progress' had been made in the divorce talks to allow the next negotiating stage to begin. The British government was, it seemed, at least united in the desire to push beyond the straitjacket of Michel Barnier's sequencing and begin discussions on a future relationship between the European Union and the United Kingdom.

Mrs May went as far as she believed she could to break the negotiating deadlock without blowing up the fragile unity of her Cabinet. She made a firm promise to meet Britain's financial obligations – stating that 'the UK will honour commitments it has made during the period of our membership' – but was studiously vague about how much she was willing to pay as part of the divorce settlement. She agreed to enshrine legal protections for EU citizens living in Britain formally in a withdrawal treaty – 'I want to incorporate the agreement fully into UK law and make sure British courts can refer directly to it' – and even accepted that the European Court of Justice would have a role in policing them, declaring, 'I want UK courts to be able to take into account the judgments of the European Court of Justice with a view to ensuring consistent interpretation.'

The idea of a transitional period to follow Britain's formal departure from the Union – she still insisted on calling it an 'implementation' period – had been floated by the chancellor at the end of July and advanced in talks with the EU in August; in the Florence speech it was finally formalised as British government policy, justified on the grounds that without it the two sides would 'not be able to implement smoothly' any new arrangements between them. The prime minister proposed it should last for two years so that 'people and businesses would benefit from a period to adjust in a smooth and orderly way'. She accepted that 'the current structure of EU rules and regulations' would apply during such a period, but insisted that after 29 March 2019, all new EU citizens arriving in Britain would have to register with the authorities.

The speech made a big splash in the British press, but Europe was growing weary. 'You can see that the speech of May was covered nowhere,' commented Guillaume McLaughlin dismissively. 'Maybe in Germany because of the elections [Germany elected a new Bundestag in September 2017], but in the newspapers at the bottom somewhere. Nobody covered it.'

The Brexit Steering Group met three days later, and Verhofstadt opened proceedings with an attempt at a joke. Theresa May had made her Florence speech in the church of Santa Maria Novella, one of the city's great basilicas, which is stuffed full of medieval and Renaissance masterpieces. Running with the historical theme, Verhofstadt began with: 'Dear colleagues . . . It is a happy day, I think . . . There was the speech of Mrs May, on last Friday. I have asked myself, why in Florence? I have the answer. In the fifteenth century Florence was exactly like the Conservative Party today. So that's the reason. The same environment. The Medicis fighting with the other families.' Somehow the gag didn't quite fly, and the group failed to react as he had hoped. 'OK, that's a joke, eh?' the European Parliament's Brexit coordinator added, a little lamely.

Michel Barnier acknowledged to the group the significance of the prime minister's shift, especially over a transition period, and he also recognised that she had made her move in the face of deep divisions in her Cabinet. 'We know that the length of the [transition] period has been the subject of much debate within the Cabinet,' he said. That was a very sober assessment of the political climate in London; in fact, in the run-up to Florence May had faced a determined assault from the leading Brexiteer Boris Johnson, her foreign secretary and, like David Davis, a claimant to her crown.

On 15 September, Johnson had published a 4,000-word Brexit manifesto in the *Daily Telegraph*, the paper to which he had, for many years, contributed a regular column. It offered, as he put it, a 'vision for a bold, thriving Britain enabled by Brexit', and, most controversially, the piece repeated the claim made during the 2016 referendum that Britain would acquire an extra £350 million a week to spend on the National Health Service by leaving the European Union: the *Telegraph* put the story on its front page under the headline 'Boris: yes, we will take back £350m from the EU for the NHS'.

The claim, which had, famously, been splashed all over the side of the Vote Leave campaign bus during the referendum, was always controversial; the figure had been calculated without taking into account Britain's EU rebate or, indeed, any EU funds spent in Britain. In September 2017, it earned the foreign secretary a rebuke from the head of the UK Statistics Authority, Sir David Norgrove, who called it 'a clear misuse of official statistics'. In his letter to Johnson, Sir David pointed out that, as well as confusing gross and net contributions, the figure 'also assumes that payments currently made to the UK by the EU, including for example for the support of agriculture and scientific research, will not be paid by the UK government when we leave'.

The manifesto brought the Cabinet's splits over the next stage in the Brexit strategy into the open at just the moment when Mrs May was trying to edge things forward to the next negotiating level. As Michel Barnier put it later in his briefing to the BSG, 'Here's a paradoxical situation; a great part of their [the British government's] energy is devoted to talking to themselves . . . There is a battle within the battle. They need to negotiate with us, not among themselves.'

Guy Verhofstadt was concerned about Mrs May's suggestion that EU citizens would have to register with the authorities in Britain during a transition period. 'For us transition means – and we've already said this in our resolution – the continuation of the whole body of accumulated European law, with all its regulations . . . you can't have a transition only for goods and services, and not citizens.' Verhofstadt, who had always regarded the issue of citizens' rights as a priority, insisted that EU citizens living in Britain, even the ones who would move there during the transition period, should continue to enjoy the same rights as they had done before Britain's departure from the EU.

A comment from his Polish colleague Danuta Hübner sug-gested that, however welcome the signs of movement from Mrs May might be, European patience was wearing thin: 'What we should have, and' – here she addressed the EU's chief negotia-tor – 'I think what you have, Michel, in the back of your head, all the time, is that actually we have a common objective: to get rid of them in March 2019.'

The next round of talks with the British negotiating team – the fourth – was due to begin later that day. Michel Barnier told the group he saw the week as a 'moment of truth', and that 'if what Mrs May has said, which I think represents interesting openings, is translated into concrete facts, that will change many things'. He would, he said, be informing David Davis that the EU was 'impatient' to see the prime minister's ideas reflected in negotiating proposals.

That afternoon brought Guy Verhofstadt a reminder of the colour and vigour of the Brexit debate in Britain, in the shape of a delegation of British MPs, the most vocal of whom proved to be Andrew Rosindell, the MP for the constituency of Romford, on the Essex edge of London. Rosindell won the seat after campaigning with his Staffordshire Bull Terrier, Spike, who was kitted out in a Union Flag waistcoat for his duties on the doorstep. In November 2016, Rosindell put down an Early Day Motion – a device MPs can use to draw attention to an issue they consider pressing – that would have required the BBC to celebrate Brexit by returning to the daily practice of ending transmissions on BBC One by playing 'God Save the Queen'. And when the government announced that post-Brexit British passports would return to their traditional blue colour, he welcomed the news with: 'The humiliation of having a pink European Union passport will now soon be over.' In the past, he has proposed a UK Borders Bill to create a special entry queue for citizens of countries where the Queen is head of state, and supported the establishment of an English Parliament. Andrew Rosindell and Guy Verhofstadt are not natural soulmates.

The moment Rosindell and the other MPs entered his office, crowding around his not too big meeting table, Verhofstadt hit him with: 'We start? You've come to tell us what is the solution for Ireland and Northern Ireland?' The two set to sparring over the Irish border, with Rosindell insisting there was no need for new controls, even though Britain was committed to leaving the single market and the EU's customs union. 'What is the purpose of these borders?' the Member for Romford demanded. 'We wouldn't set them up; so you would stop every lorry, every car, to check every box, every crate, what is the purpose of this?' Verhofstadt fired back with a question of his own.

VERHOFSTADT: What is the reason to go out of the customs union?

ROSINDELL: Because we are bound by a tariff that we want to break out of. We want to be able to make free-trade agreements around the world. The UK is a free-trading, seafaring, outward-looking global nation, why would we want to box ourselves in? And you know, the decision has been made.

Behind my camera, I couldn't help thinking of playground rows when I was a child — 'No, no, no, decided is decided, given is given, said is said, you can't change your mind any more' — and I wondered whether Edel Crosse had similar thoughts, as we both sat listening in to the discussion, she half-hidden behind a flimsy wall but with her neck craning towards the open door that separated her office from the office of her boss. Edel left Ireland as a young woman, but Ireland will never leave her.

Everyone present at the table knew that this was political theatre; Verhofstadt and Rosindell were never going to persuade one another, and the conversation wouldn't decide anything. But they did drill down to the issue that would eventually become the main stumbling block to negotiating and, especially, ratifying a withdrawal agreement. In the two years that I filmed him, this was perhaps Verhofstadt's rawest clash with Brexiteer reality.

ROSINDELL: What we want is the EU to be willing to come up with a sensible arrangement.

VERHOFSTADT: Well, I have a sensible arrangement. I would offer Northern Ireland the favour to stay in the customs union.

ROSINDELL: That is out of the question. We're a United Kingdom, so that wouldn't happen.

VERHOFSTADT: But you say that you find special arrangements between New Zealand and Australia! But a special arrangement that helps the Northern Irish and Irish economy is not acceptable for you.

ROSINDELL: The only arrangement is an EU–UK arrangement. You cannot leave bits of the UK out. We're one country and we're not going to be divided by that.

The discussion went beyond polite political banter. Verhofstadt was clearly exasperated and upset by what he heard – and the debate put him on the defensive too. Europe held Britain responsible for upholding the Good Friday Agreement, but could not accept what the British suggested as the simplest solution – we'll just let everything pass – because that would open a backdoor to their single market.

> ROSINDELL: I still don't see why there is need of even
> talk of a border. We have similar standards, we're
> a law-abiding country, all we need is a sensible
> agreement between ourselves, to continue with these
> sensible arrangements, and there's no need for any
> border. I say again, Britain will not be imposing a
> border, so you would have to; the EU would harm the
> people of Ireland by imposing a hard border.
> VERHOFSTADT: We don't want a barrier.
> ROSINDELL: So let's agree not to have it, and carry on as
> we are.
> VERHOFSTADT: Yeah, but that you don't want. Because
> you go out.

Verhofstadt laughed dryly, while another voice at the table tried to soothe the two men, saying, 'It's a fascinating discussion, very interesting . . .'

> VERHOFSTADT: Maybe it was better to have it before the
> referendum . . .

The duel then moved beyond the Irish issue to the broader Brexit debate. 'I know that you're upset with Britain leaving the EU,' Rosindell accused. 'But to politicise this decision, punish Britain, you're punishing Ireland as well, we need an open border, travel!'

Verhofstadt came back with: 'But we are punishing nobody. What we are talking [about] here is the consequence of a decision. That's the point.' And then he raised Theresa May's publicly stated negotiating bottom line. 'Take for example for one or other reason there is no deal. We have not started to talk about no deal, eh? The UK has started to talk about no deal . . . No deal is better than a bad deal, who has said that?' he demanded.

Afterwards, while Verhofstadt was switching off the lights in his office — a strange habit he has, he prefers to sit there in the half dark — Edel couldn't stop herself telling him, 'I'm most proud of you when you take on a Tory and win. He was a fucker, yeah? I was delighted.'

~

On 27 September, Michel Barnier telephoned Guy Verhofstadt to discuss a resolution the Brexit Steering Group was planning to put before the European Parliament; in another mark of the close cooperation between Commission and Parliament, the two discussed detailed amendments to the resolution. The latest round of talks with the British were now well underway, and Barnier also brought Verhofstadt up to speed on progress. 'It's been tough, the past couple of days?' Verhofstadt asked. 'I can't tell you!' Barnier laughed. The two sides had been slogging through Britain's financial commitments line by line, but Barnier was absolutely clear on one point. 'There will not be "sufficient progress" in October,' he said, and the British would have to wait until at least the end of the year before negotiations on a future relationship could begin.

The following day Verhofstadt boarded the Eurostar to

London, where he was due to give a speech on Europe's future at the London School of Economics. He bumped into David Davis as they boarded the train – Davis was returning to London after the latest round of negotiations. The two of them bantered briefly about one of Verhofstadt's pet projects; after Brexit, he wanted to turn Britain's seventy-three seats in the European Parliament into transnational seats, occupied by MEPs elected on a Europe-wide franchise. David Davis liked the idea and said he might become a transnational candidate himself. 'I would get a lot of votes,' he said. Verhofstadt retorted, 'More than in Britain.' After that, they both went to sit in their allotted seats, close to each other in business class, but not close enough to listen in to what each started discussing with their respective teams.

Verhofstadt did clock the fact that the Davis entourage included the Conservative MEP Daniel Hannan, a prominent Eurosceptic who, like Boris Johnson before he became foreign secretary, used his newspaper column to advance the Brexit cause.

Later he teased me for failing to record the other side's conversation – I had already been filming him for close to six months by then. 'I have seen there was in his [Davis's] team also Hannan,' Verhofstadt said to a more sympathetic group of British MEPs. 'The guy is not my big fan . . . His whole team was there, and we didn't listen. We could listen, but we didn't do it.' He turned and pointed at me: 'You have maybe? I'm sure that you have conversations on your tape. No? You didn't do it? Ah, you're disappointing me.' He turned away laughing; I pointed out I had only been allowed to film the Davis team for a few seconds.

On the train to London, Verhofstadt worked on his speech about the future of Europe with the help of Bram Delen and Guillaume McLaughlin. They polished his Florence joke, and when he got to his feet at the LSE's packed Old Theatre, with Sadiq Khan in the audience, it came off well. 'It is a little bit surrealistic that I give this speech about the future of Europe here in London, the capital of a country that is about to leave the Union,' he told his listeners, 'while prime minister May gave her speech on Brexit, in a European city, in Florence. But I think, I have to tell you that I also know why Theresa May gave her speech in Florence. I presume that I know it. I think that she chose Florence because Florentine politics in the fifteenth century made her feel at home. You know, back-stabbing, betrayal, noble families fighting for power, and so on. So I think that it was an environment that she recognised very well.' He got a good laugh this time, but he added – a veteran now of British press habits – 'that was a joke, eh!? I say it for the press, because tomorrow in *The Sun* . . . I see already the titles of the articles.'

Verhofstadt's new Brexit resolution was due to be debated in the European Parliament at the beginning of October. Jeroen Reijnen, his head of media and communications, worked on Verhofstadt's speech with Bram Delen, and their debate provided another warning sign of European exasperation with Britain's negotiating pace. They agreed that he should appeal for continued unity among the political groups in the Parliament. Delen tried out his draft: 'On a complex issue like the negotiation position we can transcend party differences, we can transcend national differences. It's also important as a signal to the Council, because we expect the same from them. It's important that we stick together, hold on to the timing, the sequencing of the negotiations that the British negotiation team agreed on as well, let's not forget that. It is the best way to secure the interests of all twenty-seven member states.' And then:

REIJNEN: Can we not add a sentence that it would be
good if during the Tory conference [the Conservatives
were due to hold their annual party conference that
week] they could finally decide what they want?

DELEN: Yeah, but we did a lot of Tory-bashing already,
eh?

REIJNEN: But that's not bashing.

DELEN [laughing]: So what is it? A friendly request?

REIJNEN: A friendly incentive.

DELEN: I will add it.

REIJNEN: It's lasted long enough now, eh? This soap. I
mean on Netflix also you have just two seasons. The
third season never gets better. Think of House of
Cards.

DELEN [laughing again]: Yeah, but we made so many jokes
about the Tory Party already.

REIJNEN: This is the very last one.

DELEN: Season three. And this is the last joke on the Tory
Party . . . for two weeks.

The Brexit Steering Group's new Brexit resolution was endorsed
by the European Parliament on 3 October. Thanks to the close
cooperation between Guy Verhofstadt and Michel Barnier, it
reflected the joint negotiating position agreed within the EU.
And on the issue of the Irish border it included European 'red
lines'. Section 9 of the text stated that the European Parliament

[s]trongly believes that it is the responsibility of the UK
government to provide a unique, effective and workable
solution that prevents a 'hardening' of the border, ensures
full compliance with the Good Friday Agreement in all
its parts, is in line with European Union law and fully

ensures the integrity of the internal market and customs union; believes also that the United Kingdom must continue to contribute its fair share to the financial assistance supporting Northern Ireland/Ireland; regrets that the United Kingdom's proposals, set out in its position paper on 'Northern Ireland and Ireland', fall short in that regard; notes on the other hand that in her speech of 22 September 2017 the prime minister of the United Kingdom excluded any physical infrastructure at the border, which presumes that the United Kingdom stays in the internal market and customs union or that Northern Ireland stays in some form in the internal market and customs union.

Anyone who took the trouble to read the resolution could have predicted a battle royal to come over the Irish border. But the British press does not, by and large, pay much heed to the doings of the European Parliament, and at the beginning October 2017 the attention of Britain's political correspondents and commentators was focused on a great political drama at home; it was the season of the annual ritual of the party conferences, and the Conservatives met in Manchester on 1 October amid yet more fevered speculation about the leadership.

The somewhat unlikely media star of the gathering was Jacob Rees-Mogg; a fogeyish figure in his beautifully tailored suits, he had his finger on the party's Brexit pulse, and his fringe meetings – he addressed nine in the course of the week – were packed. He compared Brexit to the great battles of Britain's past. 'It's Waterloo, it's Agincourt, it's Crécy,' he told his audience, to thunderous applause. 'We win all these things.' Before the Brexit referendum Rees-Mogg was widely regarded as an eccentric backbencher; he was now spoken of as a possible prime minister. The media had coined the term

'Moggmentum' – a pun on the Momentum movement that had done so much to mobilise support for Jeremy Corbyn – to describe his rise.

When Theresa May took to the podium on the morning of 4 October, her first task was to say sorry for that spring's election debacle. This she did quickly and graciously, addressing her personal shortcomings head-on. 'We did not get the victory we wanted because our national campaign fell short,' she acknowledged. 'It was too scripted. Too presidential. And it allowed the Labour Party to paint us as the voice of continuity, when the public wanted to hear a message of change. I hold my hands up for that. I take responsibility. I led the campaign. And I am sorry.'

Old hands at the party conference game sometimes complain that the events are now so carefully controlled that they lack any spontaneity. The first sign of Mrs May's leader's address slipping out of control came when a comedian called Simon Brodkin (stage name Lee Nelson) bounced cheerful up to the podium and handed her an imitation of a P45, the tax document that is issued on termination of employment, claiming that 'Boris asked me to give you this.' Brodkin then approached the foreign secretary with the words 'Boris, job done, I've given her the P45', and patted him on the knees. Johnson looked thoroughly discomforted, and it fell to his neighbour, the home secretary, Amber Rudd, to nudge the interloper away. May managed to recover with an off-the-cuff sally about how much she would like to give a P45 to the Labour leader Jeremy Corbyn.

But not long afterwards the prime minister was assailed by an apparently unstoppable coughing fit – it was so bad that there seemed to be a real question mark about whether she would manage to complete the remaining nine pages of her speech. Amber Rudd again came to her rescue, and could be seen in the television coverage instructing Boris Johnson to join a standing ovation designed to give Mrs May the chance to recover herself. Philip Hammond offered the prime minister a cough sweet, which gave her the opening for another one-liner: 'I hope you noticed that, ladies and gentlemen, the chancellor giving something away for free.' It was too late; a speech that should have allowed the prime minister to reassert her authority over the party would go down as a disaster. The verdict was sealed when letters began to fall off the conference slogan – Building a Country that Works for Everyone – which was displayed on the backdrop behind her.

The fifth round of direct negotiations took place the following week. At the final press conference, David Davis struggled to keep alive the possibility that Europe's leaders would accept that 'sufficient progress' had been made for the talks to move on to consider a future relationship – a possibility Michel Barnier had dismissed two weeks earlier in his phone call with Verhofstadt. 'As we look to the October European Council next week,' Davis said, 'I hope the member states will recognise the progress we have made, and take a step forward in the spirit of the prime minister's Florence speech. Doing so will allow us to best achieve our joint objectives by turning the ideas we have explored into concrete shared proposals.'

When Michel Barnier debriefed the Brexit Steering Group, he noted that 'there is no animosity with the British delegation, who are very anxious to show that things are moving ahead . . . pushing [he used the English word] to show both domestically and abroad that things are moving on, sometimes, indeed, rather more than they are in reality'. But he also repeated his verdict: 'To tell you the truth, there has not been enough progress made to move to the second phase.'

The phrases 'it's a negotiation' and 'nothing is agreed until everything is agreed' had by now become commonplace responses which British ministers deployed when they were challenged in interviews over the EU's publicly stated positions. It was true that the EU had always had a tradition of horse-trading until the eleventh hour, but Barnier's briefing to the Steering Group underlined the difference between the Brexit talks and EU business as usual.

'This is not the routine negotiation, the bargaining, that goes on over European texts, which you are all familiar with,' he said. The EU's position had, rather, a remorseless logic, dictated by the organisation's rules and endorsed by its leaders; there could be no question of making concessions on citizens' rights or the Irish border and, as far as the money was concerned, 'we are simply asking that they pay what they have signed up to while they were committed to us'. And, looking ahead to the draft agreement he now hoped would be settled two months later, in December, he added, 'Even if they keep telling us, every day, that nothing is agreed until we have complete agreement at the end, this interim agreement needs to be stable.'

There was, however, still room for political considerations. Didier Seeuws, the Belgian representative of the European Council, reported to the BSG that the EU member governments were debating whether to help the embattled Mrs May by softening their line on the progress of negotiations when the Council met. Some governments, he said, were concerned that 'the tide could turn against us and we could lose the high ground by being too rigid', and wanted to announce that, while the 'sufficient progress' threshold had not been met, the EU was at least willing to begin preparations for negotiations on a future relationship – 'internal work, among the twenty-seven, not with the UK,' he said. Other governments, he reported, were worried about the way the UK might 'spin' such a concession.

The balance of opinion, a couple of days later, came down in favour of rewarding Theresa May for the Florence speech; the Council decided to 'start internal preparations for the second phase of the Brexit talks', and the Council president, Donald Tusk, said that he hoped phase two could begin in December.

The issue of spin haunted the Council as much as it frustrated Barnier at times. In the stately Egmont Palace, at the breakfast meeting of Liberal heads of government preceding the October 2017 Council gathering, the Dutch prime minister Mark Rutte complained to Verhofstadt and the others at the table that 'In the British press it was reported that I would plead for some more flexibility [for May], which is not true. So this was just a spin.' He explained:

> I spoke with Theresa on Friday, in close conjunction with the French and the Germans, and my message was that if she would signal that she would come with a concrete proposal on the exit bill, we would not say there was sufficient progress, because clearly there is not, but we could have been somewhat more forthcoming in the language, about this second phase . . . But I told her that she has to give meat to the sentence of the Florence speech which was saying 'we will honour our other commitments' – which is the exit bill. And she then said, 'I can't do that, I'll think about it.' She spoke with Macron on Sunday, she spoke with Merkel on Monday or Tuesday, and no movement.

He added, 'I will make clear to the British press . . . that they should not listen always to the spin coming out of Downing Street.'

The British, for their part, were enraged by a leaked description of May at a dinner with Jean-Claude Juncker, the president of the European Commission. The meeting also took place just before the Council began, and what appeared to be an insider account of the evening was published in the Sunday edition of the *Frankfurter Allgemeine* newspaper. It claimed that an 'anxious', 'tormented', 'despondent and discouraged' May had come to the dinner to plead for her political life. Juncker leapt to her defence, stating publicly that 'she was in good shape, she was not tired, she was fighting, as is her duty, so everything for me was OK'. Juncker could afford to be magnanimous; the EU's negotiators were dictating the pace of the Brexit process. And sometimes it seemed Mrs May had more friends in Brussels than she did at Westminster.

7

ONE BIG FUN FAIR

November 2017

On a Tuesday at the beginning of November 2017, Bram Delen was sitting at his desk in Brussels, sweating over a press release about citizens' rights, and wondering – he admitted this to me after the documentary was released – why I was filming him. He was pretty sure I was never going to use the material I was shooting because the text he was working on was way too complicated and technical. The basis for the press release was an internal document in what he called 'bureaucratic' English, which had been floating around among the Brexit Steering Group members, who were less worried than he was by any need for clarity to outsiders. Despite his own impressive command of English, he had called on the assistance of Nick Petre, Verhofstadt's spokesperson for the UK.

DELEN: For the European Parliament to approve the withdrawal agreement, key principles and conditions must be met. Yeah? Parliament will not countenance any change in the rights that EU citizens currently enjoy with respect to family reunion. What does it mean?

PETRE: Countenance? Tolerate. Will not support.

DELEN: Will not accept a deterioration of existing rights?
PETRE: Yeah.
DELEN: Perhaps a better word for deterioration?

Nick had to think — but I can't say now what his answer was, because I stopped filming to change my camera angle. I picked up again when the really complicated stuff began.

Bram started reading it aloud, every two words followed by a sigh, and with underneath all the words the continuous rattle of his fingers on the keyboard of his computer. Both he and Nick were sitting in their suits, while I was wearing jeans and a T-shirt — so I pitied them, but then I knew they also pitied me. 'Both direct descendants and dependent relatives, I would . . .' Bram stopped and thought hard. 'Ah yeah, I would say: direct dependent relatives and descendants. No? Direct, comma. And direct dependent . . .' He stopped again, exasperated. Nick chipped in: 'Or the relatives of direct dependents?' Bram laughed: 'The relatives of direct dependents?' Nick: 'Yeah, I think that's what they actually mean.'

Half an hour later, in the doorway to the corridor, on their way to the Brexit Steering Group, Bram explained to his boss and to chief of staff Guillaume McLaughlin what he had been doing. 'This is very technical. It's like mathematics. We're trying to make it understandable for people outside. But we're not changing the tonality.' And he added that they kept track changes so that nobody had to worry about words or ideas lost in translation. Guillaume replied, 'Please, yeah.'

All this forging of fine phrases and meticulous detail work reflected the fact that for the European Parliament, the Brexit Steering Group and its president Guy Verhofstadt, the rights of EU citizens living in the UK was the most important of the three divorce issues. The financial settlement was judged to be the European Council's concern, because without a deal

Britain would not pay anything and the remaining member states would have to find more money to plug the hole, while the issue of the Irish border was to be mainly a matter for the Irish Republic – with the EU functioning like a letterbox between Westminster and Dublin, as Guillaume McLaughlin put it at one point.

Verhofstadt was worried that the financial settlement especially would overshadow the issue of citizens' rights, and wanted the BSG to issue a strong statement – the one Bram had been preparing – in reaction to a British proposal on the issue, which he absolutely did not like. 'The sixth round of the negotiations was finally agreed and will take place tomorrow and Friday [9 and 10 November 2017],' he said, 'and [here he hesitated] the prospects are not really promising.' He predicted that the financial settlement would once again top the agenda. 'It has only confirmed for me my worries that I have with the citizens' rights. That is that in the end, in the coming weeks, there could be a breakthrough in the financial settlement, and then you know how it goes in politics . . . when the deal is there, the deal will be there. And then to say, ah we don't agree with this and this, will be far more difficult. So I think if we want to react it's now.'

Verhofstadt had three problems with the system the UK proposed. The first related to the bureaucratic hoops EU citizens would have to go through to stay in the United Kingdom. 'What I mainly try to say in the text is that instead of a system in which you have to apply, and the citizens have to prove a number of things, with papers, and a driving licence, and whatever, it has to be a declarative system, the opposite,' he explained. 'And it's then [up] to the Home Office to prove that they have evidence that it is not true what you're declaring. So instead of an application system, it has to be a declaration system.' The second problem was that 'instead of being an individual system, it has to be a collective system, so, an individual can do that for his whole family'. His third objective was to ensure the new system should come into force after the transition period, not immediately after Britain's Brexit day. 'Instead of starting immediately, after withdrawal, it has to start after transition,' he declared. And he added, 'It has to be cost free, because in their proposal they want to ask £90 . . . because it will be the same cost as the passport.'

Verhofstadt's plan was 'to send that in a letter to Barnier, also maybe to Davis, why not, saying to both of them, "Sorry, there will be a problem with the Parliament." And I can tell you, there will be a problem in the Parliament, eh?'

Roberto Gualtieri agreed with him. 'We have to be extremely clear now,' he said, 'because to ask for changes after a deal has been reached would be a bit of a nuclear option.' The Polish MEP Danuta Hübner was more cautious. 'This is quite strong, this statement of today, and we are asking for things that the Brits so far have not found acceptable.' But Gualtieri cut her short: 'Everybody knows how it works. You ask 100, then if you get not 100, but 50, you can still decide it's sufficient.' Verhofstadt: 'Exactly. Now is the time to step on the gas pedal. Let's go for it, otherwise we can go home and do something different.'

The BSG got all worked up, and so it was funny but also striking, a week later, to hear Bram Delen and his colleague Jeroen Reijnen, the head of media, make their own more laid-back — but damning — analysis of the state of the negotiations. They were in Strasbourg, preparing for the press conference that Verhofstadt usually gives there.

REIJNEN: Do we have anything to say about Brexit, at the press conference tomorrow, Bram? Is there something

to shout about citizens' rights? That they should stop
bullshitting?

DELEN: The problem is these are not real negotiations.

REIJNEN: No.

DELEN: What's happening is, the Union has said: these
are the conditions under which you can leave, the door
is there, that's where you need to leave your money
that you owe us; regarding citizens' rights the deal was
always that everything remains the same; the Good
Friday Agreement, we also all agree that it needs to
stay in place, so once all this has penetrated, you can
leave the Union. That's what's happening now. And
so what do you see? The Union doesn't move, because
really, there's nothing to negotiate about, and the Brits
are making one big fun fair of it.

REIJNEN: But can't we say something tomorrow that
rises above the parties?

DELEN: Theresa May is falling apart; her government is
falling apart.

REIJNEN: And her party.

DELEN: And her party is falling apart.

REIJNEN: So we have to be careful that her country
doesn't fall apart.

DELEN [laughing]: Her country is falling apart. Come
on, what can we say? 'Rise above the parties'? One,
on our side, there are no parties, because everyone in
the Union is in agreement. And to say something like
that about the British will sound patronising. As if
you're talking about a developing country.

REIJNEN: Is that bad? Yes? Yes.

DELEN: It's putting salt in their wounds, do we need to
do that? You heard Verhofstadt earlier, didn't you? The

biggest risk for us now is that Brexit doesn't happen
any more. I also wouldn't be able to stomach that – to
take the Brits back in . . . And tomorrow it's going
to be the same thing all over again, in the BSG, with
Barnier who comes to tell that a little bit of progress
has been made.

Bram and Jeroen's observations echoed – in their exasperation with the
British – a story told by the German MEP Elmar Brok at the end of
one of the many informal Brexit Steering Group's meetings around that
time. He was discussing an attempt by the United Kingdom to link the
divorce talks to other topics by threatening to withdraw their security
cooperation unless the EU gave ground, and he related a conversation
he had had with the president of Lithuania [Dalia Grybauskaitė].
He reported that 'she told David Davis, look, David, you have to do
everything . . . anyway as a member of NATO. What has it to do with
Brexit negotiations?'

Brok also described a meeting with Britain's NATO ambassador
and 'a think-tanker' who had warned that Europe risked losing 'all
the access to British naval power, including nuclear submarines'. He
recalled to general laughter around the table: 'And I said, "I didn't know
that we have access to that."'

'It's idiotic what they play in that field,' was Brok's judgement,
but he also had a warning for his colleagues. 'And here we have to be
very cautious because people who don't know that in detail might be
impressed by these positions they have.'

The next day, with the European Parliament buildings in
Strasbourg shrouded in fog, the Sinn Féin MEP Martina
Anderson was back in Guy Verhofstadt's office to lobby about the
Irish border. Just as Verhofstadt was worried about citizens' rights
being forgotten, she was worried that Ireland's concerns might

be swept aside by the broader political objectives of bigger EU member states which were pushing to move the negotiation on.

'There has been lack of progress on Ireland,' she said. 'What do we do if the Council wants to move it [the negotiation] into the next stage, phase two, without there being sufficient progress?' And she added a warning about British tactics: 'The one thing I would share with you, there is no country, in the EU, that knows Britain, in terms of negotiations, like we do. We've been in there with them . . .' Anderson believed that the EU was underestimating the importance of Theresa May's confidence and supply arrangement with the Democratic Unionists: 'The British government . . . they're getting supported by the only party in Ireland, north, south, east and west, which was against the Good Friday agreement,' she said. 'And that's not understood.'

Verhofstadt responded with an insight into the ideas Michel Barnier and his team were trying to develop, wrestling with the language in a way that reflected the sensitivity of the issue. 'We cannot call it a customs union, we cannot call it a single market,' he said. 'But why not have a sort of range of sectoral regulatory agreements, I don't know what the name has to be, where, if you add all this, it's like the customs union [laughs] or like the single market. So you don't call it like that, but the addition of all these sectoral arrangements, gives you in fact a full-fledged customs union and single market. So that's the idea that is flying for the moment in the Commission.'

It involved, he acknowledged, the creative use of language: 'They continue to think, in the Commission, and in the negotiation team, that we need a solution in which Northern Ireland, in practice, doesn't see a change. And doesn't have a hard border,' he reassured Anderson, adding – and asking her to keep the matter to herself for the moment – 'And they call it, sectoral, regulatory agreements.' Guillaume McLaughlin confirmed that the Commission team were trawling through the areas where such agreements would be needed. 'I don't know what are the amount of areas [of] cross-border [cooperation], but they're huge, eh?' he put to her. 'A hundred and forty,' Martina Anderson confirmed.

Verhofstadt had to break up the meeting for the press conference Jeroen Reijnen and Bram Delen had been preparing the day before. His difficulty in defining the latest ideas for dealing with the problem of the Irish border was one of the birth pangs of what came to be known as the 'backstop' – a piece of political shorthand so opaque that it would require constant explaining and re-explaining in articles and broadcasts, even when it had been a commonplace of political discourse for months.

A joint mapping exercise by the EU and the United Kingdom in fact identified 142 areas where cross-border cooperation had developed as a result of the Good Friday Agreement, and, in the words of a study conducted by Belfast's Queen's University, they ranged 'from an all-island sanitary and phytosanitary regime (for animal health and welfare) and the single electricity market, to the cross-border rail service, mobile phone roaming and emergency healthcare planning and provision'. Some of the areas covered might seem a little obscure – the 'all-island marsh fritillary group', for example – but many of them had a direct and obviously beneficial bearing on people's everyday lives; there was an all-Ireland free travel scheme for senior citizens, bus services worked across the border, and so did GP out-of-hours services. As a House of Commons report later pointed out, the Altnagelvin Hospital in Londonderry (Derry to Nationalists) could 'provide specialist cancer treatment because it services 500,000 patients across both Northern Ireland and part of County Donegal in the Irish Republic', and people based around the same city might 'be earning in sterling, buy their home in euros and simultaneously own a car registered in [the Republic of] Ireland'.

It was a clever idea to try to defuse the big political issue of Northern Ireland's status by focusing negotiations on these smaller practical matters, but it could not alter the fact that some things would, inevitably, change with Brexit. As the Queen's University study noted,

> The concept of regulatory alignment as applied by the EU is one that covers:
> * the rules themselves;
> * the means of assessing conformity to them;
> * the need for cooperation and information-sharing across the border in order to uphold them; and
> * a dispute-settlement mechanism.
>
> This means that the post-Brexit UK–EU relationship must entail legal and institutional mechanisms to cover all these functions in relation to Ireland/Northern Ireland.

In other words, simply for things to stay the same, there would need to be a whole new structure of regulation and oversight.

The Good Friday Agreement – which ended the so-called Troubles in 1998 – succeeded because Northern Ireland's divided communities have been able to interpret it in different ways, and the fact that both the United Kingdom and the Republic of Ireland have been part of a bigger political entity in the shape of the EU made that easier: Northern Ireland's politics are built on a fudge. But Brexit brought political fudge up against the rigid realities of the single market – which, partly because of its size and the number of nations involved, depends on a rules-based system where fudge has no place.

Michel Barnier illustrated the clash when, with characteristic Cartesian clarity, he summed up the EU view to the BSG on the afternoon of Martina Anderson's meeting with Verhofstadt: 'On Ireland . . . my whole effort has been directed towards getting them [the British] to recognise that the positions they hold at the moment are not reconcilable. You cannot say that you are going to leave the single market and the customs union, at the same time as saying that you want no physical border on the island of Ireland, and also that you want to avoid the return of a frontier between Ireland and the rest of the UK. These three points are irreconcilable. It is as simple as that.' But the Northern Ireland political system works – when it does work – on the basis that nothing is simple and almost everyone has irreconcilable positions that somehow have to be accommodated.

Barnier had brought slides with him to guide the group through the negotiating thickets; on the other two areas of the divorce negotiations, citizens' rights and the exit bill, the talks were now deep in the undergrowth of detail. Barnier was able to report that Britain had accepted that the rights of European citizens enshrined in a withdrawal agreement would cover couples living together, parents and grandparents, and those in durable relationships that pre-dated Brexit. The rights of children born in a marriage contracted after Brexit remained at issue.

As for the financial settlement, Barnier reported that he had used the sixth round of negotiations to repeat his demand for 'clarity' on what he called the second phase of the commitments Theresa May had made in her Florence speech. The first phase covered the years 2019–20, and May had accepted that during that period no country should, as Barnier put it, 'pay more or receive less'. But the second phase related much more broadly to long-term commitments to which Britain had signed up as an EU member. Here, Barnier reported, there had been less progress, although he added that he regarded this area as one which allowed some political wiggle room: 'I believe that my mandate for negotiations with the British includes the payment method, a spreading of the payment which would make the presentation of the financial settlement more accept-able to them.'

Barnier wrapped up by saying that he hoped to agree a common text with David Davis by the end of November or early December which would provide what he called an *état des lieux*, a phrase often used by French estate agents to mean a stock-taking, or report on the state of the fixtures and fittings. One of the main obstacles, he reported to the group, remained the fluidity of David Davis's diary. He told the Belgian MEP Philippe Lamberts, 'You cannot imagine the difficulties we have had – speaking between ourselves – in agreeing and con-firming dates, and knowing when Davis is ready to come. Last time he came on the Friday morning [the last day of the nego-tiating round].' Lamberts came back with: 'If I understand the position correctly, fifteen days before the deadline for decid-ing whether there is "sufficient progress", you still aren't sure whether you will be holding talks in the coming weeks?' 'If we don't talk there won't be [sufficient progress],' Barnier replied.

Michel Barnier's relentlessly detailed slide show had taken its toll on one member of the group; by the end of the meeting the veteran Christian Democrat Elmar Brok had closed his eyes, his chin on his chest.

~

Four days later, the European Union's leaders – including Theresa May – met in Gothenburg, a university city and port on Sweden's west coast. The summit gathered heads of state and government and representatives from businesses and trade unions. There, the European Parliament, the Council and the European Commission proclaimed the European Pillar of Social Rights. It was an EU manifesto for equal opportunities, fair working conditions and social inclusion; this was the kind of project that should, in the view of true EU believers like Guy Verhofstadt, occupy the Union's attention and energy, instead of Brexit.

But the Gothenburg summit was to be remembered for a very different landmark; it was the moment when the debate over the Irish border broke onto the public political stage as a fully fledged diplomatic row.

As he arrived at the summit, the Irish prime minister, Leo Varadkar, delivered a broadside against Theresa May's 'red lines'. If the United Kingdom could 'unilaterally' remove membership of the customs union from the negotiations, he said, then Ireland would set some 'parameters' of its own. 'They've taken that [the customs union] off the table before we've even talked about trade,' he said. 'What we want to take off the table before we even talk about trade is any idea that there would be a hard border, a physical border or a border resembling the past . . . Then we'd be happy to move on to phase two.' And there was a sting in the tail of his comments: 'It's eighteen months since the referendum, it's ten years since people who wanted a referendum started agitating for one. Sometimes it doesn't seem like they thought all this through.'

The same day, his foreign minister, Simon Coveney, met the British foreign secretary Boris Johnson in Dublin and, with Johnson standing beside him at the press conference, stated flatly that there was an 'impasse' in the negotiations over the border, and that while everyone wanted the talks to move on to a second phase, 'we are not in a place right now that allows us to do that'. Boris Johnson later met the Fianna Fáil leader Micheál Martin, who supported Varadkar's judgement that Britain's Brexiteers had not thought through the implications of leaving the European Union. 'They use this language, "We need to have control, we need to be part of a big global world free trade" et cetera, et cetera,' he said. 'But there is no sense of any blueprint for that. There is no sense of people having worked through the practical implications of all that. And that was clear this morning.'

To complicate the picture further, the Irish government was, in the week following the Gothenburg summit, caught up in a domestic political crisis of its own. Varadkar's deputy prime minister, Frances Fitzgerald, faced accusations that she had interfered in the case of a police whistle-blower who had made allegations of corruption in the Garda (Ireland's national police and security service). Like Mrs May's Conservatives, Leo Varadkar's Fine Gael was in power thanks to a confidence and supply arrangement – in his case with Ireland's other main centrist political party, Fianna Fáil. And the Fianna Fáil leader Micheál Martin threatened to withdraw his support over the issue. Ms Fitzgerald resigned to avoid the risk of a general election at such a sensitive moment in the Brexit negotiations (she was later cleared of any blame in the whistle-blower affair), and the Varadkar government survived. But it was a reminder that Theresa May was not the only politician involved in the negotiations whose room for manoeuvre was constrained by political pressure at home.

On the evening of 20 November, Mrs May chaired a meeting of what was officially known as the Cabinet Exit and Trade (Strategy and Negotiations) sub-Committee in Downing Street. The group included the leading Brexiteers Boris

Johnson, Michael Gove and Liam Fox, and they agreed to allow Mrs May to make a substantial financial offer towards settling Britain's outstanding EU commitments. The offer was framed in terms of a methodology for adding up the bill, and there was no overall figure put on the total – certainly not in public – but the BBC reported that it was 'up to £40 billion'. The Office for Budget Responsibility, the government body set up to provide independent analysis of public finances, later estimated that the actual bill would be £37.8 billion, covering Britain's budget contributions up to 2020, a percentage of the future commitments the EU had agreed but not yet paid while Britain was still a member, and liabilities which included pension payments for EU staff.

Reports of the new offer provoked a hostile reaction from some hard-line Brexit supporters on the Conservative back benches, but all that brave talk about telling the EU to 'go whistle' for its money faded without much fuss. When Barnier's deputy Sabine Weyand met the Brexit Steering Group on 27 November, she was able to reassure them that the heat had gone out of the argument about money; the British Cabinet and Parliament had, she said, 'digested the money. The money is an issue with the tabloid press, but not with the parliamentarians.' She added, though, that 'until we have it in writing and signed off by Theresa May in blood, you know, you never know'.

Sabine Weyand's style was very different; she was just as precise as her boss, but witty, even harsh when occasion demanded.

The negotiations had moved into a new gear. The system of distinct rounds of talks had been designed to allow Barnier to keep all the interested parties on the EU side closely informed – another illustration of how carefully the EU's institutions were coordinating their approach.

'Why did I impose this system of rounds?' Barnier said to the BSG when he was challenged about the process. 'Because I needed time to come back to you and report. To verify with the Council, and with you, after each round.' But with negotiating deadlines pressing more than ever, the talks had become an almost permanent to and fro between Brussels and London.

Verhofstadt took Sabine Weyand through the areas where he felt the European Parliament might object to the emerging interim agreement. On the issue of citizens' rights, he remained concerned about the language being used; he didn't like the term 'settled status' to describe the position of EU citizens who decided to remain in Britain after Brexit – because it made it sound as if they were 'settlers', in an epic, trekking-through-America sense, with wagons and horses on trails full of hardship.

He hammered home his argument that EU citizens in the UK should not be asked to 'apply' to have their position regularised. 'They [the British] want application,' he told her. 'We say no, no, call it a "declaration". It's also wording, but I can tell you, wording in politics, in my little experience, is fundamental.' And he returned to his objection to the fact that EU citizens would have to pay to have their status decided. 'People didn't ask for it [Brexit],' he pointed out. 'People lived there, and it's because of a decision of the Brits that they now have to apply, and they have to pay £70, multiplied by the number of their family members.' The fee was in fact set at £65 (half that for those under sixteen), and much, much later, while she was struggling to get her withdrawal agreement though Parliament, Theresa May dropped it altogether.

Verhofstadt also warned that Parliament would react very badly to the idea that children born of relationships that began after Brexit would not be covered by the agreement, whereas children born before Brexit would. 'It's so symbolic,' he said. 'You know, in a family you [could then] have two types of children. That's against our nature.' Weyand explained that the British negotiating team viewed such children as 'hypothetical children of hypothetical couples', adding, 'At the moment their line is "we protect life choices made before Brexit, and not after".'

The British side had also tried to get agreement that British legal qualifications would still be recognised in the EU, and that allowed Weyand an opening for the razor-sharp sarcasm at which she excelled:

> WEYAND: The UK wants to protect lawyers, but they don't want to protect children. Politically speaking that is not really a good message to send. And that's what we're trying to drive home.
> VERHOFSTADT: It could be worse, eh? Bankers and children.
> WEYAND: I think they want to do bankers, lawyers, but not children. But maybe they will protect the children of bankers and lawyers.

The whole room laughed – but Weyand quickly returned to a more serious tone. Her overriding message for the Brexit Steering Group was that the negotiating team felt they had got as far as they realistically could in reaching an accommodation on this area of the divorce talks. 'On citizens' rights we are now of course zooming in on the outstanding issues,' she said. 'But that should not distract from the fact that we have achieved quite a lot in these negotiations. Because remember where we started. The UK said: all this will be spelled [out] by UK immigration law . . . We have now an agreement with the UK [that] all this will be based on EU law concepts, and that all EU citizens lawfully residing in the UK at the time of withdrawal can continue to do so. We have obtained lifetime guarantees.' She concluded with: 'Ninety-five per cent of our demands have so far been satisfied . . . But you are quite right, there are still a number of outstanding issues.'

Verhofstadt still did not like what he heard – and appreciated what followed even less. 'On proofs by the applicant or by the Home Office,' Weyand told the group. 'At the moment it is already the citizen who has to provide some proof that they are legally resident, and I think that we cannot change. The fact that first of all the applicant has to show that he has been in the country legally for a while, I think that is fully in line with EU law, and that's why we cannot really change that.' Verhofstadt and the Brexit Steering Group were basically being told to back off – and the coordinator's face turned dark. It was maybe the reason that Weyand replaced her boss that day.

The meeting moved on to the issue of the Irish border, which was now clearly identified as the main obstacle to progress. 'We still have problems on citizens,' Weyand told the BSG, 'and I'm certainly not in the process of belittling them, but I think there's probably more of a willingness to move on that, with some push, but on Ireland it's very delicate . . .'

She was pressed on Theresa May's willingness to compromise; did some of the more hard-line views expressed in the British press reflect her thinking? Weyand, who was reported to have developed a close working relationship with her British opposite number, Olly Robbins, replied, 'I think that those who have spoken in the press, on the UK side, are not people involved in the negotiations. That's what I can say. I think that as with all other issues it is only the prime minister who can in the end commit the government. What we know is that she is really, really very keen to have sufficient progress at the December European Council. And we are now testing how far that keenness takes her. Both on the citizens' rights and on the Irish issue.'

It seemed there was a real possibility that within a week Barnier would be able to declare sufficient progress on the three divorce issues, to allow the start of talks on a future relationship. But Weyand warned, 'As regards the future, we're in a delicate phase there, because the UK has not done anything in terms of telling. They have not clarified their own thinking about what they want from the future relationship. They have told us what they don't want. They don't want a customs union, they don't want the single market. They don't want Norway [membership of the European Free Trade Association and European Economic Area], but they also don't want to have CETA [the Comprehensive Economic and Trade Agreement between the EU and Canada] . . . But they have not landed. They're still in cloud cuckoo land.'

The EU negotiators were not minded to help Britain out by making proposals of their own. 'It would be dangerous for the EU to rush ahead with a list of things they want to address in the future relationship,' Weyand said. 'Why should we put ourselves in the position of a *demandeur*, in a situation where the UK has avoided any hard discussions?' Mrs May was still constrained by the fact that an unambiguous statement of her negotiating ambitions would risk re-igniting her party's divisions over Brexit. The complaint that Britain's position was unclear was to remain a leitmotiv of EU statements over the next year and more.

8

GOING FOR PURPLE

Late November–early December 2017

Immediately after the Brexit Steering Group meeting on
27 November, Verhofstadt hosted a smaller gathering which
included his chief of staff, Guillaume McLaughlin; Markus
Winkler, the deputy secretary general of the European
Parliament; and another senior parliamentary official, Nick
Lane, the Oxford-educated director for inter-institutional affairs
and legislative coordination. Winkler had just spent a weekend
away with Martin Selmayr, then chief of staff to the European
Commission president Jean-Claude Juncker ('I have once a
year, alcohol therapy we call it. So we go somewhere, a tranquil
weekend. And there were discussions, also including the Brexit,'
he explained), and he reported that there was now 'much more
optimism' at the Commission about reaching a deal. Winkler
also described the burden of a telephone call he had taken earlier in the day from the Brexit spokesman of the British Labour
Party, Sir Keir Starmer. 'I asked him how he's seeing things from
a Labour perspective. So I said to him openly, "Do you want this
[the interim agreement]?" He said, "Everything else would be a
real disaster on the whole process," so there they support the
government to try to have sufficient progress.'

But Verhofstadt wasn't convinced. 'On Northern Ireland and Ireland, if I understand it,' he retorted, 'they have made no progress at all.' His chief of staff Guillaume McLaughlin agreed. 'Zero,' he said. And McLaughlin, who is half-British himself, went on to explain how the British had been blind-sided by the way Ireland had blown up as an issue in the talks. 'My understanding from having spoken to the Brits last week,' he said, 'is the Brits have been caught short out on this one, because they were having this nice little technical discussion, on our agenda, eh? A nice little technical discussion, and sud-denly – claps hands – it becomes a huge political bomb, and they say, hang on a sec, we're not ready for this one.' And he laid some of the blame at the EU's own door. 'I think we have been a bit soft on the Northern Ireland issue . . . in terms of the negotiation,' he offered. 'We've been looking at technical things, [and] the conclusion of this technical thing was just to push back the fact that we knew that [at] the end of the day we're going to have a fucking huge mess [over the Irish border question]. That's what we've been doing. That's exactly what we've been doing.'

Nick Lane pointed out – with some pride – that the European Parliament resolution the previous month had laid the ground for what came to be known as the backstop, because it had raised the possibility that the border problem could be solved by either Northern Ireland or the whole United Kingdom remaining in close economic alignment with the EU.

LANE: Nobody had said that before. Everybody believed
it. Everybody thought it was OK, but nobody wanted
to say. And then we say it, with full backing of Fine
Gael members and everything, and the government,
the Irish government, then started to get tough.

MCLAUGHLIN: And then they started to wake up. And
then the Commission put out their paper where they
said the same thing at the end.

McLaughlin also pointed out that the British government's
anxiety to see the European Council give its blessing to the
idea that there had been 'sufficient progress' for the talks to
move to phase two made this the moment when the Irish
government could exercise what he called 'leverage'. 'After
that the little Irish government is . . .' – and here he whistled
and made an expressive pushing gesture with his hands. 'Out,
yeah,' Verhofstadt chimed in.

Everyone understood that the first phase of negotiations were
entering the endgame, and the pressure built on all sides.

On Friday 1 December, the leader of the DUP, Arlene
Foster, fired a warning shot with an article in the *Belfast
Telegraph*. 'In the past forty-eight hours there has been much
speculation around a possible deal between the UK government
and Brussels on how to prevent a hard border after Brexit,'
she wrote, before laying down her own clear red line. 'The
United Kingdom voted to leave the European Union as one
nation and we are leaving as one nation. The government have
a clear understanding that the DUP will not countenance any
arrangement that could lead to a new border being created in
the Irish Sea.'

On Sunday 3 December, a group of senior Conservative
Brexiteers – including the former party leader Ian Duncan
Smith and the former chancellor Nigel Lawson – published a
letter to the prime minister with a whole new set of red lines of
their own, including demands that both freedom of movement
and the role of the European Court of Justice should end when
the transition period began. And they tried to reopen a debate

the EU had thought was settled, arguing that Britain should refuse to pay the divorce settlement until these demands were met. The negotiations had, of course, moved well beyond all this, but it was a warning of the difficulties Mrs May might face in selling any agreement to her own party.

There was tension in the European camp, too. In a phone call with a journalist, Bram Delen shared his fears that the Parliament, the weakest of the three big European institutions, would back down, especially over the Irish issue. 'The essential discussion is now, how do we as a Parliament still weigh on the final, you know, on the endgame of phase one. Because you hear everywhere now that they [the main negotiators] want to land . . . but what we have on Ireland is far from enough. We need a binding statement so that we know that we can enforce on Great Britain later on what we need on Ireland.' He judged that Michel Barnier was in a mood to compromise because he 'wants to be seen as the man who can strike a deal', and 'the Council have their money, so they want to go to the second phase', but he worried that 'we're putting Ireland in an impossible, in a very difficult position'.

Delen recounted a debate at the Brexit Steering Group between Elmar Brok and the Italian Roberto Gualtieri. Gualtieri, he explained, had argued that 'we have to keep playing hard ball to get as much as possible out of the first phase', but Brok took the more relaxed view – and here Delen put on a German accent – that 'if we have 95 per cent we can ask that the 5 per cent will be resolved at the end of the deal'. Delen was inclined to agree with the harder line, but he worried that 'if we push too hard, and we really go for the full Monty, and it all leaks out in the press, and we stand alone as like the only institution who's still causing the problem to go to the second phase [shrugging his shoulders here], that's also a very weak position to be in.'

Delen recognised that one of the EU's foundational principles – that small member states can count on the support of the
Union – was at stake in the way Ireland's concerns were treated.
'If we lose,' he said, 'if we stop supporting Ireland on this issue,
it's yet another reason for the Irish people to say, "Fuck the
EU, we're a small member of this big club, but if the big boys
don't stand up for us and don't support us in essential and vital
questions, what's the use to us, I mean, to be part of the club?"'

*Bram's frustration had a personal, emotional side, inspired by Edel
Crosse, the Irish office manager, with whom the team felt they needed
to stand shoulder to shoulder. In her own inimitable style she shared
her fears about Ireland's interests being abandoned with her colleagues.
'Excuse me, but once the EU get their money, I'm very fucking sceptical
that they might throw a lot of other stuff to the walls,' she declared,
'and that was something I was always nervous about, the moment they
got the cash in hand . . . they're treating Ireland like this little kind
of breastfeeding child who's suddenly going to be ripped right off the
breast, and thrown – and then the EU is just going to stand there
saying, 'How are we going to sort [this out]?'*

*She added her doubts about whether Ireland's prime minister, Leo
Varadkar, had the mettle to stand up for Ireland's interests. 'If he doesn't
get the support from the EU, he will buckle. He's already a West Brit,
the guy is half fucking English for all intents and purposes [Varadkar's
Indian-born father and Irish mother met and married in the United
Kingdom] . . . The first time he went to No. 10 Downing Street, he
took pictures of himself, because his favourite film is* Notting Hill *. . .
or* Love Actually, *that's it.'*

*'There's nothing wrong with rom coms,' Bram Delen interjected. You
could, he declared, be a real player in the Brexit saga 'and love rom
coms at the same time, I want to make that clear for the record here'.*

Bram, Edel and the rest of the team wanted their boss to make a strong statement about Ireland. But Verhofstadt was about to leave for Amsterdam. 'We can't let him go,' Jeroen Reijnen said. Edel pointed at Verhofstadt's office: 'Yeah, I'll lock him in there.' In the end — not that day, but over the weekend — they managed to persuade Verhofstadt to put out a tweet, saying, 'Ireland decides. EU must fully unite behind Ireland. #IamIrish.'

Monday 4 December 2017 must surely rank as a nadir of modern British diplomacy.

Theresa May was due to meet Michel Barnier and the EU Commission president Jean-Claude Juncker for lunch to set the seal on the agreement the EU and UK negotiating teams had finally managed to reach on the three divorce issues. There was, of course, a long way to go before it could become a fully fledged treaty, but the EU was ready to accept that 'sufficient progress' had been made for the talks to move on to the future relationship between the two sides. The meeting was going to take place in the Berlaymont building, the EU Commission's Brussels headquarters, which is about a kilometre away from the European Parliament.

At the Parliament, the nervousness was tangible from very early in the morning. When I came in to film, Guillaume McLaughlin was already on the phone, walking, talking and gesticulating. 'Formally speaking it's absolutely the case the Parliament has its yes or no at the end of the process — and . . . no capacity to decide at this moment,' he conceded. 'However it's pretty clear that if you want to make sure the Parliament gives a positive answer in the end, you better make sure you listen to what it has to say during the process.' Otherwise, he pointed out, 'you might be surprised by the answer you get from the Parliament, especially three months before the European elections, that are happening in May 2019'.

It was still dark outside. Verhofstadt's croissant was waiting on his desk, placed there by his personal assistant, Erik Janda. The cleaning crews had not gone through all the offices yet.

Bram was sitting on a green trunk next to Edel's desk — one of the thousands of trunks the European Parliament uses to transport documents from Brussels to Strasbourg once a month. Verhofstadt as always didn't turn up before he was absolutely needed — which was at nine, when the Brexit Steering Group gathered for an informal meeting in his office to discuss what they had learned from Barnier over the weekend, in bits and pieces, via short phone calls and text messages.

The frustrating reality was that Verhofstadt and the Brexit Steering Group were at one remove from the heart of things on this critical day. They knew that in the end they would either have to accept a deal done between Barnier and the British, or risk blowing up the whole process by declaring that in their judgement the 'sufficient progress' threshold had not been reached. And as the senior parliamentary official Markus Winkler put it, 'If you want to have a mediatic nuclear bomb, you decide that it's not sufficient progress.'

The Italian MEP Roberto Gualtieri was disposed to maintain a united front, but he also had a complaint. 'If Barnier and Juncker consider that this is the moment to say there is sufficient progress, I think we should support them,' he told the group. 'But first we need to see the text.' The lack of hard information pushed up everyone's anxiety levels.

'The problem is that the Commission has not provided us [with] the exact wording,' Gualtieri said. 'I want to see the declaration . . . How it's written there . . . Not to be the difficult one, but I will kindly ask them to have . . . slightly more detail than this SMS [at this point he showed his phone] that we got. We even got two different versions of the same SMS.'

Guy Verhofstadt was still agonising – almost obsessively – over some aspects of the agreement on citizens' rights, although he accepted that there had been significant progress. 'On content everything is solved, all the rights are OK. No discrimination. Benefits for the family. All this is solved,' he said. '[But] the remaining problem is – from day one – the procedure.' He reported letters had been pouring in from EU citizens in Britain who were worried that the Home Office might unilaterally put a cap on the number it accepted for 'settled status'. 'And there [are] more and more letters . . . coming in from the 3 Million [the lobby group set up by EU citizens living in the UK], saying: the settled status, we have to apply, this is shit, a piece of shit. We don't want it.' The other complaint coming through the postbag was over the phrase 'settled status' itself; 'we aren't settlers', his correspondents were telling him. 'Settlers were those British who went to the United States. That's not us.'

On the Irish issue, Brussels seemed to have effectively delegated power to Dublin; the EU Council president Donald Tusk had said publicly over the weekend that if Britain's proposal on the issue of the border 'is unacceptable to Ireland it will be unacceptable to us'. The Irish government had been in direct negotiations with the government in London, and the Irish Cabinet was meeting that morning to consider the outcome of those talks.

Edel Crosse need not have worried about her boss holding the line. 'I think for the Irish border the benchmark is the Irish government, eh?' Verhofstadt suggested to the BSG that morning. 'If they don't have an agreement, they don't have an agreement, and it will not go forward. And if they have an agreement, then the problem is solved. We have also to check if it's more or less in agreement with what we think, but if the Irish government is in agreement, it will be completely in accordance with what we want.' The Irish prime minister Leo Varadkar later confirmed that he had been in touch with Jean-Claude Juncker and Donald Tusk on the morning of 4 December to give the draft agreement a green light.

At 10.30 a.m., the Brexit Steering Group was called into the Berlaymont building for a meeting with Barnier and Juncker, during which they would be briefed on the final details of the deal, but without being allowed to see the actual document. Just before driving off there, Verhofstadt implored his BSG colleagues not to just sit and listen, but to still make some extra demands. He wouldn't be Verhofstadt if he hadn't done that. 'If we ask nothing, they will ask nothing [of] Mrs May at the table either, eh?'

I wasn't allowed to film the meeting, and had to wait outside for the BSG members to come back out, with the rest of the press pack. When Verhofstadt appeared, he told camera crews and journalists, 'For the moment there is no agreement, no deal.' But he was optimistic 'that it is possible, 50/50'.

Later that day he would tell the BSG, 'Somebody asked me this morning when I came out, what do you think. I said 50/50, because I thought if you say 50/50, you're always right. You always give the impression that you're an intelligent man.'

They all laughed – after a day during which they had all laughed a lot less. Because while Verhofstadt was driving away from Berlaymont to give a speech in the Netherlands in the afternoon – the fact that he did shows the very real confidence that there was going to be a deal – events unfolded in a way that nobody had expected.

While his boss was away, Guillaume McLaughlin, who had been allowed to accompany Guy Verhofstadt into the Barnier briefing, discussed what he had learned with the rest of the team. The meeting had been relatively short, and no one had been allowed to take away a copy of the draft agreement, so not all the details were clear. The role of the European Court of Justice in protecting the rights of EU citizens had been resolved with a fudge (a 'kind of ombudsman thingie' was the way McLaughlin described it); British courts would be able to request a view from the ECJ, but would not be forced to, and the arrangement would be time limited. The inclusion of that sunset clause angered Bram Delen. 'They're giving it all away?' he demanded. 'Congratulations.'

But it proved really very difficult to judge who had won and who had lost in the negotiation on the basis of their limited information. Nick Petre, the British press spokesman, took the view that the EU could have been tougher with Britain. 'They're in such a weak position, the Brits. Terribly weak,' he told Bram Delen. 'The only thing we need to do is squeeze them a bit further. You know, they're only red in the face, we could go for purple, but we didn't. We're letting them off the hook. It's a strategic mistake.' But then he talked to a press contact. 'I spoke to *The Guardian*, and he said that the Brits have given up on everything,' he told Bram Delen and the head of media Jeroen Reijnen. 'Well, if nobody's happy, then maybe it's a good compromise,' Reijnen offered.

The first sign of real trouble came when a sharp-eyed Nick Petre noticed that the Belgian Green Party member of the Brexit Steering Group had been talking publicly about the Barnier briefing. 'Philippe Lamberts told *Sky News* the British government has agreed to a special situation for Ireland,' Petre announced to the team in Verhofstadt's office. Lamberts had stated that Britain had accepted there could not be 'regulatory divergence' between the North and South of Ireland after the United Kingdom left the European Union.

'The pie is almost ready,' he said. 'It was a surprise to me, but it is a matter of [Britain] facing reality. I think agreement is there.'

'A special situation for Ireland' was just the kind of phrase likely to ring alarm bells with the Democratic Unionists, and the DUP's take on the way events were unfolding was very different from Philippe Lamberts'. They had only seen the text of the draft agreement that morning, and as they watched the way the story was playing (the Irish broadcaster RTE was also running a leaked version), they made a dramatic public intervention. 'We will not accept any form of regulatory divergence which separates Northern Ireland economically or politically from the rest of the United Kingdom,' the DUP leader Arlene Foster told a press conference at the Stormont Parliament Buildings. 'The economic and constitutional integrity of the United Kingdom will not be compromised in any way.' And she quoted some of the assurances given by Theresa May: 'The prime minister has told the House of Commons that there will be no border in the Irish Sea. The prime minister has been clear that the UK is leaving the European Union as a whole and the territorial and economic integrity of the United Kingdom will be protected.' For good measure she threw in an accusation that the government in Dublin was 'clearly seeking to unilaterally change the Belfast agreement without our input or our consent'.

Twenty minutes later, Theresa May was hauled out of her lunch with Jean-Claude Juncker and Michel Barnier to speak to the DUP leader on the telephone – instead of negotiating with the European Union, she was forced to negotiate with her own partners in government back at home. It was reported that the call lasted for more than an hour, and she took over Jean-Claude Juncker's office while she talked.

The mood music from both sides had been so optimistic in the morning that everyone had been expecting an early agreement over lunch, but as the time ticked by, the Verhofstadt team became increasingly anxious about what was happening. When Jeroen Reijnen suggested the team also had lunch, at a local Italian restaurant, Guillaume McLaughlin took the view that, 'Maybe it's not a good idea to go and have lunch for an hour and a half.' And he was right, but also not right. Because they (we) stayed and missed lunch while they (we) could have gone, waiting instead for news that continued to refuse to come — it was a hungry afternoon.

'What the fuck are they discussing?' Guillaume McLaughlin demanded, noting, at four in the afternoon, that the meeting of May with Barnier and Juncker had lasted for an hour and a half longer than it should have done. 'If she'd agreed that text, then it was just a question of Varadkar saying yes or no. And presumably she would have spoken to Arlene Foster before she landed in Brussels? She knew what the text was, since the weekend, yes? And she just needed Varadkar, in the nine o'clock Cabinet meeting today in Dublin, to fix it. So what the fuck are they doing?'

What they were doing was coming to terms with the fact that the DUP would not support the text Theresa May had agreed with the Irish government and the European Commission. She eventually had to concede defeat; the deal would not be done that day, and she would have to return to London without it. The news reached the Verhofstadt team in a text from Barnier's aide Georg Riekeles. 'There's no deal. No deal. Georg says there is no deal,' McLaughlin announced to the group. 'That's what Georg says: no deal.'

As the details of what had gone wrong filtered through, McLaughlin's anger burned more brightly. The first target for his rage was the Belgian MEP Philippe Lamberts, whose indiscretion had contributed to the day's debacle. 'What an idiot!' he said, as he watched a television news piece. 'It's pretty clear you don't come out and say everything that happened in one of these fucking meetings . . . They show you the documents . . . that are going to be discussed an hour later at the fucking lunch – with the PM, and you go out and say "It's all this . . ."'

But most of his ire was directed towards the British prime minister.

MCLAUGHLIN: That she got on a plane to Brussels without having cleared it with the DUP, I mean, what the fuck is wrong with her?

PETRE: That's the point.

MCLAUGHLIN: I mean it's insane! She's there, she's at this meeting, so the first question is: 'Mrs May, what does Arlene Foster think?' 'Oh, I don't know. I haven't spoken to her. Oh yeah, yeah, that's a good idea – I hadn't thought of that one . . .' I mean come on; I think what Lamberts did was pathetic and slightly irresponsible, it's really pathetic, but it has nothing to do with this, which is just ridiculous . . .

Real life briefly intruded into this world of high political drama when Edel Crosse announced that she was calling it a day. 'I'm going home to my little one,' she said. Challenged by McLaughlin about abandoning ship 'in the middle of a fucking Brexit collapse, run by the fucking Irish', she responded that 'the organic grocery shop near me closes at six, and I need to make it . . . otherwise my kid will have to eat that supermarket shite.'

The political addicts on the team stayed on to chew over the day's events. 'The marrow of life doesn't come richer or better than regulatory alignment,' Nick Lane remarked. Bram Delen, Guillaume McLaughlin and Eva Palatova, Verhofstadt's Czech foreign policy adviser, ruminated on the dilemmas Brexit had created.

DELEN: But the point is, Guillaume, they will never walk away from the table.

MCLAUGHLIN: The Brits?

DELEN: No British PM in his or her right mind will leave the table and choose . . . a hard Brexit.

PALATOVA: But again, what happens if the talks break on the Irish issue? They will have to put a border across the island, in the middle. Hard Brexit for Ireland means a border in the middle. And we will have to put it there. Or the Irish. To control the border somehow. It's unfortunate, but we are more interested in it than the Brits. The Brits don't give a fuck.

MCLAUGHLIN: That's the problem, they don't care. We need to put [up] this fucking border.

Then McLaughlin got on the phone with Verhofstadt, who was on his way back to the Parliament from the Netherlands. For a few moments Ireland suddenly seemed less important; the boss's take on the day was that the European Parliament had been slighted.

PALATOVA: And what does Hoff say?

MCLAUGHLIN: Hoff is absolutely livid because, he says, you can be sure the finance text was checked with the Council, and we know for a fact that the text on the Irish was checked with the Irish government, not only checked, they had a fucking Cabinet meeting this

morning on the fucking text. And was the citizens'
rights text checked with us? Did you, me, or Winkler
receive a copy of the proposed text that they had
drafted? No. So Hoff is absolutely fucking hopping mad.

PALATOVA: But did they show it to you? I thought they
showed it to you [this morning when you went to see
Barnier and Juncker at Berlaymont]?

MCLAUGHLIN: No, no. They showed us the Irish stuff.
They showed us the Irish stuff. Can you explain to
me why the Irish stuff is more important than the
rights of the citizens? . . . Hoff is pissed, and I fucking
sympathise with him. They could have at least shown
us the fucking text beforehand.

PALATOVA: So you were sitting there for an hour, looking
at that Irish text, without having seen the citizens'
text?

MCLAUGHLIN: No, no. We had a long discussion about the
citizens' thing, where Hoff insisted again and again that
we need that declaratory, blablablablabla . . . First of all
Mr Barnier gave a state of play of what the situation was,
he explained the situation, and then Hoff responded,
that's all very well, but on the citizens' rights there's still
missing this, this and this, and what are you going to do
about it? I think it's important. Juncker said kinda yes,
yes, let's try to push that, OK.

Verhofstadt returned to the office at eight, bearing news that the
prospects for solving the latest impasse looked discouraging. He'd
talked in the car to both David Davis and Jean-Claude Juncker.
'They [the British] will come back, probably on Thursday,' he
reported. 'With what, is not such an easy thing [to say]. Because
from the Irish side, the Irish PM's side, he said: there is no way

that I will change a word on that [the draft text], because that was an agreement with the UK government, and all the [Irish] opposition parties backed it, so we now have to go back, and say this or that word, this or that sentence, that is . . . impossible.'

Guillaume McLaughlin asked, 'And May wasn't playing games, showing that she was a tough fighter, here in Brussels?'

VERHOFSTADT: You never know, you never know.
MCLAUGHLIN: It's not very likely, it's not her kind of exercise, of May.
VERHOFSTADT: I don't know.

~

At the end of a very long day it still was not entirely clear what had happened. There were pieces of a puzzle, but also a lot of blanks still — questions, guesses and misgivings. There had never been a lot of trust lost between the two negotiating sides; now there was even less.

Late that night, the BSG's oldest member, the German Christian Democrat Elmar Brok, gave his verdict on what had happened — and he surprised me with how emphatic he could be. 'Can you imagine?' Brock mused. 'You're prime minister of the UK, of Great Britain and Northern Ireland, and you're sitting in Brussels, with the negotiator, to negotiate for your country, and the deal is nearly ready. And in the middle of that meeting you get a phone call from your coalition partner, that they're taking the energy away from you! She went out for one and a half hours, trying to convince them. It must have been a very, very painful situation for her, personally. A terrible situation. I can only feel sorry for her.'

The EU's strategy of close coordination during the negotiating process had held together; Theresa May had paid the price for failing to square away one of her most important groups of supporters. And European exasperation gave way to that most devastating of emotions in politics: pity.

9

A VASSAL STATE

December 2017

The next morning Eva Palatova, Guy Verhofstadt's foreign policy adviser, looked like she had a hangover. 'I don't know, I'm not sure I will survive today,' she said. It wasn't booze — that's simply not her — maybe it was an emotional hangover, after a day that had unexpectedly been turned upside down. But a hangover is a hangover, and so the always exuberant — and half-English — chief of staff Guillaume McLaughlin prescribed alcohol as a remedy. 'Get her a gin and tonic, immediately!' he ordered. And while Eva sat massaging her neck, he added tenderly, 'Poverino' ['Poor guy']. Guillaume didn't have the best of nights either; he could have killed his alarm clock in the morning, he said.

At their respective desks, Edel Crosse and Bram Delen also seemed pretty worn out. But Guy Verhofstadt, who'd been driven in from his home in Ghent by his driver, looked perky. He spent his morning mainly making phone calls, until at midday Michel Barnier turned up, with two advisors in tow, Georg Riekeles and Nicolas Galudec. Barnier was, as always, immaculately dressed, and looked his usual unfathomable self, even if he too had had a day he wouldn't soon forget.

'Can I sit down for a moment or two?' he asked, without taking off his dark grey coat and light brown scarf.

'You can sit down, and we can even offer you some coffee or water,' McLaughlin offered.

'Yesterday things blew up in a completely unforeseeable way,' Barnier reported. 'She [Theresa May] arrived at midday with just one point to negotiate – on the ombudsman and the [European] Court of Justice.'

'So everything was closed as far as you were concerned?' McLaughlin asked. 'Everything else had already been nailed down?'

'She told us at midday that it was fine,' Barnier confirmed. 'And then, in the middle of lunch, a first message, a second, and then a third message . . .'

Barnier's visit had a casual air to it – as if he was just passing by, but to Guy Verhofstadt it was important. The day before he'd become very angry – 'livid' was Guillaume McLaughlin's word – when he realised that the Irish government had been allowed to see the part of Barnier's (botched) deal with May that concerned them in advance, while the European Parliament hadn't been allowed to see exactly what was in the deal on citizens' rights. Barnier had come over to make amends of some sort.

He explained that he had brought a copy of what was in the deal on citizens' rights, but, since the document was not yet fully agreed with the British, he was unwilling to leave the copy with them. He told Verhofstadt and McLaughlin that they could read the document, but couldn't keep it. 'I can't leave here a joint paper that is not yet joint,' he argued. 'It's a document that will be binding for both sides, so as long as both sides haven't approved it . . .' And he added, so as to make sure they realised he was doing them a big favour, that he would not even be showing it to the European Commission when he met them the following day. His wariness was the result of the previous day's diplomatic debacle.

Barnier had become more anxious than ever about leaks. Everyone in the room knew about the way the BSG member Philippe Lamberts had given the game away in his television interview, but new intelligence had *surfaced about another leak. 'The Irish apparently gave the text [about the Irish border] to RTE [the Irish public broadcaster],' Verhofstadt said.*

Georg Riekeles nodded. 'Tony Connelly [RTE's Europe editor] had a tweet with the paragraph.'

'The Irish government gave it to him?' Guillaume McLaughlin asked.

'Of course,' Barnier answered.

'And what about the DUP?' asked McLaughlin. 'Were they really not informed by May?'

'I think there was someone who made the deal with the DUP, when May was looking for her majority, six months ago, and she had charged that person with consulting with the DUP, and that person had said it's OK,' Barnier said.

'Things like that happen,' Verhofstadt, with his decades of experience, added laconically.

In a final reflection on the events of the previous twenty-four hours, Barnier remarked, 'I have seldom seen a country take such a serious decision about its future without having a majority for what it is doing.'

'True,' said Verhofstadt. 'And it's being demonstrated all the time.'

~

In London, Theresa May was enduring some of the worst reviews of her time in office; she was condemned by newspapers on the two sides of the Brexit debate. The Eurosceptic *Daily Telegraph* headlined its account of the day in Brussels 'May's Push for Deal Ends in Chaos', while the determinedly Remainer *Financial Times* opted for the wordier but similar 'May Forced into Reversal in Brussels after Northern Ireland Allies Scupper Draft Pact'.

There was also a warning from her backbenchers that the backstop – no one was using the phrase just yet, but that is what it was – would prove a fatal impediment to the withdrawal agreement. As the *Irish Times* reported, 'Speaking after a meeting with the prime minister's chief of staff at Westminster, Conservative MPs on both sides of the Brexit debate rejected a proposal that regulation in both parts of the island of Ireland should continue to be aligned after Brexit. "We are not going to trade on distinctions between Great Britain and Northern Ireland. That would be completely intolerable. We are the Conservative and Unionist party after all," said Jacob Rees-Mogg.'

And especially alarming to No. 10 were the signs that parties in other parts of what Mrs May liked to refer to as 'our pre-cious union' would seize on the deal over Northern Ireland to demand special treatment for themselves. The *Independent* web-site reported, 'Nicola Sturgeon [the first minister of Scotland] was fast out of the blocks, insisting that, if Northern Ireland was to be allowed to "effectively stay in the single market", then so should Scotland. The First Minister's call was quickly echoed by Carwyn Jones, her counterpart in Wales, and London mayor Sadiq Khan, who both demanded bespoke Brexit deals.'

The Scottish Conservative leader, Ruth Davidson, whose standing in the party had been greatly enhanced by the relative success of the Scottish Tory Party in the June general election, said that the country must not be 'divided by different deals for different home nations'. Davidson appeared to suggest she would like to see the whole of the United Kingdom remain in a single market and a customs union: 'If regulatory alignment in specific areas is [a] requirement for a frictionless border,' she stated, 'then [it] must be on a UK-wide basis.'

The Democratic Unionists poured oil onto the fire. The par-ty's leader, Arlene Foster, told RTE that they had been trying to get hold of a copy of the text of the draft agreement for five weeks, and that when they had finally seen it the previous morn-ing it came as a 'big shock'. 'When we looked at the wording [on regulatory alignment] and had seen the import of all that, we knew we couldn't sign up to anything that was in that text that would allow a border to develop in the Irish Sea,' she declared.

After he had escorted his boss out of the Parliament building in Brussels, Georg Riekeles, Michel Barnier's diplomatic adviser and team leader on inter-institutional affairs, returned to Verhofstadt's offices on Floor 5½ and spent the next hour playing a game of political hard-ball with Verhofstadt's chief of staff, Guillaume McLaughlin. They were going to read through the text of the deal together, but when McLaughlin tried to make a joke about not being allowed to keep a copy — 'So no scan, no pictures, no filming even [pointing at me] . . . you guys are not very advanced, technologically' — Riekeles reacted grumpily. The negotiations, he warned, were on a 'razor's edge', and the stakes were very high.

The possibility of Britain leaving the EU without a withdrawal agreement suddenly looked very real. 'If she [Mrs May] doesn't come back in a few hours, or by the end of the week, to sign up, the most probable scenario is that we end this fucking Brexit with a no-deal scenario,' Riekeles predicted. 'That would mean that all citizens would find themselves without rights. It would mean that to cover Europe's budgets in the coming years we would have to go to court, it would mean a bloody mess in Ireland. That's the reality of where we are now. And if it all goes "kaput" in the next few days it is not at all certain, indeed it's most improbable, that we'll be able to pick up the pieces.'

Like Sabine Weyand in the run-up to Theresa May's lunch with Barnier and Juncker, Riekeles wanted to ram home the message that the negotiators had pushed the British as far as they would go in the area of citizens' rights. The British Home Office, he explained, would have 'an obligation to work with the applicants [for settled status], to help them prove their eligibility — so it [the draft agreement] goes a long way, not just in the burden of proof, but also in the burden of facilitating, of providing help.' Their ambition, he explained, was to 'put things in the withdrawal agreement that will move towards changing the culture' of the Home Office and the way it dealt with such matters.

When they broached the much-debated 'declaration' or 'application' question, the process EU citizens in the United Kingdom would have to go through to confirm their right to stay, the confrontation turned rough:

MCLAUGHLIN: You say you took this thing as far as you could, and I don't want to put in doubt your commitment, or your work, but we think there should be another system.

RIEKELES: Yes, but it's not possible.

MCLAUGHLIN: That's your judgement . . . but it's a question Mr Verhofstadt will have to decide on for himself, together with his colleagues, whether they want to push on or not.

RIEKELES [taking back the document they had hardly started reading through]: He [Barnier] does this to build a relation of trust with Verhofstadt. If Verhofstadt afterwards wants to say, 'No, all this is worth nothing,' you can do that in your [parliamentary] resolution. Barnier doesn't care, because he's convinced that you're wrong. No problem, if you want to make a show of it, everybody takes his responsibility. But you can't use something that has been given to you in confidence . . . in a way that does not serve the negotiations.

Riekeles made the case that the Brexit negotiations, which were, from the Brexiteer perspective, supposed to free Britain from EU interference in internal affairs, were, in this area, having the opposite effect. 'There are elements in here you would never find in a European directive,' he claimed, waving the document they were discussing. 'If you put things like this in directives, the first thing that would happen is that at the Council you would have twenty-eight member states saying, "Hang on, who do you take yourself for? You, the EU, are getting into something very far-reaching in the way a member state manages and administers itself."'

Riekeles was clever enough to acknowledge that the European Parliament had played an important role in keeping up the negotiating pressure. 'Getting this kind of language out of the British is the fruit of our work,' he said. 'But also of your insistence, time and again, over the months, that "Parliament will never accept this, we need more, we need more, we need more, we need more."' But he was anxious that Verhofstadt and his colleagues might jeopardise the whole agreement if they continued to push too hard.

He was particularly concerned about a meeting due later that week between Verhofstadt and the British home secretary, Amber Rudd. 'There's an issue of trust here,' he told McLaughlin. 'Barnier isn't showing you all this so that you can go and see Amber Rudd and say, "We must have this, blablabla, blablabla," because it could screw things up in London all over again.' The problem, he explained, was that Theresa May might not have told her own team about everything she had given the green light to. 'Not only are there things in here which we can't be sure Amber Rudd and the Home Office agree with,' he said, 'she simply doesn't know about them. [The] threshold for shit-stirring is very low [and] if you begin to discuss specific elements with Amber Rudd I think you will stir up the shit.'

~

There were difficult conversations going on in London, too, on Tuesday 5 December. Theresa May made phone calls to the DUP leader Arlene Foster and the Irish prime minister Leo Varadkar, while the Northern Ireland secretary James

Brokenshire and the government's chief whip, Julian Smith, opened talks with a DUP delegation in the chief whip's office at 9 Downing Street. The DUP have a reputation for digging in for the long haul when they negotiate and, unlike the prime minister, they were in no hurry to do a deal. The *Sun* newspaper quoted a DUP source as saying, 'We won't be bounced into anything. We're going to slow it all down.' They added, in an unusually graphic political metaphor, 'This is a battle of who blinks first, and we've cut off our eyelids.' The talks dragged on until late that night and all day Wednesday too.

By the morning of Thursday 7 December, Guy Verhofstadt's hopes were draining away. 'I don't expect that she comes here tomorrow, or after tomorrow,' he told his visitor, the veteran British Liberal Democrat – and last leader of Britain's old Liberal Party – David Steel. 'There will be simply no deal with the DUP.' Lord Steel concurred: 'The DUP are terrible people,' he offered. 'They are . . . the reverse of liberal.' Guillaume McLaughlin chipped in: 'Somebody coined the phrase that they are the Reactionary Front of the seventeenth century.'

Verhofstadt returned to his familiar complaint about the way Brexit was dominating the EU's agenda. 'A lot of negative energy is put into this,' he said. 'We should be busy with shaping a reformed Europe in this world that is more insecure than ever.'

Steel and Verhofstadt discussed the transition period, during which it was envisaged that the United Kingdom would continue to follow the EU's rules but, having formally left the Union, would have no voting rights. Verhofstadt noted that it was due to end before Britain's next scheduled general election. 'That's exactly what Boris Johnson wants,' he suggested, 'so that the new system, whatever it is, will be in place at that moment and it is irreversible.'

But he speculated about the possibility of drawing out the

transition period for longer: 'Maybe we can continue that for a few years, and then you can say to the Conservative Party: fantastic, you did your job well, you're still a member of the customs union, you're still in the internal market, the only thing that changed is that we have no say any more. We pay, we are in, and we have nothing to say about it. Well done [here he clapped his hands], Conservative Party.'

One of the aides present chipped in: 'The UK becomes a colony.'

'Protectorate. A protectorate of the EU, completely crazy,' Verhofstadt responded.

'A vassal state,' the aide offered.

Verhofstadt concluded: 'And all this because of the internal battle in the Conservative Party.'

David Steel found himself apologising on behalf of his country. 'It's a mess, and I'm sorry about it,' he said. 'I've never known a situation ... you know, I've been in politics for a long time [he was elected to Parliament in 1965], but I've never known such chaos.'

VERHOFSTADT: That's true.
STEEL: Nobody knows what they're doing.
VERHOFSTADT: No plan, no strategy, no roadmap ...

Later, Verhofstadt's French spokesman, Yannick Laude, asked for a 'clear' assessment of 'where we are'. 'We are nowhere!' Verhofstadt declared. 'We are waiting for Madame May, the return of Madame May. And I don't think she'll come.'

Laude asked about David Davis. 'He's in a scandal of his own,' Verhofstadt replied, in a reference to a row that had blown up in London about whether the government had adequately researched the economic effect of Brexit. 'First saying that impact assessments had been made, and then having to admit there weren't. It's completely crazy. Normally, if someone does something like that, he's out straightaway. But now she [Mrs May] is so dependent on all these forces within the Conservative Party that she lacks the power to do so.'

~

The UK home secretary Amber Rudd eventually cancelled her meeting with Verhofstadt, so Georg Riekeles need not have worried. Some of the waiting hours — and they were long hours, and, indeed, days — were filled by Madeleina Kay, a British writer, illustrator and political activist from Sheffield, who, in her role as EU Supergirl, became Young European of the Year 2018. Dressed up in a blue and yellow Supergirl suit, covered by a thick orange fire brigade coat, because of the cutting cold outside, she brought Verhofstadt a bag with mail from Brits who deplored Brexit and begged the EU to help them.

The office diligently prepared the boss for her visit as they would have done for any other visitor; Edel Crosse gave Verhofstadt a selection of leaflets and lapel pins to have a look at before Supergirl arrived. One of the colourful pins puzzled him. 'Bollocks to Brexit,' he read. 'What does that mean?'

'Bollocks means your balls,' Edel informed him. 'It's a curse word.'

EU Supergirl also brought Christmas gifts for Verhofstadt: an illustrated guide to what the EU does for the UK — 'If David Davis can't find his impact assessments, we can give him this,' Verhofstadt remarked — and EU socks, blue with yellow stars, which he offered to wear in his Brexit meetings.

The Democratic Unionists finally signed off on an agreement in the small hours of the following morning, Friday 8 December. At 4.30 a.m. Theresa May flew from RAF Brize Norton to Brussels, arriving in time for breakfast with Jean-Claude

Juncker and Michel Barnier, to pick up the conversation they had had to abandon at lunch four days earlier. The key change to the draft agreement was the addition of a paragraph reaffirming the British government's commitment to the indivisibility of the United Kingdom.

Paragraph 49 of the new agreement text preserved the language originally agreed with Dublin, which included an explicit provision for a backstop – a default position which would come into play if future trading arrangements between Britain and the European Union did not remove the need for a hard border in Ireland. It read:

> The United Kingdom remains committed to protecting North–South cooperation and to its guarantee of avoiding a hard border. Any future arrangements must be compatible with these overarching requirements. The United Kingdom's intention is to achieve these objectives through the overall EU–UK relationship. Should this not be possible, the United Kingdom will propose specific solutions to address the unique circumstances of the island of Ireland. In the absence of agreed solutions, the United Kingdom will maintain full alignment with those rules of the internal market and the customs union which, now or in the future, support North–South cooperation, the all island economy and the protection of the 1998 Agreement.

It was, on the face of it, difficult to see how that could be reconciled with the new paragraph 50, introduced after those hours of talks with the DUP at 9 Downing Street:

> In the absence of agreed solutions, as set out in the previous paragraph, the United Kingdom will ensure that no new

regulatory barriers develop between Northern Ireland and the rest of the United Kingdom, unless, consistent with the 1998 Agreement, the Northern Ireland Executive and Assembly agree that distinct arrangements are appropriate for Northern Ireland. In all circumstances, the United Kingdom will continue to ensure the same unfettered access for Northern Ireland's businesses to the whole of the United Kingdom internal market.

Bram Delen, Guy Verhofstadt's speechwriter, very quickly identified the difficulty which, a year later, would make the backstop such an obstacle to British parliamentary approval of the final withdrawal agreement. 'It's becoming hilarious, taking back control becomes even less control now,' he observed, because the only obvious way to resolve the contradictions between those two sets of commitments was for the whole of the United Kingdom to be forced into precisely the kind of economic relationship with the EU that Theresa May had vowed to escape when she laid down her red lines at the beginning of the year.

At this stage, the EU regarded the contradictions created by the DUP's new paragraph as Britain's problem; as Guillaume McLaughlin put it while he worked through the text, 'We don't really care about the East to West . . . issue [the movement of goods between Great Britain and Northern Ireland], because going into the UK, it will be the UK that has to put controls or no controls. They can decide to waive controls.' But Verhofstadt, like his speechwriter, could see the long-term implications of the backstop very clearly.

VERHOFSTADT: In [paragraph] 49 it says 'no hard border between Northern Ireland and Ireland. And in

[paragraph] 50 it says 'no hard border between the UK
and Northern Ireland'.

MCLAUGHLIN: Those two things are not compatible.

VERHOFSTADT: They are if the United Kingdom stays in
the customs union.

When the Brexit Steering Group met later, Verhofstadt was
insistent that their statement should simply say that 'sufficient
progress' had been made to move the talks on, and not that the
progress was 'sufficient to approve the withdrawal agreement'.

All the messy detail buried in the draft text was blown out
of the headlines in the British press by the adrenaline rush and
drama of Mrs May's early morning dash to Brussels. After
the months of trench warfare – which Britain seemed to be
losing – there was at last something to celebrate. 'Done Deal,'
declared *The Sun*. 'Theresa May finally secures Brexit deal
after late-night diplomacy . . .' And the *Daily Mirror*'s front
page carried the splash 'It's a Deal! Theresa May wins dawn
breakthrough in Brexit talks as EU says she's finally cleared
first phase of negotiations'. The *Daily Express* welcomed a 'Huge
Brexit Boost at Last', and the online *Independent* reported that
'the beaming smile Theresa May wore as she shook Jean-Claude
Juncker's hand yesterday morning bore out the relief she must
have felt after finally locking in a settlement for the first phase
of Brexit talks'.

Standing next to Juncker at a joint press conference following their breakfast, Theresa May declared that the agreement
had involved 'give and take on both sides', but described it as
'a hard-won agreement in all our interests'. The Council president Donald Tusk said that the deal was 'a personal success
for Theresa May', but he also warned that 'the most difficult
challenge lies ahead'. Like Michel Barnier, Tusk had an eye on

the clock. 'We all know that breaking up is hard,' he said. 'But breaking up and building a new relationship is much harder. Since the Brexit referendum, a year and a half has passed. So much time has been devoted to the easier part of the task. And now, to negotiate a transition arrangement and the framework for our future relationship, we have *de facto* less than a year.'

And things began to fall apart very quickly indeed. That weekend's British Sunday papers reported that Theresa May's aides had been briefing senior Brexiteers – Boris Johnson and the environment secretary Michael Gove were mentioned – that the British concessions were 'meaningless', and that the concept of full alignment 'doesn't mean anything in EU law'. And when the Brexit secretary, David Davis, appeared on the BBC's *Andrew Marr* programme that morning for his first interview since the deal had been done, he said, 'This was a statement of intent more than anything else. It was much more a statement of intent than it was a legally enforceable thing.' He later claimed he was referring simply to Britain's ambition to avoid a hard border in Ireland, but the comment was ambiguous, and could have been taken to refer to the interim agreement as a whole. And when Marr pressed him about the United Kingdom's commitment to maintain 'full alignment', he was evasive:

MARR: The Taoiseach [Irish prime minister] thinks that
he has got that full alignment in his back pocket.
That is an absolutely firm promise from Theresa May
and yourself and the British government. He may be
watching this. Can you look in the camera and say that
we absolutely commit ourselves to that?
DAVIS: What we say is we commit ourselves to
maintaining a frictionless invisible border. That's what
we undertake . . .

'That bloody bastard' was Guy Verhofstadt's reaction when the Brexit Steering Group met two days later, early in the morning, to agree on a response to Davis's interview. The Brexit coordinator of the European Parliament read from the statement that his team had prepared: '"[The European Parliament] believes that negotiations must be conducted in good faith." That's good that we are saying that. It's saying that Mr Davis isn't in good faith.' His Italian colleague Roberto Gualtieri took the view that the burden of their message should be: 'This is serious, you shut up saying stupid things, you have now to act on the basis of this act, that you signed; this is a legal act.'

Gualtieri's remarks were not entirely accurate, as Verhofstadt was quick to point out. The agreement between the EU and the United Kingdom – the 'joint report' as it was officially called – included a recognition of the familiar British mantra that 'nothing is agreed until everything is agreed'. Verhofstadt drew Gualtieri's attention to paragraph 96: 'This report is . . . agreed by the UK on the condition of an overall agreement under Article 50 on the UK's withdrawal, taking into account the framework for the future relationship, including an agreement as early as possible in 2018 on transitional arrangements.' The document was indeed not, as David Davis had put it, 'a legally enforceable thing' – at least not yet.

The BSG members wanted to ensure that the concessions the United Kingdom had made were bankable, that they could be locked down behind doors that could not be reopened further down the line. But they struggled with the language they needed:

VERHOFSTADT: That the UK government fully respects the commitments and that they are translated into . . .
GUALTIERI: Consistently translated in the draft withdrawal agreement.

PHILIPPE LAMBERTS: Accurately.

VERHOFSTADT: No, not accurately, because that's
  an interpretation. Fully translated into the draft
  withdrawal agreement.

GUALTIERI: Maybe we could use faithfully?

The Christian Democrat Elmar Brok came back with a dig at
Verhofstadt's political tribe. 'Liberals have no understanding
of faithful,' he remarked, and Verhofstadt accepted: 'We
have no faith.' Brok cut through to the political thrust of
their message – and his accusation was a grave one: he told
the group, 'We should say that people like Davis destroy the
trust that we have found now in the negotiations. Something
like that.'

VERHOFSTADT: I like it.

PALATOVA: You want to mention him by name?

VERHOFSTADT: Yes . . . We're [a] political body reacting
  to a political thing, we're not diplomats saying
  pom-pom-pom . . .

LAMBERTS: You could never have been a diplomat.

Later that morning Verhofstadt was challenged by a journalist
during his usual monthly Strasbourg press conference about
the implications of David Davis's comments. 'Some people
have said today: it's an own goal,' he replied. 'Because I think
everybody likes [a] football metaphor. It's clear that the EC
[European Council] will be more strict now . . . I see a hardening of the position of the Council, and there will be a hardening
of the position of the Parliament.'

~

I'd done a lot of filming already that morning in Strasbourg, where the inner courtyard was adorned with a huge Christmas tree, but my day wasn't over yet, because while I was queuing for a sandwich, ten minutes' walk away from Verhofstadt's office, I got an excited phone call from Bram Delen, Verhofstadt's speechwriter. 'You have to come up now,' he said, 'because David Davis is going to call Verhofstadt.'

For a politician to call another politician, to explain himself, was even for Bram a rare thing, not to be missed. I sensed the team considered it a bit of a victory, too. So I dropped my plans for a sandwich and headed back upstairs where Edel was just finishing a phone call with David Davis's office. 'He's going to call in five minutes,' I heard her saying. 'His clarification was that it was the Irish border specifically he was talking about . . . I mean that's what the Daily Mail *is saying . . . OK, thanks a million, bye.'*

When she hung up she suggested that Verhofstadt should watch a recording of Davis's interview before taking the Brexit secretary's call. And to fortify their boss, his chief of staff Guillaume McLaughlin made him an espresso, while Edel poured a glass of his favourite Sicilian 'digestif' Averna. Guillaume came in with the coffee, shouting, 'Watch out for the coffee, it's hot, it's hot. Tada. I hope you got this on tape. One little coffee, one Averna for the president. And who says we don't care, eh?'

CROSSE: He's gone into the loo, and David Davis is
    supposed
    to call.
MCLAUGHLIN: He took his phone.
CROSSE: Yeah, but we can't listen in if he's in the toilet.

Seconds later Bram Delen and Jeroen Reijnen also arrived. Reijnen wanted to take away the Averna — 'It looks really bad on camera' — but Edel Crosse thought he meant that David Davis was going to be able to see it. 'They're not on WhatsApp.' While Reijnen held his hand in front of my camera — briefly — Verhofstadt came back out of the toilet.

Then Verhofstadt's phone rang. It was a +44 number — had to be Davis. Everybody wanted to hear what the UK Brexit secretary was going to say — Bram had even tried to get Verhofstadt to put his phone on speakerphone — and what Verhofstadt was going to reply. But once he got his phone, Verhofstadt turned away and went into the small meeting room behind his office, to talk in private there. I was also shut out, but then Bram pulled my arm, took me to the door, opened it, pushed me in, and closed the door behind me again. Everyone needs a guardian angel, and so does a documentary maker.

But the phone call itself was a disappointment for me — a short and very polite chat between two gentlemen. Once again, I learned that what is interesting in such negotiations are not the negotiations themselves, that very formal ballet, but what precedes the ballet, and follows it, off stage, behind the scenes.

When David Davis came through on the phone, Verhofstadt mainly tried to impress on him the damage done by the way his words had been picked up in the European media. 'You have to know that . . . the use of your words were in the whole European press two, three days now. No, really, really,' he insisted. 'And the statement of intent now in another newspaper [be]comes then an intention, and in the third newspaper it [be]comes then "they are only intentions", and, before you know it, it's a huge thing.'

~

There was a real negotiating cost to be paid for the episode. When Sabine Weyand briefed the Brexit Steering Group the following day, she noted that 'a very important point, which I think is dominating discussion not only in the EP right now, but also in the other institutions, and also among member

states ... is obviously that the way that some members of
the British Cabinet ... have commented on the outcome, has
raised some doubt as to the good faith with which the joint
report will be translated into the actual text of the agreement'.
She said she was referring to politicians who 'have mainly been
more observers in these negotiations than actors', so she perhaps had Brexiteers other than David Davis in mind, but she
made it clear that the question of trust would be a factor in the
way the EU approached the next stage.

The Council's next set of guidelines, she revealed, would
include 'reinforced language' designed to ensure 'a good faith
effort on the UK side'. 'I think it would be useful to have from
all institutions the caveat that if there is an agreement on sufficient progress, this is not a carte blanche, to do whatever they
[the British] like in the second phase,' she told the group. 'But
that this is linked to a no-backsliding obligation. And this is
something that Mr Barnier has been very clear that he will be
very vigilant [about] and he will ring the alarm bell the first
moment he detects the UK walking back from the negotiations.'
Those warnings were borne out when the European Council
published its blueprint for the next stage of Brexit negotiations
two days later. The Council underlined 'that negotiations in
the second phase can only progress as long as all commitments
undertaken during the first phase are respected in full and
translated faithfully into legal terms as quickly as possible'.

And the paragraph in the guidelines on a transition period –
the next order of business to be conducted – read more like
an instruction than a basis for negotiation. The document
laid down that

[s]uch transitional arrangements, which will be part of
the Withdrawal Agreement, must be in the interest of the

Union, clearly defined and precisely limited in time. In order to ensure a level playing field based on the same rules applying throughout the single market, changes to the acquis [the accumulated body of EU law and regulation] adopted by EU institutions, bodies, offices and agencies will have to apply both in the United Kingdom and the EU. All existing Union regulatory, budgetary, supervisory, judiciary and enforcement instruments and structures will also apply, including the competence of the Court of Justice of the European Union. As the United Kingdom will continue to participate in the customs union and the single market (with all four freedoms) during the transition, it will have to continue to comply with EU trade policy, to apply EU customs tariffs and collect EU customs duties, and to ensure all EU checks are being performed on the border vis-à-vis other third countries.

When Michel Barnier followed this up with the announcement that the transition period should end on 31 December 2020 – making it three months shorter than Theresa May had proposed – the impression that the EU was now dictating rather than negotiating was confirmed. The date marked the last day of the EU's seven-year budget period, so the duration of the United Kingdom's transition was being decided for the EU's convenience, not the UK's.

While Brussels reworked its negotiating strategy, the government in London was absorbed by yet another challenge to its authority; a senior backbench Conservative MP, the former attorney general Dominic Grieve, put forward an amendment to force a so-called meaningful vote on any deal Theresa May brought back from Brussels. Mrs May opposed it, but it squeaked through by 309 votes to 305.

Verhofstadt, proud to be a champion of parliamentary rights, welcomed the development: 'We [the European Parliament] were always to give approval at the end of the whole process,' he told a journalist, 'and this is exactly what the British Parliament will do now . . . I'm a parliamentarian, I defend parliamentary democracy – and I think we can only be positive about it.'

The amendment was, of course, hugely consequential. Gina Miller's court case to force a Commons vote on Article 50 had very little impact on the Brexit process, despite all the controversy it caused, because MPs overwhelmingly supported the government when it wanted to trigger the article. But this time MPs would use the power they had given themselves. Together with the backstop, the amendment would be the means by which Mrs May and her government were repeatedly humiliated; the road to Britain's political deadlock at the end of 2018 was fully mapped out during these December days a year earlier.

10

SNARED IN SOVEREIGNTY

New Year–early March 2018

After galloping along with the Brexit hordes for nine wild months, I felt, at the start of 2018, in those quiet, lightless first days of the year, that I needed to make a round-up for myself. Between sequencing, financial settlements, settled statuses, the acquis and other regulatory alignments, I'd started to really appreciate what Bram Delen had said back in November 2017 when he was wrestling with 'direct dependent relatives and descendants': '[Brexit is] like mathematics, we have to make it understandable for outsiders.' For all my filming, I remained an outsider, left gasping at the technical and political complexity of the EU–UK divorce talks. Where did I come from, and where was I heading – and where was Brexit bound for? As it happened, Barnier made the round-up for me, with a multitude of explanatory slides, during the first Brexit Steering Group of the year, in the Brussels headquarters of the European Parliament, on 10 January 2018.

The previous day Michel Barnier had celebrated his sixty-seventh birthday, and Guy Verhofstadt had sent him a half-case of English sparkling wine. When the Brexit Steering Group met, Verhofstadt noted, in a reference to the EU's jealously guarded rules of origin (one of the many bolts still to be unscrewed in the negotiations with the UK), that the bottles he sent 'cannot be called champagne, of course; that is completely forbidden'.

'Happy New Year,' Barnier responded. 'Thank you for our dialogue over past months, and thank you for my birthday present. When you reach a certain age it is best not to celebrate birthdays, but I was touched. Yesterday I was in The Hague; so tulips. I gave them to my wife, and we shall drink the champagne [breaking the EU's own rules by using the term] together.'

Then it was back to business – the round-up, which Barnier started with a nod to Verhofstadt's gift. 'I've sent you a letter, which you will not have received yet, in which I say that the gift encourages us to deal very quickly with the issue of protecting the geographical identity of products in the withdrawal agreement. It was,' he pointed out, one of the 'many issues that haven't been negotiated yet, on which we simply do not have a British position.'

The deal that the United Kingdom and the EU had agreed in December 2017, the so-called 'joint report', was sometimes referred to as the 'progress report', because its goal was to show that sufficient progress had been made on the three main divorce issues – finances, citizens' rights, and the Irish border – to allow the European Council to declare that the next phase in the negotiations could begin. But Barnier underlined that progress on those three main issues did not mean they were completely settled. The final withdrawal agreement was still a long way off.

A lot was left to be done. 'And these are not small issues,' the EU chief negotiator said, with emphasis, pointing at his slide. 'The way the agreement will be governed or controlled, needs to be sorted out, Euratom [the organisation that deals with nuclear matters within the EU], intellectual property and geographical indications – I wasn't joking earlier on – there are really a lot of things still to be dealt with.'

In his methodical manner, Michel Barnier explained he was

calling this his first of four *chantiers*, French for construction sites, for the coming months. And he stressed that the EU would have to be firm with the British while dealing with these issues. 'We must be vigilant,' he said, observing that 'the way they [the British] are still talking to themselves about Brexit, without listening to us, without paying any attention to us, concerns me, frankly, preoccupies me.' And his message for the United Kingdom was steelier than ever. 'We respect your desire to regain your autonomy,' he said, addressing them as if they were present somewhere in the room, 'your sovereignty, your freedom, but we will not compromise our own autonomy. Never. Do not ask us to change because you are leaving.'

Left-over issues were the first *chantier*. Barnier's second *chantier* concerned the translation of what had already been agreed on in the joint report, about citizens' rights, finances and the Irish border, into a legally binding agreement: a 'restrictive treaty text [the so-called withdrawal agreement], which would allow for no reversal.' Barnier's choice of words reflected the suspicion of Britain's good faith, which was a legacy of the events leading up to Christmas. The Irish backstop, in particular, needed to be hammered into legal language that spelled out exactly how it would work.

Barnier said he hoped to have his work on the first and second *chantier* completed by the beginning of the following month. That was a tight deadline, but the pressure was necessary, in his opinion, to push the British to move, to reveal what they wanted on all the issues that were still open. 'To be precise, I believe that I am capable, together with my team, to put a draft treaty [the withdrawal agreement] on the table, by the beginning of February,' Barnier explained. 'For the big issues [citizens' rights, finances, Irish border] this draft treaty will be based on what is in the joint report. For all the other issues, that have not yet been talked about, we will put our position.' He added, 'I've often noticed during these negotiations that the British weren't able to give us their positions, so what they did was to come back on ours, and use ours as a basis for negotiation. Since time is short . . . we shall put the whole text on the table and see how they react.'

On a colourful slide about the *chantiers* prepared by the Barnier team, the work on the draft treaty was given the colour yellow in the timeline. Below, there were two more horizontal bars, in orange and green.

The orange bar was the *chantier* for the transition or implementation – as the UK continued to call it – period. The green bar concerned the negotiations about the United Kingdom's future relationship with the European Union. Barnier wasn't planning to start that last *chantier* just yet. The prize Theresa May's government so desperately wanted at this stage would not, Barnier explained, begin until after the European Council meeting of 23 March 2018. But in the meantime he wanted to prep the European Union, the Council and the Parliament, with seminars on all the important fields that would have to be dealt with during these talks. The slide used the term 'scoping' and Barnier explained, 'The aim of these seminars is to create a feeling of collective appropriation or understanding [of what is at stake]. Not all member states are always on the same wavelength. The unity we found among ourselves, that surprised us and that was the key to our success, has to be constructed every day.'

I sat through and filmed most of these long collective appropriation seminars – they were many and mind-boggling. 'I will briefly take you through the regulatory issues in the automotive sector,' one of them would start, typically, after which a half-hour lecture (with slides) by a technical expert followed. 'There is a mutual recognition principle, so once a car is approved in one member state, it can freely circulate on the market of twenty-eight member states, thanks to the certificate of conformity. What are the consequences of the UK becoming a third country? First of all their approval authority will lose its status. So it will no longer be able to issue car approvals' and as a result 'manufacturers can no longer issue certificates of conformity'.

Thirty minutes later a meat expert took over, with the 'specific example of a piece of steak':

> If you need to reassure citizens that their steak is safe in Europe, you need to be constant with the regulatory system to ensure that that animal has an individual ear-tag, a passport, its herd was registered, you need to know the feed that that animal was fed with, what it contained, what veterinary products it was treated with, the conditions under which it was reared, the conditions under which it was transported and slaughtered, and subsequently the hygiene conditions that brought that steak to your plate. That requires a highly sophisticated regulatory train. And we're unapologetic, because that's what you require to reassure citizens. To identify what the UK will need to do [in the absence of a trade agreement] we simply have to identify what Botswana does. Or what Indonesia does. Because the conditions will be entirely the same. There will be mandatory checks at the points of entry to the EU, so-called border inspection posts, where all consignments with animal parts and live animals will be subjected to documentary, physical and identity checks. All this is well known and established.

Well known and established? For whom . . . I wondered.

Once the talks on the future relationship did begin, Barnier stated with emphasis in front of the BSG, they would be based on the principles that had been agreed by the three EU institutions at the outset, first among them that 'a third country should never be able to put itself in a position that is equal or more favourable than [being] a member state of the Union.' The other principles were 'a balance between rights and obligations, the requirement of a level playing field, the respect of relations we already have with other, third countries, and naturally, of course, the integrity of the single market, the indivisibility of the four freedoms [of goods, capital, services and labour], and the autonomy of the twenty-seven [member states].'

Barnier also pointed out that, unlike the withdrawal agreement, the future relationship talks would not end in a legally binding treaty. The most it would be possible to achieve, by October 2018, which was at that time still the end date he had in mind, was a common political declaration in which both sides expressed how they saw their future relationship. 'So the aim is, at the moment when they sign the Brexit treaty [the Orderly Withdrawal Agreement], to have a declaration on the side, that they also approve of, that describes the future relationship in enough detail, that is restrictive enough, so that they [the member states] are not surprised by the later [real] negotiations.'

What Barnier said that morning was crucial, although it took me time to realise how crucial. However detailed, the Political Declaration on the future EU–UK relationship would not be legally binding – only the Orderly Withdrawal Agreement would be legally binding. Yet there were elements in that Orderly Withdrawal Agreement that touched upon a possible future relationship – specifically, the backstop solution for the Irish border (regulatory alignment, later to evolve into a temporary UK-wide customs union). As a consequence, the backstop would or could, by legal treaty, bind the UK into a solution that set ground rules for the future EU–UK relationship before the real talks had begun, and certainly before they produced a new trade agreement. That is why the Irish border backstop became such a battleground.

Barnier ended his lecture to the Brexit Steering Group that morning with one last colourful slide, which showed, in the shape of a staircase, his view of the UK's options for a future relationship with the EU. Each step, going down, showed flags, to refer to countries the EU already had a relationship with, which might become a model for the future EU–UK relationship. And beneath each step Barnier had laid out the UK red lines which, he judged, made the models impossible to accept for them, and which were therefore taking the United Kingdom down to the bottom of the staircase.

First came the flag of the EU itself, but that option was out because the UK was leaving the EU. Second came the flag of Norway, but that option was impossible for the UK because it wanted regulatory autonomy and wouldn't accept the jurisdiction of the European Court of Justice, free movement of people or a substantial financial contribution. The third step showed the Swiss flag – Switzerland has a web of bilateral treaties which allow it to participate in the single market. The fourth was that of Ukraine – which has a political and economic Association Agreement with the EU. The fifth step flew the white crescent and star of Turkey, which is in a customs union with the EU – and even that step would not do for Britain because Mrs May was determined to pursue an independent trade policy. The United Kingdom's companions at the bottom of the staircase, finally, were the flags of Canada and South Korea, which both have free-trade agreements with the EU (Japan would soon join them on this step; its own free-trade agreement with the EU came into force in February 2019).

Next to the staircase, behind a dotted line, loomed the words 'no deal'.

'At the moment they're at the top [of the staircase],' Barnier explained. 'Underneath I put the red lines that the British themselves formulated. Doors that they open or close themselves. I find it very important to explain to the outside world that it's them who open or close doors, not us.' Barnier was proud of his slide. He had already used it with the heads of state and government at the European Council. 'It had quite some success. I like this slide,' he said. In fact, he was so proud of it that he did not really notice Verhofstadt teasing him with 'they become more and more colourful'.

'Yes, yes,' Barnier replied. 'But that way people understand better.'

Verhofstadt wouldn't laugh for long though; a couple of days later he asked his own team to make a slide he could use at another meeting with Barnier, and the task turned out to be anything but simple. I found Guillaume McLaughlin, Edel Crosse and Bram Delen (who was the handiest at the computer) struggling with it until very late at night. They sat huddled together in Edel's tiny office, their faces reflected in the windows looking down into the inner courtyard of the European Parliament building in Strasbourg, now dark, and silent without its usual daylight clatter.

MCLAUGHLIN: I have the feeling that the reaction of Mr
    Verhofstadt [shows] that he's not going to use it, Bram.
DELEN: That's why I'm going to stop here.
MCLAUGHLIN: If you want to know the fullness of my
    thoughts, knowing the man just a touch. Plus, he's in
    competition, Bram, in direct, head-on competition
    with Barnier. Who is the fucking . . .

CROSSE: The dog's bollocks of.

MCLAUGHLIN: PowerPoint fucking king.

CROSSE: Yeah, he is.

DELEN: Well, at least if he decides to use it, it's not a complete . . .

MCLAUGHLIN: Yeah, we don't have to hide our heads in shame for ever. Unfortunately, I announced to Barnier that we would have a slide.

CROSSE: Oh no, you didn't, you created anticipation, that's the worst thing you could have done. Crazy bad idea.

MCLAUGHLIN: Yeah, it's a bit stupid, I recognise this. But I didn't realise it was going to be quite so challenging.

In the end Verhofstadt didn't use — as Guillaume had predicted, knowing the fullness of his boss's thoughts — the slide that Bram had made. Barnier retained his title as the PowerPoint king.

~

Most of Guy Verhofstadt's time in January 2018 was occupied with the question of what to do with the seventy-three British seats (out of 751) in the European Parliament once the United Kingdom had left. Were they just to be abolished, resulting in a substantial reduction in costs? Or could they instead be used for something else, the realisation of an old dream of Guy Verhofstadt's: the creation of transnational seats in the European Parliament? A limited number of extra seats, to which members are elected, not by their own national constituencies or regions, as is the practice today, but by transnational voters, in one Europe-wide constituency?

Verhofstadt saw it as a way to strengthen European democracy. As he expressed it in a speech, 'So that we lift our democracy to a continental scale. Europe is more than just the sum of twenty-seven national democracies.'

He explained the system to the Maltese prime minister Joseph Muscat like this: 'You receive two ballot papers. One for your national [representative], that's the actual [existing] system. And you receive a second ballot paper, with twelve, fifteen names, or whatever number on it, and where every party has its candidates coming from the four corners of the European Union.'

But of course, and here enters Verhofstadt, the political haggler with forty years of experience: 'If you create transnational seats without Brexit, you have to take them from other member states. So that's a non-starter. Now you have seventy-three beautiful gifts on the table. What do you do with it? And so our idea is . . . that we try to make a deal.' Some of the British seats should, he argued, be simply abolished to bring down the overall size of the Parliament – 'ideally the new total should be 699' – and some of them could be used to ease the difficulties thrown up by what is known as 'degressive proportionality', the system the EU uses to allocate seats to its member states.

Degressive proportionality means that smaller states are allocated more seats than they would get in strict proportion to their populations – or, looked at the other way round, that in bigger states like Germany, France or the UK, one MEP can be elected per over 800,000 inhabitants, while on the opposite side of the scale, Malta gets one MEP per 77,000 inhabitants. The idea is to ensure that smaller states have a real voice in the European Parliament and that the big members cannot dominate its decisions.

But as populations fluctuate over the years, the numbers and proportions of course need to be adapted regularly – meaning that states can sometimes lose, or gain, a couple of seats. Such an adjustment was due in 2019, and what Verhofstadt had in mind was to use Brexit and some of the seventy-three abandoned British seats to make that less painful for the remaining member states: no one would lose any seats, and states who should get more seats would get them from the lost UK contingent. In return he hoped that they would allow him to set up his system of transnational seats with the twelve or fifteen seats he estimated would still be available. Three birds with one stone.

Verhofstadt talked about his transnational seats to everyone he met, big or small, with an enthusiasm that made him look half his age. Everyone in the EU knew what he was up to, and fighting for, Michel Barnier included, who asked him about his transnational seats at the end of a Brexit Steering Group meeting in an exchange that reflected, in just a few words, the difference between the two men.

BARNIER: So you think they will work, these transnational seats?

VERHOFSTADT: Here [in the European Parliament] it will work, I think. We buy the French delegation, the Spanish . . .

BARNIER: You don't buy, you discuss . . .

VERHOFSTADT: No, we buy, with seats, not with euros or bitcoins, but with seats. [Both politicians laughed heartily.]

BARNIER: OK, I'm off.

In the two years that I followed Verhofstadt, I never saw him more engaged and emotional than during this period — the transnational seat saga. His idea had to be voted on twice, first in the Institutional Affairs Committee of the Parliament (AFCO) and later in the plenary. On his way to the AFCO vote he sighed, immensely nervous: 'It's like going to an exam.' But he won, and afterwards he slapped his chief of staff Guillaume McLaughlin on the shoulder. As two old friends they walked back to his offices, where Verhofstadt immediately started texting the French president, Emmanuel Macron, whom he knew was a supporter of his idea.

VERHOFSTADT: Guillaume, can you come for a second? Look, here: 'Monsieur le Président, the AFCO committee voted seventeen against eight in favour of transnational seats. Next step, the vote in the plenary. It won't be easy. Have a nice day and see you soon, Guy.'

MCLAUGHLIN: Perfect.

VERHOFSTADT: Is it OK?

MCLAUGHLIN [imitating the sound of sending a message]: Ping!

But the saga did not end well. It proved impossible for Verhofstadt to convince the European Christian Democrats to support his plan, and without them, he knew he was lost. On the eve of the final vote in the plenary, Verhofstadt received a phone call from a politician with whom he had over the years developed an, at first sight perhaps, unlikely friendship. The former Green MEP Daniel Cohn-Bendit was a student leader during the unrest of May 1968 in France, known during that time as Danny the Red, because of both his politics and the colour of his hair. Verhofstadt was sitting in Edel Crosse's office, lonely, biting his nails. 'Missed call, Danny.' He sighed and dialled. 'Danny, ça va? I had a nightmare. Really, a nightmare, this morning at three o'clock. I thought we had lost the vote on the transnational seats. A real nightmare. What a shit. I just can't take it any more. Just now when we can do it, the Parliament doesn't dare, for purely party political reasons.'

On the day of the vote itself, I put on the same T-shirt I'd worn on my first day of filming Verhofstadt – black, short-sleeved, with 'Parental Advisory, Explicit Content' emblazoned on the front. I told him it was my lucky charm T-shirt, partly because I wanted to make him feel good (he'd seemed so miserable with his nightmare – Stockholm Syndrome, I guess). But I also had an ulterior motive, namely to test something that Bram Delen had told me: that his boss was slightly superstitious, which was the reason they always went to the same restaurants in Strasbourg (at one restaurant they had once prepared a speech about the Greek crisis, addressing the Greek prime minister Tsipras, that would become his most successful speech ever on Facebook, so from that moment onwards they continued to go there).

The charm didn't work – Verhofstadt lost the vote – but the test did, because when Verhofstadt came back to the office afterwards, the first thing he said to me was, 'Your T-shirt doesn't work, jong [Dutch for youngster]. You can throw it in the garbage.'

~

On 6 February, one of Britain's most prominent pro-European political figures visited Guy Verhofstadt in his Strasbourg offices. Sir Nick Clegg had a background, rare among British politicians, within the EU bureaucracy; he joined the Commission staff in the mid-1990s and was later hired as a speechwriter and policy adviser by Leon Brittan, the former Conservative Cabinet minister who became a Commissioner in 1989. Clegg had also been an MEP before winning a seat at Westminster, and as Liberal Democrat leader he had served as deputy prime minister in David Cameron's 2010–15 coalition government. His predictions in February 2018 have stood the test of time remarkably well. 'The twenty-seven will be faced with a terrible dilemma,' he said, 'which is that you might have a country, in GDP terms equivalent to seventeen existing [states], basically, in a state of political paralysis. Chaos. Not able to decide how to go forward. Not able to decide how to go backward.'

The former Liberal Democrat leader warned that 'it will be very chaotic. The turmoil will be terrible,' but he pleaded with his hosts 'to find some mechanism to give us time, simply to give us time', because he believed there was 'a possibility that out of that chaos emerges fresh new flowers of hope, a re-alignment of British politics, brave leadership of the Labour party, a new generation'. At the same time, he said that he understood Europe's impatience; he quoted 'my 82-year-old Dutch mum' who 'keeps saying to me: De Gaulle was right' – a reference to the French leader's decision to veto British membership of the old European Economic Community decades earlier.

The grand old man of the Brexit Steering Group, Elmar Brok, was similarly clear-eyed about what the future held, but without Clegg's optimism. Discussing the Irish backstop with Michel Barnier later the same day, he mused, 'I must say: my fantasy [imagination] is not good enough to see how this result of December will be put into practice . . . Do you think that Theresa May has the strength and the courage to bring that through in Britain? I'm very pessimistic.'

Barnier was debriefing the group on a working lunch in Downing Street the previous day, and he reported that, despite the great push by the British side to move negotiations on to the future relationship between the United Kingdom and the European Union, David Davis had been reluctant to engage on the subject because the British government still had not agreed its ambitions. 'To be quite clear,' he said, 'at this lunch we didn't talk about the future relationship at all because he wasn't ready to. So, we know that there are internal debates – [for example] a customs union or not a customs union – but I wasn't able to discuss that as David Davis was clearly not minded to, and nor was Madame May, whom I met for twenty minutes before lunch.'

The meeting had, however, identified 'many points of difference' over the way the transition period should work. One of them had to do with Guy Verhofstadt's cherished area of citizens' rights; the EU wanted the withdrawal agreement to apply to any EU citizen who arrived in the United Kingdom until the end of the transition period, while the British argued that the cut-off point should be Brexit day, when the transition period would start, and Barnier judged them 'extremely resistant on this subject'.

Barnier also reminded the group that on 29 March 2019 the United Kingdom would automatically leave 750 international agreements which flowed from its membership of the EU. These covered everything from trade to agriculture, transport to customs arrangements, fisheries to regulatory cooperation, and the British negotiators wanted them to be 'rolled over' when the United Kingdom left the EU. But Barnier reported that 'we know many of our international partners are not at all open, or not very open, to what's being called a rolling over of these agreements without any change or compensation'. A number of countries wanted to use the opportunity to seek more advantageous terms, and Barnier was resisting the idea that it was the EU's job to sort this out on Britain's behalf.

Finally, the EU's chief negotiator also told the BSG, in his most schoolmasterly manner, that he had once again ticked off the British for sending ministers and ambassadors around Europe's capitals in the hope of outflanking the official negotiating team. 'I told them all that was not very productive,' he said. 'It will either end in failure for them or it will divide the twenty-seven, and if the twenty-seven are divided there's a risk there'll be no agreement.'

~

On 19 February, Verhofstadt was visited by members of the awkwardly named Exiting the European Union Select Committee
of the House of Commons, the nearest the Westminster
Parliament had to a British version of the Brexit Steering Group,
which was chaired by Hilary Benn, a former Labour Cabinet
minister, and one of the most influential pro-European voices
on Labour's back benches. Just before Christmas, Benn had
given the Brexit secretary, David Davis, a fierce grilling over
the research work the government claimed to have done on the
economic impact of Brexit – an episode which led to Davis being
publicly rebuked by the Speaker of the Commons. Frustrated
by the lack of clarity from their own government, Benn and his
colleagues turned up in Guy Verhofstadt's Brussels home base in
search of enlightenment. The committee chair asked their host
to 'flesh out the outstanding issues'.

Verhofstadt spelled out some basic truths about the European
Parliament's red lines (including citizens' rights, again), and
warned them about European reaction to the talk of Britain
becoming a low-tax 'Singapore-style' off-shore economy – 'a sort
of free tax haven, somewhere just outside the EU . . . some financial heaven, where everybody says, "OK, let's go there first."'

But the most revealing passage of the exchange, viewed
with the hindsight offered by subsequent events, came over
that 'meaningful vote' which the British Parliament had
secured for itself before Christmas the previous year – Hilary
Benn had been one of the most consistent champions of cross-
party efforts to force the government to accept the need for
parliamentary approval of the final deal Theresa May would
eventually agree with the EU. The MPs wanted to know
whether Verhofstadt believed that that deal would include 'a

sufficient amount of detail to be able to make an informed decision about the future relationship between the UK and the EU'
when they voted. Some of them were already looking ahead to
the fact that the future relationship was only going to be dealt
with in a non-legally-binding political declaration, which might
include lots of fudge.

The MPs challenged Verhofstadt over the possibility that
the European Parliament might reject an agreement. But
Verhofstadt came back with what turned out to be the much
more pertinent question of what would happen if the British
Parliament said no. 'Maybe there could be a crisis then?' he
offered. 'A government crisis . . . unknown territory.' And he
added, 'I can be pretty sure on the European Parliament . . .
if there are problems, we will flag them beforehand.' The way
the European institutions had designed their negotiating structure was, he explained, intended to avoid precisely the kind of
impasse the British Parliament would become bogged down in
at the end of the year.

'We are very close to the negotiator,' he explained. 'He
receives his directives from two bodies: the Brexit Working
Group, that's the Council, and the Brexit Steering Group,
that's the Parliament. What Mr Barnier is doing is always in
accordance and preparation with these two bodies.' The contrast with the often-hostile relationship between Hilary Benn's
House of Commons Brexit Committee and David Davis could
not have been more marked. Traditionally, the British system of
government has fostered a close relationship between executive
and legislators, because British governments depend on their
parliamentary majority, while the European Union has built
tension and institutional rivalry into its decision-making process, often denying the European Parliament a more influential
role. Brexit had turned both systems on their heads.

~

Michel Barnier's hope of turning the December 2017 joint report into a legal text by early February 2018 proved overly optimistic, but when he briefed the Brexit Steering Group towards the end of the month, the document was taking shape; he promised 'around 100 pages, with plenty of annexes on top of that, and 168 articles'. The British, he reported – the two sides had just completed a further two days of face-to-face talks – were still not fully engaged with some areas because they remained 'snared in the issue of sovereignty'. 'They don't want to become a vassal state,' he told the group, 'and at the same time they want to continue to take part in all the decision-making structures as if they were a member state.' So he had done what he'd explained he would do to the BSG when he set out his four *chantiers* shortly after New Year: include paragraphs with the EU position wherever there was no British position available yet, to give the UK a push. 'We've run out of time for general commentaries and political texts,' he declared, 'we need to work, between now and October, on a legal basis . . . I think presenting a full draft treaty might force them to take positions on points where they as yet have no position.'

He specifically had the Irish border in his sights. 'The text on Ireland in the joint report is a text characterised by constructive ambiguity,' he said, 'but we must not allow things to develop so that only the ambiguity remains, and the constructive element disappears. So we have chosen to push things along, to lift this ambiguity, to escape from the ambiguity. It is an especially sensitive subject, so we are taking a risk. But I think it is a risk we have to take at this stage to push things forward.'

Barnier was also able to report encouraging news for Guy Verhofstadt; he saw the prospect of the United Kingdom giving way on the status of EU citizens who arrived there during the transition period – not because Mrs May's government had become any less hawkish on immigration, but because the Home Office simply did not have the capacity to manage an extra layer of complexity in Britain's immigration system. 'They are already,' Barnier suggested, 'in their heart of hearts, very worried about the procedures and administration that they need to put in place to create two classes of citizen . . . It may be impossible for the British civil service to manage two different systems. I think that on this question they are going to come round to a simpler and more pragmatic view.'

Barnier was back with the BSG a week later, and by then the draft treaty text was ready for release. He was frank about the fact that it was intended to be provocative. 'I want to provoke them,' he told the MEPs. 'I want to force them to give a view on our texts.' And, as he had indicated during his previous meeting with them, the Irish issue was the negotiating target. 'The only really new thing in this text is about Ireland,' he said. The 'specific protocol' included in the draft would, he explained, 'realise the option of the "backstop", the option which will insure that the commitments made in the joint report come into force as soon as [the United Kingdom] withdraws.'

And he expanded on it: 'Our responsibility is to say now that we need to put the possibility of "backstops" in the withdrawal agreement, and the approach we have chosen is to create an area of regulatory alignment on the island of Ireland, so that we can avoid a hard border and at the same time preserve the integrity of the single market. But he added that 'regulatory alignment alone is not enough – we also need the Union's customs code to apply to Northern Ireland.'

The draft treaty was published the following day, 28

February 2018. The 'ambiguity' introduced into the pre-Christmas interim report by the DUP's cherished Article 50 had almost entirely disappeared. The draft included only the briefest of nods to the continued integrity of the United Kingdom of Great Britain and Northern Ireland, and it put Britain's relationship with Northern Ireland on a par with its relationship with the Republic, referring to 'the commitment of the United Kingdom to protecting and supporting continued North–South and East–West cooperation across the full range of political, economic, security, societal and agricultural con-texts and frameworks of cooperation, including the continued operation of the North–South Implementation Bodies'.

The document laid the responsibility for the Irish problem squarely at Britain's door ('the United Kingdom's withdrawal from the Union gives rise to substantial challenges to the main-tenance and development of North–South cooperation') and it insisted that the EU's own system should be protected ('the rights and obligations of Ireland under the rules of the Union's internal market and customs union must be fully respected'). In the absence of anything else – a technological solution to the border problem or a trade agreement which would remove the need for border checks altogether – the document bound the two sides to a 'common regulatory area comprising the Union and the United Kingdom in respect of Northern Ireland . . . The common regulatory area shall constitute an area with-out internal borders in which the free movement of goods is ensured and North–South cooperation protected.' That was followed by a long list of areas where European Union rules and regulations would apply 'in the United Kingdom in respect of Northern Ireland'.

The draft was published on a Wednesday, when Prime Minister's Questions takes place at Westminster. And the

Democratic Unionist MP David Simpson was soon on his feet demanding that the prime minister should confirm that she would never agree to a border between Northern Ireland and the rest of the United Kingdom. In her reply, Theresa May rejected Michel Barnier's proposals for a withdrawal agreement in the most emphatic terms possible, telling the House of Commons, 'The draft legal text the Commission have published would, if implemented, undermine the UK common market and threaten the constitutional integrity of the UK by creating a customs and regulatory border down the Irish Sea, and no UK prime minister could ever agree to it. I will be making it crystal clear to [European Commission] President Juncker and others that we will never do so.'

If Barnier's ambition was – as he had told the Brexit Steering Group – to provoke, he had succeeded in spades; whether the provocation had quite the impact he intended is another question. Reaction in London duly boomeranged back to Brussels, and he faced tough questions from the press about the draft. 'Are you trying to force Mrs May into saying that she will stay in a customs union?' asked one journalist. 'And aren't you risking toppling her government by meddling?' 'Do you not accept that a border will have to emerge on the Irish Sea?' demanded another.

Barnier played a dead bat. 'I'm familiar with the British political situation, and I respect that,' he said. 'We're not here to give lessons to anyone.' And in a line that must surely have raised an eyebrow or two among members of the BSG – who had heard him say precisely the opposite the previous day, he claimed, 'I'm not trying to provoke or create any shockwaves.' He added, in a reference to some British press coverage, 'Contrary to what I read there is no arrogance here. I am not being arrogant in any way.'

I I

THE ELEPHANT IN THE ROOM

March 2018

On 4 March 2018, Sergei Skripal, a Russian defector and former officer in the Soviet military intelligence organisation the GRU, was poisoned with his daughter Yulia in the cathedral city of Salisbury. The setting for the crime could not have been more English, and the story seemed straight out of a Cold War novel. Skripal had been imprisoned as a double agent by the Russian authorities in 2006, but in 2010 he was allowed to leave for Britain as part of a spy swap, and he bought his Salisbury house the following year. He and Yulia were found 'slipping in and out of consciousness on a public bench', and the nerve agent used against him was quickly identified as Novichok, which was known to be manufactured in Russia.

Ten days later, Theresa May accused Moscow of the crime and expelled twenty-three Russian diplomats from London. The United Kingdom's allies rallied round; by the end of the month more than 150 Russian diplomats had been sent home, many of them expelled by other members of the European Union. It was a striking moment of EU solidarity with Britain amid increasingly scratchy relations over Brexit. Guy Verhofstadt tweeted his support: 'We stand shoulder-to-shoulder with the

British people. It must be made clear that an attack against one EU & NATO country is an attack on all of us.'

The tweets that came back to Verhofstadt reflected Britain's divisions over Europe. The archly named Miss Feasance replied, 'How humbling. To still have friends after behaving so despicably deceptive and causing such a pointless fuss.' But a Maurice Dickinson was less impressed: 'Keep the useless #EU out of it. We have NATO to deal with Russia if needs be. We don't need a host of useless bureaucrats taking us into a war where they will be safe in their bunkers in Brussels while the rest of us are locked outside.' And Verhofstadt – true to himself – was not unambiguous in his support. In a second tweet he wrote that 'Brexit weakens the UK and us on the international stage,' and he added a link, with an endorsement, to a *Washington Post* piece headlined, 'The nerve agent attack on British soil has exposed London's isolation'.

On 6 March, Verhofstadt was in London for a meeting with Theresa May and her Brexit secretary David Davis. The full political and diplomatic implications of the Skripal affair had yet to take shape – counter-terrorism officers took over the investigation from the Wiltshire police later that day – so Brexit was still at the top of the agenda.

Crammed into a minivan with darkened windows, Guy Verhofstadt and his team were bantering like boys on a school trip as they were driven through Trafalgar Square on their way to Downing Street. Verhofstadt was accompanied by his chief of staff, Guillaume McLaughlin, and two senior civil servants at the European Parliament, the institutional affairs director Nick Lane and the deputy secretary-general Markus Winkler.

MCLAUGHLIN: So we have a light start.

LANE: David Davis.

VERHOFSTADT [laughing]: A light start, David Davis.

MCLAUGHLIN: I wonder, do you think he still does Brexit?

LANE: He's not in Brussels this week. We can ask him: why are you here?

The boys also speculated about the whereabouts of Olly Robbins, Theresa May's chief negotiator:

LANE: I'm not sure if he's not lurking in Brussels.

VERHOFSTADT: He likes it maybe there!

While the driver crawled through the morning traffic, under a spiritless grey sky, the four men in the back of his van fell silent. But not for long. Guillaume had been checking his phone and announced that 'They have a Cabinet meeting this morning at nine thirty, in Downing Street.' To which his boss reacted with dry humour:

VERHOFSTADT: Ah, we can enter, eh? Do you have problems here?

MCLAUGHLIN: Want some help?

VERHOFSTADT: Need some help?

The chief of staff reassured Verhofstadt that his visit had been picked up by one of the go-to websites for Brexit addicts: 'In the Politico London Playbook [Slogan 'What's driving the day in Westminster. Politics and policymaking in the UK capital'] it's all announced, your visit.' Verhofstadt had already checked it out. 'Yeah, I've seen,' he replied.

The van stood still more than it drove, so there was time to look around. The conversation turned to Verhofstadt's second favourite subject — cars:

WINKLER: Another Bentley.

VERHOFSTADT: Another Bentley? Not an Aston?

WINKLER: They really made something out of it.
Imagine, twenty years ago, this was quite boring.

MCLAUGHLIN: Yeah, it's true.

WINKLER: And now they are exciting cars. Isn't it owned
by BMW?

VERHOFSTADT: Nooooo! By Piëch [Ferdinand Karl
Piëch, an Austrian business magnate], Porsche,
Volkswagen, Audi.

WINKLER: And Rolls-Royce?

MCLAUGHLIN: Rolls-Royce is BMW, no?

VERHOFSTADT [laughing]: It was the Rolls-Royce for the
poor, the Bentley. And it's Piëch who bought it and
Piëch bought also Lamborghini, it's also from him.
It's why in the Audi V10 and in the Lamborghini is the
same engine also. And Bugatti is also his brand.

But as much as I was allowed to film in the car, once we arrived in Downing Street I was shut out. Despite repeated requests, made from multiple vantage points, by Verhofstadt's team as well as by my UK production company Films of Record, I was not granted access to the meetings with May and Davis. Instead I had to spend long, cold hours with the press pack outside. I filmed them hanging around in the nasty wind that blew from the Thames to St James's Park, all through London's most famous street. I filmed the brown and white Downing Street tabby, Larry, lazily loitering. And at one point I also managed to get one shot of Guy Verhofstadt and David Davis walking like best friends, chatting, from Davis's Brexit offices in 9 Downing Street, which his department shared with the chief whip, to the PM's home, where every movement at the door made the press pack look up, nervously, and then relax again. In the distance, outside the gates, a group of protesters kept warm waving European flags and shouting 'Stop Brexit! Save Britain!' Or maybe they kept Britain warm.

The agenda for Verhofstadt's meetings at Downing Street on that Tuesday had been framed by Theresa May's address at the City of London's Mansion House the previous Friday. The speech, the climax of six 'Road to Brexit' addresses by senior ministers, was yet another attempt to provide an overarching vision for the United Kingdom's future relationship with Europe – 'our economic partnership' as she now called it. And it represented a significant step down the road towards accepting that Brexit – certainly a Brexit defined by Mrs May's red lines – would carry a cost. 'The reality is that we all need to face up to some hard facts,' she said, citing in particular the inevitable impact of Britain's departure from the single market. 'Life is going to be different,' she recognised. 'In certain ways, our access to each other's markets will be less than it is now.'

In a series of apparent concessions to Brussels, Mrs May accepted that the United Kingdom would have to continue to meet the EU's regulatory standards if trade was to continue freely over 'as frictionless a border as possible between us and the EU', and that the EU's competition rules, which ensure a level playing field between their economies, would have to remain. She also recognised the 'hard fact' that 'even after we have left the jurisdiction of the ECJ [European Court of Justice], EU law and the decisions of the ECJ will continue to affect us', that there would have to be an 'arbitration mechanism' to police any long-term trade agreement, and that 'given the close relationship we envisage, we will need to have an ongoing dialogue with the EU, and to ensure we have the means to consult each other regularly'. It was a long way from the 'purist' vision of Brexit espoused by some of those who had applauded her Lancaster House speech just over a year earlier.

Mrs May continued to maintain that an 'off-the-shelf' model would not adequately reflect the future relationship. She opposed 'the Norway model, where we would stay in the single market', because it 'would mean having to implement new EU legislation automatically and in its entirety – and would also mean continued free movement', but she also rejected the idea of trading on World Trade Organization terms or under the kind of free-trade agreement recently negotiated between the EU and Canada because 'these options would mean a significant reduction in our access to each other's markets'.

Theresa May's proposals for replacing the customs union included that complicated idea of the United Kingdom collecting tariffs on the EU's behalf – the EU side had expressed deep scepticism about this when it came up the previous summer, partly because they took a dim view of the United Kingdom's record on the control of goods crossing its borders – and also a somewhat ill-defined 'highly streamlined customs arrangement, where we would jointly agree to implement a range of measures to minimise frictions on trade, together with specific provisions for Northern Ireland'.

The speech still contained a significant element of what the Europeans judged to be 'cake' – the term had become EU code for impossible British demands following Boris Johnson's statement that the government's policy on cake was 'pro having it and pro eating it' – or, to use Michel Barnier's favoured phrase, 'cherry picking'.

Verhofstadt had laid out his concerns about the speech during his Eurostar journey to London, when he briefed his team on a meeting he had had with the UK's permanent representative to the EU, Sir Tim Barrow. He cast those concerns in terms of the long-standing tension between British pragmatism and the more conceptual approach of continental European politicians, of whom Barnier was a prime example: Mrs May's plan was, he argued, lacking in an overarching intellectual structure. And he found that the British permanent representative agreed: 'There is no concept in the whole proposal of the British, that is what is lacking,' he was reported as saying to Barrow. 'And he [Sir Tim] agreed fully. That's typical of the British, he said, we have a problem and we try, *papapapapapa* . . .' Verhofstadt finished his sentence with movements with his fingers to suggest picking the problem to pieces. 'While, I said,' he continued, 'we from the continent, we need first of all a concept, and then we enter into the details . . . And that is what is lacking.'

Verhofstadt accepted that 'there will be cherry picking, always, there is cherry picking, it's called thematic cooperation', but complained that May's speech was '*papapapapapa*, and we want an arrangement there, and there, but there is no overview'. Sir Tim Barrow, he reported to the group, urged him to drive that message home when he met the prime minister: 'So there he was very much: yeah, you have to say that to her, because that is the problem.'

The meetings in Downing Street took four hours, of shivering and zipping up against the nasty wet wind coming from the river. Then Verhofstadt came back out again — and smilingly answered questions from the media for ten more minutes. With the world-famous door of No. 10 behind him, he knew he had to seize his moment. But back in the van he was grimmer and gave vent to his frustration with the British approach, although he was also glad, it seemed, to have been able to explain to May personally what he thought. 'On the concept, we hammered it in,' he said, with twinkling, boyish eyes. 'My point is always that you cannot be successful if there is first of all not a concept, an architecture of this relationship, and then you fill it in, while now, from their side, yeah, we want this and this and this, and we explained that in fact the consequence is that everybody sees it as cherry picking.'

The always perceptive Markus Winkler, who had been present at the meeting with May, added a note on the political reality she was confronted with: 'She always has these two elements in her head, what is good for us [the UK as a country], and what do I need to sell [to the British public], that we created a real difference, and that out means out.'

While they were still in the car, Guillaume McLaughlin picked up the Downing Street press statement about the meeting on his phone. 'The PM explained the vision for the future economic partnership,' he read, and then smiled mischievously, adding: 'I missed that bit – her explanation of the vision of the Mansion speech – maybe I was having a little nip, nap, at that moment!'

'Since there is no vision, it was done very quickly,' Nick Lane laughed.

McLaughlin: 'I closed my eyes.'

Verhofstadt's visit to Downing Street and his talk there about the necessity of a concept, a framework, had had an ulterior motive. Because the concept he was promoting as the basis for the future relationship between the EU and the UK was that of an association agreement – which is an established EU mechanism for regulating relationships with countries outside the Union, and which, according to EU law, has to be ratified by the EU Parliament. What Verhofstadt had in mind would secure a continued role for the European Parliament in the Brexit negotiations.

The idea of an association agreement was originally dreamt up in the 1950s to manage the European Economic Community's relations with the United Kingdom when the UK refused to join the group, so there was a certain symmetry in suggesting it as a way of giving shape to the same relationship now that Britain was leaving. And Verhofstadt's idea got cautiously positive reviews from some Eurosceptic sources. The *Daily Telegraph* wrote: 'At last, Guy Verhofstadt is trying to help the Brexit process ... The British have treated Mr Verhofstadt's plan with caution, undoubtedly because they fear any embrace would encourage their European counterparts to try and railroad them into accepting an off-the-shelf model that doesn't answer what they want. But at least Parliament's Brexit pointman is trying to be constructive ... the Hof deserves credit for – after months of histrionics – trying to put something serious on the table.'

But the paper also pointed out that Verhofstadt's idea was very quickly squashed by Donald Tusk, the European Council president. 'European parliamentarians are keen to talk up how seriously they have been taken by Michel Barnier and his bosses during the Brexit negotiation. But Donald Tusk poured cold water on Mr Verhofstadt's Brexit plan, telling reporters in Finland ... that "unfortunately Brexit was about disassociation not association." That may not be an outright rejection of the Belgian's proposal, but it hardly radiates enthusiasm.' The *Politico* website leapt on what it interpreted as an example of the long-standing institutional divisions which British diplomacy had played so successfully in the past. 'The transformation of Verhofstadt from hard-liner into potential UK ally would represent a remarkable turnabout,' it noted, 'and the difference between his and Tusk's approach may hint at inter-institutional rivalries in Brussels that the UK can exploit.'

Two days after Verhofstadt's trip to London, Michel Barnier gave the Brexit Steering Group *his* considered reaction to the latest British proposals – or, to be more precise, his 'double reaction', as he put it. On the positive side he welcomed 'the clarity of their red lines'; despite her attempts to compromise, Mrs May had, of course, repeated her commitment to take the United Kingdom out of the customs union and the single market, and Barnier offered the view that 'these positions lead us, logically, to a free-trade agreement'.

But he declared that he had had a 'less positive reaction' when he read the speech carefully because 'we can see in many paragraphs an ambition' – and here he complicated the food metaphors – 'for what I call double cherry picking'. He cited the way Mrs May had referred to 'managed divergence, or regulatory convergence or mutual recognition' and declared with brutal finality that 'these concepts are not compatible. Mutual recognition does not exist with third countries. Recognition answers to the logic of the internal market . . .' Placing the United Kingdom firmly back at the bottom of that staircase on his favourite slide, he added, 'At most what one can foresee for Britain is that we build a system of regulatory cooperation – which is what we have done between Japan and the EU.'

And Barnier categorically rejected the idea that the EU would delegate customs controls to the United Kingdom after Brexit, as Mrs May had suggested.

May's proposal had been made just as the European Commission accused the United Kingdom of failing to collect customs duties on goods from China on a heroic scale. The Commission wrote to the British government stating that the UK owed £2.4 billion in duties, and that it had, in the words of a BBC report, done 'too little to prevent fraud after it was warned about the problem by the EU's watchdog Olaf in 2017'. The EU investigation found that 'organised crime groups had been using fake invoices to undervalue goods being imported from China – many of which were destined for the black market in other parts of the EU.'

Barnier had just completed another round of talks with the British (though without the participation of David Davis) and the Belgian MEP Philippe Lamberts pressed him over the Irish issue, following Theresa May's emphatic rejection of the critical paragraph on the subject in the draft withdrawal agreement the EU had published the previous month.

'During your private contacts, do you get a sense that things [regarding the Irish border] are opening up?' Philippe Lamberts asked. 'Because for me that is the elephant in the room . . . it really is a very big stone in one's shoe.'

'That's a fundamental point,' Barnier replied. 'I would like to say with complete clarity that there is no question that we will leave the elephant there. Our position is that we need an operational agreement on Ireland, workable solutions in the withdrawal agreement, in October at the latest.' He said he detected movement in London on the issue, but advised that it was not the right moment to push it, because there was another priority now: a deal on a transition period.

The need for a transition period had been clear to the EU, Guy Verhofstadt and the Brexit Steering Group right back in the spring of 2017 before the triggering of Article 50, and Theresa May had formally acknowledged it would be necessary in her Florence speech in the autumn of 2017. Now it had become the most pressing matter at hand.

The British government liked to describe it as an 'implementation' period, on the grounds that it would be a time to introduce the new arrangements for the United Kingdom's future relationship with the EU. But, even in Westminster, everyone now recognised that, on the date the UK was due to leave the EU (29 March 2019), those new arrangements would not be agreed; at most, there would be a political declaration about the future, not a legal treaty. And you cannot implement what has not yet been agreed upon. The EU had, of course, always said that there wasn't going to be a future trade deal ready, hence their use of the term 'transition period', which would really be a breathing space for further negotiation – two or three years during which nothing much would change and in which the two parties could really hammer out their future relationship.

'At the moment they are pushing and pushing to get a transition agreement,' Barnier told the Brexit Steering Group, so 'if they reach reasonable positions on the transition, we need to bank them'.

Barnier sounded cautiously hopeful, and told the BSG that he sensed the same kind of urgency on the British side as he had felt in December, when the first deal, on the joint report, was reached. But Danuta Hübner, the Polish member of the group, challenged his short-term optimism with long-term pessimism, wondering whether any agreement with the United Kingdom would ever be durable. Looking back to Theresa May's Mansion House speech, Hübner pondered, 'She said . . . that they want durability of the solution, so they want something that should be strong, deep and durable, and then . . . that [the] next government can change everything. So the instability is already in their minds. I don't understand.' She asked whether the chief negotiator had similar concerns.

Barnier replied with an anecdote about his British counterpart. 'I remember a conversation I had in Downing Street last year with David Davis,' he told her. 'He said to me, "Don't worry, on D-Day, the day we leave, thanks to our Great Repeal Bill, we'll transpose everything into British law." Very good, thank you. And what happens on D-Day plus ten? And his answer was "That's another story", and for us it isn't another story.'

~

On 19 March 2018, David Davis stood next to the 'dog's bollocks of PowerPoint fucking king' in front of a huge colour-coded slide display, as Michel Barnier took the press in Brussels through the state of play in the talks on a transition agreement and the broader issues that would be covered in a withdrawal agreement. The sections of text marked in green were agreed, yellow indicated continuing discussions, and those areas where the British had yet to respond to the EU's proposals featured in plain black and white.

'Oh, a PowerPoint! Barnier, his favourite thing,' remarked Edel Crosse as she watched the press conference from Verhofstadt's offices in the European Parliament. 'It's mostly yellow,' she noted – continuing discussions. But there was enough green there for David Davis to claim a kind of triumph; crucially, the terms for Britain's transition period had been settled. 'In December we reached an important milestone by achieving an agreement on the first phase of the negotiation,' the Brexit secretary told the press conference. 'And today we took another significant step by reaching an agreement on the next phase, which I'm confident will be welcomed by the European Council when it meets later this week. Businesses need not delay investment decisions or rush through contingency plans based on guesses about the future. Instead they now have certainty.'

Davis welcomed especially the news that the United Kingdom would be able to negotiate and ratify – but not implement – new trade deals during the transition period. 'The UK will be able to step out, sign and ratify new deals, new trade deals, with old friends and new allies, for the first time in forty years,' he declared, glossing over the possibility that the United Kingdom's trading partners might be cautious about negotiating new agreements until the country's long-term relationship with the EU was settled.

Both in Britain and in Europe, the press put a rather different spin on the transition deal. A Belgian newspaper, *De Standaard*, summarised the position like this: 'While on 29 March 2019 at midnight they will officially leave the European Union, the British will *de facto* continue to abide by all the EU rules until 31 December 2020. That's in a nutshell what's in the deal signed yesterday by the EU Brexit Secretary David Davis and EU chief negotiator Michel Barnier.' The *Daily Telegraph* headlined the story, 'Theresa May accused of Brexit climbdown as UK agrees to free movement in transition period', and *The Guardian* described the agreement as a 'pyrrhic Brexit victory', judging that 'the UK has paid a high price to get to this point. A series of once-unimaginable concessions are now baked into the withdrawal agreement, with more likely to come if Britain wants to avoid everything falling apart again in nine months.'

In the words of a later press release from the European Commission, the transition agreement meant that

> during this period, the entire Union *acquis* [laws and regulations passed to date] will continue to apply to and in the UK as if it were a Member State. This means that the UK will continue to participate in the EU Customs Union and the Single Market (with all four freedoms) and all Union policies. Any changes to the Union *acquis* will automatically apply to and in the UK. The direct effect and primacy of Union law will be preserved. All existing Union regulatory, budgetary, supervisory, judiciary and enforcement instruments and structures will apply, including the competence of the Court of Justice of the European Union.

Some of the sharpest comment was prompted by the fact that the transition agreement meant Britain would remain part of the Common Fisheries Policy until the end of 2020. The

Financial Times reported, 'A fiasco over fish: Hard Brexiters are livid that UK will remain in the CFP during transition period.' And when the environment secretary, Michael Gove, accepted in the Commons that the agreement was a 'disappointment in fishing communities', *The Sun* splashed the headline, 'WHAT A LOAD OF POLLOCKS! – Fury as Gove refuses to give promises on fish'. In an ominous sign of trouble to come, thirteen Conservative MPs and one from the DUP wrote to the prime minister threatening to vote down the agreement when the time came unless the deal on fish was reversed. Jacob Rees-Mogg warned that Britain had become a 'joke nation', and Nigel Farage (now a regular radio presenter) staged a protest on a boat opposite Parliament, throwing two crates of dead haddock into the Thames.

While Barnier and David Davis said their goodbyes on the television screen where their press conference had been showing, the members of the Brexit Steering Group started pouring into Guy Verhofstadt's office to fillet Barnier's colour-coded overview together. Verhofstadt wondered why the colour green had been chosen to indicate what was agreed, and Edel Crosse knew why: 'Ireland, Ireland.' Guillaume McLaughlin chipped in with, 'It's Saint Patrick's Day', though of course Saint Patrick is celebrated not on the 19th but on 17 March.

When Elmar Brok came in, he complained that he had not been able to print the overview in colour, whereas Verhofstadt and the Parliament's deputy secretary-general, Markus Winkler, apparently had.

BROK: Why do ordinary MEPs have no . . .
WINKLER: Colour printer?
BROK: Colour printer.
MCLAUGHLIN: It's a scandal.
WINKLER: I ask, why do we have MEPs?

They all laughed. The atmosphere was celebratory, because of what, rightly or wrongly, they regarded as an almost total British surrender on the issue of citizens' rights. 'I cannot believe that they've just given in on everything,' commented Roberto Gualtieri. Crucially, the introduction of a new immigration system would be delayed, and full freedom of movement was to continue throughout the transition period. The BSG's efforts to ensure that future spouses of EU citizens settling in the United Kingdom should be covered by the withdrawal agreement had not borne fruit, but most of their objectives had been achieved. 'On financial settlement, everything done. On citizens' rights, more or less everything done,' Verhofstadt told the group.

But when they met Michel Barnier the next day, the EU chief negotiator seemed tired. He'd arrived late, looking haggard, running to the European Parliament from a previous meeting at the European Council.

First, Barnier went over the progress that had been made (and not made) on the Orderly Withdrawal Agreement. Following up on the rationale he had laid out to the group the previous month, he said that he had intended the publication of a draft treaty text to act as an 'electric shock' to force negotiations forward. Member states had come back with some 700 questions on the text, which had all been answered by his team before the proposed agreement was formally submitted to the British negotiating team so that they could – here he smiled – 'colour it in'. His strategy, he felt, had worked. 'Number one,' he told the group, 'the British have negotiated on the basis of our text, which is always better in a negotiation, and secondly we've used the political momentum, which you must have noticed when you were in London the other day [turning to Verhofstadt], the need to get results.'

Nailing down what was agreed upon, in the green sections of his overview, had meant working through the evenings and much of the nights on the previous Friday, Saturday and Sunday, and he 'rendered homage' to Olly Robbins and the British negotiating team. 'Perhaps one day they will reveal what they thought of what they were doing,' he remarked, 'but it was good work, day and night, to finalise this document which has given us an agreement which Mrs May has just signed off on.'

Barnier identified several European victories and one continuing battlefield. We have 'definitively and legally settled the financial settlement', he said. The issue of citizens' rights – 'your priority since the beginning' – had, Barnier revealed, been the most complex issue to crack, and they had had 'extremely hard' debates with the British over the previous Friday and Saturday. Barnier's team had, he explained, given up on the issue of future spouses because the cost of fighting that battle 'was too high to pay'. As for the transition agreement, the British had, he declared, accepted 'almost all our conditions'.

Ireland remained the most troublesome issue. 'On Ireland, I think that, speaking objectively, I am both sure about what we yesterday recorded as progress and sure about what is still up in the air,' Barnier reported. He recalled that a fortnight earlier Mrs May's reaction to the draft treaty had been 'violent', and in answer to a question from Elmar Brok, he underlined the importance of the way she had moved since then; she had, he told the group, accepted the need for a backstop in the withdrawal agreement, even if 'perhaps not the backstop in detail as we have proposed it'.

The meeting broke up because Barnier had a date – 'lunch with the king of the Belgians'. As always, Barnier was precise, even in that short announcement, because the Belgian king is indeed not the king of Belgium, the territory, but the king of the Belgian people living there. When Belgium became an independent country in 1830, the

Belgians didn't really want a king. But a king was forced upon them by the nations, including the United Kingdom, around them – and so as a compromise they decided that this king, Leopold I, would be their guest; he would be allowed to govern them, together with a Parliament, but he wouldn't be given, not even in a symbolic way, the ownership of their lands.

~

Two days later, Theresa May joined her fellow EU heads of government at the Union's regular summit in Brussels, in the Council building that lies just a stone's throw away from the triumphal arch at the Jubilee Park, built to celebrate Belgium's independence.

For the first time since she became prime minister, her time at the meeting was not completely dominated by Brexit; the Skripal poisoning occupied an even more prominent place on the agenda. Mrs May was afterwards able to report to the House of Commons that the summit conclusion stated that the Council 'agrees with the United Kingdom government's assessment that it is highly likely that the Russian Federation is responsible and that there is no alternative plausible explanation'.

As a result, fifteen member states, along with the United States, Canada and Ukraine, were undertaking 'the largest collective expulsion of Russian intelligence officers in history'. For once she found herself on the same side as her fellow EU leaders. 'In my discussions with President Macron and Chancellor Merkel, as well as other leaders,' she reported, 'we agreed on the importance of sending a strong European message in response to Russia's actions – not just out of solidarity with the UK but recognising the threat posed to the national security of all EU countries.'

12

A SUBMARINE IN MUDDY WATERS

Mid-April–early June 2018

One week after he celebrated his sixty-fifth birthday, Guy Verhofstadt was in Strasbourg, early in the morning, and edgy. As a consequence, his team was also tense, and Bram Delen, on top of that, felt nauseous. The night before he'd eaten something that didn't agree with him, and he feared now that stuff was 'going to come out both ways'. Chief of staff Guillaume McLaughlin tenderly told him, 'We love you very much, Bram, but . . .' Then their boss broke in with changes he wanted to make to an important speech he had to deliver later that morning in a plenary session of Parliament, addressing the French president, Emmanuel Macron, and they got to work.

They were in Edel Crosse's tiny office on the sixth floor of the main oval Parliament building in Strasbourg, with Bram as usual in front of the computer, typing, Edel sitting next to him, commenting, Guillaume hovering behind, also commenting, and Guy Verhofstadt pacing around from his own office to Edel's and back – discussing changes, eating his croissant, rehearsing, and in general being pretty annoying, but also, nevertheless, still inspiring to his team. The time limit for his speech today was seven minutes – and he had still quite a lot of sentences and words to lose.

The European Parliament had invited Emmanuel Macron for a

debate on the future of Europe and – as a guest – the French president could talk for as long as he wanted. After he'd finished, Manfred Weber, the leader of the biggest political group in the European Parliament, the Christian Democrats, would get ten minutes to reply to him, followed by Udo Bullmann, the leader of the second group, the Socialists, who got five. The British Tory Syed Kamall, of the third group, the European Conservatives and Reformists, had been allotted four and a half minutes, and Philippe Lamberts, of the Greens, five. So with his seven minutes, his boss was 'within the norms', Guillaume said.

As far as I understood, Verhofstadt got seven whole minutes, despite being the leader of only the fourth group, the Liberals, because speaking time had been deducted from other Liberal speakers later in the debate.

The speech Verhofstadt was to give in the presence of Macron was important because he wanted to make an alliance with the French president and his – until then – very successful movement En Marche, to create a new, bigger and stronger group in the Parliament, after the European elections of May 2019. It wasn't certain that he was going to succeed, because Macron was also courted by other groups. He was Europe's new hero after all, who had turned the tide after Brexit, stopping a possible Frexit by defeating with a pro-European agenda the extreme right, nationalist and populist Marine Le Pen at the French presidential elections.

For once, the European Parliament plenary was filled to the brim – with MEPs and with the public. Even the cleaning ladies came to take pictures, although they were quickly chased out again – not even the presence of my camera filming the scene could prevent that.

Macron got many rounds of applause during his speech, but the highlight was undoubtedly when he said:

In this world and in this difficult moment, I believe deeply that European democracy represents our best hope. The very worst of mistakes would be to give up our model – I'll even dare to call it our identity. Faced with the authoritarianism that surrounds us, the answer is not authoritarian democracy but the authority of democracy. A Parliament like yours, ours, indeed, is a European miracle; to gather the elected representatives of the peoples of Europe to deliberate together in peace, despite all the powerful and weighty differences of their histories and what has sometimes divided them, is a unique model for the world. I belong to a generation which has never experienced war, and I belong to a generation which is allowing itself the luxury of forgetting what its forebears lived through. But I do not want to belong to a generation of sleepwalkers, I want to belong to a generation which has decided, with determination, to defend its democracy, this European sovereignty, because it is something we fought for, because it is the foundation which will allow generations to come to choose what sort of future they want for themselves.

Verhofstadt, who wanted to make an impression on Macron, used an old rhetorical trick to create, in the midst of a thousand onlookers, his own private moment with the French president. 'I have one thing I want to say to you in this debate. It is to encourage you to persevere. To persevere because, and I must say this to you, conservative forces in Europe are still strong. There are too many people who say, "Let's keep the status quo, we don't need to do anything, keeping power is more important than using it." And I should also say to you, just between the two of us, that my sense is that compared to Europe's conservatives, even the SNCF is a great bastion of reformers.' The French national rail company SNCF was mired in strikes over the government's plans for reforming employment conditions, and Verhofstadt got a smile from Macron, and laughter from the hall. He concluded, 'Don't hesitate. Don't abdicate your responsibilities. [When elections come] in 2019 there will be many of us to support you. To paraphrase [the French revolutionary leader] Danton, "Boldness, more boldness, always boldness and Europe [instead of Danton's *la Patrie*, the Fatherland] will be saved." Thank you.'

~

It was a rough descent, a week later, from the high clouds of European dreams, back to the Brexit marshlands, and a UK Home Office pres-entation at the European Parliament in Brussels – of a phone app, with which EU citizens who wanted settled status in the UK after Brexit would have to make their application (in the end it had remained an application, not a 'declaration' as Verhofstadt had hoped).

At the appointed hour, a British delegation of eight civil servants was ushered in, who did their very best to impress everyone with how simple the procedure was going to be. They'd brought a PowerPoint (they too), with moving images even. I wasn't allowed to film it though, and nor was anyone else allowed to take any pictures. Guy Verhofstadt – halfway through the presentation, spoke up: 'This is an in camera *meeting, so I'd like to ask no one to make pictures of the presentation. My mistake, I should have mentioned that beforehand.'*

The civil servants told their EU audience: 'We believe that this system will be genuinely easy to use for the vast majority of EU citizens in the UK. What we're very conscious of, is that there will always be a small percentage of people, however small, who will find it harder. And whether that is digital skills, access to documentation, language barriers, those are things we are working through at the moment, with specialist user groups. We're building a system here, where our default position is:

we want to grant status to EU citizens. We don't want to catch people out. If you pass a simple test, we want to say yes.'

There were, in fact, three tests they explained. 'First, important to us, we need to prove that this EU citizen is actually an EU citizen. What we don't want is people using fraudulent identities, from outside the EU. The second set of tests is about eligibility. And that's just about saying: were you resident here before the end of 2020, and how do we help you prove that, in order that we can grant you status.'

The final test, on criminality, they ranked as the most important. 'This is absolutely about making sure we are not granting status to serious criminals, or persistent criminals,' they insisted. 'This is not about minor criminality. Speeding fines, et cetera. This is really about making sure that people who have serious criminal records or are persistent criminals, we don't grant status to. We will ask a very simple question . . . in terms of a self-declaration: have they committed any serious crimes? If they answer yes, there will be more questions to determine what type of offence. We will check within the UK, and if someone declares they have been a criminal across the EU, we will also do a check against the EU member state databases.'

I have to admit that I had to smile when I heard this. Criminals declaring themselves, knowing that as a consequence they would be refused status in Britain. Sounded like a plan. And then I hadn't heard about the app yet, via which EU citizens would have to apply.

CLAUDE MORAES [Labour MEP]: 'You say iPhones are not included, and Android *only* is. This may sound like a trivial question, but the moment you start saying things like this . . .'

CIVIL SERVANT: 'Any device will do the application. The

only bit that Apple devices can't do, is the reading
of the biometric chip on the passport. And there's
nothing the Home Office can do [about that]; it's the
way Apple have designed their operating system. So
if someone wants to use an Apple device, they have
a choice: they can either borrow someone's Android
phone, just to do that one bit, no information is stored
on the device, so it's perfectly safe, or they can choose
to send us their passports.'

Right.

~

When Michel Barnier met the Brexit Steering Group the following week, he compared the Brexit negotiations to a submarine.
'You dive, you often find yourself in waters that are far from
clear,' he told them. 'You resurface for meetings of the European
Council and parliamentary resolutions, and then you dive again.'

His assessment of the current state of play was downbeat. 'At
the moment we are in a dive,' he said, 'and we can't see where
we are going very clearly.'

Guy Verhofstadt picked up with, 'Won't the periscope go
high enough?'

'Perhaps the waters are too deep,' Barnier responded. And
he warned the BSG about what he called the 'flight forward'
strategy of the UK. 'They will only talk about the future relationship,' he said, 'and keep trying to put arrangements for
their departure to one side.'

Still, for all his frustration, Barnier recognised the importance of the future relationship talks for the UK and he gave
an example to illustrate it. 'The other day I met the president
of BMW,' he explained:

And we discussed the consequences of the absence of a free-trade agreement. All the cars BMW make in Bavaria contain elements [parts] made in the United Kingdom – especially the engines. And the cars are exported from Bavaria to Japan, South Korea etc. in accordance with our trade agreements with those countries, and each of those agreements includes rules of origin thresholds for products [parts] coming from within the single market and from outside it. When the United Kingdom leaves the single market, all the cars will be affected, because the likelihood is that for every line of car they [BMW] will have to reduce the proportion of products [parts] coming from the United Kingdom.

There was no question, Barnier added, of renegotiating these trade deals because of Brexit, so 'BMW are preparing to screen all their production lines in case there is no trade deal.'

Despite the urgency of problems like that, the chief negotiator was determined not to back down on the sequencing strategy the EU had set out from the first, still insisting that real talks about the future relationship could only start once all the divorce issues, including Ireland, were settled. Because he still judged that to mix the two would lead to what he had warned about on many occasions: grand bargaining, trying to buy a future deal with debts from the past. 'To talk about the future relationship, the British proposed to open thirty-two tables of negotiation,' he said. 'There can be no question of that; not of negotiating [the future relationship], nor of thirty-two tables.'

An image popped up in my head, of a vast hangar with thirty-two tables where politicians and civil servants sit huddled over piles of documents. The pressure the negotiators were under had to be huge. We created such a complex world for ourselves – that they now had to map out in every detail and discuss with each other. If I learned one thing from filming behind the scenes of the Brexit negotiations, it is how daunting a task it is to govern our societies. The experience made me more respectful for those we charge with taking on that burden, but it also raised a difficult question, in the first place for myself: in the face of such complexity, how can one expect a general public not to prefer simple, reductive answers from their politicians, newspapers and TV-stations ? What if populism is just unavoidable, and a book like this, just a vain (in both senses) attempt at fighting the impossible?

Barnier's principled position on sequencing, the order of the negotiations, was a reminder of the deep clash of cultures at play in the Brexit negotiations, one that Guy Verhofstadt had referred to when talking to Sir Tim Barrow, and which reflected an even deeper difference in the histories of the two unions. The United Kingdom's political system, which has evolved over centuries, famously has no written constitution; it is governed by conventions which have proved useful and successful, and the habit of not writing things down is part of the British political DNA. The European Union, contrastingly, is based on rights and obligations precisely spelt out in a series of treaties over the past five decades – and has to be so because it involves an agreed pooling of sovereignty. Twenty-seven otherwise independent nations need to feel bound by them.

The Brexit negotiations were also a staring contest. While the EU kept explaining that their founding principles could not be flouted, the UK was negotiating as if there were no founding principles.

On 3 May 2018, the EU Commission president Jean-Claude Juncker urged Belgium to grant citizenship to the British EU staff – 500 people – worried about their post-Brexit status. That same day, in a speech in the European Parliament in

Brussels, Guy Verhofstadt touched upon another point of historical contrast between the UK and mainland Europe: a very different experience of the wars that had raged on the continent for centuries. As a former prime minister of Belgium this was something he was acutely sensitive about – and his message was the same as the one Macron had conveyed.

'For the Belgians, Flemish, [French-speaking] Walloons and citizens of Brussels, all mixed up together, being pro-European is our identity,' he said. 'It is not a matter of choice; it is an existential question. Our lands have for too long been the battlefield of Europe, squeezed as they are between Germany on one side and France on the other . . . [O]nly Europe can save us from the misery of the past – everything else is a lie.'

Verhofstadt's address involved him in one of his periodic spats with Nigel Farage.

The former UKIP leader – now working as a radio presenter – reacted with, 'There are two parts of Belgium, they speak different languages, they dislike each other intensely, there's no national TV station, there's no national newspaper, Belgium is not a nation.' To which Verhofstadt replied in a tweet: 'Today, Nigel Farage said Belgium is not a real country. He'll see how real Belgium is when we play England in the World Cup! But perhaps he's still exploring German citizenship and will be rooting for "die Mannschaft".'

That last jibe was a reference to an incident in 2016 when Britain's *Spectator* magazine and BuzzFeed both quoted a Facebook post that Farage was seen in a queue at the German embassy, standing alongside other people who were hoping to secure dual citizenship before Britain formally applied to leave the EU. Farage has been married to a German, Kirsten Mehr, since 1999, although they no longer live together. When telephoned and asked whether he was queuing to apply for German citizenship, Farage had replied, 'None of your business' and then hung up, BuzzFeed reported.

As to the World Cup, Belgium beat England both in their group match (1–0) and in the play-off for third place.

~

Meanwhile, local elections in London and English unitary authorities brought some relief to Theresa May. Despite the divisions within the government, the Conservatives lost only thirty-five seats, out of 1,365 they were defending. Labour increased their total by seventy-five, and UKIP was the biggest loser with 123 seats gone.

The *Daily Telegraph* reported:

THERESA MAY URGED TO PURSUE HARD BREXIT AFTER STRONGER THAN EXPECTED SHOWING IN LOCAL ELECTIONS

The Tories saw off Jeremy Corbyn's challenge . . . on what Mrs May described as a 'strong night' for the Conservatives . . . The fact that the Tories' best showing was in areas that had backed Leave showed that Brexit is both 'an issue and an opportunity', according to the former Conservative leader Iain Duncan Smith. He said: 'Leave voters have stayed with her and that's really important, but they also have a demand, and that is why messing around with these complicated models for Brexit is wrong. If we end up making massive compromises and if we keep caving in we are going to lose these people.'

The BBC's election guru, Professor Sir John Curtice of Strathclyde University, confirmed that Brexit remained a

vote-winner for the government: 'The Tories were performing relatively well in areas with a substantial Leave vote in
the 2016 referendum,' he noted, 'where they are picking up
votes from UKIP, which did not stand candidates in many
areas, while Labour were performing better in places where
the Remain vote was stronger and with a higher proportion of
younger voters.'

But the *Financial Times* concluded the outcome would not
alter the course of the Brexit negotiations. 'The overall consequence is that these results will entrench the main parties'
strategies,' it declared. 'Neither has done badly enough to
change course.' And the veteran political commentator Adam
Boulton in *The Times* judged that 'The UK remains politically
paralysed . . . Just as the prime minister's position stabilises,
her party's civil war is sapping her ability to exercise power.
Tory business managers are desperately trying to delay any
serious parliamentary votes on Brexit until after the summer
recess because they can't be sure of winning in the Commons.
Indeed, a growing number of MPs on all sides shake their heads
and say they cannot see any form of agreement that could command the support of a majority.'

By mid-May 2018, Michel Barnier's mood was growing more
and more sombre. He explained to the BSG that there was
another negotiating round due the following week – including
'many technical meetings' – and Barnier expressed the hope
that it would allow him to highlight more areas of that slide of
his in green. But he was wary. 'We are in a situation, to tell
the truth, where anything could happen. We can hold on to
the positive gains we made in March – 75 per cent of the draft
[withdrawal] treaty is now agreed in principle and there's no
question of going back on that.' But 'the remaining 25 per cent

is extremely difficult.' And he warned, 'If there is no progress in June, I think the risk of failure will become more serious.'

The Irish border backstop especially was turning into a very tricky issue, Barnier said: 'You know the situation. Theresa May agreed that the [withdrawal] agreement contains a backstop. But until today we haven't seen the British negotiators make any effort to translate what Mrs May consented to [in the December 2017 joint report] into operational, precise, practical proposals. We need concrete, practical, specific solutions now for the unique situation in Ireland.' According to Barnier, the UK negotiators had changed tack on the backstop. 'They try now to expand solutions for Northern Ireland to the whole of the British territories.' And he figured he knew why. 'You can see that the British have a strategy that consists in mixing up the issues at stake in Ireland with issues that have to do with the future relationship, through creative solutions that are not coherent, though, with the reality of the situation the United Kingdom will be in, that of a third country.' It was the first indication of the structure of the Irish backstop which would eventually emerge in the final withdrawal agreement; a UK-wide customs union that would minimise the need for the control of goods between Great Britain and Northern Ireland.

The British had two plans for this customs union, Barnier said. The first was something they called the New Customs Partnership. A second proposal 'they call Max Fac, Highly Streamlined Customs Arrangement. Neither proposal is operational and acceptable for us.'

In the New Customs Partnership the United Kingdom would collect tariffs on the EU's behalf – or, as Barnier put it, 'we [the EU] would agree to give the British a kind of public service delegation, so that they could exercise the Union's customs controls at their borders, even though they will no longer be a member of the single market.' Barnier reflected, 'We know this idea all too well, since it was included in the British proposals made in August last year,' and he damned the concept with the French expression *'une usine à gaz'* – a 'Heath Robinson machine' is probably the best English translation.

The Highly Streamlined Customs Arrangement would employ new technologies, including some that still had to be developed, and automation, to remove the need for physical customs checks – with the aim to create as frictionless a customs border as possible, rather than to remove it altogether.

He detected – to use another very English metaphor – an *Alice in Wonderland* character in the political debate about these two proposals in London. 'What strikes me,' he told the MEPs, 'is the political capital and energy currently being deployed in London' over ideas which the European Union would not entertain. 'What's more,' and here he added an extra element of complication, 'the British government itself knows these options could not be introduced before the end of the transition period, and so somewhere, behind these options, lies the idea of prolonging the transition. And that's why we are seeing a third idea appear; a temporary continuation [of staying] in the customs union.'

Guy Verhofstadt started laughing at this point.

Barnier then listed other ideas about the future relationship which worried him. 'They [the British] want to opt in to areas where they did not play a part even when they were a member state,' he said. 'I couldn't help smiling when I was reading their paper on internal security yesterday – although it's not really funny – because I reflected that it was written as if by a state that was in the process of joining the EU.' He itemised the programmes the UK wanted to be part of despite leaving the EU, including the European Arrest Warrant, Europol, databases which were only used by members of the Schengen free travel area, joint investigation teams and cooperation in prisoner transfers.

Barnier ended with a now-familiar warning about British tactics. The British team, he said, 'are still good diplomats' and were 'negotiating channels on all these subjects with many parliamentarians in many member states, and if people listen to them we'll find ourselves tied up in some thirty parallel negotiations'.

At that point, Elmar Brok's mobile started ringing loudly – a sign that it was time to wrap up. Walking back to his office, Guillaume McLaughlin said to me, 'C'était intéressant, hein?'

~

On 16 May 2018, Guy Verhofstadt received the new British home secretary, Sajid Javid, who had replaced Amber Rudd after she resigned in April in connection with the Windrush *deportation scandal. Verhofstadt was still pressing for more British concessions on the status of EU citizens in Britain after Brexit. But the more attractive footage I captured that day came from before and after his meeting with the new home secretary.*

Before the meeting, when Markus Winkler, the deputy secretary-general of the European Parliament, arrived with his assistant François Javelle in tow, Guy Verhofstadt said he had a toy for them. It was a stress ball, in the shape of a Donald Trump head. I'd brought the toy myself that morning, not for Verhofstadt, but as a gift for Edel Crosse, who surely deserved a present – I'd caused her quite a lot of extra work and worry for more than a year now. But somehow the Trump head stress ball had ended up on Verhofstadt's desk, and he now showed off with it.

CROSSE: But it's my toy, it's my toy . . . It's a stress ball.
Don't throw it.

WINKLER: That's a cool one.

CROSSE: It's good, isn't it?

WINKLER: We can do one with . . .

CROSSE: Tajani [the president of the European
Parliament].

WINKLER: For the administration we can do one with
Klaus Welle [Winkler's boss].

François Javelle pointed out that I was recording all this.

WINKLER [laughing]: Please erase this. This ends my
career. We can do a Guy Verhofstadt one.

VERHOFSTADT: There [probably] is already one. But they
never showed me.

*The other moment came after the meeting, when Guillaume McLaughlin
was sitting on Verhofstadt's sofa with Markus Winkler, and together they
were trying to figure out what was awaiting them in the months ahead.
Winkler said: 'I met this [Gavin] Barwell, the chief of staff of Theresa
May, three weeks ago. And he is quite interesting. This guy was testing
how much room on the timeline they have. How far they can move it
in the later autumn.'*

*And Winkler continued: 'And yesterday I had a conversation with
Selmayr [Martin Selmayr, the secretary-general of the European
Commission] and he said Barnier was trying to accelerate everything
because in his personal timeframe he would have wanted to have a
deal in September.' Barnier's timeframe, he explained, was dictated by
his desire to be the main candidate for the presidency of the European
Commission – the so-called Spitzen-candidate for his political
family, the Christian Democrats. But Winkler reported that 'Juncker*

[Jean-Claude Juncker] and Selmayr, they are much cooler, and they say: we have to bring it [Brexit] to an end, to a solid result, and if this is November, it's November, yeah.'

So even the inscrutable Michel Barnier was human, after all – a man of ideas also has personal ambitions.

Two days later Guy Verhofstadt tweeted from Rwanda, where he had gone to commemorate the genocide: 'At the beginning of my career, I was very much a nerd of figures. The atrocities of 1994 made clear to me that the core of politics is not the numbers, but the ethical issues, the questions of identity, of multiculturalism, of peaceful coexistence with one another.'

That too was human, courageous even – admitting to have been wrong in the past. And I saw more of Verhofstadt's human side soon after, on the day Erik Janda, his personal assistant for many years, retired.

I wanted to capture Erik's last day at work on camera, and so at six thirty in the morning I stood waiting for him on the shore of the River Ill, which runs through the city, outside the campervan he always slept in when he came to Strasbourg. EU workers receive money to cover their stay in Strasbourg when the European Parliament moves there every month, and while most people book hotels or rent a room or a flat, Janda chose to make savings and slept in a camper. He used a parking space very near the Parliament, which also made it easier for him to get to work early in the morning – to go and buy his boss a croissant at the Parliament canteen, and make him an espresso ready for his arrival.

Erik closed the back door of his camper, walked to the Parliament, passed security checks, bought his boss's croissant, took the elevator to the sixth floor, unlocked their offices, warmed up the coffee machine, and washed some cups that had been left dirty the day before. Then together we waited for his boss to arrive.

Meanwhile, Erik's wife Marleen called him.

In a soft voice, Erik told her how the previous evening he'd been busy at his desk with his retirement dossier, when Verhofstadt came to sit with him. Erik said, 'For the first time ever I saw his eyes get wet, for the very first time, just inside his eyes, you know how that looks. And he didn't say a word, it was a very weird moment, he just sat there, quietly staring at me. One minute, two minutes, that's long, eh? And I looked at him, and I kept looking.'

Then a message came in from the garage downstairs, sent by Verhofstadt's driver, Gaetan, that Verhofstadt had arrived. Erik finished his call and made coffee – and I filmed how he served it, together with the croissant he had fetched earlier.

It wasn't the first time I'd filmed Verhofstadt having breakfast at his desk, so he asked, 'Why are you filming this, again, now?'

And I replied: 'Because that's the very last croissant Erik will ever buy for you.'

Verhofstadt stopped chewing, gaped at me, and, lost for words, grinned sheepishly. Then – while behind him Erik was coming into his office to check whether his boss needed anything else – he said, 'In two weeks' time we will be travelling to the House of Commons in London, eh?'

Verhofstadt and personal emotions – not a simple thing.

~

On 24 May, Michel Barnier gave another briefing to the Brexit Steering Group in Brussels – and he was once again irritated by the blame game he said the UK was playing. As one of his assistants explained – paraphrasing the British on the subject of post-Brexit security collaboration, 'If the EU does not give us the cooperation [we want] there will be a big consequence and responsibility on the EU side for any potential atrocities that might happen.'

Barnier was determined to avoid 'this British spinning, as if *we* have to deal with the consequences of *their* decision to leave'.

Not for the first time he insisted, 'We are not going to change the way the EU works just because the British are off. It is not about punishment,' he said, 'or revenge. It is simply a matter of calmly explaining the consequences of Brexit, and you will see these consequences spread through every sector.'

He was also piqued by comments he had read from David Davis. In a formal government response to a report by the Commons' Foreign Affairs Select Committee about the implications of a no-deal Brexit, the Brexit secretary had written:

> We have made further significant progress in recent weeks, reaching agreement on the majority of the Withdrawal Agreement issues and on the time-limited implementation period. Recognising this, the European Council has confirmed that we are able to move on to discussions on the future relationship between the UK and the EU. In the light of these milestones, I am increasingly confident that we will secure a positive and mutually beneficial deal with the EU, and that the prospect of a 'no deal' outcome in March 2019 has receded significantly.

Barnier dismissed this as 'wishful thinking', declaring they were 'nowhere' on the issue of how the withdrawal agreement would be policed, and 'not very far on Ireland'. He said this optimistic gloss reflected the political pressures on Theresa May, but vowed, despite his annoyance, 'to make use of this lever' in the hope of achieving progress. 'I think the week of 4 June will be decisive,' he said. 'Because the British are convinced of the importance of the European Council next month, and, as ever, they want to show there's been progress.'

Roberto Gualtieri asked 'what level of progress' he expected before the Council meeting. 'If we can move from 75 per cent to 85 per cent in the draft treaty being "greened",' Barnier said, 'that will be a result.'

On 3 June, the *Sunday Times* claimed that officials in Davis's Brexit department and the departments of health and transport had drawn up a secret report with scenarios for a no-deal Brexit – a mild one, a severe one, and one dubbed 'Armageddon'. The newspaper wrote that the scenarios predicted 'Britain would be hit with shortages of medicine, fuel and food within a fortnight if the UK tries to leave the European Union without a deal'. The newspaper also cited a source saying, 'In the second scenario, not even the worst, the port of Dover will collapse on day one.' *The Independent* quoted another (or perhaps the same) source saying, 'The supermarkets in Cornwall and Scotland will run out of food within a couple of days, and hospitals will run out of medicines within two weeks.' And it wrote that 'The source added that the RAF would have to be used to transport emergency medicine to the far corners of the UK and warned that the country would also quickly run out of petrol.'

These alarming quotes were dismissed by the new home secretary, Sajid Javid, who told the BBC's *Andrew Marr Show*, 'I have to say I don't recognise any bit of that at all, and as home secretary, I am deeply involved in "no deal preparations" as much as I am in getting a deal – I'm confident we will get a deal. From the work that I have seen and the analysis that has been done, those outcomes . . . I don't think any of them would come to pass.'

But in the weeks and months ahead, more and more alarming reports would start surfacing, about the cost and dangers of a no-deal, or even just a bad-deal Brexit. In a statement after a Downing Street meeting, a group of business leaders, including representatives of BP, BMW, Nestlé and Vodafone, said that a trade deal with the EU had to be as 'frictionless as with a customs union', and they warned the prime minister they might cut investment without more clarity over the terms of Britain's EU exit. They told May, 'Time is running out.'

The move Theresa May eventually made on 7 June 2018 set in train the sequence of events that would eventually drive her out of Downing Street.

The United Kingdom officially proposed a new version of the Irish backstop which went beyond the principles the two sides had agreed in the December 2017 joint report. It envisaged that, in the event that there was no trade agreement which removed the need for a hard border on the island of Ireland, the arrangements originally envisaged for Northern Ireland should be extended to the United Kingdom as a whole. This new plan would mean the United Kingdom as a whole would effectively remain in the customs union and part of the single market if the backstop was triggered.

The EU had known for a while what was cooking, so May's move didn't come as a surprise.

To complicate matters, however, the proposal also included a time limit on the backstop, which had been included at the insistence of David Davis; the proposal stated that the backstop was 'expected' to run out by the end of 2021. *Politico* reported 'a tortuous twenty-four hours of back and forth' between May and Davis. 'Theresa May emerged Thursday lunchtime with an Irish "backstop" plan for Brussels that Downing Street hopes will form the beginning of a breakthrough in the Brexit talks,' according to the website's account. 'And she got there without any Cabinet resignations. Yet.'

Guy Verhofstadt immediately made his team prepare a tweet that questioned both May's proposal as such, and the David

Davis time limit. 'Difficult to see how UK proposal on customs aspects of IE/NI [the Republic of Ireland and Northern Ireland] backstop will deliver a workable solution to avoid a hard border & respect integrity of the SM/CU [single market/customs union],' it began, following that up with a sentence that went to the heart of the dispute: 'A backstop that is temporary is not a backstop, unless the definitive arrangement is the same as the backstop.'

Barnier was – as ever – more diplomatic on his Twitter account: 'I welcome publication of #UK proposal on customs aspects of IE/NI backstop. We will examine it with 3 questions: is it a workable solution to avoid a hard border? Does it respect the integrity of the SM/CU? Is it an all-weather backstop?'

'No, it wasn't' was the answer of Leo Varadkar, the Irish prime minister, to that last question. 'The principle that's in the existing Irish protocol, the existing backstop which is supported by 27 EU member states including Ireland, is that it applies at least until there's an alternative in place, until there's a new relationship between the EU and UK that prevents a hard border. It's not something that can be just time limited by date. It has to be what they say: "All weather".'

One of the sharpest comments on this development came from Jonathan Powell, who served as Tony Blair's chief of staff throughout his time in Downing Street and was one of the architects of the Good Friday Agreement. In a *Financial Times* column he wrote:

Thursday June 7 2018 may go down in history as the day hard Brexit died. It has tripped over the conundrum of the Northern Ireland border, as it was always going to do. The only reason there isn't more noise is that the Brexiters do not realise it yet. There was only ever one possible answer to avoiding a hard border, and that is either Northern Ireland or the UK as a whole staying in the customs union and the single market for goods. Finally, the British government has accepted the inevitable in its 'backstop' proposal: the UK will stay in the customs union, although it will be called something else, and we will have to negotiate regulatory alignment by remaining in the single market for industrial and agricultural goods.

May's proposal meant that the future relationship – which Michel Barnier still did not want to talk about until the divorce was settled – became part of the negotiations on the withdrawal agreement. Whether May intended this or not is an open question, but, as she was to discover, it carried a significant risk. Because the withdrawal agreement would be a legally binding treaty, anything it said on the UK's future relationship with the EU would be set in stone; there would be no room later for fudging what it said or interpreting it in different ways.

The day after May announced her new backstop plan, BuzzFeed released a recording in which the foreign secretary Boris Johnson criticised his own government's Brexit talks strategy, saying it lacked 'guts', and suggested Donald Trump could do a better job.

Johnson – speaking to around twenty people in a private room after an Institute of Directors reception – warned that the UK could remain 'locked in orbit around the EU' and claimed the Irish border issue had been allowed to dictate 'the whole of our agenda. It's so small and there are so few firms that actually use that border regularly, it's just beyond belief that we're allowing the tail to wag the dog in this way,' he said.

'I will be prepared to compromise over time, but I will not

compromise over the destination,' the foreign secretary told his audience. 'The Remainers in government are so worried about the potential for short-term disruption after Brexit that they're blind to the long-term benefits. What they don't want is friction at the borders. They don't want any disruption of the economy. So they're sacrificing all the medium- and long-term gains out of fear of short-term disruption. Do you see what I'm saying? The fear of short-term disruption has become so huge in people's minds that they've turned into a quivering wreck.'

It was a harbinger of a very rough passage indeed for the May government; the foreign secretary's reservations would soon take him out of government and set him on the course that would see him competing to replace her just short of a year later.

13

IF THEY DON'T KILL EACH OTHER AT CHEQUERS

Mid-June–mid-July 2018

Early in 2018 the Tory MP Andrea Jenkyns revealed that her son had been nicknamed 'Brexit' because he had been born on the day Article 50 was triggered. She and the child's father, her fellow Tory MP Jack Lopresti, are both committed Brexiteers, and Jenkyns was to become one of the most outspoken opponents of Theresa May's withdrawal agreement. As a member of Hilary Benn's Exiting the European Union Committee, she was able to interrogate Guy Verhofstadt when he appeared before the group at Westminster in mid-June.

'Regarding the 38 billion divorce settlement from the EU, when is the EU expecting to receive the 38 billion?' she enquired. Verhofstadt answered that the EU expected the money at the time of Britain's departure from the Union. But 'if this is truly a two-way negotiation, what is the EU prepared to give up for the UK?' came Jenkyns's follow-up.

Verhofstadt explained that the EU view of the negotiations was rather different. 'It's not a classical negotiation, like between two political parties for example, sitting around the table to make a government and to give in on their principles,' he said. 'It's a country leaving the Union. We have to do [this in] the rules-based way described in the [Lisbon] treaty . . . We will never accept a trade-off, for example, between "Oh, we are going to give you a good cooperation from the British side on internal security and external security, if you give us a good deal on trade and economics." We will not accept that, this is not a classical, political trade-off, dealing and wheeling between political parties . . .' The exchange underlined another fundamental difference of approach which had marked every phase of the negotiations; the EU believed the United Kingdom should settle the so-called 'divorce' issues as an obligation, rather than using them as negotiating tools.

Verhofstadt had flown into London from Vienna, via Heathrow, and in the cab on his way to the city centre, his phone rang. It was his mother of ninety-three. 'Yes, hello. What are you saying? I'm in England, in London. I just arrived here from Vienna, in Austria, and now I'm in London. That's my job, eh?' His mother called to check on her son's teeth. She'd heard from her granddaughter Charlotte that there was a problem. 'It was an infection in my tooth, but it's solved now,' her son explained. 'Yes, I'm still taking antibiotics. No, it doesn't hurt. They cleaned everything up, I went to see a specialist. OK, dada, joehoe, ciao.' Verhofstadt laughed, went on to discuss a strange block of houses we passed along Talgarth Road, a row of eight Arts and Crafts-era studios – which took us both some digging on our mobiles to find out about – and then he turned back to the dossier Guillaume McLaughlin had made for him, in preparation for his parliamentary committee hearings.

In the Grimond Room at Portcullis House, Verhofstadt faced a cannonade of hostile questions from two committees, the

Exiting the European Union Committee, and the Home Affairs Committee. The Barnier-inspired metaphor of submarines lost in murky water and unable to communicate seemed more apposite than ever. 'Isn't the problem here that your idea of compromise is to put something on the table that falls far short of what could be possible?' accused the former Conservative Cabinet minister Stephen Crabb. 'When you're talking about compromise all we see on this side, from the UK perspective, is just this very hard application of cold logic about what it means for Britain to be a third country.' Verhofstadt suggested in response that 'maybe if you're a little bit flexible on your red lines it could also be a little bit easier, don't you think so?'

'There are things that are possible and things that are not possible,' he explained in response to another challenge, citing as an example the debate over the system of European Arrest Warrants, which Britain wanted to remain part of after Brexit. 'It's of course impossible for the UK to stay in the European Arrest Warrant, because it is the arrest warrant of the EU,' he said. 'But what we can do . . . is make an extradition agreement where . . . we try to go as far as possible to have the flexibility that is in the European Arrest Warrant.' For much of the time it seemed he and his interrogators were talking past each other rather than to each other. 'The problem is not the EU,' he told the Labour MP Stephen Kinnock. 'The problem is how you marry the red lines of the UK with what Michel Barnier is always calling . . . the ecosystem of the EU, the rules-based system of the Union.'

Afterwards Verhofstadt complained to me that he had felt tired and found the hearings trying. He wasn't completely satisfied with his performance and wished he'd been sharper. But the visit did at least give him the opportunity to lay out once more the logic of (and his

*enthusiasm for) an association agreement. He warned that a whole series
of separate agreements between the United Kingdom and the European
Union — 'one on trade, one on internal security, one on external security, one on Euratom, one on this, one on that' — would create what he
called a 'Swiss situation, in which tens and tens of different agreements'
would need ratifying at national and European levels, leading to 'the
nightmare of a ratification period in the EU that will last years, if
not decades'.*

The confrontational tone of much of the questioning Verhofstadt faced reflected the way the political temperature at
Westminster had risen. Mrs May's latest device for clearing
a path through the Brexit thickets was a White Paper setting
out the government's ambitions for a future relationship with
the EU, but even the date of its publication proved a hot political issue.

The White Paper had first been promised back in mid-May,
and the government's stated ambition was to bring it out in
advance of the next meeting of the European Council at the
end of June. They promised a 'detailed, ambitious and precise'
explanation of their hopes for a final agreement on the future
relationship, and David Davis talked up the aspirations for the
document; he identified it as the 'most significant' government
offering since the 2016 referendum, and claimed, 'It will communicate our ambition for the UK's future relationship with
the EU, in the context of our vision for the UK's future role
in the world.'

But in the second week of June, while attending the G7
summit of industrialised nations in Quebec, Mrs May told
reporters that she had decided to delay publication of the paper.
'I'll be going to the June European Council, where we'll be
talking about finalising the withdrawal agreement, but also

pressing on the future relationship,' she said. 'After that, I'll be bringing my ministers together for an away-day at Chequers to finalise the White Paper we're going to be publishing.'

The Irish prime minister Leo Varadkar described the delay as 'disappointing but not entirely surprising'. Mrs May was caught between two political imperatives; because of that ticking clock there was huge pressure building at Westminster to move the Brexit process forward, but she also knew that laying anything out in detail carried great political risk.

On 26 June, Michel Barnier gave the Brexit Steering Group his analysis of British thinking at this delicate stage, and his interpretation of the new British proposal for a backstop to avoid a hard border in Ireland. He identified a 'double tactic'. The first he called an 'isolation process' – what he had earlier described as 'cornerisation' – by which 'all the other issues would be sorted out, while the Irish question would be left open until the last moment, in the hope that the twenty-seven heads of state and government would not jeopardise an orderly withdrawal for the sake of Ireland'. The second he character-ised as the 'instrumentalisation' – weaponisation might be a better translation – of the backstop proposal to give the whole of the United Kingdom access to the customs union and part of the single market.

Barnier allowed himself to speculate on the likely contents of the White Paper, prefacing his remarks with the observation that 'in the war cabinet' – here he smiled – 'meaning of course Mrs May's Cabinet' there were 'many conflicting trends'. He identified two, and considered them both to be 'extremely destructive for what we [the EU] have done together for the past sixty years'.

Barnier judged that David Davis, 'whom I saw last Monday for half an hour, for the first time in three months,' favoured

' a sort of mini-Union, between the EU . . . and the UK, as if we were on an equal footing, between two blocks, more or less equal', with some kind of third-party ombudsman to police the relationship and resolve any disputes between the two sides. The problem with this – from Michel Barnier's perspective – lay in the fact that 'if we are on an equal footing, whenever we want to change something, we'll have to ask their permission'.

The second model – which Barnier said Theresa May championed – involved Britain effectively remaining part of the single market, but for goods alone. The risk there, he argued, was posed by the fact that a significant element in the value of most goods – Barnier put the figure at between 20 and 40 per cent – is based on services or research, so allowing Britain freedom to regulate its service sector, for instance, would give it a competitive advantage in the market for goods – Barnier called this 'an open door for regulatory dumping'.

And he suggested that the British would try to exploit the Irish backstop to achieve that objective. So – in a truly *Through the Looking Glass* twist – Barnier's worries about the backstop in the summer of 2018 precisely mirrored those of Eurosceptic Tory MPs six months later: both believed it could be used as a mechanism for determining the broader relationship between the EU and the United Kingdom.

The chief negotiator also reported an episode which eloquently evoked the culture clash between his cerebral style and the more rambunctious world of Westminster politics. He described, in shocked tones, 'a truly astonishing meeting with the secretary of state for Northern Ireland, Karen Bradley'. He was convinced she had 'come just to be able to say she had come', because she had brought only 'slogans', declaring, 'We cannot accept a solution which divides the United Kingdom.' Barnier relayed his reply: 'Madame, we no longer have time for slogans. We are not having a debate; we are in the process of constructing a treaty . . . this is about finding solutions to the problems you have created with Brexit – no more and no less.'

Barnier allowed himself a smile when Verhofstadt informed him that David Davis had told him he would be 'making a tour of capitals with the White Paper during the holidays, and he complained that he would have to use his holidays for a European tour'.

Barnier: 'It's normal, I'm going to do the same thing, but I'm not going to complain about it.'

But Barnier wrapped up the meeting on a serious, even sombre note: 'What will allow us to finalise things in the autumn – at least this is my view – is the certain risk of "no-deal". "No-deal" would be a really serious problem for the British economy, and for British politics. I believe, indeed I know, that Mrs May doesn't want to take that risk. And let me remind you, my dear friends, that no-deal means no transition. It is the cliff edge in March.'

~

One week later, the European Parliament moved to Strasbourg again, where the summer had started, and girls and women in short skirts, and boys and men in short trousers, leisurely flocked in parks, near fountains, on terraces and along the River Ill. Some of them also came queuing for a tour of the Parliament, and their excited shrieks were audible from the courtyard below, while Verhofstadt and his team prepared for his last press conference before the holiday break.

'OK, *allez*, let's start this bloody shit!' was Guy Verhofstadt's opening salvo on that Monday 2 July. 'Is it necessary to say something about Brexit?' he wondered. Mrs May's away-day at Chequers – at which she planned to unveil her White Paper to her Cabinet – was planned for Friday, and that provided a convenient escape from the subject. 'You could also say, on Brexit, I will not continue on Brexit, because we're expecting the White Paper of the British government on 7 July,' Verhofstadt suggested. 'If there are still ministers then. If they have not killed each other in Chequers.' The divisions between Mrs May and her Brexit secretary David Davis – and indeed within the British Cabinet more broadly – were now an open secret. Michel Barnier had identified one fundamental difference over strategy, but almost every aspect of the Brexit process was now being fought over, and ministers were finding it increasingly difficult to maintain the fragile unity of the past few months.

The possibility of ministers killing each other at Chequers didn't seem exaggerated. '*Voilà*, that's nice,' commented Jeroen Reijnen, his head of communications. The group played with the wording for a while, with Verhofstadt insisting that they were painting an accurate picture of the infighting in London. 'You can do that, with a joke, no?' he suggested. 'Yeah, and it's also true, eh?' responded his foreign policy adviser Eva Palatova.

The main focus of Verhofstadt's attention that morning was not Brexit. It was Europe's own infighting, and more specifically the migration crisis – or rather, as he insisted it should more properly be called, a 'political crisis on the back of the migrants'.

The origins of the migration row that blew up towards the summer of 2018 went back to the huge wave of migrants who had arrived in Europe three years earlier. The numbers had dropped dramatically since then, but the political impact was still shaking the EU, fuelling support for political parties which Verhofstadt viewed as dangerous populists. On 1 June, Matteo Salvini, the leader of the right-wing *Lega* or

League, a successor to the regional party previously known as the Northern League, was sworn in as interior minister in Italy's new coalition government, and immediately set about introducing radical policies to curb immigration. Italy was of course the natural point of arrival for migrants crossing the Mediterranean from North Africa, and the EU's failure to come up with an effective mechanism for sharing the migrant burden was widely resented among Italian voters.

On 11 June, Salvini prevented the rescue ship *Aquarius*, carrying 629 migrants who had been saved from the sea, from docking at any Italian port. He argued that 'France pushes people back at the border, Spain defends its frontier with weapons. From today, Italy is also starting to say no to human trafficking, no to the business of illegal immigration.' The ship and its human cargo were diverted to Spain. Subsequently another charity ship, *Lifeline*, was also refused entry to Italian ports. It was eventually able to dock in Malta after eight EU countries agreed to take the migrants on board.

Europe's leaders recognised that the migrant issue posed a grave threat to the European Union – one perhaps even more serious than Brexit. The German chancellor Angela Merkel warned, 'If we are unable to come up with a common response to the migration challenges the very foundations of the EU will be at stake. Action is really needed.'

Verhofstadt's tactic – and he was already looking ahead to the possibility that nationalist and populist parties would make big gains in the 2019 elections to the European Parliament – was to respond by pointing out that while Europe's right-wing parties might all agree on the principle that migration was a bad thing, in practice they seemed only to want to solve the problem in their own country, no matter what happened elsewhere, even in countries where their allies were in power. 'Salvini, who closed the port for a boat, didn't want the refugees for himself, but [has no problem with them] in other countries, Germany, Austria, Hungary. And Mr Orbán [the Hungarian prime minister] doesn't want them in Hungary, he wants them in Italy, Austria or Germany. And Mr Seehofer [Horst Seehofer, the leader of the Christian Social Union, a sister party of Mrs Merkel's Christian Democrat Union] doesn't want them in Germany, he wants that they go to Austria, Hungary or Italy.'

The only 'unanimity of our nationalists', Verhofstadt concluded, was 'not in my backyard'. But he was also critical towards the European Council and other European countries. 'Even in Spain, after one boat, the solidarity was over.'

Verhofstadt, who'd been sitting at first, almost hanging in his chair, annoyed and bored at the start of the meeting with his press team, ended up standing, rehearsing out loud the good lines he'd found – waving his hands as if addressing a stadium, and not just his staffers, Bram, Jeroen, Eva and Guillaume.

It was time and again amazing to see how quickly he could get worked up by his ideas, dreams and frustrations. This time the topic was migration, but his vexation went far deeper. A month earlier he'd addressed the plenary in Strasbourg in a scathing tirade, saying, 'For me, the next European Council can talk and talk and talk, and discuss and write conclusions on whatever item you want: Brexit, the reform of the Eurozone, the defence union, the emerging new world order . . . you name it . . . but there is one item, one crisis on which I urge you not just to talk, but to act now. And that is the ongoing migration and refugee crisis, especially in and around the Mediterranean Sea.'

'It's a disgrace what is happening there,' he declared:

A scandal, for years now. Again, again and again . . . Since 2014, since the start of this [parliamentary] mandate, almost 10,000 men, women and children drowned in the Mediterranean. It has become the largest graveyard of Europe. I will not point my finger to any individual country . . . No, I am pointing the finger to all of them, to all member states, assembled in this so-called European Council. The tragedy in the Mediterranean is their fault, their collective responsibility . . . Member states still refuse to give to Europe full responsibility to protect our external borders. Better, we outsourced it all to Erdoğan [the president of Turkey] and now even to criminal gangs terrorising Libya. When will the European Council really take responsibility? When? Was that not why on earth we created the European Council, as an official institution of the European Union, to take responsibility, to steer the Union?

And Verhofstadt had recalled the photograph of a dead three-year-old lying on a Turkish beach which had caught the world's imagination during the 2015 refugee crisis. 'For me, dear colleagues, the picture of the year will not be the image of our six European leaders humouring Mr Trump who sits on his chair, arms crossed. No, the picture of the year will be another little Aylan [as in 2015]. And if you, the Council, is not able to prevent this, well then you should resign. Collectively!'

What Verhofstadt hated most about Brexit was that it was draining energy and attention away from other, more important, reforms that Europe needed. But Brexit was not over yet.

Far from it.

~

'Cabinet ministers' phones are routinely locked away when they arrive at Downing Street for weekly Cabinet meetings, to prevent the potential for espionage by hostile states,' *The Guardian*'s website reported on 6 July 2018, but 'As ministers gathered at Chequers at the end of a heated summer week of leaked letters, biting texts and secret huddles in the Foreign Office, the policy had another use: to prevent the potential for yet more Brexit hostilities.'

The ground for Theresa May's away-day at the prime minister's official country residence was prepared with almost theatrical care. The *Daily Telegraph* reported a Downing Street warning to Eurosceptic members of the Cabinet; one of those anonymous 'sources' briefed that 'A select number of ego-driven, leadership-dominated Cabinet ministers need to support the PM in the best interests of the UK – or their spots will be taken by a talented new generation of MPs who will sweep them away . . . it is a cold world outside government.' The chief whip, Julian Smith, met several junior ministers on the eve of the gathering to discuss their ambitions, lending credibility to the threat of a reshuffle.

And just to ram the point home, it was made clear that any minister who did resign would immediately lose access to the usual ministerial perks. 'The most Machiavellian tactic employed by Downing Street was a tip-off to the Politico website that business cards for a taxi firm called Aston's had been left in the foyer of Chequers for any minister who decided 'they can't face making the right decision for the country', the *Telegraph* reported. 'Number 10 was making the point that ministerial cars would be immediately forfeited by anyone who quit, meaning they would need a taxi for the 40-mile trip back to London.' The paper added that 'inquiries by the *Daily Telegraph* revealed that Aston's is no longer trading, suggesting that Downing Street had either got its facts wrong or, even more darkly, that it gives ministers a number for a non-existent taxi firm to make them think again if they try to quit'.

Ministers were instructed to attend wearing business attire

despite the July heat, and they were warned it was going to be a long day. Liz Truss, the chief secretary to the Treasury, tweeted a picture of a slice of pizza she had eaten by way of 'fortification' before the 9.30 a.m. start.

The first order of business was a briefing from Olly Robbins, Mrs May's chief negotiator, on the current EU position. The main action of the day, a discussion of Mrs May's plans for the United Kingdom's future relationship with the EU, began at 2.00 p.m. after a buffet lunch. And in the end, the *purdah*, with phones kept under lock and key, did not take too long. By early evening, everyone had, it seemed, signed up to the thrust of the White Paper.

'Mrs May briefed the media at 6.45 p.m. on Friday that the cabinet had agreed a collective position to create a "UK–EU free-trade area which establishes a common rulebook for industrial goods and agricultural products",' the *Financial Times* reported – a participation in the EU single market, but not in all the four areas it covered: goods, services, finances and the free movement of people (the EU single market's four freedoms). 'The plan would see Britain commit in a treaty to adopt new EU rules for goods – an approach viewed by some Tories as leaving the UK as "a vassal state",' the *FT* wrote. 'Parliament could break the treaty, but trigger severe market reprisals from the EU if it did. Mrs May also announced "a business-friendly customs model" intended to help secure an open Irish border while also allowing Britain to strike its own trade deals around the world.'

The *Daily Telegraph*'s headline read, 'Cabinet signs up to May's Brexit deal – Ministers agree plan to keep close ties with EU after day locked away at Chequers', and it described the outcome as 'a significant victory for Remainers in the Cabinet, as it keeps Britain closely aligned with the EU Customs Union and Single Market and is largely the "soft" Brexit they sought'. May had called her plan, which built further on the new UK-wide backstop proposal she had launched a month earlier, 'broader in scope than any other that exists between the EU and a third country'. But underneath this ambition lurked a huge political risk – to be seen by harder Brexiteers to keep the UK 'locked in an orbit around the EU', as Boris Johnson had said. The *Daily Telegraph* reported that 'there were no resignations from Leave-supporting ministers, but some Eurosceptic Tory MPs viewed the deal as a "total betrayal" by both the prime minister and the Cabinet'.

The outbreak of unity lasted for the weekend. *The Guardian* gave the Chequers Agreement – as it quickly became known – a fighting chance of success. A headline in the comment pages read, 'May's Chequers victory averts disaster – for now at least – PM seems to have reached a very saleable political stance without bloodshed, but it is not yet a done deal', and the columnist Martin Kettle judged that 'May's victory was impressive'. In a reference to England's football manager, who was bringing the English team rare and welcome success in the World Cup, he added, 'She seems to have taken a leaf out of the Gareth Southgate playbook by insisting on "owning the process" at the cabinet awayday.'

The Guardian's Sunday sister paper, *The Observer*, did, however, include an ominous warning for Mrs May in its report: 'The Tory MP and leader of the European Research Group (ERG) of hard-line Brexiters, Jacob Rees-Mogg, questioned whether signing up to elements of the EU rulebook would amount to Brexit at all. He warned that abiding by a common rule book could make "trade deals almost impossible", adding that "it is possible that this deal is worse" than a "no-deal" Brexit.'

Andrea Jenkyns, the Brexiteer backbencher who had been one of Guy Verhofstadt's most challenging inquisitors during his London trip the previous month, was also promising trouble, saying, 'The danger is that British business would "continue to be a rule-taker from the EU".' *The Observer* reported that 'Jenkyns indicated she would back a leadership challenge against May if she concluded that the plans agreed by the prime minister amounted to a watering down of Brexit.'

Government unity ended with David Davis's resignation late on Sunday night. There had been repeated rumours that he was on the brink of standing down for much of his time in the Brexit secretary job, and in his resignation letter to the prime minister he confirmed that they were true. 'As you know there have been a significant number of occasions in the last year or so on which I have disagreed with the Number 10 policy line,' he wrote. 'At each stage I have accepted collective responsibility because it is part of my task to find workable compromises, and because I considered it was still possible to deliver on the mandate of the referendum, and on our manifesto commitment to leave the customs union and the single market.' But the Chequers plan, he argued, 'is making that look less and less likely', and he warned that 'in my view the inevitable consequence of the proposed policies will be to make the supposed control by Parliament illusory rather than real'.

David Davis's departure introduced, or at least accelerated, another dynamic in this already tortuously complicated process. The real possibility of a leadership contest to replace Theresa May had – as Andrea Jenkyns's comments suggested – been hanging over Tory politics ever since the 2017 general election. Chequers would clearly be seen as one of those moments that define a candidate, and Boris Johnson concluded that if David Davis was standing down over the Chequers Agreement, he would have to do the same. So on the afternoon of Monday 9 July, the foreign secretary gave his own resignation letter to the media – contrary to the convention that No. 10 releases ministerial letters of this kind once the prime minister has received them.

Johnson's letter echoed the comments he had been secretly recorded making the previous month. He claimed that the 'dream' created by the referendum result 'is dying, suffocated by needless self-doubt'. He warned that 'we are truly headed for the status of a colony', and described the state of negotiating play in the sort of colourful language familiar to readers of his columns in the *Daily Telegraph*. 'What is even more disturbing is that this is our opening bid,' he wrote. 'This is already how we see the end state for the UK – before the other side has made its counter-offer. It is as though we are sending our vanguard into battle with the white flags fluttering above them.' Steve Baker, a junior minister at the Department for Exiting the European Union, also resigned that day, bringing the ministerial casualty count since Chequers to three.

The White Paper agreed at Chequers was formally published on 12 July. The proposals for a new customs relationship with the European Union – now called 'a facilitated customs arrangement' – still involved the EU delegating the collection of tariffs to the United Kingdom; even if that idea had, of course, been greeted with scepticism by EU negotiators nearly a year earlier and was categorically rejected by Michel Barnier when it came up again in the spring of 2018. Chequers further alienated Brexit hard-liners in London without offering a realistic path ahead to Brussels. But because the Chequers Agreement at least appeared to represent a more realistic approach by the British government, and because it had been bought at a significant political cost, Europe's negotiators and politicians were reluctant to weigh in too heavily against it.

The dilemma over how Europe should react to Chequers gave the Brexit Steering Group a happy morning at one of their favourite pastimes – drafting a reaction. The senior parliamentary civil servant Markus Winkler wanted something 'in the OK zone, in the positive form, saying this is progress, it's a first step, et cetera', arguing, 'If you compare this paper to a few months ago, you have to admit that they made a really bold step.' Verhofstadt asked him laughingly whether he was 'working for the British embassy'.

Roberto Gualtieri countered that while 'Politically it's a move in the right direction, on the substance there is still a lot of cherry picking, or fantasy things, that can never work, so you have to be balanced between these two things.' Verhofstadt suggested their text 'welcomes the statement and the White Paper of the UK government as contributions to the process', and then wondered, 'As contributions to the process? Or as useful contributions to the process?' Guillaume McLaughlin chipped in with, 'If we say useful, we'll be asked which bits are useful!'

After batting phrases back and forth for a while, the group were joined by Elmar Brok: 'I was two hours late with the plane, because the toilets were blocked,' he reported. He suggested, in his usual wise way, that their response to Chequers should be qualified as a 'first reaction', allowing them a little room for manoeuvre down the line.

At the end of the meeting Markus Winkler asked, 'Would it be useful if we also got a resignation of a BSG member, just as a reaction to the . . .?' To which Verhofstadt replied, 'I know somebody, I know somebody.' He left me guessing as to whom exactly he meant, but the group seemed to know. They all laughed.

Then everybody got up . . . only to sit back down again.

Because there was more to talk about. While the British political world was still consumed by the impact of the Davis and Johnson resignations, Europe's capitals had already begun to look at the rocks and squalls ahead. Guillaume McLaughlin was just back from a trip to Paris, and reported concerns in the French capital about the possibility

that the United Kingdom would want to extend the Article 50 nego-
tiating process beyond the departure date of 29 March 2019. The
French, he said, were worrying that 'if there was — as a hypothetical
[here he threw his arms in the air] — if there's a fall of the government
in October, November . . . and there's a new government, a new British
prime minister might have to be given more time to sort things out.'

MCLAUGHLIN: All the heads of state will let the new PM
   have a bit more time, to do that.
VERHOFSTADT: It's not an abnormal reaction, eh?
MCLAUGHLIN: Of course not, but if we have European
   elections [in May 2019] . . .

Here Marek Evison — Brok's assistant — chimed in.

MCLAUGHLIN: Two months later, you will have Brits
   in the Parliament again. Marek, the Brits will get
   seventy-five UKIP representatives elected, you
   will have twenty, thirty AFD elected in Germany,
   minimum, twenty, thirty Le Pen.

Guillaume was already predicting the way nationalist and populist parties
in Germany and in France, as well as the UK, would exploit problems in
the Brexit negotiations: 'Brussels, the Brussels bureaucrats have stopped
the people speaking. They wanted to leave, and they have been stopped
by Brussels . . . So we have to be really, really, really careful.'

VERHOFSTADT: You cannot imagine that we are giving
   six months more for Article 50, and that we are stuck
   for five years, with seventy-five Brits again.
MCLAUGHLIN: The political damage of elections 2019
   with the Brits still in . . .

EVISON: For us it's a disaster . . . Steve Bannon [Donald
Trump's former chief strategist] has organised
yesterday a meeting of the so-called Eurosceptics in
London, briefing them on Trump, and there was Le
Pen, obviously Farage, the alternative of Europe . . .

Later that day, 12 July 2018, Verhofstadt welcomed Sabine
Weyand back to the Brexit Steering Group with a dig about the
lack of progress in the negotiations. 'I thank Mrs Weyand [for
being] present for an update on the state of the negotiations' –
at this point Weyand began laughing – 'That will be very short.'
He welcomed the fact that the new British proposal was framed
in terms of his concept of an association agreement, but added,
to more laughter from Weyand, 'We shall have to see if they
have the same understanding of what an association agreement
is, naturally.'

Weyand was replacing Michel Barnier because the chief
negotiator was on official business in Washington. She began
by laying out the reasons the negotiating team had taken 'a
very low-key approach' in reaction to the Chequers proposals.
'We don't want to do a knee-jerk reaction. We don't want to
shoot from the hip. We have to recognise that there has been
a serious discussion in the UK, and we have to recognise that
the situation is febrile,' she told the group.

The strategy she offered was to combine public reticence
with private firmness: 'Let's not shoot this down, but we
should also be firm in the message of saying, "This can be the
start of a more constructive phase in the relationship, but it's
a start, this cannot be the landing zone."' And she appealed
to the members of the BSG for their support: 'The UK has
asked everyone, please don't shoot this down, and as I said, we
shouldn't, but at the same time, we should also make it clear

in private contacts with the UK, and we all have contacts with them, we should say: "We are ready to give this a shot, but be aware, this is the starting point of serious negotiations, and not the end point." I think that would be very useful.'

The short phrase 'the UK has asked everyone, please don't shoot this down' was and remains one of the most striking things I heard over the two years that I followed the Brexit Steering Group. It sounded so humiliating to me – to have to ask your opponent (and we're talking of people who consider themselves world powers, still) to be careful and gentle with your proposal. What a mess the UK had to be in. But I also like the humanity of it – the sense, revealed in that short sentence, that at both sides of the table sat people, human beings, fellow sufferers.

Weyand suggested two possible readings of the central Chequers proposal – which had been floated in the United Kingdom's June initiative for the Irish backstop – that the arrangements envisaged for Northern Ireland should be extended to the whole United Kingdom. The first was that 'they saw this as the only way to deliver on no border between Ireland and Northern Ireland.' This interpretation was based on a reading of the political arithmetic at Westminster, proposed because 'they couldn't, or this government felt that they can't, deliver on that [an open border] through a NI-specific solution, because they have the DUP but also the unionists within the Tory party, and so they have structured the future relationship to get to this point.'

The second, more Machiavellian, reading was the one Michel Barnier had suggested in his briefing before the White Paper came out: that 'they have instrumentalised the Irish issue in order to get to the future relationship that suits them best'. In other words, that Mrs May still wanted the advantages of some kind of customs union – even if she had ruled out membership of the existing customs union in her Lancaster House speech – and was using the argument over the backstop to achieve that objective.

And, again like Barnier, his deputy warned that the Chequers model of single market participation for goods but not services (nor the other so-called freedoms) could give the United Kingdom a commercial edge. She cited as an example:

> If they want to export chemical products to us, they have to respect the EU's products standards, but they would not have to respect all our environmental conditions for production in the UK, because they would be free to set those rules. So they're not doing this for the blue eyes of the Irish, they're also doing it because they look at competitive advantage. So we should not be naive.

But Weyand also expressed the view that Britain had 'moved in certain areas' with the Chequers Agreement, and her plan for the next stage of negotiation was extremely sophisticated. She identified the link between the legally binding withdrawal agreement and the non-binding political declaration on a future relationship between the EU and the United Kingdom as 'crucial', because she judged that the declaration could provide 'political cover' to get the withdrawal agreement through the British parliament. 'I think we have gone almost as far as we can on the withdrawal agreement,' she explained, and argued that to get British approval would mean using the political declaration to frame the backstop in the context of a longer-term relationship, which would mean it would never be needed.

This strategy involved accepting that the two sides would have the political room to interpret the declaration in different ways. The British government could be expected to use it as a way of selling what it had signed up to in the withdrawal agreement: 'We will again be in a situation where we have to let the UK say: we have agreed to the backstop because we are confident that we will not have to use it, because in the context of the future relationship we will find a better all-UK solution,' Weyand explained. The EU, on the other hand, could feel confident about the treaty obligations enshrined in the withdrawal agreement, so, as she put it, 'We on the side of the EU 27 will say, "Of course we have great ambitions for the future relationship, but for us this is OK, because we have the legally certain operational terms in the withdrawal agreement of the backstop, the all-weather insurance policy that we need."' She described this as 'the sort of presentational fudge we will have to live with, and frankly, I don't care about that, as long as the operational solution is in the withdrawal agreement. They will say things that you will find outrageous, [it] doesn't matter. As long as we have the legal text.'

Weyand's strategy was possible precisely because the political declaration would be a joint expression of intent, not a full-blown treaty. 'The withdrawal agreement can have no ambiguity. It's a legal text, it has to be crystal clear,' she pointed out. 'The future relationship [declaration] should not . . . mislead people either, but it should not pretend that in October, November 2018, we are able to decide the outcome of negotiations that haven't even started, for which we don't even have a mandate yet. Ambiguity, fudge, can help.'

Towards the end of her presentation she gave an equally sophisticated assessment of the political situation at Westminster. She reported that Theresa May was determined to get her deal through Parliament by relying on her own party and its DUP allies, because Labour would not support it. She recognised that May would need the votes of hard-line Brexiteers to do that, but 'if you kill a PM who negotiated all this, at the end of the process, you have no alternative, then you can no longer run away . . . then these guys have the responsibility for the cliff edge. I think they will blink. If what's on the table is a good and fair withdrawal agreement, a sufficiently vague, but still nice-sounding political declaration, I would want to see the people who run away from that, and take the responsibility for jumping off the cliff edge.' She added the logic of Barnier's ticking clock. 'The Brexiteers are running scared of any rumour that there might be a delay in the actual Brexit . . . for them the most essential [thing] is to be able to dance in the streets on 29 March and say, "We are out, we are free from the shackles of Brussels."'

It was a sophisticated analysis, but it turned out to be wrong. Within a week, Tory Brexiteers were on manoeuvres in the House of Commons. One amendment to the Trade Bill made it illegal for the United Kingdom to collect EU customs tariffs unless the EU did the same for the UK; another ruled out Northern Ireland becoming a 'separate customs territory to Great Britain'. Together they were designed to kill both the Chequers version of the Irish backstop and the EU's.

The Brexit bubble, I sometimes called the long technical and tactical discussions that I filmed, in meeting rooms hidden at the end of long corridors — even after more than a year I still could not always find them.

Sixty-six million people in the UK and 445 million people living in the rest of the Europe depended on both sides making the negotiations work, in the nine months now left before the UK would officially leave the Union.

Half a billion people — so many, depending on so few.

14

A TACTICAL MISTAKE

Early September–early October 2018

Guy Verhofstadt spent his summer holidays in Umbria, where his daughter Charlotte got married and the garden around his villa was filled with candles for a fairy-tale wedding party. Probably because of the marriage, he returned to Brussels cleanly shaven, which was not always the case, according to his speechwriter Bram Delen – his boss often came back from holidays with a firm stubble or even a full beard. But not that morning, a few minutes before nine on Monday 4 September 2018.

Nobody else had arrived yet at the offices in Brussels, Verhofstadt for once was first, and so he got annoyed. 'Where are they all? Come on, guys,' he complained, out loud, as if they could hear him in the distance. 'Damn. I'm starting at nine. I still have to take my pills. I need my stuff, and nobody is here.'

Then Edel Crosse arrived, followed by his chief of staff Guillaume McLaughlin – who had grown a beard, at his wife's request – and he quietened down.

Fifteen minutes later, the Brexit Steering Group started dripping into Verhofstadt's office. Not the whole group, just the core members and their assistants – the core members being the representatives of the two most powerful groups in the European Parliament, the Christian Democrat Elmar Brok and the Social Democrat Roberto Gualtieri.

Together with Verhofstadt they always had a pre-BSG before the whole BSG gathered.

While coffee was being served, Verhofstadt immediately set the pessimistic tone of the day. 'It doesn't go well, eh? [In an hour] we are going to hear Barnier explaining where we are, after three rounds of negotiations [over the summer] now. Three rounds of two days, eh? Not so long, but three rounds. And I personally think that there comes a moment, and I have already spoken with Barnier about it, that there will be [a] need from the European side to do [a] type of last offer. To them. To the British side. A last offer in the sense that, to avoid a no-deal, here's a proposal . . . so that we put the ball in the camp of Britain.'

Verhofstadt was concerned that the EU's softly-softly strategy in response to the Chequers proposals might have backfired. 'We didn't react very fiercely to Chequers,' he reminded the Group, 'but now we have seen that Barnier in a more vocal way said that Chequers will not fly. Because for two months in Britain they thought that it would fly. So maybe it would have been better to say from day one [and here he slapped his hands together, whistled, and pointed his finger at the side of his head]: crazy.'

Fifteen minutes into their first meeting after the holidays, and they were debating the paradox that would haunt the autumn; the fact that for the EU May's Chequers proposal was an unrealistic plan that would probably not even command a majority in Britain, but if it was just part of the non-legally binding political declaration, Europe (and even the UK, there was still hope in the BSG) might let it pass. There was, not for the first time, a surreal quality to the conversation:

VERHOFSTADT: The Chequers plan has no majority in
    Britain . . . The Chequers plan is a minority issue
    of the Conservative Party, where the Brexiteers are
    against . . . and the pro-Europeans are against. So, it's

really . . . and for tactical reasons the whole Labour
is against, the Liberal Democrats are against, SNP is
against.

GUALTIERI: And also we are against. So everybody is
against . . .

VERHOFSTADT: Everybody is against.

GUALTIERI: It's a great fiction. But still, according to the
baseline strategy of us, that's where we are putting
our fishes. This fiction will prevail because in the end
nobody – she's [May] getting up in the polls – nobody
wants to get rid of the PM or has . . . the power, the
Brexiteers in the end, with blood on their fingers will
have to vote for this . . . and we will buy it, pretending
that we agree but we disagree, and everything is just a
big theatre to make them accept this bloody Brexit. So
that's the scenario we're looking at . . .

VERHOFSTADT: Yes, that's the scenario.

In September 2018, there were seven months to go until the
departure date the UK had set for itself – 29 March 2019 – and
with the need for a ratification process on both sides, EU chief
negotiator Michel Barnier felt he only had 'six to eight weeks'
left to finalise the withdrawal agreement and negotiate a political declaration on the future relationship. Right in the middle
of these six to eight weeks, both Theresa May's Conservatives
and Labour were due to hold their annual party conferences,
with the usual surge in the political temperature.

But at least, Barnier told the complete Brexit Steering
Group, in a spacious, elongated meeting room in Brussels, at
a table that looked like a long double blade, they were now
engaged in 'a process of more regular meetings' with the new
Brexit secretary, Dominic Raab, 'which is something that used

to be extremely difficult'. Around the time of David Davis's resignation, it had emerged that Davis was spending an average of forty minutes a month with his EU counterpart. 'Michel, once every six months was also regular,' remarked Philippe Lamberts. 'Indeed; I said MORE regular,' Barnier replied. 'We would work with Olly Robbins and his team almost every week, but the minister in charge [Davis] came once a quarter. Now we are dealing with a minister, Raab, who is fully aware of what he needs to do and who comes every week.' However, this could create, he noted – choosing his words with care – 'difficulties of coordination within the British team, where evidently other routines had been established'.

Barnier sketched out his impressions of the new Brexit sec-retary, describing him as 'much more direct, less sophisticated, less the politician' than Davis. He took the view that, again in contrast to Davis, Raab 'has no immediate personal agenda in the United Kingdom' – which proved to be a misjudgement, as Raab would before very long be a candidate for the Tory leadership. But Barnier correctly judged that Dominic Raab 'was on a pro-Brexit ideological line, much more clearly than some others. For the moment I find him someone who tries to talk about everything, but does so with lots of rhetoric and slogans – in rather a general manner. We have no more time for slogans [though] – we now need to find solutions.'

Those 'difficulties of coordination' in the British team were also picked up on by the British press. The *Financial Times* noted 'one looming issue for Mr Raab, 44, is that he may find the job as frustrating as Mr Davis because key decisions on the UK's plans to leave the EU are taken by Mrs May and Olly Robbins, her chief adviser on Brexit'. The paper said that Raab's appointment was aimed at 'maintaining the delicate status quo between Eurosceptics and Europhiles in Theresa

May's cabinet'. ITV News called Raab 'one of the staunchest Brexiteers on the Conservative benches, calling for EU withdrawal long before the referendum'.

The new Brexit secretary had a striking back story. He was the son of a Czech-born Jewish father who came to Britain as a refugee just after the Munich Agreement, which handed control of Czechoslovakia to Hitler. Raab junior collected degrees from both Oxford and Cambridge and – as he reminded Tory MPs when he later stood for leader – a black belt in karate. He had worked for a blue-chip law firm and the Foreign Office before standing for Parliament. At the time of his appointment, *The Guardian* suggested that 'some of his past comments could come back to haunt him, including branding feminists "obnoxious bigots" in 2011'. The paper ended its profile with a gossipy reminder that 'Raab was in the news earlier this year when it emerged one of his researchers was selling sex while working for him at the Commons. She also revealed he liked to have the same lunch every day, which she dubbed the "Dominic Raab special" – a chicken Caesar and bacon baguette, a superfruit pot and a vitamin volcano smoothie.'

Much later, after my documentary had come out in May 2019, I was surprised to find out that a clip from the BSG meeting where Barnier talked about Raab, was being used by Raab's supporters in the Tory leadership contest. It was cited as evidence of his willingness to take a tough line with the EU, and was extracted from Michel Barnier's account of a confrontation between the two negotiators over the Irish border.

One ReadyForRaab tweet said: 'The documentary, Brexit Behind Closed Doors, *revealed that Dominic Raab stood up to the EU in Britain's national interest.' The tweet showed a clip with Barnier saying: 'On the issue of Ireland, there was a moment of extremely high tension, when Raab said, "If you don't accept our demands in the Chequers White Paper, the UK-wide solution", the cherry picking, "then you're responsible for the disagreement, for no-deal, and it is you who creates borders, because we want to leave it as it is, without borders." I [Barnier] stopped him there and told him very, very clearly: your prime minister Theresa May never dared say this to us.'*

There the clip as it was used in the tweet ended, making it sound as if Raab had indeed stood up to Michel Barnier, where PM May hadn't dared to do so. But the tweet omitted the rest of what Barnier had bluntly told Raab during the meeting and in the documentary: 'My dear Dominic, your prime minister, Theresa May, has never dared to say that to us, never. On the contrary, she has reaffirmed that the United Kingdom understands the problem it is creating by leaving the EU and the single market, and understands its responsibility. The idea that it would be the Europeans' fault, and that it would be up to us to introduce border controls is absolutely unacceptable to us, and if that is the British position you had better say so now, and I shall report to the European Parliament and Council that our discussions have come to a halt – that negotiations have failed.' And Barnier added, 'They [the British, including Raab] immediately backtracked, saying that this was not what they wanted to say. He's not a great one for nuance, Dominic Raab, and we are dealing with matters where you need to be able to demonstrate an understanding of nuance.'

By omitting the second part of what Barnier said, the ReadyForRaab tweet reframed the scene for their own purposes. The Brexit Party and the DUP used other clips from the documentary in a similar way.

After filleting Raab, Barnier turned to May's Chequers plan, and argued that it showed his earlier warnings about the 'instrumentalisation' of the Irish issue had been justified – that Theresa May was indeed now leveraging it to extract a better deal for the United Kingdom – 'using the proposal made specifically and as an exception for Northern Ireland for a UK-wide solution, which creates an enormous amount of problems', he said. He read the Chequers proposals as a prime example of the 'cherry picking' he had always warned about: a bid to set up a customs arrangement that kept the UK close to the EU – as was the plan for Northern Ireland – but without accepting full regulatory alignment, only following the rules where it suited them, thus creating competitive advantages to the UK.

He interpreted the plan as an attempt to smuggle through a softer form of Brexit. 'Those who support these ideas,' he observed, 'Mrs May and a section of her majority in Parliament, want to lessen or suppress the economic consequences of the Brexit they are pursuing.' The plan was not acceptable, and formally, therefore, the EU still stood by the original Irish border backstop plan, agreed on in the joint report of December 2017, which would see Northern Ireland – and Northern Ireland only – remaining in the customs union and aligned to parts of the single market.

Like Brok, Gualtieri and Verhofstadt in their pre-BSG chat, Barnier recognised that he would have to discuss the Chequers plan with the British side, even if he did not approve it and, to make things more complicated, did not believe it would necessarily command the support of the British Parliament. 'The position of Rees-Mogg, David Davis and others is that it's a Trojan Horse,' he said, 'and they are trying to get together seventy British MPs to knock down the British position – to knock down Chequers in the weeks to come.' Just to make these dizzying political calculations even more vertiginous, he could not negotiate the one solution which he believed *would* get through Parliament: a full-blown customs union. 'The paradox', Barnier told the BSG, 'is that if there was a vote in the Commons on the idea of a customs union with the European Union [a vote where MPs could just decide what they preferred and didn't have to vote along party lines], I think there would be a majority.'

Barnier had had an opportunity to gauge the way political opinion was moving in Britain when he met members of the House of Commons' Exiting the European Union Committee over the summer. He described the committee chair, the former Labour Cabinet minister Hilary Benn, as 'very competent', but was less flattering about Jacob Rees-Mogg, whom he had met for the first time. 'Rees-Mogg – he's pretty extraordinary,' Barnier remarked, and told the BSG members about the speech the Tory backbencher had given at the party conference the previous year, which he described as 'absolutely astonishing'.

'It's really something,' Barnier said. 'He appealed to the spirit of Agincourt, said that "we must rediscover the spirit of Trafalgar, Waterloo, the determination of Nelson".'

'The Dardanelles too?' asked Philippe Lamberts, in a reference to the disastrous Gallipoli campaign during the First World War.

'Agincourt,' Barnier mused, 'you can't go much further back than that.'

'Hastings?' Lamberts mischievously suggested.

'That one is a bad memory,' Barnier noted.

Because at this stage the EU was still sticking to the idea of a backstop that was specific to Northern Ireland, the issue of a so-called 'border in the Irish Sea' – or anything remotely resembling one – was a highly sensitive matter in British politics. Barnier explained he had given the Exiting the EU Committee several examples of why the EU believed controls on what arrived in Northern Ireland from the UK were

273

necessary. The first related to a possible future trade deal between Britain and the United States, which, Barnier argued, demonstrated the problems created by keeping the Irish border open. And he allowed himself a moment of sarcasm: 'In the context of the sovereignty they have recovered, they will probably have to accept chlorinated chickens in the UK,' he suggested. 'Mr Trump talks about that to everyone he speaks to. Where would one control that? No way do we want them in the European market . . . and once they arrive in Northern Ireland they would be in our common market.'

And Barnier gave the Committee three more examples: cloned beef, Thai shrimps treated with antibiotics forbidden in the EU, and Chinese bicycles which are subject to EU anti-dumping taxes; if the UK decided not to raise such a tax, the bicycles would enter the EU, via Northern Ireland and then Ireland, very cheaply.

'Who would control this?' Barnier asked again.

His strategy at this stage was to, as he put it, 'de-dramatise' the issue of controlling goods coming into Northern Ireland from Great Britain, by approaching it in a pragmatic way, to show that it 'really isn't a border. We are ready to work to simplify controls thanks to electronic [methods],' he said. 'And on our side we are looking at what controls are really necessary, who can do them, how and when.' They need not all be done in one place, he explained, but could be dispersed, with some done on board ships or at the port of Liverpool. And he pointed out that there were already some controls in place – mainly veterinary controls on livestock. 'So I have been asking the British: how and where are you doing the controls that exist already? In Belfast, at the airport and in the Belfast harbour? But for now the British won't give us this information.'

His team had, however, been able to establish that 60 per cent of all the goods that are shipped from the UK to Ireland, or vice versa, pass via Dublin. 'So there we can already control,' the EU chief negotiator finished, with what looked like a mischievous twinkle in his eyes. Beyond trying to find a negotiated solution, he was also, already, it seemed, preparing for the eventuality of a no-deal, when the EU would have to organise controls on its own.

But Barnier still believed that the consequences of the United Kingdom leaving the EU without an agreement would be so grave that no British government would ever allow it to happen. 'The risks . . . of a no-deal are so vast, for the UK, and unpredictable, and what's more they haven't even been fully explored, in every area, that a no-deal is not, is not . . .' So inconceivable, it seemed, that he got lost for words.

Then everyone got up to run to other meetings – because Brexit was not the only issue on their plates. Barnier as always went to shake hands with everyone, individually, and afterwards walked out together with Guillaume, whom Barnier too had noticed had grown a beard.

BARNIER: The beard – it makes you look older.
MCLAUGHLIN: My wife says the opposite.

A few days after the meeting, there was a reminder that at least one senior British politician was indeed willing to contemplate leaving the EU without a deal. Writing in the *Mail on Sunday*, Boris Johnson claimed that, with the Chequers plan, 'We have wrapped a suicide vest around the British constitution – and handed the detonator to Michel Barnier. We have given him a jemmy with which Brussels can choose – at any time – to crack apart the union between Great Britain and Northern Ireland.'

The former foreign secretary slammed the negotiating position of the government of which he had, until two months earlier, been a member. 'At every stage in the talks so far, Brussels gets what Brussels wants. We have agreed to the EU's timetable; we have agreed to hand over £39bn, for nothing in return. Under the Chequers proposal we are set to agree to accept their rules – for ever – with no say on the making of those rules. It is a humiliation. We look like a 7-stone weakling being comically bent out of shape by a 500lb gorilla.'

But there was also a steady drumbeat of warnings about the likely consequences of a no-deal Brexit in the British press. *The Times* reported that 'house prices would fall by 35 per cent over three years after a chaotic no-deal Brexit, according to a stark briefing given to the cabinet by the Bank of England governor, Mark Carney'. And in an interview on Sky News, the chief executive of Jaguar Land Rover, Ralf Speth, warned that tens of thousands of jobs in the UK motor industry were at risk if the UK left the EU without an agreement. Increased and uncertain processing times at the border, causing queues at Dover, could force firms to rethink their supply chains. Speth said the lack of clarity about Brexit meant he did not know if his plants would be able to function after 29 March 2019, and told Sky News, 'Just one part missing could mean stopping production at a cost of £60m a day. That is a huge risk. We depend on free, frictionless, seamless logistics.'

Experts from the think tank The UK in a Changing Europe warned – according to *The Guardian* – that a no-deal would mean 'the disappearance without replacement of many of the rules underpinning the UK's economic and regulatory structure', and as a consequence, food supplies could be temporarily disrupted. The beef trade, for instance, could collapse, as Britain was heavily reliant on EU imports and would be forced to apply tariffs in accordance with World Trade Organization (WTO) rules. European health insurance cards, which allowed British tourists free healthcare in the EU, would be invalid from Brexit day.

The Guardian reported that 'in the longer term, The UK in a Changing Europe's experts say, the UK would have time to normalise its trading status, and agreements could be struck with the EU27 to tackle many practical challenges. "It should not be assumed that the damage, while real, will necessarily be long-lasting," the report says, [but] in the short term, and particularly if talks broke down acrimoniously, making it polit-ically difficult to negotiate measures to mitigate the risks, the disruption would be significant.'

In an comment article published in the *Daily Telegraph*, Dominic Raab denounced what he saw as alarmism. 'We shouldn't give succour to those scaremongering for political ends,' he wrote. 'It's nonsense to claim that UK supermarkets would run out of food. Our diverse sources of food – 50 per cent home-grown, 20 per cent imported from non-EU coun-tries – provide us with a high degree of food security, and EU farmers will still want to sell to the UK. Nor should our advice to pharmaceutical firms, to stockpile six weeks of additional medicine supplies, scare people.' Like Johnson, he was willing to contemplate a no-deal departure from the EU:

As WTO Director General Roberto Azevêdo recently said, leaving the EU with no deal would not be 'a walk in the park', but it would 'not be the end of the world' either. There would be some countervailing opportunities. We could negotiate and bring into force new free-trade deals straight away. We would see the immediate return of full legislative and regulatory control – including over immigration. And the government would not pay the terms of the financial settlement, as agreed with the EU as part of the Withdrawal Agreement. There's no deal without the whole deal.

But Raab was not convincing everyone. The government published a series of notices – twenty-five in August, twenty-eight in September – spelling out what might happen in the event of no-deal between Britain and the EU. And the *Financial Times* commented, 'Mr Raab wants to convey the impression that the government is increasing efforts to cope with a "no deal" outcome if it arises. But Mr Raab and his colleagues are going to find it hard to convince people outside government, especially British business, that the UK is remotely prepared for such a stark eventuality . . . there is little evidence that Whitehall is anywhere near committing the extra resources or personnel that would be needed for a no-deal scenario.'

The paper gave an example:

Take the issue of driving licences. This week's technical notices describes how, in the event of no deal, UK nationals driving on to the continent will need a separate document called an International Driving Permit. However, delivering these IDPs to the British public looks like a logistical nightmare. At present, 89 post office branches issue around 100,000 IDPs annually. If there is no deal in March, up to 4,500 post offices may need to issue between 100,000 and 7m IDPs in the first year. But the NAO recently said it has not seen any detailed plans from the Department for Transport on how to deliver this.

On 14 September, Dominic Raab and Michel Barnier had a thirty-minute phone call, and afterwards the Brexit secretary issued an upbeat statement: 'This morning, I had an extended phone call with Michel Barnier. We discussed the latest progress our teams have made on the withdrawal agreement and the framework for the future relationship. While there remain some substantive differences we need to resolve, it is clear our teams are closing in on workable solutions to the outstanding issues in the withdrawal agreement, and are having productive discussions in the right spirit on the future relationship.'

The EU's side saw things rather differently; Michel Barnier's tweet in response focused more on the 'substantive differences' than the progress.

And when the two next met, Barnier reported to the Brexit Steering Group, the British representative was leaping well ahead of the current negotiating position. 'His first point was to talk about the governance of the future relationship,' he said, '. . . that we needed to find [a] mechanism to manage . . . a common rule book.' Barnier said he had 'listened attentively and taken good note' of Raab's comments, but had explained that 'all that was very premature, because it would mean discussing the governance of an agreement when we did not yet know what that agreement would be'. He said that Raab appeared crestfallen. 'He was very disappointed by my answer,' Barnier reported. 'I said, "You can't really have expected that I would say anything else."'

Barnier also came back to the information he had asked for from the British about the way they exercised those controls which were already in place for goods coming into Northern Ireland from Great Britain. This time he had been given the explicit response that 'they had instructions not to give me the figures. So I said to them that if we were going to continue on this course we were heading straight for deadlock on this question of the backstop, and therefore for a failure in the negotiations.'

There was progress in some areas, although much of it

underlined the sheer complexity of the task of unknitting the relationship between the United Kingdom and the European Union. Euratom, which dealt with all nuclear matters on EU territory, has the same membership as the EU but was established under a different treaty. Barnier reported that the two sides had almost reached agreement on how the United Kingdom's role in the organisation would operate after Brexit; it would be, he explained, 'a bilateral collaboration between Euratom and the United Kingdom', along the lines of an arrangement that allowed the Swiss to participate in the project. But the negotiations had thrown up a couple of unexpected problems. 'It's not an easy issue for them,' Barnier said, 'because they will have to build a national institution for managing fissile material.' On top of that, he explained, it turned out there was a Euratom installation in the United Kingdom which would have to be decontaminated, and the British wanted the EU to pay for that. 'It's not a considerable sum,' he added. 'So I hope we can settle this.'

More irritation – there was always more irritation than good news, it seemed – was caused by a letter London had sent to the transport ministers of the twenty-seven remaining member states, stating that the UK was ready to have bilateral discussions with them on country-to-country arrangements to avoid disruption in the crucial aviation and transport sectors. The letter had earned another Barnier ticking off: 'I said to Dominic Raab in no uncertain terms, roughly even, that there would be no mini-deals. If there is no [overall] deal then confidence will have gone, because they'll refuse to pay the financial settlement, and we won't know what to do for citizens, and we are not going to get involved in negotiating little deals which will replace the [main] deal minus the financial agreement.'

This was a point of principle for Barnier. Because of the collapse of confidence a no-deal outcome would involve, each side would, he declared, make its own unilateral contingency plans. The message was directed at 'supporters of a no-deal', who believed that 'in the end it would not be so serious'. He added, 'I think even Mrs May has said it wouldn't be the end of the world. And why would it not be too serious? Because [they think] they can negotiate mini-deals with Europe, putting the bill and Ireland to one side.'

At that point, Elmar Brok intervened. 'And now they are trying to blackmail us. Rees-Mogg – Marek [his adviser] just showed me that – is calling if there is no final deal, not to pay the 39 billion pounds. So they put now the pressure more on us. As if we would be the main loser if there's no deal.'

Brok was concerned that 'some member states might lose their nerves' and detected (once again) what he called 'the special bilateral diplomacy of the Brits' at work. 'This is exactly the plan they had from the very, very beginning of our nego-tiations . . .' he said. And he suggested that it might be easier for the Parliament rather than Michel Barnier to draw a line in the sand with a public statement. 'And let's see then who will lose the nerves,' he suggested. 'Probably those who will lose the most. Which is also very clear who it is.' The Parliament should, he argued, make it clear that the EU was not about to 'fall into that trap they're preparing for us' by issuing a firm message. 'Sometimes you have to be very simple in such situa-tions – to achieve something,' he declared.

Barnier wholeheartedly supported him. 'I could not be more completely in agreement with what Elmar has said,' he responded. 'That is why I say, Elmar, that Parliament, which has the final word [on any deal], has a very important role to play. I think that if you send out a very clear message it will be extremely important for the success of this negotiation.'

And with that, and a half-weary, half-ironic smile in his eyes, Guy Verhofstadt ended the Brexit Steering Group meeting for that day, saying, 'If there are no other questions, we will see each other next week.'

~

Verhofstadt went back to his office, where it was time for another, equally serious and unpleasant task: the last preparations for a vote the next day against Hungary and its populist prime minister, Viktor Orbán. Orbán was accused of breaching the EU's core values in his migration policy, his attacks on the independent media and his campaign against the Hungarian-born Jewish businessman and civil society supporter George Soros.

Verhofstadt had a personal history with Orbán that went a long way back. He likes telling that he met him for the first time twenty-five years ago, right after the fall of the Berlin Wall, in a hotel in Budapest.

I forget the name, but what I do remember is that he was a convinced liberal in those days. Fidesz, the party he led then and still does, was nothing more than the student organisation of the liberal party, SZDSZ, the party of such eminent intellectuals and writers as Imre Kertesz, Peter Esterhazy and my friend Gyorgy Konrad . . . I know that's hard to believe, but in his first term as prime minister he reformed pensions, cut taxes, passed progressive legislation. He was a true liberal.

But then, in 2002, 'he lost the elections. He went in opposition. And to regain power he renounced his principles and he became a populist, replacing liberal values by a "dictatorship of the majority". The majority has it always right. Even when human rights and democratic principles are trampled.'

In 2017, in a speech in plenary, addressing Orbán directly, Verhofstadt asked him with a voice full of venom, and contempt – but

also frustration: 'How far will you go? What is the next thing? Burning
a book or so, on the place [square] before the Parliament in Hungary?'

One year later, Verhofstadt (together with many others) had finally
managed to push the European Parliament to take action against the
Hungarian prime minister.

Before the vote, Orbán defended himself in a speech of his own
to the European Parliament. 'You want to denounce Hungary
because the Hungarian people have decided that our homeland
will not become an immigrant country,' he accused. 'With due
respect, but in the strongest possible terms, I reject the threats,
the blackmail, the slander and fraudulent accusations levelled
against Hungary and the Hungarian people by the European
Parliament's pro-immigration and pro-migrant forces. I respectfully inform you that, whatever decision you come to, Hungary
shall not bow to blackmail: Hungary shall continue to defend its
borders, stop illegal immigration and defend its rights – against
you, too, if necessary.' The appeal failed; by an overwhelming
majority (448 voting in favour of the motion, 197 against and 48
abstentions) the European Parliament voted to censure Hungary,
setting in motion a process that could lead to the country being
stripped of its voting right in the European Council.

The British Tory MEPs voted against the motion, which
led to accusations that they did so because they were seeking
Brexit favours. Michael Gove, the UK secretary of state for
environment, food and rural affairs, did little to dispel this
criticism when he refused to condemn Orbán on *The Andrew
Marr Show*, saying he did not believe that 'individual criticisms
of the kind you are understandably tempting me to make
don't necessarily help us in ensuring we get both solidarity on
the issues that count and the best deal for Britain as we leave
the EU'. In fact, although some of Orbán's Eurosceptic ideas

echoed those of the Brexit campaign in Britain, all the polls in Hungary recorded continuing, strong support for remaining in the European Union, and the Orbán government has shown no sign of following the United Kingdom out.

~

On Tuesday 18 September – two days before the British prime minister, Theresa May, was due to defend her Chequers plan in front of her twenty-seven colleagues at the European Council, Guy Verhofstadt and his chief of staff were discussing the way Chequers still seemed to have so much traction in the British political debate. 'I saw a *Panorama* about Brexit yesterday,' Guillaume McLaughlin commented. 'It was a real publicity campaign for Mrs May and her Chequers [Plan] . . . without ever explaining what was in Chequers or why the EU is against it.'

'That's the problem,' Verhofstadt replied, returning to an earlier theme. 'We made a mistake – tactically – in not saying at once, after Chequers, this won't work.' The two of them picked up on the suggestion Elmar Brok had made at the previous meeting of the Brexit Steering Group.

VERHOFSTADT: . . . and so we must make . . .
MCLAUGHLIN: The Brok statement.
VERHOFSTADT: The Brok statement, what we call the Brok statement. And we must prepare it; a short statement with plenty [here he raised his fist] on the real negotiating position.

As things turned out, the need for a Brok statement was overtaken by an equally powerful Instagram message from the president of the EU Council himself, Donald Tusk.

15

OH, FUCK OFF
(WITH A HISTORY)

Late September–early October 2018

On Thursday 20 September 2018, EU president Donald Tusk posted a picture of himself and the British prime minister, Theresa May, on Instagram. He was wearing a light blue suit over a white shirt, with a blue tie. She was dressed in red, also over white, with a heavy-looking silver chain around her neck. Both smiled, looking at a tray with tiny cakes that Tusk was holding up. On the right-hand side of the picture, the blurry pointing finger of an otherwise unidentifiable man seemed to either say 'be careful' to Tusk or 'I would take that one' to May. It was just another snapshot of two political leaders at the informal European Council summit in Salzburg, Austria – exchanging pleasantries after the lunch they had just been served. That was, until the EU president launched the snapshot on his Instagram account with the caption: 'A piece of cake perhaps? Sorry, no cherries.' Then it became a bigger picture.

Theresa May had come to Salzburg to present her Chequers plan, stating just before the event that it was the only credible plan to allay concerns about the Irish border and avoid trade disruption. But her presentation was given a very chilly reception. The EU did not like her plan.

The EU's leaders had not wanted to say that explicitly. In fact, as the BBC's Europe correspondent Katya Adler reported, 'Their Brexit aim for this summit was to go as far as they could with words and gestures to throw Theresa May a lifeline.'

Adler explained: 'The EU's "support Theresa" effort was actually launched the day before the summit with chief Brexit negotiator Michel Barnier, suggesting a "new, improved" proposal on the key sticking point of the Irish border. With the intention of directly addressing UK concerns, Mr Barnier also made explicit assurances that no one in the EU wanted to break up the constitutional integrity of the UK.'

None of the media in Salzburg were able to report what this new and improved Barnier proposal exactly consisted of.

But, Katya Adler reported:

Their [Barnier's and the Council's] tokenistic effort was a misreading of Theresa May's political position – especially ahead of what is likely to be a difficult annual conference with her own Conservative Party. The prime minister swiftly and bluntly rebuffed the Barnier Irish border suggestions – thereby misreading EU leaders right back. There was huge irritation in EU circles – and that's how this summit began. EU frustration only grew when the prime minister then arrived in Salzburg insisting unequivocally that her Chequers Brexit proposal was the only way forward. Theresa May's uncompromising tone was then matched note by note by the EU and here we are now.

The transcripts of what was said in the Brexit Steering Group meetings in the weeks leading up to the Salzburg summit, which are recorded in the previous chapter, suggest at least some on the EU side understood Theresa May's position all too well – that was why Barnier had tried to offer a lifeline.

But when May wouldn't take it, the EU leaders snapped.

Donald Tusk sent out his *Sorry, no cherries* Instagram post and told the press, 'There will be no withdrawal agreement without a solid, operational and legally binding Irish backstop. And we continue to fully support Michel Barnier in his efforts to find such a model.' And he once again reported solidarity on the European side: 'Everybody shared the view that while there are positive elements in the Chequers proposal, the suggested framework for economic cooperation will not work. Not least because it risks undermining the single market.' Tusk declared that the 'moment of truth for Brexit negotiations' would be the next gathering of the European Council the following month: 'Then we will decide whether conditions are there to call an extraordinary summit in November to finalise and formalise the deal.'

The French president Emmanuel Macron was especially unyielding in his comments:

We've got to be clear, straightforward and calm on this issue because there's a great deal of nervousness; clear and straightforward in saying that the British government proposed a number of steps forward in the summer in its Chequers plan. I had the opportunity of discussing them at length with the British prime minister at the beginning of August. It's a good thing and a courageous initiative from the prime minister, which I want to welcome here. But I also want to say very clearly – and there was a consensus on this at noon today – that the proposals put forward as they are today are unacceptable, especially on the economic front, and, as it is, the Chequers plan can't be a take-it-or-leave-it plan. We're duty-bound to defend the single market and its coherence, and we reaffirmed our determination not to yield an inch on this point.

And there was a sting in the tail of his post-summit press conference: 'Brexit has shown us one thing – and I fully respect British sovereignty in saying this – it has demonstrated that those who said you can easily do without Europe, that it will all go very well, that it is easy and there will be lots of money, are liars. This is all the more true because they left the next day, so they didn't have to manage it.' That last sentence appeared to be a dig at Boris Johnson, who famously pulled out of the Tory leadership election after the 2016 referendum at the very event staged to launch his campaign.

Press reaction in Britain was full of perhaps predictable outrage. The *Daily Mirror* told its readers that May's plan was 'brutally' dismissed as a 'non-starter' and that May was left 'shaking with anger'. And Tusk's cake snapshot was called a 'barbed' Instagram. The *Express* stated that May had been 'rebuffed by a vengeful EU' as they told her that 'your Brexit deal is a dud', and reported that 'Downing Street officials felt the prime minister had been ambushed by the EU at the gathering'. On a front page that showed Macron and Donald Tusk mocked up as Prohibition-era gangsters carrying tommy guns, *The Sun* headlined, 'EU Dirty Rats – Euro mobsters ambush' and declared, 'We can't wait to shake ourselves free.'

The *Daily Telegraph*'s Europe editor, Peter Foster, represented the Salzburg summit as a reality check for the British government. 'It was death by a thousand cuts, but when Donald Tusk administered the coup de grace on Theresa May's Chequers plan in Salzburg yesterday, there was still a

sharp intake of breath among those who had – encouraged
by delusions in Downing Street – clung to the belief it could
survive,' he wrote:

> Until yesterday, Downing Street has been in denial. It
> believed that when Mrs May got her fellow EU leaders in the
> room, they would show more flexibility than Michel Barnier
> and the 'theologians' in Brussels who she blamed for such
> a narrow, blinkered approach to the negotiation. But the
> chiefs have spoken, and they have apparently come to the
> same conclusion as Mr Barnier – that the customs and trade
> part of Chequers was 'cherry-picking' and posed a systemic
> threat to the economic and political future of their union.

In Downing Street, the day after Salzburg, Mrs May, who did
indeed seem somewhat shaken, fired back. 'I have always said
that these negotiations would be tough – and they were always
bound to be toughest in the final straight,' she declared in a
statement:

> Yesterday Donald Tusk said our proposals would undermine
> the single market. He didn't explain how in any detail or
> make any counter-proposal. So we are at an impasse. As I
> told EU leaders, neither side should demand the unaccept-
> able of the other. We cannot accept anything that threatens
> the integrity of our union, just as they cannot accept any-
> thing that threatens the integrity of theirs. We cannot accept
> anything that does not respect the result of the referendum,
> just as they cannot accept anything that is not in the interest
> of their citizens.

She added an acerbic postscript:

Throughout this process, I have treated the EU with nothing but respect. The UK expects the same. A good relationship at the end of this process depends on it. At this late stage in the negotiations, it is not acceptable to simply reject the other side's proposals without a detailed explanation and counter proposals. So we now need to hear from the EU what the real issues are and what their alternative is so that we can discuss them. Until we do, we cannot make progress. In the meantime, we must and will continue the work of preparing ourselves for no-deal.

Four days later, Guy Verhofstadt was sitting on the Eurostar to London, together with Guillaume McLaughlin, Nick Petre – Verhofstadt's spokesperson for the UK – and the senior parliamentary civil servants Markus Winkler and François Javelle. They were on their way to a meeting with Theresa May in Downing Street, which had been arranged before the Salzburg blow-up.

WINKLER: You're the first guy seeing her after Salzburg.
VERHOFSTADT: That's by accident, eh? [laughs]
WINKLER: Yeah, but sometimes accidents are interesting.
MCLAUGHLIN: But nobody seems to know. Nick? Does anybody know we're going?
VERHOFSTADT: No.
MCLAUGHLIN: Shouldn't we do a nice little tweet . . . A little photo, with your folder and your biro, preparing for your meeting with Mrs May later today?

Markus Winkler added: 'In a rush to see her before the general election,' which drew laughter.

The group then started to try to piece together exactly what had happened in Salzburg. The fireworks had also taken them by surprise. According to McLaughlin it all started with a meeting that Donald Tusk had with Theresa May, privately.

> MCLAUGHLIN: Actually, the meeting she had with Tusk was before Tusk did his press conference. And I think maybe even before the Instagram, I'm not sure. She could have said, 'Donald, OK, I didn't quite expect such a push back, you know, between four walls, let's look at this.' No, she went back on the attack with Tusk. Didier was there. [Didier Seeuws, the Brexit coordinator for the European Council, and Verhofstadt's chief of staff when he was prime minister of Belgium.]
>
> VERHOFSTADT: Yeah? Didier was there?
>
> MCLAUGHLIN: And she said nothing conciliatory at all. Nothing to suggest there was a change of . . . that she felt that maybe she should adjust, nothing.

Later, in the car on their way through London, McLaughlin also shared more information about that mysterious last-minute 'new' proposal that Barnier had made, just before Salzburg. Nobody, it seemed, was sure of what had really been in it.

> MCLAUGHLIN: The new Barnier proposal is not public, and has not been transmitted to the Brits. The main elements have been explained at . . . the technical level with Olly Robbins, and Michel Barnier with Raab . . . Maybe they should publish, eh?
>
> VERHOFSTADT: Yeah, but if [the idea] is to publish [simply] to have a rebuttal from the British side, what is then the need to publish it? [It seems] only [useful]

when you continue the fight for the public opinion? Or
to start the fight for the public opinion.

MCLAUGHLIN: Yeah.

JAVELLE: She said in her statement on Friday that the
latest Barnier proposal for a backstop would be tearing
the UK apart, that's what she said.

Verhofstadt suggested that she must have been referring to
Michel Barnier's ideas for 'de-dramatising' the backstop issue
by ensuring that checks on goods moving to Northern Ireland
from Great Britain could be dispersed rather than being
concentrated in a way that suggested a border in the Irish Sea —
'scanning containers on the ferry between Glasgow and Belfast'
and 'increasing the number of phytosanitary controls [checks
on plant health] in the port of Belfast, that is mainly what this is
about, eh? If I understand it well, the Barnier proposal is about
that. Controls, no borders.'

'He [Barnier] is actually using the same language the
Brits were using in their "maximum facilitation proposal",'
Guillaume McLaughlin noted.

But Verhofstadt pointed to an important distinction between
a so-called 'border in the Irish Sea' and setting up border
controls on the island of Ireland — the second involved a much
more direct risk of a return to terrorism. 'Yeah,' he responded,
'with the difference that nobody will blow it up in the Irish Sea
when you scan a container, while you do the same thing on the
ground between Northern Ireland and Ireland, you can be sure
that, BAF, they blow it up [laughs]. That's the difference.'

*I was wondering, there and then in that car, whether anyone involved in
the Brexit talks still had a complete overview of all the proposals that were
floating around. Barnier's submarine came to my mind — and despite the*

*sunny weather outside, murky waters. There was not one submarine; there
was a whole flotilla. And one of them looked like a cab today.*

*A cab crawling through the London traffic, giving Verhofstadt and his
team plenty of time to tackle yet another aspect of the negotiations —
although I have to be careful what I say here about time passing, because
the transcripts of what I filmed have, in all the details they contain, a
misleading feel to them. They betray the often rapid-fire succession of
thoughts and issues I — as an outsider — was subjected to, and sometimes
drowned in.*

Still in their car, Verhofstadt and his team had turned to another
aspect of the Chequers plan, the common rule book — the plan
envisaged for harmonising areas of standards and regulations
so that the United Kingdom's 'frictionless' trade with the EU
could continue. Part of the EU's objection to this idea was, as
Verhofstadt pointed out, precisely that it would only apply in
some areas, but beyond that he saw a threat to the EU's sovereignty. 'Common rulebook means, together,' he said, 'so we have
then to make common rules. That can be European rules, that
can be their rules, if we accept their rules, that can be new rules.'
Agreeing new rules in the future would mean negotiating with
Britain as an equal partner — the British on one side of the table
and the EU 27 on the other — and as François Javelle pointed out,
'that would give them more power than any member state', so
they would, in the EU's eyes, be rewarded for leaving.

That view was a mirror image of the reasons many Brexit
supporters in Britain also objected to the common rule book —
they saw it as a mechanism for giving Brussels a continuing say
in British regulations and standards. With the rule book proposal, Mrs May had pulled off the remarkable trick of putting
the EU and British Brexiteers on the same side of an argument.

As we got closer to the centre, the attention focused on how it was all going to end. Verhofstadt and his team were in a betting mood. And the coordinator of the EU Parliament remained optimistic. He was going for 'with a deal, and three months late'. As ever, he had his eye on the electoral timetable: 'That means the day of going out will be pushed just the day before the European elections.'

JAVELLE: Sounds a risky bet.

VERHOFSTADT: It's not a risky bet . . . because it's middle way, it's not going beyond the dates [of the election timetable] and . . . if you have three months more, you take three months more. If you can find a way out in three months, you take them. It's not a beauty contest, such a deal.

I joined in the conversation, thinking of our agreement that I would broadcast my documentary once Britain was out of the EU. 'When do I finish my film then?' I asked.

VERHOFSTADT: Ah, your film . . . you have to wait for five years later [laughs]. And if they don't go out, you make a second film.

WINKLER: Wait until you heard my scenario, I think they will stay in.

ME: So, the conclusion is that nobody knows?

WINKLER: Exactly.

VERHOFSTADT: But that's easy, eh?

WINKLER: Like always in politics, at the end we explain very precisely how it went and how we forecasted the whole thing.

Then finally we arrived in Downing Street, where I was once more not allowed to accompany Verhofstadt and his team inside. Luckily, this time, the weather was bright, and the driver a chatty fellow. The gated UK government street was quiet and almost empty, with just a minimal press pack on standby behind their fence, and no sandbags in front of No. 10, yet, however embattled Theresa May was these days.

But when Verhofstadt and his team climbed back into the car, their comments were dripping with frustration as they ran through their conversation with Theresa May and her team.

MCLAUGHLIN: So it's funny, eh? Northern Ireland is a
    principled question, but the customs union between
    the EU and the UK is one we have to be practical
    about . . . Pragmatism is a thing, except when
    you're talking about Northern Ireland, then it's not
    applicable.
VERHOFSTADT: Then we are . . .
MCLAUGHLIN: Then we are very principled.
VERHOFSTADT: Very principled.

There was a lot of sighing in the car, and tangible exasperation. Following the rejection of the Chequers plan, the British side were at an impasse.

MCLAUGHLIN: They're really stuck, eh?
JAVELLE: They're going nowhere.
WINKLER: They're stuck. Yeah. And she was super-
    stressed, did you see it? She was really . . .
MCLAUGHLIN: Last time we saw her it was exactly the
    same.

David Lidington had also been present at the meeting. Theresa May's de facto deputy, formally known as the minister for the

Cabinet Office and chancellor of the Duchy of Lancaster, had supported Remain during the 2016 referendum campaign and was known to be one of her most pro-European ministers. Verhofstadt reported that he had taken the opportunity to suggest a way out to him: 'I said to Lidington . . . "Look a little bit in[to] an existing system like Norway-plus [so including membership of the European Free Trade Association and membership of the European Economic Area] with the customs union, and try to find out how far you can stretch it [so that it's still acceptable]. Look a little bit in[to] that, because otherwise we are not going to make a lot of progress."'

Verhofstadt said he'd avoided making the same suggestion to Dominic Raab for the obvious reason that it was not the kind of idea that would appeal to a committed Brexiteer and because, acutely aware of political nuance as ever, he had picked up that 'on Brexit . . . it's Lidington who is doing the thing, inside the Cabinet. If she [May] is not in charge, it's Lidington who's in charge.'

So despite their misgivings about the impasse the British were in, and the lack of hope they had exuded when re-entering the car, they still had tried to get some work done. Although the overwhelming feeling among the group remained that the negotiations were caught in a repeating loop.

WINKLER: But it's really going nowhere.

JAVELLE: Yeah, it's depressing.

WINKLER: They tell us the same stuff as half a year ago, you know?

JAVELLE: It's exactly as if Salzburg never took place last week. They just don't pay attention that it was bluntly rejected by the twenty-seven.

MCLAUGHLIN: They still want it to be explained. That's
     what she said. She wants it to be explained why it was
     rejected.
MCLAUGHLIN: What a bloody mess!

*When Markus Winkler mused again 'they will stay', Guillaume
McLaughlin declared, to general laughter, that that would be 'the worst
possible outcome'.*

*François Javelle enquired what had happened to the BSG's plans for a
'Brok statement', the strong statement about Chequers Verhofstadt had
wanted to prepare a week ago, at their last meeting before Salzburg and
the cake and cherry blow-up there.*

MCLAUGHLIN: Tusk did it.
VERHOFSTADT [laughing]: He did more than that, he
     did a Brok plus, a super-Brok, he did a super-Brok
     statement. The BSG takes too much time; I'm going to
     phone Donald [Tusk]. Donald, can you do something?

The following day, in Brussels, Michel Barnier came to give
the Brexit Steering Group his version of what had happened
in Salzburg – and, despite his words, he seemed genuinely
agitated. 'I am still calm, and I am going to stay that way right
until the end,' he said, 'but I find it absolutely out of order
that Mrs May and Mr Raab should say they had received a
negative answer without any explanation. It isn't true. It isn't
true. We have said in a very precise way, and often, since the
publication of Chequers, that there was a clear problem, of
cherry picking . . . half of the customs union and a third of the
single market.'

What Theresa May had proposed in Salzburg, Barnier said,
'is not a backstop, it is a UK-wide solution, and this UK-wide

solution is, easy as pie, cherry picking.' In his view, it was clear evidence of their 'strategy of instrumentalising the Irish question', turning the backstop, a solution for the very specific situation in Ireland, into an arrangement for the whole of the UK, and a blueprint for the future relationship – one which in the eyes of the EU was not workable, and anyway had no place in the withdrawal agreement. And so he concluded that 'we don't actually have a solution for Ireland. That is where we are, in strategic terms. And therefore I don't find it right or fair that they say to us, in public, "the Europeans have not given us any explanation".'

Didier Seeuws, the Brexit coordinator for the European Council, was also present at the BSG. Soft spoken, and a much younger man, his analysis of the Salzburg disaster had a certain fatalism. 'I think that the "moment of dramatisation" [so the opposite of Michel Barnier's efforts to "de-dramatise the Irish issue"] had to happen,' he suggested. 'Whether it happened before Salzburg, or after, it had to happen. I think the Brits were victims of a mismanagement of expectations.'

Seeuws identified the source of the British miscalculation in its traditional diplomatic strategy. 'For months,' he said, 'they were basically saying that we [the different EU institutions] would be in different places, that the heads [of government] would take over, and that our negotiation, although it was based on a governance that we all agreed upon, would be put aside, and that the member states would be in a different place. Well, the result was, no, we were not in a different place. The member states were solidly behind the negotiator.' He said that on the very day of the Salzburg summit the British had been talking to individual member states they believed might have their own views about the direction of negotiations, only to find that those governments 'of course . . . confirmed that they were in no different place at all'. And he concluded in his turn: 'So I think mismanagement of expectations was definitely one of the reasons they were "surprised" [he used his fingers to mime inverted commas here] about that.'

The way Seeuws characterised Theresa May's approach echoed what Guillaume McLaughlin had told his fellow travellers on the Eurostar to London the previous day. 'She came to the European Council with the message: it's Chequers and nothing but Chequers, and by the way I'm not going to do a second referendum, and by the way there is no other plan,' he'd said, suggesting a contrast between Theresa May's intransigence and the more pragmatic approach of Michel Barnier, 'whereas the approach of our negotiator was to go pedagogically [through it] and explain with very practical examples why this model is unworkable – it's not an ideological repulsion, it's unworkable.'

Seeuws's verdict on the continuing and, if anything, growing gap in understanding between the British and their European interlocutors was harsh:

> I think it's still staggering that after months of negotiations, notwithstanding the very pedagogic and detailed explanations by Mr Barnier, they think that there is somewhere in between Norway and Canada [shorthand for a close or more distant, free-trade relationship with the European Union], a formula which is not even a single market for goods, it is a selective single market for goods. As if one [any European] Parliament would ratify such a model. This will never happen. But, very well . . . as I said, the moment of dramatisation had to happen.

~

Four days later, the Conservatives gathered in Birmingham for their annual party conference. Here the deal that Brussels had rejected as cherry picking was regarded by many party members as a compromise too far. Boris Johnson electrified the gathering with a speech on the conference fringe on Tuesday 2 October; party members and Brexit-supporting MPs formed long queues to hear the former foreign secretary demand that the government should 'chuck Chequers', because 'this is not what we voted for, this is an outrage. This is not taking back control, this is forfeiting control. If we cheat the electorate – and Chequers is a cheat – we will escalate the sense of mistrust. If we get it wrong, my friends – if we bottle Brexit now – we, the people of this country, will find it hard to forgive. If we remain half-in half-out, we will protract this toxic, tedious business.'

Headlines about Mrs May's precarious position were by now almost routine, but Johnson's barnstorming performance pushed them up a gear; the *Daily Mail* carried pictures of the prime minister and her former foreign secretary on its front page with the words DAGGERS DRAWN splashed across them.

Jacob Rees-Mogg, who had been elected as the chairman of the hard-line Eurosceptic European Research Group (ERG) since the speech at the previous year's conference which so shocked Michel Barnier, positively embraced the idea of a no-deal Brexit. He told *Chopper's Brexit Podcast* that 'a no-deal would help poorer families', because 'getting rid of tariffs on food, clothing and footwear will help the least well-off in society the most'. The *Daily Telegraph* reported Rees-Mogg's view that leaving the EU would benefit London because EU regulation was making it 'less competitive than the rest of the world', and that it would make Europe safer by strengthening the role of NATO in the face of the threat from Russia. He accused the EU of undermining the North Atlantic Alliance by developing its own plans for an army, and argued that 'our leaving will reinforce NATO because it will be clear that that is the major defence system for continental Europe'.

Members of Theresa May's Cabinet remained publicly loyal, but some were already positioning themselves for the leadership battle they believed was coming. Jeremy Hunt, who had replaced Boris Johnson as foreign secretary, campaigned for Remain during the 2016 referendum, but he now spoke with a convert's zeal:

> Our friends in Europe need to understand that 52 per cent of the country [the proportion of Leave voters] aren't rabid populists trying to build Fortress Britain. We fought for peace on our continent so none of us will ever turn our back on history. But nor, and I want to address our European friends directly now, should you. At the moment, you seem to think the way to keep the club together is to punish a member who leaves. Not just with economic disruption. But even by breaking up the United Kingdom with a border down the Irish Sea.

And Hunt went on to compare the European Union to the Soviet Union. 'What happened to the confidence and ideals of the European dream?' he asked in his conference address.

> The EU was set up to protect freedom. It was the Soviet Union that stopped people leaving. The lesson from history is clear: if you turn the EU club into a prison, the desire to get out won't diminish, it will grow, and we won't be the

only prisoner that will want to escape. If you reject the hand of friendship offered by our prime minister, you turn your back on the partnership that has given Europe more security, more freedom and more opportunities than ever in history, and a setback for the EU will become a wholly avoidable tragedy for Europe.

The comparison with the Soviet Union drew a rare rebuke from the European Commission; the chief spokesman, Margaritis Schinas, declared, 'I would say respectfully that we would all benefit – and in particular foreign affairs ministers – from opening a history book from time to time.' Guy Verhofstadt called the comments 'offensive and outrageous', and Lord Ricketts, a former head of the British Foreign Office, tweeted, 'This rubbish is unworthy of a British foreign secretary.'

There was more fighting talk about the United Kingdom's history, although Mr Hunt drew on the twentieth century rather than the Hundred Years' War and nineteenth-century precedents favoured by Jacob Rees-Mogg. The allusions to the Second World War were followed by a reference to one of Margaret Thatcher's most famous performances at the despatch box, when Hunt said: 'We understand the EU wants to protect itself. But if the only way to deal with the UK leaving is to try to force its break-up, as someone much more distinguished than me once said, the answer is: No, No, No. Never mistake British politeness for British weakness. Because if you put a country like Britain in a corner, we don't crumble. We fight.'

The leader's speech is, by long tradition, the conference climax, and on Thursday morning Theresa May shimmied up to the podium to the sound of Abba's 'Dancing Queen', one of the disco anthems of her Oxford years in the 1970s. It was a bold, half-ironic reference to her not entirely fluent dance moves while watching children perform during her African trade tour the previous August, and it worked; the Tory audience lapped it up and she got off to a good start.

'There we go,' said Guillaume McLaughlin, who sat watching the spectacle on television in the office he shared with Edel Crosse in Strasbourg. 'Make Britain great again,' Edel chirped in. The Tory conference had been closely monitored in Brussels, as EU officials tried to assess whether Mrs May would survive to complete the final negotiating furlong.

Outside in the courtyard a brass band was playing, adding an extra layer of music, while May started her speech with a reference to the Great War. 'This year marks a century since the end of the First World War,' she told her audience:

> Just a few hundred yards from this conference centre stands a Hall of Memory, built to honour the sacrifice of men and women from this city in that terrible conflict. Inscribed within it are some familiar words: 'At the going down of the sun, and in the morning, we remember them.' We do remember them. We remember the young men who left their homes to fight and die in the mud and horror of the trenches. We remember the sailors who shovelled coal into hellfire furnaces in the bowels of battleships. We remember the selflessness of a remarkable generation, whose legacy is the freedom we enjoy today. But the builders of that Hall of Memory also wanted us to do something else. Alongside a commitment to remember, they inscribed a command that still calls to us today: 'See to it that they shall not have suffered and died in vain.'

McLaughlin, who knows a thing or two about speeches, having worked for Verhofstadt for so many years, nodded in appreciation. He knew a good speech when he heard one. 'She's really managing [a] great, great job,' he said.

In a reminder that there was life also outside Brexit, May also spoke about the need for the Tories to be a party for the whole country, long-term plans for the National Health Service, the decision to send the RAF to Syria, and the expulsion of twenty-three Russian diplomats over the Skripal poisoning.

And then, but then, came Brexit.

> MAY [on television]: No one wants a good deal more than me.
> MCLAUGHLIN: Aha.
> MAY: But that has never meant getting a deal at any cost. Britain isn't afraid to leave with no deal.
> MCLAUGHLIN: Oh, fuck off.

Both Edel Crosse and Guillaume McLaughlin pulled faces at me, while the audience in Birmingham started applauding.

When this scene appeared in my documentary, many viewers with a heart for Britain and Brexit found it offensive. It was cited and lambasted on social media — used and abused there. Guillaume's 'fuck off' went just too far. But for me it was a 'fuck off' with plenty of history — the stickers Guillaume put on British cars as a six-year-old with his parents, a lifetime of believing in Europe, and now almost two years of disheartening talks, prepared and rehashed, talked through once more and analysed again, in the small, suffocating office where Guillaume and Edel were now watching May on screen.

MAY: We need to be honest about it, leaving without
a deal, introducing tariffs and costly checks at the
border would be a bad outcome for the UK and the
EU. It would be tough at first. But the resilience
and the ingenuity of the British people would see us
through.

CROSSE: Oh that war spirit.

MAY: I have treated the EU with nothing but respect.

MCLAUGHLIN: Oh, fuck off.

MAY: The UK expects the same.

MCLAUGHLIN: Oh yeah.

MAY: When we come together there is no limit to what
we can achieve. Ours is a great country. Our future
is in our hands. Together, let's seize it. Together, let's
build a better Britain.

*Despite McLaughlin's visceral reaction to parts of the speech, he and
Edel Crosse gave the performance a good review.*

CROSSE: It was good. I have to admit.

MCLAUGHLIN: What she did well . . . the whole Cabinet,
they were there, and they had to clap [here he clapped
himself] Chequers.

CROSSE: I think that in terms of silencing [the opposition
within her own party], she did a great job, that
worked.

An hour later, at the start of the Brexit Steering Group, the
Italian Social Democrat Roberto Gualtieri was less impressed.
He held up his smartphone to Guy Verhofstadt, saying, 'When
Barnier enters we should play "The Winner Takes It All". And
film that with this.' Verhofstadt laughed and agreed. 'Instead of

a written statement, something like that would be more sexy.' But a statement was what he had in mind.

> VERHOFSTADT: I think that we have to make a little statement, saying, 'Now that this is finished, can we start?'
> GUALTIERI: Now that this two-year-long congress [party conference] of the Tories is over . . .
> VERHOFSTADT: Can we now really start?

When Barnier arrived, he began with 'a few words on Mrs May's speech, which I listened to with great care', judging that 'she has certainly survived this conference and created a margin of stability for herself in the coming days and weeks'. Barnier also hoped that the way she had shored up her position would allow her to focus on the negotiations now.

But he warned the group to be ready for a game of diplomatic chicken, a test of whose nerve would break first. Barnier pointed out that there was nothing new in what the prime minister had said about Brexit, and that although she had not used the word 'Chequers' she was still defending the substance of the Chequers plan. And he quoted a passage he described as 'revealing of the position that she will hold fast to, right until the end': in her Birmingham speech Mrs May had rallied her party troops with, 'What we are proposing is very, very challenging for the EU, but if we stick together, and hold our nerve, I know we can get a deal that delivers for Britain.' Michel Barnier looked around the group of MEPs with gravity: 'So, we are warned. When I read this passage it did not surprise me; the broad [message] is: if we keep up the lobbying campaign we've long been engaged in, if we keep our nerves and the Europeans lose theirs, we'll get a good deal from the Europeans.'

Barnier said he understood that the British political timetable meant that an agreement in late November or early December would be too late for Mrs May, so he calculated that he had a 'window of opportunity' of a fortnight to see whether there was a deal to be reached – not to settle things finally, but to establish the kind of progress that would be decisive. That would take the negotiations up to the 'key moment' of the next European Council meeting on 17 October 2018. May's conference speech was on 3 October.

And he returned to the fundamental political fact he believed would drive the British to compromise; the fear of a no-deal Brexit. He underlined:

> Since right at the beginning of the negotiation, it's been my belief that the economic and political risk for the United Kingdom associated with a no-deal is so substantial – and all the [negotiating] teams know it and Philip Hammond knows it better than anyone. And so I can foresee the possibility that she [May], having given herself a bit of oxygen at the Conservative Party conference, will use it to avoid a no-deal. Because she knows what a no-deal would mean for her politically, and for the British economy, and for business, which is opposing it and is in revolt . . . the panic there is beginning.

But that panic should not affect the EU, he cautioned. 'Our public line must be clear and simple; we shouldn't become sentimental, accommodate, mollify. Without any doubt, I will [in the end] have to look for a compromise, that is logical and objective. But I'm not going to say that publicly now.'

The stage was set for the final showdown.

16

THE TUNNEL

Early October–mid-October 2018

After her 'Dancing Queen' act and the applause Theresa May received at the Tory Party conference on 3 October 2018, Michel Barnier felt he had two weeks to make what he called 'decisive progress' before the European Council on Wednesday 17 October 2018. But in reality Barnier's 'window of opportunity' was smaller, because the heads of state and government in the Council do not like last-minute proposals. They wanted the deal – if one was reached – ready a couple of days earlier, by Monday 15 October at the latest, so that their advisors could pore over it and tell them whether to approve it.

Which left Barnier and the British team twelve days, at most.

So he decided to go into lockdown. His deputy, Sabine Weyand, laid out the plan for what she called a negotiating 'tunnel' at a meeting with ambassadors from the member states – minus, of course, Britain – on Friday 5 October in the Council's Europa Building. *The Guardian* later reported that she 'told the room of diplomats that she wanted to take the negotiations out of the public eye, and talk intensely with the British, without the usual consultation with the member states laid down in a hefty book of rules of procedures.'

The *Guardian* story stated that 'the small core group of negotiating teams' would set up home on the fifth floor of the European Commission's Berlaymont building 'to throw around new ideas, some of which were potentially highly controversial, to try to break the deadlock'. Weyand appealed for the trust of the member states, saying, according to the report, 'We don't know where we will land but it is worth exploring . . . What we would really like to do is go into a tunnel and then come back to brief you about what happened just before the next European council.' Until then, everyone not directly involved would be kept in the dark about the doings inside the tunnel, and that included Guy Verhofstadt and the European Parliament's Brexit Steering Group.

Barnier's tunnel strategy gave Verhofstadt the chance to travel to Umbria, where his 2018 harvest of grapes was ready to be picked. His wife Dominique, his children Charlotte and Louis, and their childhood friend Manel came with him to help. But when they arrived, the hilltop villa was shrouded in patches of mist – and a persistent drizzle had made the grapes too wet to be collected. Picking them now would add too much water to the future wine. Verhofstadt, true to himself, was hopeful that tomorrow was going to be better and that the pickers – four local women, led by a man – would be able to come back then. 'Tomorrow we will try, tomorrow we'll all try, we have to hope that tomorrow the weather improves.' His daughter Charlotte laughed. 'Ah yes, because to do nothing, that's forbidden.'

As it turned out, the weather didn't improve. The drizzle turned into a steady downpour, and Verhofstadt tended his rose garden instead, stubbornly pulling weeds in the rain, refusing the coat that his wife Dominique brought out – while I stole an image of her giving him a tender kiss.

My film was about a divorce, after all.

On Wednesday 10 October, with now only eight days to go until the European Council meeting, Verhofstadt was back in his offices in Brussels. His guest that morning was the leader of Northern Ireland's Democratic Party, Arlene Foster, who was in Brussels for what one British website described as 'a bid to break the Brexit deadlock ahead of a looming no-deal deadline'. Like Verhofstadt, Ms Foster was outside the negotiating tunnel, and neither seemed clear what was going on inside it. Although that may just have been the impression they gave to each other, the conversation was also a bit like a fishing party, with both sides angling for morsels of extra information.

VERHOFSTADT: OK, where we are?

FOSTER: Where we are, where we are? We had a meeting as you know with Mr Barnier yesterday, we were trying to establish where we are at the negotiations. Our own government are putting forward, we understand, a new . . .

VERHOFSTADT [interrupting her]: But it has been seen, I understand, by nobody?

FOSTER: That's correct.

VERHOFSTADT: Also not by you?

FOSTER: That's correct, yes.

VERHOFSTADT: OK, and they are going to discuss it, if I understand it well, tomorrow or after tomorrow? At a Cabinet meeting?

FOSTER: I think it's next Tuesday, yes. I think there are discussions, but no text as yet.

Verhofstadt probed a little for a reaction to the plan Michel Barnier had been working on since the summer, to take the heat out of the issue of the backstop by developing an unobtrusive system for controlling goods arriving in Northern Ireland from Great Britain. He did not have to probe very far.

VERHOFSTADT: And in your meeting yesterday with Barnier, Barnier has explained [to] you his idea of this, er, how to call it . . . de-dramatised [laughs] regulatory controls or something?

FOSTER: The current text doesn't work for us and I think he understands that very well, because of the fact that it creates this border down the Irish Sea. Some of his de-dramatisation, as he calls it, still involves checks, which means that there still is a difference between us and the GB. And that's where the problem lies.

In public Arlene Foster was describing her red lines as 'blood red', and after her Brussels trip the DUP threatened to bring down the government by withdrawing support at Westminster if those lines were crossed. She and Guy Verhofstadt discussed the idea of a customs union to get round the problem – Verhofstadt again laid out the EU's objections to the Chequers plan – but with the real action still being played out in that negotiating tunnel, there was a limit to how far they could get.

VERHOFSTADT: The idea I thought was that Barnier will come forward with a proposal.

FOSTER: I thought he was going to publish his proposal this week?

VERHOFSTADT: No, for the simple reason that I think both sides, the UK side and the EU side, have decided to . . . not publish things, neither on the backstop by Britain, neither on the future relationship by EU, that make[s] things worse . . . I think it's a very sensitive

period, in which it's best that we work behind the
scenes, and you only come forward with texts at the
moment when you feel it can work. Or that it has a big
chance to work.

FOSTER: Do you have a timescale for that? I'm impatient.

VERHOFSTADT: I'm impatient for already more than a
year.

When Guillaume McLaughlin discussed the meeting with his
boss afterwards, he suggested that 'No-deal, and turning down
a deal, is going be a hell [of a] lot worse for the Northern Ireland
economy, than accepting a deal that may be bad . . . They have
to make that calculation.' But he also focused on what he called
the 'terribly worrying' point Arlene Foster had made about
the medium-term future. If Northern Ireland remained close
to the EU, it was bound to develop an economic system that
was increasingly different from that operating in the rest of the
United Kingdom. 'Of course, there's going to be divergence,
[it will] increase the difference [between Northern Ireland and
the UK], that's the real . . . problem,' he said, drilling down to
the hard political fact behind the technical discussions about
the way a backstop would work. From the DUP's perspective
the backstop looked like a step towards a united Ireland, and,
as Verhofstadt understood, 'they are against the reunification of
the island'. Guillaume nodded emphatically: 'And that's exactly
what people like her have been campaigning about for generations, to prevent. And [he showed his fists, clashing] there's no
answer, there's no solution to that problem.'

Michel Barnier escaped from the tunnel briefly that day to
give a speech to the closing session of the so-called European
Parliament of Enterprises, a two-yearly event which brings 751
(matching the number of MEPs) business leaders to Brussels,

and he used it to float his idea for 'de-dramatising' the border issue once more, saying that 'the EU proposes to carry out these checks [between Northern Ireland and Great Britain] in the least intrusive way.'

Barnier had been due to brief the Brexit Steering Group as well, but after the group again fell under suspicion because of a leak to the press, he had decided to stay away.

In the corridor outside Verhofstadt's offices, Guillaume McLaughlin discussed the leak with Edel Crosse and Jeroen Reijnen, the head of communications. Guillaume commented that 'I think the complaint of Barnier about the leak is exaggerated — a), and b) is a good excuse for him not to come.'

There had indeed been a leak, in The Guardian *it seems, but they didn't know who had leaked — was it someone from their own team, maybe? The way they discussed the issue gave a rare glimpse of how they saw their relationship with the media.*

MCLAUGHLIN: If you want to leak, you don't go to *The Guardian*, you speak to Bruno Waterfield and then it gets in The Times and then it gets somewhere.

CROSSE: No, you go to Politico, if you have a proper leak. You go to Politico.

REIJNEN: To be honest, if you leak, *The Guardian* is not a bad leak. Why? Because there is no pay wall. So people can share it on their . . .

MCLAUGHLIN: Did you leak then?

CROSSE: Did you leak?

REIJNEN: Of course not.

Barnier's tunnel strategy was fraying nerves elsewhere in the EU. Sabine Weyand had told the European Council ambassadors that it could only work if everyone was willing to trust the negotiating team, but trust is never in ample supply among the big European institutions. 'When you speak to the people in the Council, they're very anxious,' Guillaume told Verhofstadt, after another phone call, one of many that Wednesday. As chief of staff he was his boss's antenna.

The fact that everything was being kept secret until the last moment made the EU member governments even more tense than usual. Guillaume continued:

Everything will be kept completely under wraps until Monday. The first time the member states are going to see the outline of this is Monday. And they're very nervous about that because they think it's too short. This is under the assumption that we're going for a deal on Wednesday, Thursday [when the European Council was to meet], which should be a deal on everything. And maybe they will need a few commas here and there, but the global deal will be done. But they're worried of course that the member states won't have enough time between the Monday and the Wednesday evening . . . to be able to [digest the] result. And I say, yeah, we're in the same situation, we just need to trust Barnier; Barnier knows exactly the parameters [Guillaume showed some distance with his fingers], he knows what the space is. Because if they start consulting member states before Monday, they will be all over the place.

Towards Wednesday evening, Verhofstadt did get an update from Barnier after all. I'd left the premises by then, but Bram Delen filmed for me on his iPhone. As always, the phone call did not come as a surprise, but was organised half an hour earlier, to the exact minute, giving Bram the time to install himself.

VERHOFSTADT: Allo? Michel, how are you? No, not at all, I am in my office, I have just finished a meeting with Arlene Foster . . . No, you are the one who is the enemy! I am just a parliamentarian doing my best. [laughs] But they are unbelievable, eh? [sighs]

Verhofstadt, apparently echoing Barnier, followed that up with the even harsher judgement that the DUP were 'unbearable'. 'Each time they repeat their thing, their mantra,' he said, 'about "the indivisibility of" and now, as you said, they're especially using the economic argument.'

The call didn't last long, but afterwards, as he briefed Bram and his chief of staff Guillaume McLaughlin, Verhofstadt sounded optimistic. He outlined the likely choreography of closing the deal:

VERHOFSTADT: So, they are going to continue working right through the weekend. And then [here he whistled] Mrs May will meet her Cabinet on Monday morning.

MCLAUGHLIN: Monday morning?

VERHOFSTADT: Monday morning . . . to 'zip' [he made a slicing movement with his hand], get this through, and once it's passed, Mr Raab will get on a plane [here he whistled again] fly here from the Cabinet meeting to bring the news of the Cabinet's agreement, and then there'll be a joint press conference – on Monday afternoon.

MCLAUGHLIN: The member states won't like that very much, eh?

VERHOFSTADT: He [Barnier] will keep them up to date, one way or another, I don't know how. So there we are; he says they are working on the same elements from our ideas, but also the fact that Great

Britain becomes part of a customs union, because
otherwise . . . [he stirred his coffee] but he didn't give
me much detail.

MCLAUGHLIN: He can't say anything.

VERHOFSTADT: He can't say anything because each time
he does it gets out and then it's 'kaput'.

MCLAUGHLIN: The problem is . . . that English
journalists are capable of making him say things he
didn't say.

VERHOFSTADT: One word, one word, one little word –
that's enough to say that he's said such-and-such, and
then they put it in a headline.

MCLAUGHLIN: The main news is that they are really
slogging away at getting a deal for Monday.

VERHOFSTADT: Yes.

DELEN: With our backstop in there?

VERHOFSTADT: With 'a' backstop, I don't know what
they are looking at in terms of a system – but it will
be a system that is anyway, one way or another, linked
to the continuation, temporary or not, of a customs
union with the UK, because otherwise . . .

*He trailed off and didn't finish his sentence. Guillaume McLaughlin
picked it up: 'A temporary customs union which will continue in a way
that is not at all temporary until the moment when the two parties
agree that it should end, either because of a better new relationship,
or because we need to fall back upon the backstop – so it's a double
lock – and it's temporary until the two parties decide to end it.*

VERHOFSTADT: Yes. And malicious tongues will say that
it is unlimited. And then of course there'll be pretty
phrases about the future [relationship].

MCLAUGHLIN: Lots of pretty phrases. The future will be wonderful.

In the end, what Michel Barnier and the British negotiators had to reach an agreement on was a text — but a text can either be crystal clear, or cloudy, with fudge. To reach a deal both kinds of language would probably have to be used. The withdrawal agreement had to be an unambiguous legal text. The lawyers — including, notably, the United Kingdom's attorney general — would trawl through every detail. But in the political declaration on the future relationship that accompanied it, fudge could be used, leaving a lot of room for interpretation.

Verhofstadt's faith in the power of words is unlimited, and given his qualities as an orator, that's no surprise. But perhaps, on that Wednesday 10 October 2018, he had fallen into precisely the trap he often felt the Brits were vulnerable to — of being so wrapped up in the optimistic mood on his own side that he ignored the reality of what was happening on the other.

The way opinion was moving in London was as opaque as the tunnel in Brussels. Also on Wednesday 10 October 2018, *The Guardian* ran a story under the headline 'Senior Tories launch concerted attack on May's Brexit plan — Brexiters warn against fresh concessions to Brussels as PM faces calls to change course'. It reported that the former Brexit secretary David Davis warned that Mrs May's negotiating position could cost her party dear; in a letter to all Tory MPs, he wrote, 'If we stay on the current trajectory we will go into the next election with the government having delivered none of the benefits of Brexit, with the country being reduced to a rule-taker from Brussels, and having failed to deal with a number of promises in the [election] manifesto and the Lancaster House speech.'

But other reporting painted a picture that chimed more

closely with Guy Verhofstadt's view that a deal was in the offing. On Thursday 11 October, *The Times* informed its readers, 'Today the prime minister is due to meet a group of senior cabinet ministers, including the foreign secretary, Jeremy Hunt, the home secretary, Sajid Javid, and the defence secretary, Gavin Williamson, to brief them on the negotiations.' And the *Financial Times* interpreted the meeting positively, for the fact alone that it took place, reporting that 'one official close to the Brexit talks said: "The prime minister never brings the cabinet together to tell them what's going on. That's not her style. It feels to me like the deal is practically done."'

The *FT* also seemed to know what was going to be in the deal – how both sides were going to compromise. 'Mr Barnier is set to agree Britain's demand for the backstop to include references to a customs union to the whole UK, which would avoid a customs border in the Irish Sea while a more comprehensive UK–EU trade agreement is completed. Mrs May has accepted that there should be no firm end date to the backstop, although language will be found to say that it will be a temporary arrangement with "a clear pathway" to a final trade deal, intended to create frictionless trade.' To anyone keeping score, it sounded like a one–all draw; the EU had accepted Mrs May's case for a solution to the Irish problem, which would involve the whole of the United Kingdom – despite all Michel Barnier's concerns about 'cherry picking' – while she had accepted that the backstop could not be time-limited.

The 'language' about the length of the backstop did not convince Jacob Rees-Mogg. 'It is worth remembering that income tax was introduced as a temporary measure,' he said. 'Without an end date, we could be in the customs union for ever.'

There was a growing consensus in London – even without certainty about the details of the agreement that might shortly emerge from the tunnel – that May was likely to face a real challenge in getting a deal through Parliament. According to the *Financial Times*, the government was, even before the deal became public, putting out feelers to Brexiteers on the other side of the aisle. 'The accepted wisdom in Britain is that Theresa May is far from certain to win a parliamentary vote on whatever deal she manages to agree with the EU this autumn,' the paper reported. 'This perhaps explains why, along with a small gang of Brexit-supporters on the opposition benches, Downing Street advisers have been chatting discreetly to Labour MPs who they believe could support the government when it comes to the crunch . . . Up to 30 Labour MPs could defy their party's line to vote for Mrs May's Brexit.'

The *FT*'s assessment of the way opinion on the Tory back benches was moving is worth quoting as an illustration of the way the volatility of Westminster politics was now rewriting conventional wisdom. The paper reported that

the government whips' office is crunching the numbers to figure out how many Tory rebels can be peeled off. There have been suggestions that there could be up to 80 rebels on the government benches, which would spell disaster for Mrs May. Yet as the classic political adage has it, when talking of rebellions, halve the numbers, then halve them again . . . At the crucial moment, many ERG [European Research Group] MPs may lose their nerve and side with the government. There is growing confidence in the cabinet that Mrs May will strike a deal and that parliament will approve it.

That 'classic adage' would soon be proved profoundly wrong; as things turned out, the figure of eighty rebels proved to be a significant underestimate.

Inside the tunnel, though, on Friday 12 October, the canaries were still very much alive and not giving any warning signs of calamities to come. According to the later *Guardian* account of the way this act in the drama unfolded, Sabine Weyand told EU ambassadors gathering in Luxembourg that last day of the week that the talks were progressing well. The paper quoted an EU diplomat as saying, 'The Wedding Knot is tied.' Further scraps of detail about the substance of a deal were emerging, too. According to the same paper, it included 'secret plans' for a year's extension of the transition period (from two years to three years) during which the EU and the UK were to negotiate their future relationship; the idea was to create more space to settle the long-term economic framework in the hope that the backstop would never be needed. As *The Guardian* put it, 'The expected offer of an extension is designed to convince Arlene Foster, the leader of the Democratic Unionist party, that the "backstop" plan to avoid the creation of a hard border on the island of Ireland will never come into force.'

The way that turbulent week unfolded brought home the consequences of the negotiating processes the two sides had developed. Despite the nervousness behind the scenes which Guillaume McLaughlin had reported to Guy Verhofstadt, there was no public sign of unease in Europe's institutions and the twenty-seven member state capitals about what might be happening in the tunnel. During the fourteen months since Theresa May had triggered Article 50, Michel Barnier had amassed significant political capital which he could now afford to draw down on. He had kept solidly within the negotiating mandate that the Council and Parliament had endorsed, and he had been scrupulous about keeping the lines of communication open with both – his phone call to Verhofstadt that week was an example. So both members of the Council and Parliament could be confident that Barnier would not bring anything out of the tunnel that was wildly at odds with the fundamental positions agreed within the EU.

Theresa May, by contrast, had always had her room for manoeuvre limited by the fact that any detailed exposition of her negotiating ambitions carried huge political risk, because it was almost always bound to provoke anger on one side or the other of the Brexit divide within her party. Verhofstadt himself had direct experience of the way the British prime minister liked to keep things to herself. In December 2017, while they were trying to save the botched first deal with May, the joint report, the Barnier team had warned him that the British prime minister might not have told her then home secretary, Amber Rudd, about some of the agreements that had been reached on the rights of EU citizens living in the United Kingdom. In the end, this approach could only undermine the trust May needed from her party, and as the expectation of a big reveal in Brussels mounted, the political atmosphere in London turned poisonous with cries of betrayal.

One of the bitterest denunciations came from the pen of Charles Moore, a former editor of the *Daily Telegraph* and, as the official biographer of Margaret Thatcher, a figure of considerable consequence among Conservatives. 'Theresa May cares, above all, about "burning injustices",' he opened his regular Saturday *Telegraph* column. 'She often tells us so. Yet she seems determined, next week, to ignite the biggest injustice yet. She goes to Brussels ready, it seems, to frustrate the result of the EU referendum.'

Moore's account of the 'weary months since the negotiations began' was a litany of capitulations. 'Mrs May has doubled the money she proposes to pay to the EU and more than halved the things she insists on in return. She said at first that the

European Court of Justice (ECJ) would not have the last word over the rights of EU nationals living in this country after Brexit. Then she gave in. She said that we would make our own trade deals: now, because of the terms of the transition, we can't. She agreed to a crippling Northern Ireland backstop without even seeming to grasp what it means.' Moore asked rhetorically: 'Please could someone remind me of any significant concession the EU has made in return for Mrs May's? As we approach the moment of truth, is there anyone, on either side of this argument, who can whole-heartedly commend her plan?'

On Sunday morning David Davis, the former Brexit secretary who had now become one of the most vocal leaders of pro-Brexit rebels on the back benches, also passed judgement on the yet-to-be published deal – in an apocalyptic call to arms. 'It is time for the cabinet to exert their collective authority,' he declared in the *Sunday Times*. 'This week the authority of our constitution is on the line.' And that same day's *Sun on Sunday* reported, on the basis of a 'leaked memo', that there was an 'EU plot to do a secret deal today'. The paper quoted the former Cabinet member Priti Patel, who said, 'This memo reeks of a secret, precooked backroom deal. If the details are true, it stinks, and most MPs will find it totally unacceptable.' The paper added, 'Another senior figure described the proposed deal as "a pile of vomit".'

The Sun's former political editor and veteran commentator Trevor Kavanagh was sulphurous, and he reached even further back into history than Jacob Rees-Mogg had done to make his point. 'Brexit's our worst defeat since 1066,' he declared. 'For two nail-biting years, wide-eyed optimists like me have put our trust in Theresa May's promise: "Brexit means Brexit." This week, there is a whiff of betrayal in the air.' Kavanagh declared that, 'barring a last-minute revolt by Tory Brexiteers, Brussels has won and we have lost', and reported that 'sniggering can be heard across the capitals of Europe, with France guffawing loudest. The British Lion is a toothless kitten and we are the laughing stock of Europe.'

~

At four o'clock in the afternoon on Sunday 14 October, Dominic Raab arrived in Brussels. Despite all the fury in the Eurosceptic press, reporters were still writing stories about 'crunch talks' which were 'expected to last late into the night'. There was a widespread expectation that he had come to settle the last details of the deal that Barnier and the British negotiators had been preparing in their tunnel for the previous ten days. Michel Barnier himself later confirmed to Guy Verhofstadt that he understood Dominic Raab was coming to finalise things.

But, just before a quarter to seven that evening, Barnier sent out this tweet: 'We met today @DominicRaab and UK negotiating team. Despite intense efforts, some key issues are still open, including the backstop for IE/NI [the Irish Republic and Northern Ireland] to avoid a hard border. I will debrief the EU27 and @Europarl_EN on the #Brexit negotiations.' In the light of the dramatic detail that emerged in subsequent days about the way talks had broken down, it was a remarkably neutral description of what had happened.

~

Early the next morning, Guillaume McLaughlin stood in front of Verhofstadt's desk in his office in Brussels, and the Brexit coordinator of the European Parliament told him, 'Can you imagine? There's nothing! They [the British] went down there [came to Brussels] to say "OK,

everything we've been talking about these last few days, pfffft, it's no
good, there you go then, bye.'"

There was no deal.

MCLAUGHLIN: But that means that she hasn't got it over
    the hurdle of her Cabinet.
VERHOFSTADT: No, no.
MCLAUGHLIN: That's a really bad sign.
VERHOFSTADT: A really bad sign.
MCLAUGHLIN: She's hesitating, she's really hesitating.
VERHOFSTADT: I don't think she's hesitating, but that
    she doesn't have a majority in her own Cabinet. Well,
    what to do then? If half of those sitting there, say no?

When the rest of the core team arrived – Bram Delen, Jeroen Reijnen,
Eva Palatova and Edel Crosse – Verhofstadt told them: 'There is no Brexit
any more, cheers, finished, over.' He laughed cynically and added that he
had heard it said that 'we [are] going to now do negotiations Wednesday
evening [at the Council meeting] to find a breakthrough. But it doesn't
work like that. It is not that there is a sort of fine tuning to do, you know.'

A deep rift had to be resolved, about Ireland, and Verhofstadt didn't
see how that could be done very quickly. What's worse, if the Council did
try to resolve it, the result might be disastrous, because, in Guillaume's
view: 'Half of the member states don't give a fuck about Northern
Ireland. They don't even know there is a problem there. They say, build
a fucking wall. Build a fucking wall.'

The team then sat down around the meeting table in Guillaume's
office, without their boss, and with played naivety – that could have
been mine – Jeroen Reijnen asked, 'So it's not going to get solved this
week?' Everybody laughed, but bitterly. They had all really been hoping
that the long negotiating slog might be over.

DELEN: Jeroen, you are a bit too joyful with the fact that
this shit is going to continue for the next three years.

MCLAUGHLIN: I was prepared to go through this week,
excessive Brexit crap, because then it would be done.
In my mind I was mentally prepared to be writing
resolutions, and spend ten days, really, and then it's
finished. But it's not finished, aaaaahh . . .

DELEN: Let's hope for a hard Brexit then, that they don't
come back to the negotiation table.

CROSSE [born in Ireland]: As [the] Irish, we're in a
difficult position then.

MCLAUGHLIN: Yeah, terribly difficult.

CROSSE: It just doesn't bear thinking about. I can't really
laugh at it for the moment . . . And I normally laugh at
anything.

Later that morning, Guy Verhofstadt gathered the Brexit
Steering Group in his office, to share what intelligence he
could. Perhaps most alarmingly for those still hoping that the
negotiations could be brought to a head, he reported they had
actually gone backwards.

Verhofstadt explained that the meeting between Dominic
Raab and the Barnier team had only lasted an hour and ten
minutes, and that when it began, 'immediately Raab attacked,
and put in question a number of issues that were 100 per cent
agreed'. Olly Robbins, Mrs May's Europe adviser, tried to push
back against the Brexit secretary, 'saying, "Don't do that, this
is agreed, this is not about that, and that question."' But Raab's
message was blunt; the solution Michel Barnier and Robbins
had been working on did not command the backing of the
Cabinet and would not fly politically. Verhofstadt reported that
he declared 'it's not possible for us in Britain', and proposed

once more that the issue of Ireland be pushed off into discussions on the future relationship.

'There will be a need of a new drama, a new Salzburg moment,' Verhofstadt judged, 'but with this difference; that it's clear now that in the British government there is no majority, it's blocked there, but in a serious way. It's not that it's one, two guys making it difficult.' The Parliament's director of inter-institutional affairs, Nick Lane, chipped in with an estimate of eight members of the Cabinet threatening rebellion. 'Eight or nine' was Verhofstadt's analysis, and he added, 'This is not about: this phrasing is not good, this wording is not good, this paragraph is not in the right place. It's really about the approach that is completely different.'

Not for the first time, the members of the Brexit Steering Group found themselves confounded by the weakness in Mrs May's political position, and her incapacity to 'push through the Olly Robbins deal – let's be honest, it was the Olly Robbins deal, eh?' as Verhofstadt remarked.

'It's incredible,' Roberto Gualtieri said, 'because she won the congress, the party congress [party conference], now she has the authority, so really I'm astonished [by] how she does not use the fact that she is in power. She can force.'

Evidently, she could not.

And in the fallout from Sunday's abortive negotiations, some of the flak was directed at the man who – according to Guy Verhofstadt – continued to be Mrs May's main representative at the negotiating table, Olly Robbins. While Verhofstadt debriefed his colleagues in Brussels that Monday morning, *The Times* was reporting that 'in private some right-wing Tories have suggested that Mr Robbins has an almost Rasputin-like hold over the prime minister, filtering the messages coming from Brussels and skewing official advice to aid a soft Brexit.'

The paper's letter columns included a highly unusual public defence of Mr Robbins from the acting Cabinet secretary and head of the civil service, Sir Mark Sedwill, who said that those responsible for the 'sniping' against the former should be 'ashamed of themselves'.

Michel Barnier gave his account of what had happened to the Brexit Steering Group on Tuesday. It was early in the morning – the cleaning ladies were still busy with their tour of the offices – and while the BSG members arrived one by one, the chief negotiator was already pouring his frustration out to Guillaume McLaughlin:

> BARNIER: We have a problem, eh? We have a problem. Because, because she, in fact she refuses a backstop now. She had accepted a backstop two times, in December and March, by letter. And [now] she refuse to put a backstop.
>
> MCLAUGHLIN: That's what it amounts to. That's the result.
>
> BARNIER: Because, any backstop, any backstop – even if we never use a backstop, because a backstop doesn't have to be used, it's a safeguard – any backstop means controls, customs, border, control between Great Britain and Northern Ireland. Any backstop.

His efforts to 'de-dramatise' the control of goods arriving in Northern Ireland from Great Britain had failed, foundering on the hard political facts at Westminster; any semblance of a division between mainland UK and Belfast was unacceptable to the Democratic Unionists, and the DUP was keeping Mrs May in power.

Over coffee and croissants, Barnier repeated to the Brexit Steering Group where he thought they stood. 'We have made huge progress for everything else,' he said. 'In fact we were ready on Friday, to make this agreement, but it blocked, it blocked clearly on the backstop.' But Barnier still believed that there was more to the British position than the political arithmetic in the House of Commons. 'For me there is a strategic and tactical reason also,' he said, echoing comments he had often made before in this forum, 'which is to use Ireland for the future negotiations. To isolate Ireland, and not to close this point, and to leave it open for the next two or three years. And in that case we will face clearly a permanent pressure on the negotiation for trade, the single market, because of Ireland.'

And Barnier reminded the BSG that 'from the very beginning, remember, they tried to merge everything, the budget, and the future relation[ship], to buy part of the single market and pay by the debts of the past . . . and now they try to postpone the Irish case, to have this leverage during all the . . .' And Guy Verhofstadt finished his sentence for him, because this was an assumption they all shared – '. . . the negotiations afterwards.'

The European Council was due to meet the following day and, again not for the first time, Barnier expressed his fear that the united front he had worked so hard to sustain would begin to fray; that ticking clock which had in the past served as his ally in putting pressure on the British might, with the negotiations now in a state of crisis, become an enemy and not a friend. 'We have to be careful what will be the reaction of the European Council and the member states,' he said. Verhofstadt asked him whether his fear was 'that some countries will say, "Let it go, this Irish issue"?' Barnier nodded wearily. 'Yes. Between us I can tell you, one of the ministers told me, if there is no deal, we will be obliged to implement controls, so why don't we put in the control[s], and [get on] with the deal?'

Elmar Brok, the German Christian Democrat, shared Barnier's concerns. 'I'm really afraid that in the mixture of pressure, member states fall apart. [And then] exactly what they [the UK] [have] wanted [for] one and a half years will be achieved in the last moment. They always said, we will make it politically at the end.'

'She [May] phones everyone,' Brok observed.

'Everyone,' Verhofstadt confirmed.

The Brexit deal had been intended as the centrepiece of that week's Council meeting, and the parliamentarians began to worry — allowing themselves a little irreverent levity — about what sort of mischief Europe's leaders might get up to with time on their hands if the centrepiece fell away. 'And there is an additional danger: that they have nothing to do for two days. The member states,' noted the Italian Roberto Gualtieri, 'in a place with a very light agenda, and nothing big to discuss.'

Verhofstadt noted, 'That's not good.'

'They can play cards,' Philippe Lamberts suggested. Verhofstadt, his mind perhaps returning to Umbria, added, 'We can send them wine.'

As the group mulled over possible ways round the impasse it became apparent that every solution threw up new problems. Barnier's adviser Georg Riekeles pointed out that a backstop in the form of a temporary customs union 'would hold up our own trade negotiations, because we wouldn't be able to say what happens with the territory of the UK'. Barnier himself mused that 'the problem with a temporary customs union is that you have to have a trade deal on the side, because things like fishing need to be sorted.'

They also discussed the idea that had escaped from the tunnel and made it into the pages of *The Guardian* at the end of the previous week – prolonging the transition period during which the United Kingdom negotiated its future relationship with the EU. Since the UK would have to be required to abide by all the EU's laws and regulations during that period, the problem of the Irish border could be avoided for as long as it continued.

BARNIER: Prolongation of the transition is then a smarter solution.

VERHOFSTADT: But is then the route to prolong the transition not the route in the coming days?

RIEKELES: Mrs May, in an answer to a question from Boris Johnson yesterday in the House of Commons, he said, 'Will you confirm that we will no longer [be in transition] at the end of 2020?' She didn't confirm.

But prolonging the transition could not provide a long-term solution to the border problem. 'Even then, even if we prolong, after that we need the backstop,' Philippe Lamberts pointed out.

'We know, because of the political situation in the UK, that it cannot be an indefinite prolongation,' Barnier replied, and when Roberto Gualtieri pointed out that 'legally it is not possible' the chief negotiator looked ahead to a development they all feared: a Boris Johnson premiership. 'Legally, we run the risk that Boris Johnson or some other [prime minister] put[s] us in front of the court [if we prolong the transition for too long]. And we can lose. The prolongation is a phasing-out period. It could be several years more, but not indefinite.'

Verhofstadt floated one more possible ploy: 'But it's not

indefinite if you say: until we have an agreement on the future relationship. Because the prolongation of the transition gives you all the security.'

Barnier did not think that ruse would fly either. 'I'm not sure that an indefinite prolongation of the transition could reach an agreement in the House of Commons,' he concluded.

The Polish MEP Danuta Hübner, returning to the temporary customs union as a backstop solution, asked what progress the talks had made towards ensuring a so-called level playing field? Was there an agreement in sight on baseline economic regulations between the two sides which would ensure they could compete fairly – something the EU insisted must be a precondition of any form of customs union? 'Nowhere,' Barnier stated flatly, adding the warning: 'If we give them the temporary customs union without the guarantee of the level playing field, officially, we are lost, eh?' Because, Verhofstadt chipped in, 'they are going to say, that's very good, for the future also, thank you very much.'

But the idea of using talks about the future relationship to fudge the issue of the backstop had clearly not been completely dismissed. Barnier's adviser Georg Riekeles explained that the EU and British teams had been discussing 'the possibility of keeping our backstop, a permanent backstop, because we need that permanent backstop', in the legally binding withdrawal agreement, while at the same time introducing into the non-binding political declaration 'some language, that there will be another backstop, or something that kicks in before that, which is a customs union, but without saying this is temporary'. 'Plus regulatory alignment,' Barnier added, the details man to the last.

That combination was the foundation of the compromise over the Irish backstop which eventually emerged, but when the negotiators went back into their tunnel, they would have to travel one further, crucial, mile before they got there.

I filmed, quietly, every so often changing my position, but not very often, while this discussion was going on, and on – and to be honest, afterwards I didn't recall a single word of what had been said. Of course, I had the excuse that I had been busy with my images. But not really understanding everything also didn't help to remember things. In fact, even when I made my transcriptions later, I found it hard to grasp what had been discussed.

I wondered, though: was I the only one? Or were at least some of the people around the table that day in Guy Verhofstadt's office equally confused? One would wish they weren't, of course, but then again . . . maybe one would also wish they were – human beings, groping along together in a misty swamp, or on a narrow path that skirts perilous mountain ridges, trying to survive together the ordeal they have been landed in.

In times of a certain predilection for strong all-knowing leaders, it could be my alternative definition of democracy.

Michel Barnier ended the meeting on Tuesday 16 October 2018 with his now-routine pleas for confidentiality, and was rewarded with a somewhat unusual remark from the European Parliament's second most senior civil servant. 'Thank you for keeping the BSG alive,' said Markus Winkler.

BARNIER: What?
WINKLER: Thank you for keeping the BSG alive. We feared a bit that we would disappear from this bit onwards.
LAMBERTS: Not with Michel.
BARNIER: I'm ready to work with you in the next few

days . . . but give me the margin for negotiations,
eh?

HÜBNER: So you still think that it's feasible?

BARNIER: Yes, yes.

VERHOFSTADT: It's the building up of the necessary
pressure.

BARNIER: I thank you to protect me, and to protect the
negotiation. Many thanks to all, and many thanks for
that margin.

Barnier went back to work; one more heave would be needed.

*I packed up – wondering what Theresa May told her Cabinet ministers
at the end of their meetings.*

17

ARMISTICE

Mid-October–mid-November 2018

The Grand Place in Brussels is one of those great open-air drawing rooms that are such a hallmark of European city civilisation – a huge cobbled rectangle surrounded by buildings emblazoned with elaborate ornament. On the evening of Wednesday 17 October 2018, Emmanuel Macron, Angela Merkel, the Belgian prime minister Charles Michel and the prime minister of Luxembourg, Xavier Bettel, joined the drinkers there and, according to the *Reuters* news agency, downed their beers with French fries in the best Belgian tradition. A Croatian journalist, who caught the four beer-drinking leaders on camera, tweeted that he had spoken to a group of visitors who had had a chat with Mrs Merkel. They had asked her about Brexit. 'Please, it's a wonderful evening,' she replied. 'Let's not spoil it.'

Earlier in the evening Theresa May had been given fifteen minutes to lay out her position on the deadlocked Brexit talks to the twenty-seven other heads of government in the European Council, and she did her best to reassure them that she remained committed to reaching an agreement. She appeared open to the possibility of extending the transition period as a way of getting round the backstop impasse, but most reports of the meeting suggested she had come with no substantial new ideas. After a quarter of an hour Mrs May then left her fellow leaders to their dinner – 'pan-fried mushrooms, fillet of turbot cooked in wheat beer and a trio of fruit sorbets' – and they reviewed the state of the negotiations in the wake of the high drama of the previous weekend.

The statement issued by the Council the following day was neutral but firm in its tone, and was clearly designed to kill once more any remaining British idea that they could circumvent Michel Barnier and his team by appealing directly to individual member governments. 'EU27 leaders reaffirmed their full confidence in Michel Barnier as the negotiator and their determination to stay united,' it read. 'They also noted that, despite intensive negotiations, not enough progress has been achieved. The European Council (Art. 50) called on the Union negotiator to continue his efforts to reach an agreement in accordance with previously agreed European Council guidelines. The leaders declared their readiness to convene a[n extra] European Council, if and when the Union negotiator reports that decisive progress has been made.'

The Brexit-supporting *Daily Telegraph* summarised the EU response with the headline 'EU ignores UK's plea with message: it's your problem to sort out'. But this summit was clearly not going to see a repeat of the theatrics of Salzburg. And that, as Guy Verhofstadt explained when he discussed the state of play with a group of British MEPs he trusted the following week, was quite deliberate.

He had invited them for a briefing on his latest intelligence about what had been happening inside the British Cabinet (it was one of the oddities thrown up by the Brexit process that UK MEPs could, it seemed, get a clearer picture about this from a fellow member of the European Parliament than from their own government).

Verhofstadt's analysis of the deal-that-never-quite-made-it was that Mrs May had failed to stand up for it when the crunch came. 'Apparently she [May] didn't defend it, around the [Cabinet] table, but presented it,' he said. Verhofstadt reported that when the deal came under fire from Dominic Raab and the attorney general, Geoffrey Cox (who was to emerge as a key player on the British side), 'There was no real . . . "my team did it, and [these] are the advantages"; that didn't happen. So that means that at the end of the meeting suddenly there were [laughs] eight, nine ministers against the proposal that was put on the table.'

Then Raab came to Brussels, and 'within five minutes I got Barnier on the phone saying, "He came here to say it doesn't work,"' Verhofstadt explained. The one thing the two sides had been able to agree on was Barnier's dry, informative tweet that announced the deadlock to the world – 'That's today's politics, eh? Agreement on a tweet,' Verhofstadt remarked with a laugh – and that had at least helped to avoid things blowing up in the way they had at the Salzburg summit. 'Because we knew in advance, on the Sunday evening, that it would not fly,' he said, they had been able to 'de-dramatise' the European Council and 'avoid in fact a second Salzburg. Everybody went to Salzburg . . . saying . . . "There it's going to happen, they will come out," and nothing came out. On the contrary, it was a big disaster. That didn't happen this time because in advance there was communication to say there is no agreement, so we have to work further on this.'

Verhofstadt wrapped things up with his view that there would eventually be a deal – but he had a caveat. His prediction of how things would unfold would prove bull's-eye accurate:

'At the end, there will be a deal. But I'm not so sure that the deal will fly in Westminster. That's another story. So there are two different stories, eh?'

While Barnier and the British negotiators rolled up their sleeves again, Verhofstadt returned to the routine business of the EU's institutional rivalries once more. The EU's heads of government at the Council had not, in his view, done anything useful at all at their October summit, even with Brexit off their hands, and as he prepared for his monthly speech at the plenary session of the European Parliament in Strasbourg, he role-played the case for their prosecution with Guillaume McLaughlin. Bram Delen was typing as usual, while Edel Crosse listened in and offered her comments.

VERHOFSTADT: I'm asking myself if two weeks ago it was
     really necessary to hold a European Council? If it was
     not a waste of time? On Brexit, no-deal, but that was
     expected. On migration . . . no agreement too. On
     the governance of the Eurozone, no progress either.
     I'm very disappointed. Four months ago, in June, you
     promised a lot, but little has been delivered . . . Public
     opinion is still doubting that our external borders
     are seriously protected . . . We are waiting already
     two years . . . You find that normal, Mr Guillaume
     McLaughlin?
MCLAUGHLIN: It's scandalous.
VERHOFSTADT: I thought you gave that impression . . .
     It has now been ten years since the outbreak of
     the financial crisis, and no new governance for the
     Eurozone has been put in place.
MCLAUGHLIN: Yeah.
VERHOFSTADT: Really, Mr Tusk, the way you and your

colleagues in the Council evade your responsibility, is
de—

MCLAUGHLIN: Dereliction.

VERHOFSTADT [struggling with the diction of the word
and asking his team for help]: . . . dereliction of
duty. You have not another word? Sleepwalking to
catastrophe. So [my] question to you [is]: when are you
going to change your method? When are you going
to lock your colleagues into a meeting room? No new
clothes, no new underwear. Until they have taken
their responsibility. Until they have reformed our
migration and Eurozone policy. It's not five minutes
before, it's five minutes after twelve.

DELEN: That's what my mum used to say to my brother
always. 'It's not five to twelve, it's five after twelve, for
you, eh, comrade?'

CROSSE [laughing]: Even Verhofstadt knows your mother.

*Verhofstadt didn't laugh, but sighed — because he knew that he was
going to say things he'd said a thousand times before. Each time he had
to find a new dressing for the same message, and that morning, he was
tired of doing so, it seemed. He was always making the same points.*

*He told me, while putting on his tie: 'If you do that every time, you
end up with one word per point, and then with just one word in all. And
then you ask yourself, what was that word again? I forgot.'*

Then he did laugh.

Two weeks later, on 11 November 2018, the beer-drinkers
of the Grand Place gathered for an altogether more solemn
occasion; to commemorate the 100th anniversary of the end of
the First World War. Donald Trump, Vladimir Putin, Angela
Merkel and more than sixty heads of state and government

joined the French president Emmanuel Macron at the Tomb of the Unknown Soldier beneath the Arc de Triomphe in Paris. Theresa May was not among them, opting instead to attend the ceremony at the Cenotaph and a service at Westminster Abbey: she had visited war graves in Belgium and France the Friday before Armistice Day, and David Lidington deputised for her at the Paris ceremony.

The gathering heard Emmanuel Macron warn of the dangers of resurgent nationalism, and praise the United Nations and the European Union for their contributions to peace. In a speech reminiscent of Guy Verhofstadt's 'to be European, for us, is an existential question', he cautioned against the return of Europe's 'old demons', and declared that 'Patriotism is the exact opposite of nationalism. Nationalism is a betrayal of patriotism.' Macron questioned whether the Paris gathering would be remembered as 'a symbol of lasting peace or the last moment of unity before the world falls into disorder', and he told his fellow leaders that the answer 'depends on us'.

Afterwards, in the forest of Compiègne where the Armistice was signed in a railway carriage, the Frenchman Macron warmly hugged the German Merkel. The picture of this moment became the symbol of the memories and hopes they shared.

Michel Barnier attended the commemorations in Ypres, the Flanders town which was the focus of three great battles during the First World War. The first, fought in the autumn of 1914, was a devastating demonstration of the casualties that war fought with modern weapons could exact, and British, French and Belgian troops fell alongside one another. The first German use of gas, in the spring of 1915, marked the beginning of the second battle of Ypres. The third battle, in 1917, which is better known as Passchendaele, led to half a million casualties.

When Barnier turned up at the Brexit Steering Group a couple of days after the centenary commemorations, he explained that he had chosen to spend Remembrance Day in Ypres because 'it was there that the largest number of British were killed in the whole war'. He reported that 'there were many English people there, and they were very moved'.

Verhofstadt reflected that 'the Last Post is still sounded every day'. 'Every night, at eight o'clock, from day one, 1918,' Barnier confirmed.

Ypres was where I was taken as a schoolboy, many times, to hear the bugle call of the Last Post, and in the fields and hills around, to visit the trenches and to wander through the war cemeteries, often still divided by nationality, but united in their silent grief. The memories of those visits are among the most vivid of my youth, together with the stories I was told by my parents, of how they were born and spent their first years of life in a country occupied by German troops, during the Second World War.

I've often wondered, over the past two years, whether this is not the biggest rift between mainland Europe and the United Kingdom: the fact that none of us on the continent won that Second World War, like Britain did – we all lost, but we managed to build upon that, creating a new reality for ourselves, whereas Britain just carried on as it had always done, believing that it could keep on winning.

I really hope that, long after Brexit, the bugle call will continue to spread its message – that the cost of believing that wars can be won is terrible.

18

TORTURE FOR THE BRITS

Mid-November–late November 2018

On 13 November 2018, Guy Verhofstadt organised a closed, secret session of the Brexit Steering Group, with Michel Barnier and all the usual politicians involved — Elmar Brok, Roberto Gualtieri, Philippe Lamberts, Gabi Zimmer and Danuta Hübner — but without the aides who normally accompanied them. The two high-ranking civil servants Markus Winkler and Nick Lane were also invited, as was Verhofstadt's chief of staff Guillaume McLaughlin. Everyone was shovelled into the narrow room behind his office on the sixth floor of the Parliament building in Strasbourg, where a very large table left just enough space for the chairs.

When I turned up as well, with my camera (Bram Delen had informed me of the meeting), Verhofstadt raised his eyebrows. He warned me that I was probably not going to be able to film. Barnier wouldn't allow it.

I suggested that I just install myself in the room, and if Barnier wanted me out, he could say so.

Verhofstadt agreed. And Barnier, eventually, didn't object. The EU chief negotiator was on the brink of finally, really reaching a deal with the United Kingdom.

Maybe he was too happy or too relieved to object. Or too proud.

The negotiating teams 'worked all weekend. I can tell you that my team is impressive, eh?' Barnier told the restricted BSG gathering. 'The team is exceptional, all the DDs [deputy directors] were there. Mobilised. Deputy of the Commission, legal services, the team. We have worked with the Brits all the weekend, until three o'clock at night yesterday, all day yesterday, we are working today.'

Their efforts had borne fruit; there was a deal – at least as far as Barnier and the chief UK negotiator Olly Robbins were concerned. But now the 'key person' Olly Robbins had gone back to London with 'a dozen points where he needs to get the agreement of Mrs May, and if Mrs May agrees, she has to convince the Cabinet before the end of this week'.

Michel Barnier was clearly elated on that Tuesday morning, but at the same time still 'sure of nothing'. Indeed, he was well aware that even if Theresa May said yes, her Cabinet might still say no. 'We are not yet there,' he said. 'Everything is difficult, linked to the incapacity of Mrs May to be sure of the support of the government.' He picked up on the widely reported meeting of a cabal of Brexiteer Cabinet members in London the previous evening: 'Yesterday night, seven ministers met between themselves, Raab and some others, the Brexiteers within the government . . . we can be concerned by the fact that she can face a lot of difficulties in the government.' And his usual warning to the group had added urgency: 'First point I want to make, is [that] to help me as a negotiator, and to help yourselves . . . be very careful in the next hours, and the next days.'

Sitting very quietly behind my camera, trying not to get noticed at all – although truth be told Barnier was sitting right in front of me, just two metres away – I wondered what had changed. Two weeks earlier, I had heard Guy Verhofstadt explain to a group of sympathetic British MEPs where the negotiations had foundered at the last attempt.

'As you know we were working . . . Barnier especially, very hard, to find a way out, the week before the Council meeting [in October] . . . And we thought, OK, we had a proposal on the table,' he reminded his audience. The proposal, as Verhofstadt laid it out, was that Britain's transition period would be prolonged and that at the same time there would be 'the possibility of a UK-wide customs union as a follow-up on that'.

This approach presented a real challenge, Verhofstadt explained. It didn't 'mean that all the problems were solved,' he said, 'because, if there's a UK-wide customs union, we want to have certainty about regulatory alignment and a level playing field, [those] are two things that are absolutely also linked to that.' In other words, the EU wanted to ensure that if the United Kingdom did stay in some sort of customs union with the EU, it did not do so on terms that gave it a competitive edge. 'We cannot say, "Customs union, but your products can have different standards – environmental, social, et cetera." That's really important for us,' Verhofstadt stressed, adding, 'For a few months you could do that, but I'm not sure if it's for a few months, eh? [Laughs] It could be that it is for years and for years, so we have to be absolutely sure.'

The proposal had still included a backstop specific to Northern Ireland – sometimes referred to as an 'all weather' backstop, or as Mrs May put it in the House of Commons, the 'backstop to the backstop'. But the proposal minimised the chances that it would ever be needed because, as Verhofstadt put it, 'in such a system there is no real reason that it would be used . . . First of all, because you prolong the transition, and secondly because you fall into a UK-wide customs union.' That was the position when the talks broke down so dramatically.

What had changed?

It seemed a switch had been made in this fiendishly complicated *piece of diplomatic engineering. Barnier had given up on his original idea to limit the backstop to Northern Ireland only, and accepted May's proposal to include a UK-wide solution – in the form of a customs union – in the withdrawal agreement. It was something the EU's chief negotiator had always fought against, because it blurred the line between the 'divorce issues' and the future relationship between the EU and the United Kingdom. In return, May had had to accept a far-reaching set of rules to regulate the custom union solution.*

'We have taken [matters] back to the point where we were fifteen days ago, and that Mrs May refused at that time,' Barnier explained to the BSG. 'And we work[ed] on this base, which is clearly to re-write the protocol on Ireland, on the base of a . . . customs union, but a specific customs union, to solve most of the problem of Ireland. A UK-wide solution, but not a complete customs union . . . only what we need to solve as far as possible the customs issue.'

There were still elements specific to Northern Ireland in the new proposal; Northern Ireland would have to continue to follow many single market regulations to avoid a hard border returning. But the great advantage of this solution was that it would, as Barnier put it, 'avoid . . . a divide of the custom territory of the UK', so the need for controls between Northern Ireland and the rest of the United Kingdom was minimised.

Barnier declared, 'We have . . . how do you say: *habiller?*'

'Dressed up,' his adviser Georg Riekeles chipped in, although in fact *habiller* usually just means 'dress' rather than 'dress smartly'.

'. . . dressed up the backstop in this new protocol,' Barnier nevertheless repeated, 'which means we will offer, at the end of the transition, as a backstop, a customs union.'

Barnier then turned to the challenge that Verhofstadt had

identified; the need to ensure that the agreement included guarantees of a level economic playing field so that the integrity of the EU's internal market was not compromised by British membership of a customs union. 'We need[ed] to put at the same time, in a very operational and binding way, all the framework of [a] level playing field. Everything,' he said.

This was a truly formidable task. The way the negotiating team had achieved 'in a very few weeks' work which 'usually needs one year' was, Barnier said, 'the reason I'm very impressed [by] my team'. Thanks to their work, he stated, 'we have put in an annex to the protocol, in an annex to the treaty, all the level playing field'. His adviser Georg Riekeles drove home the scope of what was involved: 'It's the minimal substantial rules that we accept they continue to adhere to, in the different areas, so it's what we expect, or agree, in terms of competition policy, what it means for them, from state aid control to merger control, it is what we expect in the field of fiscal standards, it is what we expect in terms of environmental standards, et cetera, et cetera.' 'Dynamic alignment' was the way Barnier characterised it.

Both sides had moved significantly to reach this point. The new backstop proposal gave Theresa May the UK-wide solution she wanted, but with the catch that the UK would have to abide by a whole number of EU rules, to ensure a level playing field between the EU and UK economies.

On the European side, Barnier had long resisted this solution because a customs union, any customs union, even if it was only meant as a backstop – an in-theory never-to-be-used insurance policy – went a long way towards defining the future relationship between the UK and the EU. Under the logic of Barnier's sequencing strategy, that was something that should only be discussed once the withdrawal agreement was signed – the future relationship belonged in the non-legally binding political declaration that was going to accompany the withdrawal agreement. But now a possible model for that future relationship had – via the backstop – been smuggled into the divorce settlement and would be enshrined in the legally binding withdrawal agreement.

Elmar Brok was quick to divine one significant political reality behind all the technical jargon. If the United Kingdom signed up to preserving many of the EU's rules in areas like environmental protection and labour standards, it would be swallowing more of that 'red tape from Brussels' which was so hated by Brexiteers. 'It must be torture for the Brits,' Brok observed. 'Torture,' agreed the Polish MEP Danuta Hübner.

In Brok's mind, May's 'victory' had come at a heavy cost. In her Chequers plan she had proposed a much looser arrangement with the EU:

> The UK would commit to apply a common rule book on state aid, and establish cooperative arrangements between regulators on competition. In keeping with our commitments to uphold international standards, the UK and the EU would also agree to maintain high regulatory standards for the environment, climate change, social and employment, and consumer protection – meaning we would not let standards fall below their current levels.

In Chequers, Theresa May had tried to keep her hands as free as possible, but in the new backstop the United Kingdom's scope for independent action was restricted; agreeing to maintain standards is one thing, but agreeing to follow someone else's standards is quite another.

Verhofstadt raised another key sticking point – one that

would, indeed, become a critical obstacle to the agreement's ratification at Westminster. In theory, the customs union backstop was designed to be a temporary arrangement that would remain in place until it was superseded by a broader trade agreement, but the issue of deciding what 'temporary' might mean was extremely sensitive. 'The key issue that remains a problem is "who can put an end to that temporary customs union?"' Verhofstadt suggested. Barnier agreed, insisting that there was no question of the United Kingdom being able to pull out of the backstop unilaterally; 'For us it is not negotiable that it would be a common decision. A common decision.' 'A common decision,' Verhofstadt chimed in, 'not a unilateral decision.' 'No, *non*, no. Never,' Barnier confirmed. And he added for emphasis, 'It was the point where we failed ten days ago, so for me it was non-negotiable. It must be and it will be a common decision.'

His determination on that point prevailed. The withdrawal agreement would state that if 'either side considers the backstop is no longer necessary, it can notify the other' setting out its reasons. The matter would then be discussed at a joint committee, but the backstop would only end if both sides agreed.

Michel Barnier then made a startling admission – and the way he put it sounded almost like a boast. He had warned the Brexit Steering Group again and again that the UK side was trying to 'instrumentalise' the Irish issue to achieve an advantageous long-term deal with the EU. And with the inclusion of the customs union in the withdrawal agreement Mrs May had, it might be argued, done exactly that. But Barnier now said that he had been playing the same game.

'You see, to be clear, what I tried to do,' he told the group. 'We know that from the very beginning the UK want to use Ireland as a leverage to get the cherry picking, half the customs union, and 25 per cent of the single market for goods. My strategy was to use Ireland, if I may say' – and here he broke into French – '*pour les emmener vers l'union douanière* [to bring them towards a customs union].' And he delivered an ex cathedra–sounding judgement to justify this strategy: 'Because if you look at the national interest, and the common interest of both sides, a free-trade agreement plus a customs union for the long term will be the best.'

Georg Riekeles wound up the meeting with the Barnier team's now familiar complaint about leaks from the Brexit Steering Group. 'Every time after we come out of this room, in the course of the day, often very early afterwards,' he said, 'we get calls from journalists, very often it's *The Guardian*, but also others, to say, "Ah Mr Barnier just said this, this, this and this . . ." And it's been exact quotes of what Mr Barnier has been saying.'

Riekeles said they kept giving the group another chance but 'every time that happens after the BSG. Every time.'

Barnier, playing good cop to his assistant's bad cop, lightened the atmosphere with a laugh, but made a plea for silence at least until after the British Cabinet meeting. With negotiations so delicately poised, the BSG were in biddable spirits; Roberto Gualtieri asked about an interview with Sky he had scheduled. 'Cancel it,' ruled the chief negotiator.

~

In London that evening, senior Cabinet ministers were called to No. 10 to read through the draft withdrawal agreement. At 2 p.m. the following day, on Wednesday 14 November 2018, the full Cabinet met to discuss the document.

By then, enough information had leaked out about the deal to provoke a barrage from backbench Brexiteers in Westminster: 'I hope Cabinet will block it, or, if not, Parliament will block it,' declared Jacob Rees-Mogg, while the former foreign secretary Boris Johnson dismissed it as 'vassal state stuff', calling the 'level playing field' guarantees 'utterly unacceptable' because they involved accepting EU rules and regulations. The DUP's Westminster leader, Nigel Dodds, denounced the deal in similar terms.

Guy Verhofstadt waited for news from the Cabinet meeting in London at his office in Strasbourg. He was irritated, because Michel Barnier had returned to Brussels, and Verhofstadt feared that all the media were also going to flock there — looking for first reactions to what he expected would be a 'yes' from May's government. The Parliament's Brexit coordinator wanted to go back to Brussels as well, first thing the next morning — if only Edel, who had a bad headache, could find him a ticket. 'We go to Brussels, we do a BSG with Barnier, the press is invited to take the pictures at the beginning, and afterwards we do a press conference with the whole bunch,' Verhofstadt told Roberto Gualtieri, waving his arms. But the Italian Social Democrat was interested in something else: the actual text of the draft withdrawal agreement. Because once again the members of the BSG had not been allowed to see it.

GUALTIERI: We will get the text this evening?

MCLAUGHLIN: Yes, after the Cabinet has
agreed.

VERHOFSTADT: Just after the Cabinet agrees, then we
have the text.

GUALTIERI: I think we should do a press conference tonight.

VERHOFSTADT: Here?

MCLAUGHLIN: You'll be asked to comment on the text, a
little bit, and you can't, on the text. Even you will not
have been able to read the text that quickly.

Verhofstadt's team had lined up a whole series of individual interviews for their boss towards the evening, so the argument that answering questions about the deal wasn't possible without having read the text did not really fly. Politicians know what to say even when they don't know what to say. Bram Delen and Jeroen Reijnen had even prepared a whole statement for Verhofstadt to pre-record for Facebook in the afternoon — well before Theresa May would be able to communicate what her Cabinet had decided.

Facebook — I learned over these past years — is a most interesting way to communicate for politicians, not only because so many people use it, but because it can be done without having to answer questions.

The Facebook recording took a while to start because the cameraman had problems with his video-prompter — and Verhofstadt's face turned thunderous. But when he was finally called to action, his serious half-smile face quickly returned.

VERHOFSTADT: Let me start by saying that I hope that one day the UK will come back home, back into the European family. But we have tried to make the best of what was in fact a very difficult decision, taken by Britain, to leave the European Union. And the agreement achieved will make it possible, I think, to maintain a close relationship, between the European Union and the United Kingdom. And for that result I would like to congratulate Michel Barnier, who has done a tremendous job, and this in close cooperation with us, with the European Parliament. Our top priority was to safeguard citizens' rights and here the European Parliament has improved significantly the outcome.

The time ticked by, but no news of the British Cabinet decision came. Verhofstadt moved from his chair behind his own desk to sit with

Guillaume McLaughlin and Edel Crosse next door, and then returned.
He checked his watch, and then did so again. 'I don't like to worry
anyone, but one government source says there are still up to twenty
people yet to speak in Cabinet,' Jeroen Reijnen came in to report. 'It
could go on for another two and a half hours.'

Verhofstadt replied: 'It's clear that they have some problems, eh?'

One by one, the whole nice spread of interviews the team had lined
up had to be cancelled. 'I can't come on TV', Verhofstadt said, 'with
the message: yes we are waiting. "And is that good news or bad news?"
Maybe yes, maybe no.'

Fifty/fifty, I thought – remembering the year before.

The team was disappointed but also annoyed, because they knew they
were in for a long evening now. Bram Delen, Jeroen Reijnen and Edel
Crosse decided to go to an Indian restaurant and wait there. Verhofstadt
went to have dinner somewhere else but ordered them to find a spot where
they could meet, have drinks and work, later at night.

Mrs May finally emerged from Downing Street at 7.20 p.m.
London time to announce Cabinet backing for the agreement;
it had taken five brutal hours to secure that outcome, and it
was reported that she had faced rebellion from eleven of her
twenty-nine ministers. She said the 'collective' decision 'ena-
bles us to move on', and declared that 'the choice before us is
clear: this deal, which delivers on the vote of the referendum,
which brings back control of our money, laws and borders, ends
free movement, protects jobs, security and our Union; or leave
with no deal, or no Brexit at all.'

In their Indian restaurant, Jeroen, Bram and Edel posted their pre-
recorded Facebook video, ate, and then went to look for a café where they
could meet their boss, plus Guillaume McLaughlin and Eva Palatova,
for a first discussion on how they were going to communicate the next

morning. They found one on the Place du Corbeau, of all places – the Square of the Raven. What was it again that I recalled from my very first visit to London, about the Tower of London? That if the ravens there fly away, the Crown will fall and Britain with it?

It was ten to midnight when Verhofstadt arrived, and once they had all ordered their drinks, with weary faces, bleary eyes, they set to work.

Guillaume McLaughlin immediately teased his boss with news about how others had communicated. 'The Greens have got a press release. Have you seen it?' he asked. And then he read from his mobile, 'Deal will put the UK in a weaker position than as EU member.' Verhofstadt reacted, 'Well, that's true.' But Bram Delen objected: 'That's not very helpful.'

As Brexit coordinator of the European Parliament, Verhofstadt could of course not say something that harsh publicly. But with his circle of close advisors around him he did allow himself to muse on an element in the deal which was politically vulnerable; even if it minimised the divisions between Northern Ireland and the rest of the United Kingdom, it did not eliminate them altogether. 'There will be some level playing field and some regulatory alignment for the whole UK. But for Northern Ireland it will go further than that. Northern Ireland will be really like in the single market. With full regulatory alignment,' he said. 'And that is the problem that the DUP [has] got.'

The deal might, he suggested, be sold as a 'UK-wide solution', but 'in fact, inside the UK-wide solution, there is . . . hidden there [that] Northern Ireland . . . goes in fact further in the regulatory alignment, and further in the level playing field, so that nothing changes. That's not the case for the rest of the UK, because the rest of the UK didn't want to be in the single market. So that's the difference . . . There is a UK-wide solution, so there is no border, but the reality is a little more [complex].'

In London, almost immediately after the 585-page text of the agreement was published at 7.45 p.m., open mutiny had broken out in the Tory ranks. The backbencher Nadine Dorries set the tone of Brexiteer reaction with her verdict: 'Catastrophe and calamity. What an utter, total mess.'

The following morning matters took a turn for the worse for Mrs May with Dominic Raab's resignation as Brexit secretary, and the day went downhill from there. *The Times* described it as a 'horror show', and its leader column opened with a vivid sketch of the crisis that had engulfed the prime minister:

It started with the resignation of her Brexit secretary, Dominic Raab, who was nominally responsible for negotiating the Brexit deal that had just been approved by the cabinet. That was followed by the resignations of one more cabinet minister and two junior ministers, with rumours that others were considering their positions. Meanwhile, Jacob Rees-Mogg and Steve Baker, leading members of the Brexiteers' European Research Group (ERG), submitted letters of no confidence to the chairman of the Tory backbench 1922 Committee, raising the prospect of a leadership challenge. All this as she faced three hours at the dispatch box in the House of Commons, where she and her deal came under sustained assault from her own backbenchers, opposition parties and parliamentary allies in the Democratic Unionist Party (DUP). It was fifty-seven minutes before anyone spoke in her support.

'It's all people who are thinking about leadership in the future,' *remarked Nick Petre, Guy Verhofstadt's press spokesman for the United* *Kingdom, as the Verhofstadt team digested the news of the Cabinet* *resignations in London. 'They know that the Tory Party members* *are Eurosceptic, so to become party leader they have to show they are* *resisting.'*

Verhofstadt agreed: 'They are busy with their careers, not Brexit.'

(Two of those who resigned that week — Dominic Raab and the work and pensions secretary, Esther McVey, would indeed stand in the Conservative leadership contest the following year.)

Verhofstadt sat at his desk in the Parliament building in Strasbourg, waiting for an interview with BBC Radio 4. He was worried because he realised that whatever he said was going to be used by one or the other side in the battle that was now raging over the deal. 'You know, this is an easy deal to defend and to sell on the European side,' he said to Jeroen Reijnen and Nick Petre. 'But having the British press is absolutely not interesting for the moment. Because they want to get from you a quote that they can use [to polarise].'

Suppose he said, in the interview, as a European: 'We have won, fantastic.' That wouldn't go down well with the Brexiteers. But suppose he was asked whether Europe had given away too much? He imagined a question: 'Shouldn't Europe have stood more firmly with the Remain camp? No?' Then that could also be used. 'Ah, you don't want to help. See, these Remainers are lunatics, because they think they can obtain something from the EU that they will never obtain.'

'Everything I say is not helpful,' he complained. 'It's a good deal, yeah, but for who?' His head of communications Jeroen Reijnen tried to give him a line that had a positive spin to it: 'It's also a good deal for them. Otherwise they can never leave.' Verhofstadt agreed: 'It's the best we can handle out for [hand out to] them, yeah. What you can say, is that it's not disruptive for British economy. It limits the disruption. It limits the disruption for British industry, British economy. That's the reality, eh?'

Verhofstadt also wanted to know from Nick Petre who was going to be at the other end of the line, for the interview with BBC. It was not going to be a debate, was it? No, it wasn't, Petre set him at rest, just a reporter asking questions.

Which was bad enough already, of course.

I never saw my main character so nervous during an interview. Verhofstadt was constantly rubbing his trousers with one of his hands, while the other held his mobile. For all the harsh jokes and rough comments that sometimes floated around the office, he was, as was his whole team, very well aware of the responsibility he carried when communicating with the outside world. As Brexit coordinator for the European Parliament he was speaking for Europe – that's what was agreed with Barnier and everyone else, from the very beginning, and even the sometimes very Einzelgänger *Guy Verhofstadt stuck to it.*

'I think that it's an agreement that makes possible that there is a Brexit, on the one hand,' Verhofstadt said on the phone, to London. 'And at the other hand that there is not too much disruption, certainly not in the first years of the Brexit, while we are negotiating the future relationship. Because let's be honest, to have the least disruption possible, for citizens, economy, is a common objective from both sides.'

The questions were not audible, but the answers spoke more or less for themselves. 'I am an optimist by nature, so yeah. Let's first wait [to see] what's happening. But yeah, this has been hammered out, there is not a lot of room for manoeuvre to say let's start again . . . so I hope everyone will understand that when they're voting.'

The last question in the interview was about whether the United Kingdom could stop the withdrawal process triggered when Mrs May invoked Article 50 of the Lisbon Treaty. Verhofstadt said no. 'I don't see this happening,' he repeated twice, adding that 'all member states would have to agree.' The European Court of Justice would, three weeks later, take the contrary view, ruling that the United Kingdom could unilaterally revoke Article 50, but Verhofstadt's answer was founded on politics, not law.

'Remainers will be furious that I say that Article 50 cannot be revoked,' he remarked after hanging up, 'but they know that that is our position, because if you say now that Article 50 can be prolonged,

then in Britain they say, "Oh, so, that's an advice not to vote for the deal."'

The interview had taken less than five minutes, but it still managed to annoy Verhofstadt. They asked, he said, '"What do you think, when it is voted down in the House of Commons, and there is a new PM, and he comes to have a new deal?"... Things like that. They are busy with that. They're not busy with explaining what is in [the deal].'

But he did what he could to counter that. 'I think I explained a bit what the advantage of this deal is, that it is limiting the disruption on both sides.'

~

Later that day, Michel Barnier was at his most magisterial when he held a press conference about the deal. 'I never had any intention of taking revenge on or humiliating the United Kingdom,' he declared. 'I simply intended to deliver on the sovereign vote of the UK to leave the EU. I may regret it, but we are delivering it.' He expressed satisfaction with the way his negotiating strategy had worked: 'For me this was never a power game between the [European] institutions,' he said, 'that's why we introduced this method of complete transparency, from the very beginning.' And he returned to the fundamental convictions that had guided his approach to negotiations: 'It was never a power game with the United Kingdom either,' he said, 'and my thinking had nothing to do with who would lose and who would win. Everyone loses, everyone loses in Brexit . . . it's lose-lose.'

But he and the EU did have their red lines. 'It is the British who decided to go,' he said. 'It is not we who are leaving the British. So they are leaving us, but they can't ask us as they leave to weaken ourselves or fracture who we are.' The bedrock of the EU's negotiating position had always been that the Brexit process should not undermine the European Union as a whole, and Barnier believed he had remained faithful to that principle.

Despite all the sound and fury that surrounded the publication of the details of the withdrawal agreement, that agreement did not, of course, settle everything between the United Kingdom and the European Union – far from it. It was designed simply to deal with the so-called 'divorce issues' of citizens' rights, the UK's financial obligations and the Irish border, and to provide for a transition period. The withdrawal agreement protocol on Northern Ireland did now include an aspiration to 'build on the single customs territory' which had been agreed as part of the backstop arrangements, but huge areas of the way the United Kingdom would trade and interact with its continental neighbours in the longer term continued to be almost as ill-defined as ever.

Right at the beginning of the Brexit process, in her Lancaster House speech in January 2017, Theresa May had laid out her ambition to complete talks on a future relationship with the EU during the two-year negotiating period dictated by Article 50. And ever since the opening of formal negotiations in June that year, her negotiators had been struggling to escape the straitjacket of the sequencing of negotiations that the EU had successfully dictated. Her acceptance of a blueprint for a withdrawal agreement, the so-called joint report, or progress report, which included the first version of the Irish backstop, in December 2017, was driven by her urgent need to move the talks on to negotiations about the future. But a year later very little substantive progress had been made towards set-tling the United Kingdom's long-term relationship with the EU. The EU had maintained the position laid out in that first European Parliament resolution on Brexit, which noted that 'an agreement on a future relationship between the European Union and the United Kingdom as a third country can only be concluded once the United Kingdom has withdrawn from the European Union.'

At a special European Council meeting on 25 November 2018, only a non-legally binding political declaration about the future relationship was due to be endorsed, along with the withdrawal agreement. But its publication generated strikingly little political or media attention during the high political drama of the autumn of 2018.

The first draft of the declaration landed on the Brexit Steering Group's table on 20 November, and Guy Verhofstadt expressed concern about the possibility of 'an attempt by the British side to put in the political declaration things that have the smell of Chequers, if I can say so, l'odeur de Chequers'. But when, two days later, he announced to the Brexit Steering Group that 'she [Theresa May] declared a few moments ago in Britain that the text is OK for her, and closed,' the news provoked little more reaction than an acid joke from Elmar Brok. Noting that Mrs May was due to come to Brussels the following day to set the seal on both the political declaration and the withdrawal agreement, Brok asked, 'And what happens tomorrow evening? Poor Jean-Claude [Juncker] has to eat with her? Because no Brits eat with her any more.'

Because the political declaration was not a legally binding treaty, neither side was especially fussed about the detail. Sweeping, broad-brush language was very much in order. The declaration stated that the two sides aspired to an 'ambitious, broad, deep and flexible partnership across trade and economic cooperation, law enforcement and criminal justice, foreign policy, security and defence and wider areas of cooperation' – almost every area covered while the United Kingdom was an EU member, in fact.

The document included references to some of the difficult issues outstanding between the two sides, but without providing solutions. It noted that 'the United Kingdom has decided that the principle of the free movement of persons between the Union and the United Kingdom will no longer apply' without saying much about what this would mean in practice, and it committed the two sides to 'use their best efforts to agree and ratify' a new agreement on fishing rights, which remained an area of especially acute sensitivity, 'by the summer of 2020', again without suggesting how this might be done.

Anyone who read it closely could see it contained potential contradictions. In a cross-reference to the withdrawal agreement, the declaration included the promise of 'ambitious customs arrangements that build and improve on the single customs territory [the backstop] provided for in the Withdrawal Agreement', but also a commitment to 'ensure the sovereignty of the United Kingdom and the protection of its internal market, while respecting the result of the 2016 referendum including with regard to the development of its independent trade policy.' An independent trade policy which involved tariff agreements with other countries was, on the face of it, incompatible with membership of an EU customs union.

And of course the whole question of a customs union remained a highly controversial party political dividing line at Westminster, where the withdrawal agreement and the political declaration would have to be ratified. Pulling out of the existing customs union had been one of the red lines Theresa May had laid down in her Lancaster House speech, while the Labour party had, after much debate, committed itself to the policy of remaining in one, although it was studiedly vague about exactly what that meant. In the context of the debate within her own party, Mrs May had taken a big political gamble by pushing for a single customs territory as a solution to the problem of the Irish border backstop.

The sensitivities and contradictions did not escape the notice of the Brexit Steering Group; one staffer commented that 'each paragraph contradicts the other'. Verhofstadt declared himself well pleased with it, however, not least because, at twenty-seven pages, it was a good deal shorter than the withdrawal agreement. 'So [all] of us read the political declaration,' he said at the BSG meeting on 22 November, 'I think a little bit easier than the withdrawal agreement. And my second conclusion was at the end when I was reading this, in saying: I have a solution for all these problems; membership of the EU.' He followed up the laughter with, 'Then all this is solved.' But Elmar Brok raised both his hands in mock horror at the thought that the United Kingdom might remain in the European Union: 'No, no, no.' Roberto Gualtieri's assistant chipped in with 'Basta' – enough.

After the long agony of the Brexit negotiations, the very last thing the group wanted was a change of heart in the United Kingdom. 'The biggest threat is a new referendum,' Elmar Brok offered. 'It's true, that's the reason we are so silent about it,' Verhofstadt acknowledged.

Imagine a new referendum, *I thought,* and the British people reversing the decision to leave the EU. *Would anyone in Europe still want that? Underneath the end-of-term banter at Verhofstadt's office table, and (still prudent) joy about the deal that had been reached, lurked a dark sense of relief. Those difficult Brits were finally on their way out.*

Or were they?

Westminster wasn't done with Brexit yet.

19

WE AUTHORISE MICHEL
TO APPLY POMADE

Late November 2018–mid-January 2019

On Monday 26 November 2018 – the day after the European Council endorsed the Article 50 withdrawal agreement and approved the political declaration on the future relationship between the EU and the UK – I took the morning commuter train from Leuven to Brussels. As always, I used my forty-minute ride to the European Parliament to make transcripts of footage I had filmed previously on my laptop. One and a half years into my shoot, I had developed a routine that even the Verhofstadt team had become aware of, so I was not surprised to be greeted by Guillaume McLaughlin, who obviously thought I did not look particularly perky, with a commiserating smile: 'It's nearly finished, eh? Don't worry, it's nearly finished. And you have to go home and watch all this shit on the computer as well. Can you imagine? What do you do, drugs, Valium, cocaine? How do you get through it?'

Finally the EU and the UK had reached a deal. But whether that deal would secure the approval of the British Parliament was far from certain. So the Brexit Steering Group had invited Martin Selmayr, the secretary-general of the European Commission, to give them an update on Europe's no-deal preparations. 'If there is one moment to work on contingency planning, it's maybe in the coming days and weeks,' was Guy Verhofstadt's ominous opening statement; the chances that the UK would leave the EU *without* an agreed and ratified agreement on 29 March 2019 were deemed to be all too real.

'Chancellor Merkel yesterday praised the deal as a diplomatic masterpiece,' Martin Selmayr said, in his very fast and efficient German-accented English, but, he added, in a reference to David Cameron's attempts to secure new EU terms for the United Kingdom in the run-up to the 2016 referendum, 'the last time a deal with Britain was praised as a diplomatic masterpiece was the deal with David Cameron, and we all know what happened afterwards, therefore we take very seriously the preparation for a no-deal.'

Selmayr warned that, in the case of a no-deal outcome, 'there are no rules. Some people don't understand that. If we don't have a withdrawal agreement, we don't have a transition.' There would be nothing – uncharted territory. 'The focus in this meeting is on contingency planning for that eventuality,' Guy Verhofstadt said, and he emphasised that this would not be a different form of negotiation with the United Kingdom. 'That means unilateral and temporary measures, taken by the EU to mitigate the most significant effects of the withdrawal without a withdrawal agreement,' he said. 'There can be no misunderstanding . . . It's not business as usual.' And he dismissed any idea that the EU and the United Kingdom could continue as if nothing had changed: 'Contingency planning is about taking measures only in the interest of the European Union, to defend our vital interests and to make sure, if there is no withdrawal agreement, [that] we reduce the disruption for our own members and our own citizens.'

Selmayr reinforced the sense of urgency, pointing out that if the United Kingdom did leave without an agreement, the relationship between the EU and the UK was likely to be rancorous: 'In such a situation, where we have a hostile divorce . . . we will not on the day after sit together and say, "Everything is fine", *hein*. Probably we will have a situation that is extremely disruptive. Politically, legally and economically . . . Therefore what we prepared for that situation is an exercise in damage limitation.'

There was also a diplomatic dimension to his message. Brexiteers in London had begun to consider the possibility of what was described as a 'managed no-deal', in which the two sides would agree ways to make the United Kingdom's departure less painful. The EU leaders and negotiators wanted to kill that kind of thinking before it took root. 'They [the contingency plans] are not negotiated measures. That is very important to add,' Selmayr stressed. 'Negotiate the no-deal? The EU is not available for that.'

'All contingency measures should be adopted unilaterally by the EU, not negotiated with the UK.' Here he made explicit reference to the advocates of a managed no-deal: 'I say that here, because if you look at the reaction at the moment [to] the withdrawal agreement, some say, there should be alternatives available, as a plan B, a plan C, a plan D. And some also say there should be a negotiated no-deal.'

As an example of what this would involve, he cited talks with the United Kingdom to ensure that planes could keep flying in the event of what he called 'a hard exit'. That concession would, he argued, undermine the EU's determination to stick by the agreement that had been so painstakingly negotiated. 'That would be not in the interest of the EU,' Selmayr insisted. 'That would go against what we have decided this Sunday; that there is only one deal on the table, the one that has been negotiated by Michel Barnier, our chief negotiator.'

Selmayr mentioned two other important principles. 'They [the contingency measures] should be temporary.' And 'they should not replicate the status of member states', he said, so the United Kingdom could not be allowed to continue to enjoy the privileges of membership. That was an echo of the principle that had underpinned the EU's negotiating position from the outset; that leaving the EU came at a cost, and the United Kingdom's position should (or could, as Edel Crosse had pointed out to Bram Delen when they were preparing Guy Verhofstadt's press conference on the day of triggering Article 50, two years earlier) never be as good outside the EU as inside it.

A list of seventy-nine notices had been published, to warn EU and UK citizens of what could occur in case of a hard Brexit, Selmayr explained. 'In every field, from what happens with my cat that I want to transport to Spain, during the holidays, to what happens to vaccines. It's basically the whole list of EU policies. If you read through that list, it's probably the best argument for ratifying the withdrawal agreement.'

But the deal was assailed on every side. A very different message came winging into London from the other side of the Atlantic. Donald Trump declared that the agreement 'sounds like a great deal for the EU' – which, from Mrs May's perspective, was the worst possible verdict he could have delivered – and that it could damage the prospects for a future trade deal between the United Kingdom and the United States.

At the same time, a long-term economic analysis published by the UK government that week warned that Britain would be poorer under any form of Brexit, compared with staying in the EU. It said the UK economy could be up to 3.9 per cent smaller after fifteen years under Theresa May's Brexit plan, while a no-deal Brexit could deliver a 9.3 per cent hit. The former Brexit secretary David Davis questioned the analysis, saying previous Treasury forecasts had been proved wrong and were based on 'flawed assumptions'.

The most serious blow to Mrs May's prospects of securing parliamentary support for her deal came from within her own Cabinet – in the shape of legal advice on the text from her attorney general, Geoffrey Cox. By convention the British government does not publish the full text of legal advice it receives, on the grounds that government law officers might feel inhibited from expressing a controversial opinion if they knew it would be made public. But Mrs May's government was instructed by Parliament that it must do so on this occasion; an unlikely-sounding alliance of Labour, the Democratic Unionist Party and some Tory Brexiteers forced a motion to that effect through the Commons on the day the deal was approved by the Cabinet. It was a mark of the collapse of parliamentary trust in the government, and MPs on all sides wanted to know what the backstop really meant, not what politicians might say it meant.

When the advice was published in full, on Wednesday 5 December, it was devastating. Geoffrey Cox had concluded that the backstop – because it was in the legally binding withdrawal agreement – could oblige the United Kingdom to remain in a customs union for ever. 'In the absence of a right of termination, there is a legal risk that the UK might become subject to protracted and repeated rounds of negotiations,' he declared.

The political damage was all the greater because the government had fought to keep the advice secret. The BBC reported that 'newly published documents show the PM was told [that] an arrangement designed to prevent a hard Irish border could last "indefinitely" and the UK could not "lawfully exit" without EU agreement'. Mr Cox's analysis, the report continued, 'said the "current drafting" of the backstop "does not allow for a mechanism that is likely to enable the UK to lawfully exit the UK-wide customs union without a subsequent agreement", and that "this remains the case even if the parties are negotiating many years later and even if the parties agree that talks have clearly broken down and there is no prospect of a future relationship agreement."' Assurances that the arrangement was supposed to be temporary cut no ice with Mr Cox. 'In international law the protocol would endure indefinitely until a superseding agreement took its place,' he ruled.

Five days later, Theresa May postponed the Commons vote on her deal; the government's whips could not promise her a majority, and rather than see the deal go down, she deferred a parliamentary decision.

I was back in Strasbourg by then, where down in the Parliament's oval courtyard a new Christmas tree stood quietly preaching peace and other more mixed messages. Up in his sixth-floor office Guy Verhofstadt greeted me with a jolly 'I don't think you will be able to broadcast your documentary any time soon, dear fellow.' He whistled and made a throw-away gesture with his right hand.

VERHOFSTADT: Maybe in a year, two years.

ME: Two, really?

VERHOFSTADT [laughing]: If things go well, eh? On our way up here, someone said to Guillaume, you know what, with this backstop? We'll make it end in 2087 — that's not eternal, it remains temporary. That way it's solved and we can stop drivelling. [That] shows the nonsense [it all is], eh?

Guillaume McLaughlin, his chief of staff, sighed and launched: 'What a fucking, fucking, fucking, fucking mess.' And while his boss left for a meeting in another part of the sprawling Parliament building, he switched on the small television in the office he shared with Edel Crosse and started watching the House of Commons debating Theresa May's decision to cancel the vote on her deal.

On the tiny screen, Hilary Benn, the Labour chair of the Committee on Exiting the European Union, was just on his feet with a question to the prime minister: 'Can she tell the House whether a single one of the EU leaders that she spoke to over the weekend indicated that they were prepared to renegotiate Article 20 of the backstop protocol, because in the absence of any such commitment, isn't cancelling tomorrow's vote just postponing the inevitable?'

'Yeah. He's right,' applauded Guillaume McLaughlin in Strasbourg.

Mrs May answered, 'I can give my right honourable friend the assurance that, having spoken to European leaders, they are open to discussions with us on this particular issue, and I'm confident that we will be able to see some further changes. Of course that will be a matter for further negotiations.'

'Huh,' Guillaume commented.

When Verhofstadt returned an hour later, Bram Delen briefed him on May's statement: 'She's saying, I'm going to do the tour of the European capitals, giving the impression to her party: I will renegotiate.' Sitting on Edel's desk, he started scrolling through his iPad, where he had prepared a reaction for his boss. 'I put in the draft speech something like . . . how did I put it? Hold on, ah, yes, here: "Mrs May can do as many tours of the European capitals as she wants, we will never . . . renegotiate the current agreement." That's a bit . . . is it too aggressive?' Guy Verhofstadt nodded, and summed up the EU position: 'Yeah, because the political declaration will be possibly re-done. But not the backstop.' That position was, in one form or another, to be stated again and again by the European Union in the following weeks and months — indeed, the EU's leaders were still repeating it when Mrs May announced her resignation half a year later.

Edel Crosse, who'd been watching the debate as well, again had words of praise for the British PM. 'She's being quite hammered,' she said. 'But, my god, she is tough. She's really tough. For hours she's been taking shit.' At exactly that moment, Theresa May could be seen on the television screen saying, 'This deal is not going to make us poorer.' From his own desk, next door, where he couldn't see but could still hear her, Verhofstadt shouted, 'That's not true. Even their own assumptions say that it makes [them] poorer.'

By then phone calls had started to come in.

Guillaume had Barnier's Norwegian adviser Georg Riekeles on the line, and he asked him, 'Georg, what are we going to do? There will be no vote tomorrow evening. May wants clarification, we have just heard. She is going to come to try and get more clarification on the backstop and the temporary nature of the backstop.' But he found some crumbs of comfort in the way the prime minister had chosen her words; at least she had not said, 'I am going to Brussels to renegotiate everything, and the whole thing's a scandal.' By sticking to the 'subtleties of clarifications' she had, McLaughlin judged, avoided 'saying the kind of things which would blow the whole thing up'.

Verhofstadt took a phone call from European Commission president Jean-Claude Juncker, and confirmed the tone that would mark the EU strategy in dealing with the UK quagmire: 'Allo? Allo? Yes, Jean-Claude, how are you?' he began. 'I am in the middle of following the debate in England. Non-binding stuff, where we say, "Yes, indeed, we will do our best over the backstop . . ." That we can do. There's no reason not to express the Union's desire not to use it. But we can't say more than that.'

Guillaume McLaughlin was soon at work trying to craft some helpful 'non-binding' language together with Marek Evison, Elmar Brok's adviser, and the way they talked about the backstop said everything about what the Irish insurance clause had become.

> EVISON: The Conference [of Presidents, where the
>   leaders of the political groups in the Parliament meet]
>   reiterates its support for an as-close-as-possible EU–
>   UK relationship, that will not require a backstop to be
>   deployed, or something like this . . .
> MCLAUGHLIN: Thereby reducing the necessity to deploy
>   the backstop.
> EVISON [laughing]: It makes it sound like a nuclear
>   weapon solution. Deploying the backstop, like a SS20.

To make things even more complicated, on the day of Mrs May's Commons statement, 10 December, the European Court of Justice delighted Remain campaigners in Britain by issuing an emergency ruling that, under EU law, the UK was able to halt the Article 50 process unilaterally. The ruling revived calls for another referendum on the United Kingdom's EU membership. Andy Wightman, the Scottish Green Party MSP who had led the legal challenge, was quoted in *The Guardian* describing it as 'a momentous ruling which now meant the UK could stay in the EU and keep all its existing benefits, including its rebate, its opt-outs and the pound'. He said, 'MPs now know that stopping Brexit altogether is an option open to them before the end of the Article 50 period.' It was a strange twist of history; just as the publication of Geoffrey Cox's legal advice strengthened hard Brexiteers in their resolve to oppose May's deal, a legal ruling by the ECJ in Luxembourg strengthened the incentive for Remainers to fight it, too.

*Guy Verhofstadt ended the day with a tweet, not about the ECJ ruling —
too tricky — but about May's delay of the vote.*

*The tweet said, 'I can't follow any more. After two years of negotia-
tions, the Tory government wants to delay the vote. Just keep in mind
that we will never let the Irish down. This delay will further aggravate
the uncertainty for people & businesses. It's time they make up their
mind! #brexit.'*

*The next morning, over coffee, a croissant and yoghurt, Verhofstadt
was happy with the result of his tweet, reporting to me (successes like
that he was always happy to share), 'Seven or eight thousand retweets.
And over 20,000 likes. And then some likes on Facebook as well, eh?
You have to do a tweet at the right moment, otherwise you're out of the
game. You can give the best speech in the world, nobody will listen.
Trump only tweets.'*

*I asked whether he didn't find that problematic — a terrible loss of
insight? Verhofstadt shrugged. But half an hour later in the BSG, he
complained about the debate in the House of Commons in a way that
reminded me of my question:*

VERHOFSTADT: Yesterday, there was in fact not a
debate, eh? There were statements of one minute.
This is just shouting. And she [Mrs May] always
answers in the same way. As for a real debate, that
didn't happen; the British Parliament simply doesn't
have much to say.

LAMBERTS: You know, what frightens me is the denial of
reality.

BARNIER: From the very first.

The tone of the meeting — which was short — was a curious mixture of light-heartedness and determination, on a course that
was very clear: no renegotiation of the withdrawal agreement

and the backstop clause, but a willingness to accommodate May with supportive but non-binding statements.

> HÜBNER: So we are behind no negotiation, no re-
> opening, but helping May.
> LAMBERTS: We authorise Michel to apply pomade.

And the group devoted a bit of time to chewing over the political balance at Westminster.

> BARNIER: At this stage the problem is to know what the
> Labour Party will do, eh?
> VERHOFSTADT: Exactly.
> GUALTIERI: The most ambiguous of course is Corbyn.
> BARNIER: He told me, in my office: I want new elections,
> and if we don't get new elections, I will move to the
> second referendum.
> VERHOFSTADT: He has to keep the election as first option
> open. So he cannot now say, the second referendum,
> because then the first option, an election, is over.
> So he burns the different stages, eh? The one after
> the other. If it is clear [in] the coming weeks, that a
> general election will never happen, for one or other
> reason, what will happen then, [is] he will move to the
> second referendum.
> GUALTIERI: And then again there's two options. They go
> to the second referendum. Or it brings the Tory Party
> together and they accept the May deal.

'Such optimism, still,' I jotted down in the margin of my transcripts, sometime later, on my commuter train.

~

Then came my last night in Strasbourg that year — on my own with
pasta and a movie on Netflix (no transcripts, please) on my laptop, in
a small Italian restaurant underneath the Notre-Dame cathedral.

Outside, throngs of people were strolling through the Christmas
market, until suddenly all movement stopped and the owner of the
restaurant locked his door with a key and closed the thick velvet bur-
gundy curtains that framed his large front windows. 'Police orders,' he
said, without giving any further explanation. But on my mobile, news
flashes started coming in. Three streets away from where I sat, a man
had started shooting people. Edel, Bram, Jeroen and Nick were having
dinner even closer to the incident.

The assailant, later identified by police as a local resident with a
long history of criminal convictions and suspected of Islamic extrem-
ism, killed five people and wounded eleven before escaping in a taxi.
It would take two days before he was tracked down and shot dead by
police. Meanwhile, in their offices the next morning, Guy Verhofstadt's
team relived what they had been through:

CROSSE: The shouting, and then you could hear the
    police. And then you could hear that silence . . .
    Silence, and then the police again. It was just,
    really . . . And not being able to move, and not
    knowing when to move. That was quite stressful as
    well. Nowhere to go.
REIJNEN: And then this website sending out fake news.
    Multiple terrorist attacks, and you read that . . .
PETRE: Multiple shooters.
REIJNEN: Multiple shooters, yeah.
CROSSE: And they were giving an emergency number,
    but the emergency number didn't work. The thing is

we didn't know whether it was multiple. So it was one guy, and we thought, there's one guy who is going to shoot, everyone runs a certain way, and there's another guy waiting for us, so we had no clue. Really, like. And nobody was telling us to leave. We weren't evacuated. Around eleven o'clock Bram went out to look and he spoke to a soldier and the soldier said, 'You are going to go now, but you can only exit this way.'

Jeroen Reijnen also had news of another colleague.

REIJNEN: Brigitte, even worse, eh? Have you heard that? Someone fell in front of her, was shot in front of her, and someone was shot behind her. So the guy must have been like two, three metres in her zone, eh? Can you imagine?

CROSSE: Fuck.

REIJNEN: She's been really lucky.

Brexit really became totally unimportant that day — for me and the team — even as in London the pressure continued to build.

∼

At Westminster, the hard-line Brexiteers of the European Research Group had been preparing a coup against the prime minister for weeks. To trigger a vote of no confidence in her leadership, they needed to persuade forty-eight MPs (15 per cent of all Tory MPs) to send in letters to the chairman of the 1922 Committee, which represents Conservative backbenchers; they finally achieved that target on 11 December. The vote took place the following day, and Mrs May survived — but 117 of her own MPs, more than a third of the parliamentary party, voted against her. The result added to the sense of paralysis at Westminster; Mrs May's authority was undermined further, but under the rules of the Conservative Party she was now safe from another challenge for the next twelve months.

In the weeks that followed, the United Kingdom, like the EU, stepped up preparations for a no-deal Brexit, but some of them proved controversial.

Just before Christmas, the Department of Transport awarded a £13.8 million contract to a company called Seaborne Freight to run a ferry service between the Kent port of Ramsgate and Ostend, to ease the pressure on the Dover–Calais route if a no-deal Brexit led to delays there. It soon emerged that Seaborne Freight had never run a ferry service and had no ferries. On 3 January 2019, the BBC reported that the firm 'has used website terms and conditions apparently intended for a takeaway food firm'. The transport secretary, Chris Grayling, defended the contract, but it was eventually cancelled altogether after a major backer withdrew its support from Seaborne.

The government also ran a pilot to assess plans for dealing with congestion on the roads in Kent in the event of delays at Dover. On 7 January 2019, a convoy of eighty-nine lorries – considerably fewer than the 150 which were planned – took part in two test runs from the disused Manston Airport, near Ramsgate, on a 20-mile route to the port. The experiment, part of Operation Brock – not named for Elmar Brok – was widely derided by politicians and representatives of the haulage industry. The Conservative MP for Dover and Deal, Charlie Elphicke, told the BBC, 'We've got to remember 10,000 lorries visit the Channel ports every single day, so a test with less than 100 is not even a drop in the ocean.'

When Guy Verhofstadt gathered his team later that same day to discuss where they stood on Brexit, for the first time in the New Year, they all rolled their eyes at the Operation Brock story. Verhofstadt wanted to talk to Guillaume McLaughlin, Eva Palatova and the senior civil servants Nick Lane, Markus Winkler and François Javelle, about the preparation of two new parliamentary resolutions. A date had finally been set for the House of Commons vote on May's deal with the EU, on 15 January, and Verhofstadt needed one resolution in case of a no vote, and another one in case of a yes – although he didn't believe a yes was in any way possible. 'There will be no approval. Why do you think there will be an approval by the meaningful vote? There will be no approval,' he told the group.

VERHOFSTADT: It's like there was no [Christmas] break. We're there at the same point as before.

WINKLER: Very often such breaks can give an atmospheric change. But I don't see it in this situation. It's simply . . .

PALATOVA: Stuck.

MCLAUGHLIN: Yeah, nothing has changed. At all.

WINKLER: Well, we lost another four weeks.

LANE: Sixty per cent of Tory Party members, those are the people Tory MPs refer to, are in favour of no-deal.

VERHOFSTADT: That's a lot, eh?

LANE [laughing]: We're only talking of 100,000 people of an average age of about eighty-six, of course. But there you go.

Guillaume McLaughlin reported that Nick Petre, Verhofstadt's spokesman for the United Kingdom, had spent the Christmas

holidays with his family in Theresa May's Berkshire constituency and found 'all the friends of his parents were in favour of
a no-deal Brexit. A clean break.' Verhofstadt made the shrewd
observation that the events of the past few weeks had 'radical-
ised both camps'. There might, he ventured, have been some
voter movement from Leave to Remain, because older people
were dying and younger ones were coming onto the voting
roll, but 'for the rest' – and here he widened the gap between
his hands – 'the split widens. And a new referendum will not
solve that.'

'Whatever happens, it's a divided society for the next fifteen years,' Nick Lane agreed, and Verhofstadt reflected that
the reaction to Mrs May's deal showed that the idea of finding
common ground between Leavers and Remainers did not
work. 'I think what you are going to see [is that] the current
party system won't survive,' Lane predicted. 'The two-party
system, the two-and-a-half-party system [including the Liberal
Democrats] won't survive. They'll split. The Tories will certainly split. And Labour might split.'

Michel Barnier, who had become a grandfather during the
Christmas break, had an equally sombre analysis when he came
to see the Brexit Steering Group the following day. The Polish
MEP Danuta Hübner asked him, 'So what's the good news?'
And he replied, 'There is no news. The vote will be next week,
and it will be lost, with 200 votes.'

He reported that Mrs May was 'still asking for clarification,
legal certainty, reassurance about the backstop' as the vote
approached. And it seemed the EU was prepared (once again)
to accomodate her somehow. Barnier said he was not yet sure
what form this would take – perhaps 'an exchange of letters' –
but it was clear that 'in any case we cannot go further than what

has been decided by you and the EC [the European Council] last time'.

I was struck by the fact that, for Barnier, apparently, it still wasn't clear – even after two years of dealing with May, indirectly and directly – whether her demand for clarification was an attempt to salvage the deal she made, and her own position as prime minister, or a ruse, a strategy to obtain a better deal for Britain. He actually seemed to lean towards the latter explanation. 'If I can speak frankly, they act today exactly as they did before Salzburg. Always and always coming back on the same arguments, with a clear strategy, in my view, to use the Irish case to get the cherry picking.'

Did the EU really still fear the British as highly skilled negotiators? Or was it just Barnier's role to always expect and prepare for the worse?

Barnier enumerated the points on which the British government wanted clarification. 'They think,' he said, 'that we are very happy with the backstop, the backstop is very comfortable for us, and they will be in that case obliged to be the prisoner [of a customs union]' – this despite the fact that Mrs May herself had requested a UK-wide customs union as part of the backstop arrangements. Roberto Gualtieri chipped in at this point with, 'I gave an interview in which I said it was very bad for us.'

Further areas where Britain required clarification included the possibility that the backstop arrangements could, as Barnier put it, 'have a negative impact on the Good Friday Agreement', reassurances on the way the European Union would look for regulatory alignment between Northern Ireland and the EU, and the EU's willingness to seek an agreement on a future relationship which would supersede the backstop.

One idea that was being floated to meet that last concern was to agree a deadline for the end of talks on a future relationship. 'In theory,' the EU's chief negotiator said, 'there is no problem [with] this, because we write in the treaty that we will do our best [to complete the talks] for 2020, and at the same time it's written that we are able to prolong the transition for one or two years. That means if we don't succeed in reaching an agreement on the future relation[ship] for 2020, we can reach [one] in '21, '22.' But the ever-cautious Barnier could see a trap ahead: 'If a new date [is added], you know there is a legal risk. We could be put into a diffi-cult position in front of an arbitration committee if the English tell us that we haven't demonstrated that we have made all necessary efforts [to achieve an agreement].' That, Barnier feared, would allow the United Kingdom to argue that 'we have justifications for pulling out of the backstop unilaterally'.

Then Barnier and Verhofstadt started debating how useful an exchange of letters would be – and what I heard was to me one of the most reveal-ing things I recorded over my two-year shoot, about the mad complexity of international negotiations.

Barnier said that the British, in May's letter, had to 'understand that they have to ask something reasonable. If they want to send a letter asking for several points that are not acceptable to us, in that case, it is not useful.' Why? Because then the EU would be obliged to reply with a negative, and that would, as Verhofstadt added, make things 'even more difficult'.

So first you tell the other side that you want to write a letter, then the other side tells you how they might respond, and warns you what they certainly don't want you to write – and only then do you actually write your letter. Barnier explained that the UK had already been 'testing ideas' with his team to work out what would be 'reasonable' to ask.

I wrote love letters like that for my friends, when we were teenagers.

But even if May wrote an acceptable letter, and got an acceptable answer from the EU in return, Barnier still held out very little hope the tactic would overturn the arithmetic in the House of Commons: 'To speak frankly, even on their side, they know that this letter will change nothing,' he said. And he reported what sounded like a mark of desperation in Downing Street: 'She [Theresa May] had a phone call with Angela Merkel, with Macron, with Juncker, with Leo Varadkar, and she was incapable [of saying] what she needs, and to give the assurance that if she gets what she needs [she may be able to win the vote].'

Barnier concluded with a prescient – it was early January 2019 – prediction: 'My feeling is today that it is very probable that we will face a prolongation of Article 50. And that could be a problem for you, eh?' And here he raised a finger, because a prolongation of Article 50, meaning a delay of the UK departure date, might clash with the European elections, due at the end of May 2019.

VERHOFSTADT: A few weeks is not a problem.

LAMBERTS: If they ask for prolongation to organise new elections or a second referendum, we can give that.

BARNIER: Sure.

LAMBERTS: But if it is because 'we cannot make up our minds' . . .

BARNIER: Exactly. Before we give a prolongation, we have to know why.

GUALTIERI: A prolongation to prepare for a hard Brexit, we cannot do that.

Like many commentators in the United Kingdom, the group fell into speculation about how the House of Commons might react to this unprecedented stalemate. Verhofstadt was

convinced that 'there are majorities' in the British Parliament
for some solutions, 'but nobody tested them, nobody is busy
with it'. Barnier had, at an earlier meeting of the BSG, stated
his conviction that a customs union of some kind would find
favour in Parliament, and he returned to it. 'If there was a vote
[in the House of Commons, with MPs voting according to what
they preferred – personally, not according to party lines] on the
customs union, there would be a majority, I'm sure,' he said.

'It doesn't happen because they have this problem of their
bi-polar political system,' Roberto Gualtieri judged, and the
conversation turned again to those fundamental differences
between the European and British political cultures which the
Brexit process had so often exposed.

VERHOFSTADT [annoyed]: Cross-party, you find a
　　majority. But there's nobody busy with cross-party.
　　Here, yeah, we are busy with cross-party, all the time.
BARNIER: This national issue of Brexit is totally prisoner
　　[to] the traditional political system.
VERHOFSTADT: And it is more important than even
　　Brexit. To win the next elections is more important
　　than Brexit.

That same evening Verhofstadt sent out a tweet, looking ahead
to the European elections, and how they might be affected by
Brexit: 'After the mess of #Brexit, the far-right won't campaign to leave the EU, they want to destroy it from within
instead. Time that all pro-Europeans start to flex their muscles.
We need a counter-movement to stop the nationalists destabi-
lising our Europe.' The way the Brexit process was dragging on
was forcing the EU negotiators to make calculations about its
impact on their own prospects and the political debate within

the EU. And, as Barnier pointed out, 'We have so many points of fragility, not only in France.'

On Monday 14 January 2019, Theresa May received the reassurances she had asked for. The letter was co-signed by Donald Tusk, the European Council president, and Jean-Claude Juncker, the president of the European Commission, and it provided a point-by-point response to the issues summarised by Michel Barnier at the BSG the previous week. But it also confirmed, once again, what the EU was not willing to do, noting, 'As you know, we are not in a position to agree to anything that changes or is inconsistent with the withdrawal agreement, but against this background, and in order to facilitate the next steps of the process, we are happy to confirm, on behalf of the two EU Institutions we represent, our understanding of the following points within our respective fields of responsibility.'

When it came to winning the meaningful vote in the House of Commons the next day, the letter, as both Barnier and Verhofstadt had predicted, helped not one jot.

20

PARLIAMENT IS NOT A CASINO

Mid-January–early February 2019

Even though they were convinced that the meaningful vote on May's deal would fail, Verhofstadt and his team still decided to make the evening of 15 January 2019 a semi-festive occasion. They had ordered sushi, and a big TV screen was installed in the meeting room behind Verhofstadt's office in Strasbourg, so that they could watch the proceedings in Westminster together. Almost two years earlier, Verhofstadt had told the BSG, raising a glass of Sicilian wine: 'If we make an agreement with the Brits, we are going to pour 100 of these.' That hope had faded now, completely, but it seemed that no one was ready to face up to the facts just yet. So while the sound of a bottle of wine being uncorked popped through the room, and Edel Crosse was taking pictures on her iPhone, Theresa May began her final plea to MPs to support the deal she'd made with the EU.

'Mr Speaker, this is the most significant vote that any of us will ever be part of,' she declared. 'A decision that will determine the future for our constituents, their children and grand-children. A decision that each of us will have to justify and live with for many years to come.' A little later she warned against the risk of rejecting the agreement: 'A vote against this deal is a vote for nothing more than uncertainty, division, and a very real risk of no-deal.'

Jeering from the parliamentary benches brayed out of the television set. 'Give her a glass of wine,' Verhofstadt interjected. Then came the vote itself. 'Sssssstt,' said Edel, in an attempt to silence her chatty team, but maybe also, from a distance, the rowdy Chamber where the vote was taking place.

John Bercow, the Speaker of the House, in his black robe, moved first to the traditional voice vote. 'The main question in the name of the prime minister,' he shouted, and asked those who were in favour to say 'aye'. '*Aaaaaye,*' part of the Chamber responded. Then Bercow asked, 'On the contrary, no.' And a thunderous '*Noooooo*' followed.

Guy Verhofstadt's team laughed at the proceedings. 'What a puppet show,' their boss said. 'This is insane,' Jeroen Reijnen added. But Verhofstadt had also attentively listened for an indication as to what the outcome of the vote was going to be: 'It was very clear that there was a no. Sorry. If you hear it, it's over already.'

It was not quite over in formal terms; the house then divided, and MPs filed through the division lobbies to settle the fate of Theresa May's deal.

Just before the result was declared, some twenty minutes later, Edel asked her team members responsible for social media whether they were ready with their tweet – it had, as always, been prepared in advance. 'The tweet is ready,' Jeroen said, while everyone was peering at the screen now, and both the Chamber and Verhofstadt's back room fell silent. 'If it's [a defeat by] over 200 it's a massive loss. The biggest ever,' Nick Petre whispered.

They watched the four tellers advance up the centre of the

Commons chamber: the result, when it came, was stunning. Mrs May's deal was rejected by 432 votes to 202 – a margin of 230 MPs. 'That's the biggest defeat [of a sitting government] ever,' Nick Petre confirmed – it was far worse than Michel Barnier's gloomy prediction a few days earlier.

At Westminster, the Labour leader Jeremy Corbyn immediately announced, with a cracking voice, that he was tabling a motion of no confidence in the government. But Guy Verhofstadt dismissed his gambit decisively: 'That's a bad move. It will not happen.'

The civil servant Markus Winkler had now arrived, and Verhofstadt asked him whether he could get Keir Starmer, Labour's shadow Brexit secretary, on the phone. Winkler obliged. 'Hi, Keir, good to talk to you. I give you Guy Verhofstadt. Guy, that's Keir Starmer.' Verhofstadt's message for Starmer was in line with his view of the no-confidence motion just tabled by Labour leader Jeremy Corbyn; rather than opposing Theresa May, he wanted Labour to start looking for common ground. And he explained that the European side would be stating that publicly. 'What we are going to do tomorrow is to say, first of all, what they need to do in Britain, is cross-party [cooperation].' And he promised that the EU would put its weight behind efforts to find a consensus, 'saying that we are ready to work further on the future relationship, and in such a way that you don't need the backstop, [that] you can avoid the backstop with the future relationship'.

The Brexit Steering Group was due to discuss the result of the vote with Barnier that same evening, and although it was now past ten o'clock already, a group of reporters stood waiting outside the room where they were going to meet. Verhofstadt was careful not to express any party political views, but he was direct in his advice – almost instructions – to British politicians.

> VERHOFSTADT: This result is the consequence of the British political system. The fight between left and right, between Labour and the Conservative Party. And there is a need for cross-party cooperation [now] so that we know what Britain wants and there is a majority in the House of Commons backing that proposal. And if that proposal goes in the direction of a more deepened relationship with the EU, we are ready to do so. Secondly, what we don't want is that this mess in British politics is imported in[to] European politics. So let's try to find a solution before the European elections.
>
> REPORTER: Can May deliver that deal or should she step aside?
>
> VERHOFSTADT: That's a question you should not ask here in Strasbourg or even in Brussels, but in London. In Westminster. But what is absolutely clear is that there is a need for cross-party cooperation so that the national interest and the interest of the EU prevails. And that is still not the case today. Today it's still a fight between the majority and the opposition, left and right, Labour and the Conservatives.
>
> REPORTER: So you're not using this opportunity to support Mrs May as the government leader.
>
> VERHOFSTADT: I'm supporting neither Mrs May nor the opposition leader.

It was another vivid example of the ironies thrown up by the Brexit process. Returning sovereignty to Westminster was one of the rallying cries of those campaigning for a 'Leave' vote in the 2016 referendum; two and a half years later, Britain's MPs were being given a frank lecture on how they should conduct themselves by a politician in Brussels.

Inside the Brexit Steering Group meeting room, once the camera crews flocking around had been led out, Verhofstadt opened the meeting with, unusually, a long declaration of his own. 'We all know that in the next two days [there] will be a no-confidence vote tabled by the opposition,' he said. 'But really, [speaking] inside this room, I don't think that will make a big difference at the end. But that's not our concern. Our concern has to be to prepare the next steps.'

The EU's strategy, he argued, should be to shore up the unity which had been such a hallmark of Europe's position on Brexit: 'It would be good that the different political parties involved in the BSG, in the plenary [the whole European Parliament], together with the Commission and the Council, have the same wording and at least the same attitude in this. There's maybe disruption in Britain, in the House of Commons, [but it is important] that there is no disruption in the European family now, between the Council, between the Commission, and the European Parliament.'

And he had further words of commentary on events at Westminster. After a long career in the coalition politics which are second nature in the Belgian and European Parliaments, Verhofstadt thought he detected a glimmer of hope: 'One thing I would like to underline is that for the first time in the intervention of Mrs May after the vote, immediately after the vote, she, for the first time, is my impression, she opened the game towards the opposition, in saying, "I will invite everybody, also the opposition, to see how we are going to proceed further."' On this point his political instinct, usually so sharp, was to be proved well wide of the mark.

Michel Barnier had been nodding at Verhofstadt's words. The two presided over the meeting like twins — and that's a description not of my own but of Verhofstadt's making, in a chat with Edel Crosse. 'Wherever I appear, he [Barnier] appears.'

Barnier elaborated on his Brexit twin's reasoning: 'Today in the House of Commons there are two negative majorities. A negative majority against the deal, and a negative majority against a no-deal [Brexit]. But there is no positive majority for anything.' He too picked up on the idea that cross-party consensus-building might offer a way ahead in the United Kingdom, 'even if one may regret that it did not emerge earlier'. And he too was hopeful. His optimism was based on a conversation earlier that evening with Sir Tim Barrow, the British permanent representative to the EU, who seemed to have confirmed what Verhofstadt had detected in May's own words, namely that she was 'at last going to begin discussions with the other parties'. Like Guy Verhofstadt's optimism, it would prove to be a serious misreading of the direction of Westminster politics.

Verhofstadt also noted another development: 'It's also important that John Bercow, the Speaker of the House, after the intervention of Theresa May, said that . . . all options will be debated and voted [on] by Parliament, eh?' The idea that Parliament would replace the government as the guiding hand behind the Brexit process was gaining momentum at Westminster, and the Barnier–Verhofstadt double act welcomed it with a sly reference to Vote Leave's referendum slogan.

'Parliament will . . .' Verhofstadt began.

'. . . take back control,' Barnier supplied as a punchline.

'"Finally," I should say, because this could already have happened one and a half years ago.'

'Absolutely,' Barnier echoed.

Manfred Weber, the leader of the Christian Democrats in the European Parliament – so someone with significant influence; at a certain stage he even became a potential new European Commission president – also attended the meeting, and he gave voice to the worry that, as the Brexit process dragged on, individual EU member states would return to focusing on their national priorities. Weber gave the example of the Polish government; in Warsaw they might 'have in mind the amount of Polish workers in Britain', he said. In 2017, there were an estimated 922,000 Poles living in the UK.

Weber also referred to a recent conversation he had had with the Irish prime minister, Leo Varadkar. 'I can imagine', he told the meeting, 'that he's considering: "Am I now forced to build a border wall between our Ireland and Northern Ireland?" It would be for him in Ireland a disaster if he [was] forced to build up a border control because of Brexit.' Weber suggested that, with the Brexit process apparently paralysed, and both the UK and the EU searching for a way out, 'everybody will now look on his special interests'.

In his reaction, Barnier seemed less worried than Weber, trusting the efforts his team had made over the past two years to create and maintain a united front on the European side of the negotiating table: 'Our great strength at the moment is that unity which we have built together, between the [EU] institutions, the twenty-seven countries and, more generally, among the various political groups. It is not artificial, because we have made this, over the past eighteen months, a joint project – building the treaty together. And that's something that hasn't been done on the British side.'

The United Kingdom's divided ambitions for the Brexit process might have offered the European Union a tactical advantage while the negotiations were on-going, but now that the terms of the withdrawal agreement were settled, those divisions were proving a real obstacle to its ratification. Barnier accepted that the Europeans could not build a parliamentary majority for a particular outcome on Theresa May's behalf, but he believed the EU could at least help her with changes in the political declaration which had been signed off alongside the withdrawal agreement. And he came back, yet again, to his conviction that the British Parliament, if given the chance, would be willing to vote for some kind of customs union on top of a free-trade agreement. 'That would not deal with all the problems of Ireland,' he recognised, but it would deal with 'part of them', so it would 'put the backstop into perspective'. He smiled at his point: 'Why do I bring up this hypothesis? Because from the first the Labour Party, like the business community, like the House of Lords, has said they are favourable to a customs union.'

'OK, thank you very much,' Verhofstadt said, ending the meeting. 'And let's not talk outside about what has been said inside.' It was close to midnight, but when the meeting room's doors were opened again, the camera crews and journalists were still there. They shouted questions at the BSG members trickling out.

To avoid the press, Verhofstadt remained seated for a few minutes more. Bram Delen and Jeroen Reijnen took up position behind him, waiting to escort their boss safely back to his office. They knew from habit that he wouldn't want to leave the Parliament straight away — first he needed a drink and a chat. There was no way they'd get to bed any time soon.

Back at his office, Verhofstadt pointed at the fridge in his back room.

'Look a bit [at] what is in there, if there is alcohol.' There were cans of beer — and I also got (and felt I deserved) one. While we pulled them open, Eva Palatova and Guillaume McLaughlin joined the conversation, which quickly returned to Corbyn's motion of no confidence in the British government.

McLAUGHLIN: Corbyn is going to lose this ridiculous
    thing, eh? It's a stupid move. He's going to come out
    losing.
PALATOVA: He lost the whole momentum.
VERHOFSTADT: It was the moment to say, 'I'm going to
    do something. The national interest has to prevail. And
    so I offer to you to look with you what the agreement
    could be.' And then in negotiating with her he can
    ask, afterwards, 'Immediately after the deal we go to
    elections.' He would have been the saviour of the day.

Bram and Jeroen took a rather more cynical view of the way the British political system works, however.

DELEN: I don't think you can make a deal in British
    politics saying, 'If I support you now, and then we go
    to elections.'
REIJNEN: No, it doesn't work like that.
DELEN: You get fucked in the ass, in Britain. You vote
    [for] Mrs May's deal and then you get fucked in the ass
    about your elections.

Eva Palatova drew on her knowledge of British history. This was about communicating to the public, in her view, 'We are fucked without a deal, so we have to come together.' Historically it was the case, no? Churchill was somehow imposed in the war . . .'

Jeroen Reijnen agreed: 'They need a war to work together.'

But Verhofstadt put the reference to Winston Churchill in perspective, reminding everyone what happened to the United Kingdom's great wartime prime minister at the 1945 general election. 'Yeah, and then, if you win the war, you [makes a sign with his hand], you're chucked out,' he said.

'They get rid of you,' Jeroen Reijnen agreed. But still, he argued, 'that would be a good line for tomorrow, eh? When were the moments when [the UK came together] . . .'

But Bram Delen felt the EU had to be careful in its communication. Putting all the onus on the UK was tricky. 'People are also going to look to our position and our contribution to a solution, eh?' said Delen. 'So it's been voted down now, OK, it's their problem, we put the ball in their camp, but the ball will come back at one point.'

Verhofstadt ended the evening — past midnight — with an observation full of cynical political venom. 'All these guys, like David Davis and Boris Johnson, will have to vote [for May] now, in the confidence vote,' he laughed — while Jeroen continued his line of thought: 'Within the Conservative Party, they tried to get rid of her, and it didn't work, because they couldn't find a majority. Now they can get rid of her, but they're not going to support that, because it's Labour who has started it.'

'Exactly,' Verhofstadt said. 'That's a good summary. These 100 stupids who wanted to get rid of her one month ago will now vote for her in the non-confidence vote.'

~

At eight o'clock the next morning the team was back at the office for their monthly Strasbourg speechwriting session — and Verhofstadt was in a foul mood. He read out loud to Bram Delen what they had prepared the day before:

Jeremy Corbyn wants to become the next PM, it's legitimate. Theresa May wants to remain PM, it's legitimate as well. That SNP wants to make Scotland independent, that's legitimate. And that the DUP wants the opposite and wants to stay in the UK, is equally legitimate. So my message today is that whatever legitimate ambition everybody has, all have to come out of the trenches. All have to transcend the binary system in which they are locked. Brexit started as a catfight within the Conservative Party, but since then it has become far more than that. It became an existential question about Britain's future, about Britain's soul.

VERHOFSTADT: OK?

DELEN: Mmmm-mm. The first sentence . . .

VERHOFSTADT [raising his voice]: Print it. I have to GO!! Don't . . .

CROSSE [putting her hand on Bram's shoulder]: You have ten minutes. It's OK. You have ten minutes. Relax. We'll get it done.

VERHOFSTADT: Oh, come on!!

Then Verhofstadt left – and Edel commented on his grumpiness with an exasperated sigh: 'Grateful, for everything we do.'

DELEN: Happy, shiny people.

CROSSE: Showered with compliments.

DELEN: Waltzing through the hallways of the European Parliament.

CROSSE: 'You're doing good, you're doing well'; 8.30 in the morning, two squashed beer cans, and that just sums up my whole feeling, basically.

~

On Monday 21 January, Theresa May made a statement to the Commons laying out her Plan B after the overwhelming defeat of Plan A. It included a very belated victory for Guy Verhofstadt; she announced that the government would waive the fee for EU citizens applying for settled status in Britain after Brexit. In a nod to the spirit of cross-party cooperation, she also pledged to maintain and enhance protections for workers' rights and the environment after Brexit.

Plan B otherwise looked very much like Plan A. Mrs May said that she would be holding talks with the DUP about the Irish backstop and would take her conclusions back to Brussels. She summarised her position to the Commons with 'my focus continues to be on what is needed to secure the support of this House in favour of a Brexit deal with the EU'.

But where was she going to find that support? After months of trying to limit the extent to which Parliament could influence the Brexit process, the government was now forced to accept, at least to some degree, that the House of Commons would have to have a role in finding a way forward. In formal terms, the prime minister's next step was to table a motion 'in neutral terms' on her position, and she added the crucial information that 'this motion will be amendable', so MPs would have an opportunity to express their views on the deal in Parliament. The votes were planned for the following Tuesday, 29 January.

In Brussels, meanwhile, it had started snowing. The fat flakes fulfilled my dream of filming the Parliament at least once in white, and, to make my happiness complete, some children had made a snowman in the public garden that can be seen from Verhofstadt's office.

I spent the morning outside, and then rushed back in for another BSG update with Michel Barnier.

'Everybody among us follows carefully what happens in the UK, and it's kind of chaos – more than chaos, general hysteria,' was his dramatic opening salvo. 'And for the first time in each camp there are also some divisions. Even in the Brexiteer camp. And there's division also among the 3 Million [EU citizens in the United Kingdom].'

He picked up on the significance of the fact that the next votes on Tuesday 29 January would be amendable: 'The point is important, in her speech . . . she encouraged the Parliament to present amendments.' His interpretation was that this tactic would allow the prime minister to delegate the task of finding a compromise without compromising her own political position. 'The line of Mrs May is clear in my view,' Barnier judged. 'She decided to stick to the Brexiteers, stick to the DUP, not to lose, herself, by her fault, the support of the DUP and the Brexiteers, and the Tory Party. I think, personally, that she wants to stick to, keep her majority, but encourage the Parliament to take the power. To move the line.'

Barnier added that the stakes were high. 'It's clear, friends,' he said with emphasis, 'if nothing moves, next Tuesday, we are going straight down to a no-deal, eh?' But his hope was that the amendments would provide the basis for a compromise, per-haps some kind of an idea about the future relationship between the United Kingdom and the EU to be included in the political declaration – which, unlike the withdrawal agreement, could be redrafted.

Elmar Brok had serious doubts about whether a compromise was going to be found – and he did not just blame the hard Brexiteers. 'The most problematic in the House of Commons are the Remainers,' he said. 'It's a coalition of the hard Brexit people, and the Remainers [that blocks everything]. If that coalition is not broken, if that negative coalition is not broken, forget everything. This is so broad, a large majority. The Remainers don't want to compromise, finish. That's the case.'

It was indeed the case that some Remain-supporting Tories – including the prominent pro-Europeans Dominic Grieve and Anna Soubry – had joined the hard-line Brexiteers and the opposition parties in the 'no' lobby. 'The Remainers are a problem,' Brok said. 'We have to say it. Please, Remainers, come up also with a compromise. That will disappoint them, because our sympathy is with them. But in this moment we have also to explain to them that internally it's time to move. To compromise.'

Guillaume McLaughlin agreed, underlining the strength of some pro-European sentiment in the United Kingdom, especially among younger voters and the MPs who represented their views. 'It's existential, eh?' he said.

> If you sit down with people like that, these young guys, it's fucking existential. These guys will go to the very end and will never compromise. They want to stay in the EU. They say it's the end of their world. Remainers are crazy. They don't believe that May will dare to push the UK over the edge. And so until the very end they will say no so that in the end they get what they want: second referendum or revocation.

Seven amendments were selected for debate by the Speaker, John Bercow, on 29 January 2019. His power to make that selection astonished Guy Verhofstadt, who called the British 'a medieval democracy' – although some of those parliamentarians who take pride in Westminster's venerable procedures and traditions may take that as a compliment rather than the reverse. But the result did little to clarify the situation in Westminster.

The opposition motions – from Labour and the SNP – were easily defeated. An attempt by Dominic Grieve, a former Conservative attorney general, to force the government to hand over control of the parliamentary timetable for a Brexit debate went down by a much narrower margin, as did two amendments from Labour backbenchers providing for the possibility of postponing Brexit.

The two amendments that succeeded – neither of them binding on the government – reflected the complex, and sometimes apparently contradictory, mix of opinion in the Commons. MPs voted by 318 to 310 against a no-deal Brexit, in an amendment brought by one Conservative and one Labour backbencher, that stated that Parliament 'rejects the United Kingdom leaving the European Union without a Withdrawal Agreement and a Framework for the Future Relationship'.

They also voted – by the slightly larger majority of 317 to 301 – for an amendment proposed by Sir Graham Brady, the Chairman of the 1922 Committee of backbench Conservative MPs, which called on the government to renegotiate the backstop so that it could be replaced by unspecified 'alternative arrangements' to keep the Irish border open. The 'Brady Amendment', as it became known, was passed with government support, and was greeted on the Tory benches as a triumph for party unity. It would soon become a further source of irritation in the relationship between Brussels and London.

Verhofstadt was intensely annoyed by the day's dealings at Westminster. He called Bram Delen and Guillaume McLaughlin into his office, to prepare a reaction, but instead they became his audience for a fierce outburst. 'We have to get angry a bit at the British,' he started. 'Well, at the British political class.' And while he addressed his staffers, it was in fact as if he was talking to the UK politicians directly. 'It's up to them to sort it out, across party, with a broad majority and a proposal supported by two thirds of your bloody House of Commons there. If you take out the real hard Brexiteers, you can have two thirds, eh?'

'A clear and stable majority, tada,' that's what Britain needed — according to Verhofstadt. 'And not depending on the choice of the Speaker who is choosing an amendment, and that is producing a majority, ten in favour, or ten against.' He was frustrated that 'an existential political issue' could be dealt with like this. 'These votes are like gambling, casino. Parliament is not a casino, eh?'

That line pleased him. 'It's going to make headlines,' he said — although Bram was already shaking his head, no too harsh.

But his boss was on a roll now. 'The British Parliament is not a casino, eh? I know the Brits like to bet, but not on the future of their country . . . Well, they're capable of anything!'

His chief of staff agreed: 'They seem to be doing it.'

Verhofstadt laughed — but didn't stop: 'You have to be a little bit kwaad *[Dutch for angry], eh? It's been enough now. On 14 February [the date of yet another Brexit debate], they will vote again, on a number of amendments, who will "pepepepe", a little bit there, and they will pass with a majority of ten, fifteen, that's what they are busy with.'*

Guillaume tried to interject: 'But I mean she [May] is right . . .'

But that only made Verhofstadt explode even more. 'Stop now with "she's right or not right". You're entering in her game. You're entering in the game of, "Oh, this amendment, oh, this amendment. Wow? Will it pass: yes, no? Oh, it passed. Ah, fifty thingies." They like it. It's like a football match. And it's always the same. It's always Man City against Man United what we are seeing, and sometimes it's City who wins, and sometimes it's United.' Guillaume and Bram Delen couldn't contain their laughter. 'But they like it. Again, 1-1, 1-2, no, now 2-1. And in the meanwhile . . . [and there he whistled]'

'. . . nothing happens,' Guillaume finished the sentence.

VERHOFSTADT: Maybe Man City and Man United can
    have one . . .
MCLAUGHLIN: . . . final.
VERHOFSTADT: No, no, not one final. That they both
    join, to get rid of Real Madrid together.

*Westminster Divided against Real Madrid: that's what the negotiations
had come down to.*

That same afternoon Michel Barnier described the situation
as 'grave and serious', pointing out that his ticking clock had
now brought the two sides within six weeks of the United
Kingdom's scheduled departure from the European Union.
'They were the ones who chose that date,' he said, 'who wrote
it into British law, and we still do not have agreement on an
orderly withdrawal. That means that as the days pass the risk
of a disorderly withdrawal grows. It's almost a mechanical process. It's not what we want, but neither is it our responsibility.
You need both sides to reach an agreement.'

And he noted that the Westminster amendment against a
no-deal Brexit did not guarantee the outcome: 'Voting against
no-deal doesn't mean that no-deal won't happen by accident,'
he said. 'To avoid a no-deal there needs to be agreement on
something positive, and the real problem with this Parliament
is that there are still two majorities which are both clearly negative – one against no-deal and one against the deal.'

The other amendment that Parliament had adopted, the
Brady Amendment, was causing not just frustration, but real
anger in Brussels. Although it called for 'alternative arrangements to avoid a hard border' in Ireland, it made no attempt
to suggest what those arrangements might be. Yet the British
government presented the Brady Amendment as an indication

of what could command a (positive) majority in Parliament, and Mrs May was now proposing to renegotiate the backstop on that basis. Since the EU's negotiators had spent a year and a half exploring every 'arrangement' anyone could think of to 'avoid a hard border', this did not go down very well.

'The backstop, my dear friends, is not a fantasy,' Barnier told the Brexit Steering Group, 'or an ideology, or a way of ensuring we create a problem with the British. It is precisely the opposite. It represents the care we have taken to find a solution to the problems created in Ireland by Brexit. It is the decision to leave the Union which has created the problem in Ireland.'

And like Verhofstadt in his rant against a 'casino parliament', Barnier seemed unstoppable – if perhaps lacking the comic flair that had made the Brexit coordinator's riff so entertaining to his staff. 'The problem in Ireland is a double one, for us,' he hammered on:

One should always remember that. Number one, peace and stability on the island – of which the British government is a co-guarantor. Mrs May has always said – and we should grant her this – that the United Kingdom is co-guarantor of the Good Friday Agreement. And the second priority, requirement, which is not an ideological one, is that of the internal market. It is necessary to repeat, calmly and in the manner of a teacher, that every product, every live animal which comes into Ireland, from the north, can wind up in Spain, in Poland, in Italy, and in Belgium – immediately. And that we have a duty to protect consumers, businesses and the whole EU. We cannot compromise on that – without excluding the Republic of Ireland from the single market.

His irritation was especially acute because 'this backstop is a British idea. It is not the backstop we first proposed, which, let me remind you, was limited to Northern Ireland. They asked for a UK-wide solution, the idea of a customs union – it was they who put that in the Chequers [plan]. So there's the paradox.'

And he again had the Brady Amendment in his sights: 'Perhaps in the future, "alternative arrangements" will be possible', he said, 'to square this circle, perhaps, but we don't have them today. We need time, time to work on them, and we have promised, in the treaty, that as soon as the withdrawal agreement is signed we will begin work on a specific agreement to deal with the question of the Irish border – to find "alternative arrangements", to find a future relationship which can deal with this issue.'

~

With the process of active negotiation effectively on hold, Barnier and the members of the Brexit Steering Group focused increasingly on divisions which went beyond the backstop – beyond, indeed, the immediate reality of Brexit.

Barnier, for instance, complained during his meeting with the BSG at the end of January 2019 that in the United Kingdom 'there had really never been an open, pluralistic debate' about Brexit, and contrasted that with the way politicians from very different traditions could 'work on what we, together, consider to be the general interest of the Union' in the Brexit Steering Group.

It was something Verhofstadt, too, had already said quite a few times.

Elmar Brok, who as a German Christian Democrat came from a political tradition that had been intimately involved in the European project from its earliest days, but which has no equivalent British political party, gave a concrete example of what Barnier and Verhofstadt meant. 'If my country would be in such a situation, the chancellor [Angela Merkel] would have invited two years ago [so, straight after the referendum] the leaders of the opposition for a decent Sunday evening dinner, to find a solution,' he said. 'They [British politicians] say all the time they have talked to each other, but they still have not . . . That is the problem: please talk and then come. Find a solution among yourself. She [May] comes back now with the same question as she came in December 2017.'

Like Barnier, Brok particularly resented the way an agreement that had been negotiated by Mrs May herself was now being framed as an EU ruse to catch the United Kingdom in a long-term economic relationship: 'It's their proposal. They have asked for a customs union – not us. We had other proposals. We had proposals which were not so dramatic[ally] big.'

The original backstop proposal, which was included in the joint report of December 2017, had indeed only contained measures specific to Northern Ireland, and had not covered the whole of the United Kingdom. The big, never-resolved question that the EU asked itself was: would the UK have accepted that first backstop proposal if May had not become so dependent on the DUP following the 2017 general election?

Roberto Gualtieri, the Italian Social Democrat – so an heir to the other mainstream political tradition in post-war Europe – meanwhile shared the frustration of his Christian Democrat colleague about the way the British had dealt and were dealing with Brexit. His verdict on the Westminster amendments was blunt: 'I think yesterday we have seen an incredible combination of weakness, irresponsibility and cynicism.'

The Belgian Green MEP Philippe Lamberts brought the group back to the reality the two sides were currently facing: the very real possibility of a no-deal outcome. The question, he suggested, was whether the European side would give way under the pressure of that damaging prospect. He thought – or hoped – that Europe would not cave in, because 'A no-deal Brexit would be costly for the twenty-seven, but destroying the integrity of the internal market would be even more costly, so do not underestimate the calculation we are making in terms of outcome. If we have to decide between two evils, we'll choose the less costly for us. And that is a no-deal Brexit. Don't underestimate that.'

Lamberts was, however, worried that some member states might lose their nerve, as Manfred Weber had suggested earlier – and this time Barnier was less dismissive of the suggestion. He still wavered between seeing the British disarray for what it was, and sensing a plan behind it.

'Theresa May's strategy is extremely clear,' he said:

It's to consolidate the unity of her party, and to force us to give way. Several of them [the Conservatives] said, yesterday or the day before, 'the Europeans will always do a deal in the end'. It was David Davis's view, which he repeated to me several times: 'At the end of the road, you always give in. You always throw in the towel, the Europeans always give in.' They think that we are in a traditional negotiation, commercial bargaining, and that we shall give way in the end. So she [Mrs May] has come down in favour of party unity – including the DUP in that, because she needs them – and based on that decision she wants us to give up on the European red lines, and to make us fold.

And the EU chief negotiator was clear about what was at stake: 'We know all too well, as you have said, Philippe, that what is involved is the integrity of the single market.'

Barnier, ever the historian, quoted the words of the 1950s left-wing French prime minister Pierre Mendès-France: 'Never sacrifice the future to the present.'

But the former East German communist Gabi Zimmer had a warning. 'My feeling [during] the last [few] weeks in Germany was that people are asking now, why do you want to punish the UK? Why is [the] EU not ready to open it, to negotiate?' she said. 'That means we have to explain from the very beginning, very carefully, and very clear[ly] . . . what is behind our positions, as a European Union.'

Guy Verhofstadt conceded: 'That's the very big danger that we have now. That in the coming days people start saying we are too tough.' To help rally support for the agreement, his chief of staff Guillaume McLaughlin came up with the idea of 'a list of terrible things, a horror list' of what might happen if there was no deal. Verhofstadt threw out a well-crafted sentence that might have made a sharp headline: 'The Brexit Steering Group publishes the Brexit horror list.'

Negotiations on the substance of the May–Barnier deal hardly moved at all from this point – but the battle for public opinion was well and truly joined.

CAN I BECOME A BELGIAN CITIZEN?

February–March 2019

On Monday 4 February 2019, Guy Verhofstadt was pacing around in his office in Brussels, waiting for the arrival of Theresa May's chief of staff, Gavin Barwell. Outside all light had long disappeared. A biting cold winter evening turned freezing later that night. The little Queen Elizabeth statue on Guillaume McLaughlin's windowsill had stopped waving her solar-powered hand.

With time to kill, the Brexit coordinator of the European Parliament took his phone and called his daughter, to talk about the renovations she was doing in her house and the ridiculous price difference – he got angry – between white and black paint. Meanwhile, I installed my camera in Guillaume's office. From there, through two open doors, I knew I would have a clear view of the red sofas in Verhofstadt's office, where he and Barwell were likely to sit down. If nobody closed the doors, as happened once in a while when someone insisted that a meeting really remained private, I would be able to film their conversation.

And I was lucky. Barwell and his team arrived right in front of me and didn't say a word about my presence. They didn't ask me what I was doing – they just went inside and left the door open.

Making documentaries is a bit like being a sniper, sometimes.

Barwell explained why he had come. 'My job, ultimately as the PM's adviser, is to try to say to her, how could you get your deal through? And at the moment I can only see two ways,' he said. 'One is, if she accepted a second referendum, those MPs that favour a second referendum would go for it, even if they don't like her deal, they would vote for it, but that would break the government apart. And the second is this package that we now try to push, some room from the EU on the backstop combined with some measures of workers' rights, the environment, that bring over some Labour MPs.'

Barwell is not a big man, but his voice was loud and clear, and he took Verhofstadt through the parliamentary arithmetic. 'We've got 115 MPs to switch [the total number of Conservatives who voted against the deal was in fact slightly higher than that],' he said, 'and about eighty-five of them are the people we should be looking at. The hard-core ones, you're not going to get to back her. But [for] those ones [the eighty-five], my judgement would be that the key test is our attorney general's legal advice.' So No. 10 was calculating that when the deal came back to Parliament, the decisive factor would be Geoffrey Cox's legal opinion; could the attorney general be persuaded to change his view by what Gavin Barwell called 'some room from the EU on the backstop'?

Verhofstadt interjected that Barwell and May also had 'to be ready to eventually lose the ten DUPs [Democratic Unionists] in a search for the majority'.

But Barwell did not agree. 'This is one of the key things that I wanted to say to everyone I met today. Don't think of the DUP as the same as the ERG [the hard-line European Research Group]. They're not the same. The ERG are people who actively want no deal – and it contains other people who would say, "Well, I'd like a deal if it's the exact deal that I want, and if you're not prepared to do that, I'm quite happy with no-deal." The DUP cannot sell no-deal in Northern Ireland. They need a deal. So this is really important.'

And Barwell explained the significance of the DUP position in terms designed to resonate with a veteran parliamentarian like Verhofstadt. 'The reason they are like a piece of litmus paper, they're like the litmus test, is because the average Conservative backbencher, what they say to the PM is: "Look, if I vote for a deal, and the DUP can't support it, that's the end of the government, or we've got a general election, and I can then lose my seat. So I'm not going to back any deal unless they say it's OK with them."'

Afterwards, for Guillaume McLaughlin, Verhofstadt's chief of staff, who thought that Barwell 'thinks what Mrs May thinks, he says what Mrs May thinks, maybe more eloquently', the conclusion was clear. 'They need us to move, and I can't see how we can move.'

Verhofstadt gloomily agreed. 'Therefore I hope he hears the same thing in every corner [of the EU, and especially the European Council]. They will not move, they will not put an end date to the backstop; that's impossible.'

Two days later, the EU Council president Donald Tusk, at a press conference with the Irish prime minister, Leo Varadkar, was in a rather more impish mood: 'I've been wondering what that special place in hell looks like, for those who promoted Brexit, without even a sketch of a plan of how to carry it out safely,' he declared.

The two men's microphones were left open at the end of the press conference, and Varadkar could be heard telling Tusk: 'They'll give you terrible trouble in the British press for that.' Tusk nodded, and both men laughed.

Guy Verhofstadt – challenged of course by Tusk's daring comment – reacted with a tweet: 'I doubt Lucifer would welcome them, as after what they did to Britain, they would even manage to divide hell.'

Shortly afterwards, while Verhofstadt was walking around in his office, again, waiting for the Irish prime minister, Leo Varadkar, this time, he started chatting to me, which didn't happen too often. Tensions between the EU and the UK were clearly running high, but Verhofstadt still didn't seem to be too worried – although he did start with a sigh.

VERHOFSTADT: Pfff, what a mess, eh?

ME: This is not going to end well, no?

VERHOFSTADT [laughing]: Is that what you think? It's always like that in politics, eh? If you start thinking it's not going to end well any more, we're coming close to the conclusion.

ME: So you think it's going to end well?

VERHOFSTADT: But of course.

ME: Tsss.

VERHOFSTADT: Surely, jong [Dutch for youngster]. Surely.

ME: Really?

VERHOFSTADT [laughing even more]: I'm telling you, yes!!

ME [with a sigh]: OK, well, it's your job, your trade, after all. You know a lot more about it than I do.

VERHOFSTADT: It's my trade, indeed. I've always known it to be like this. You don't imagine solving something like this six months beforehand? Typically, in a situation like this, everybody thinks and tries, until the very end, no?

ME: I find that strange, but . . .

VERHOFSTADT: You find that strange? Look at what
    happens with a divorce. How long does that take?

*And with that Verhofstadt strode into Edel's office to ask when Varadkar
was finally going to arrive. Not yet, apparently. So, with Guillaume
McLaughlin and the top civil servant Markus Winkler, he started on
another topic of substance: where had Verhofstadt found his nice red
sofas? In Ikea, cheaply, it turned out. But there was also lots of stuff in
his office that came from the European Parliament's cellars. 'It's a real
treasure chest down there,' Guillaume observed.*

    I wasn't allowed to film the meeting with Varadkar.

The following day's visitor was Theresa May herself. The prime
minister would not be coming to Verhofstadt's offices, and so
she would not be able to admire his nice red sofas; they would
meet instead in the European Parliament's Protocol Room.
'You have to go in thirty-four minutes,' Guillaume told his
boss. 'I'm trying to see if you can get a call from Mr Barnier
beforehand.'

    May's visit was going to be very short. 'She's coming [for]
half an hour to the Parliament, so it's just aesthetics, eh?'
Guillaume said. 'By the time they sit down, you will have
three, four minutes, I would have thought.' But even in those
few minutes it was important to give May a unified EU message – so the call with Barnier mattered.

    Meanwhile, Verhofstadt was wielding a yellow marker pen as
he went through a letter the Labour leader, Jeremy Corbyn, had
written to Theresa May. Verhofstadt was highlighting elements
he found interesting and could use in his own upcoming talk
with May. He had a positive feeling about the letter. It suited
his view that the only way out of the British conundrum was

cross-party cooperation. Corbyn set out five conditions for his party's support for the Brexit deal, and he wanted them enshrined as objectives in domestic law. The letter spelt them out: a UK-wide customs union; close alignment with the single market; 'dynamic alignment' on [social and environmental] rights and protections; 'clear commitments' on participation in EU agencies and funding programmes; and 'unambiguous agreements' on the detail of future security arrangements. Corbyn said that Labour did not believe that 'simply seeking modifications to the existing backstop terms is a credible or sufficient response' to the scale of defeat suffered by Mrs May the previous month – and he added that EU leaders had been clear that changes to the political declaration were possible if a request was made by the UK government 'and if the current red lines change'.

When Verhofstadt was halfway through Corbyn's letter, Olivier Schotte dropped by. He was a young social media manager who was slowly climbing his way up the staff ladder, and had by now reached the status where he could just pop in like this. Verhofstadt stopped reading briefly, to discuss with Olli (as he's known) the reactions to his Lucifer tweet the previous day.

Many of them came from within the UK – some supportive of what Verhofstadt had tweeted, and others lambasting him. One tweet showed the picture of a raised middle finger in the UK colours. Another referred to a speech by the fascist leader Oswald Mosley about the United States of Europe [Europe a Nation] he favoured, and said, 'Let's be clear, these people are fascists.' Gerard Batten MEP (UKIP) asked, 'Lucifer was expelled from Paradise. What does the UK have to do to be expelled from your paradise?' The EU Brexit coordinator was happy with the number of 'likes' for the tweet, but wanted Olivier to work on moving the more negative comments further down, where they'd be less visible.

To me Verhofstadt said, 'You know how many comments there are? Nearly 5,000. And they're responding to each other, eh? It's like internal battles. One who's saying you're a lunatic. And then the other, "What? A lunatic!?"' He laughed. 'It's very divisive. It was meant as a joke, but it's not seen as a joke. British humour is at its lowest level in decades.'

Checking the tweet recently, the 'moving down' of negative comments didn't work very well.

Then Guillaume McLaughlin came back in, telling Verhofstadt that Barnier was going to call in fifteen minutes, 'so put your telephone in ringing mode'. He prodded his boss for attention. 'Hello there? He will ring you in fifteen minutes. So make sure the ring tone is switched on – because sometimes you turn it off.'

Barnier had seen Theresa May earlier that day, and when he got on the phone to Verhofstadt, he reported, 'She told me that she did not want to prolong [the Article 50 process], that's the main thing I wanted to tell you.'

'That's good,' Verhofstadt replied.

Short, but important.

I wasn't allowed to film the meeting with May either, but I managed to steal – though even that wasn't really authorised – some footage of her arrival. She walked in stiffly, preceded by a Parliament bailiff with a heavy-looking silver chain around his neck, and she had at least twenty staffers in tow.

Olly Robbins was walking just behind the prime minister.

Afterwards Verhofstadt told his team that he'd broken the ice with May by telling her that the 2016 Cameron deal had been brokered in the same room they were sitting in now, but with Cameron at the other side of the table. The bad memories of that deal – the manner in which it was negotiated over long, arduous months but was almost immediately rejected by many Eurosceptic MPs – go a long way towards explaining Verhofstadt's profound scepticism about negotiating with the UK — something he shared with many prominent figures in the EU.

May had laughed at the Cameron anecdote, Verhofstadt claimed. 'We get along quite well, actually,' he said.

But what had May herself said? Had the meeting been productive, his team asked? 'She wants a backstop, only another one, by limiting it in time,' he reported. 'And I said, "Well, the only way to solve your backstop problem is to be more precise on the future relationship in the political declaration so that the backstop needs not to be used." *Enfin*, always the same.' But in a typical Belgian surrealist manner he added that sometimes you repeat things so often that in the end 'they find it: oh, that's interesting' again.

Verhofstadt also talked to Mrs May about Jeremy Corbyn's letter and cross-party cooperation, and she told him she wanted to try to secure a parliamentary majority from her own party.

The British prime minister was then treated to a lecture on the virtues of European-style coalition-building. 'I said, "But there are thirty, forty assholes" — I did not say assholes — "who will never back it,"' Verhofstadt told his team. '"In our country, in this Parliament here, the extremes are not represented in the Brexit Steering Group. Really, I don't want to give a lesson to you. [But] you have to do a cross-party [deal]. Because you have fifty lunatics on the left" — I didn't say lunatics . . .' — here Edel Crosse chipped in with 'honourable members' — '"Fifty lunatics on the left who want a second referendum. And you have fifty others who want no deal at all. So you have to make your majority there in the middle of the House."'

After Verhofstadt had taken off his tie, Eva Palatova asked whether he had the sense there was an opening to a solution that was worth exploring. Instead of an answer, she got an anecdote.

VERHOFSTADT [grinning]: After the meeting, Olly
    Robbins came to me: 'Guy, can I become Belgian
    citizen after this whole thing? Because I don't think I
    will return.'
PALATOVA: Olly Robbins?
VERHOFSTADT: He was laughing, a joke.
MCLAUGHLIN: He can't stay in the UK after this. Maybe
    it was an answer.

~

'Why do I say that the situation is serious?' Barnier asked the
BSG a week later in Strasbourg. 'Because we are now at forty
days [from Brexit].' And still, he said, there was none of the
clarity or movement from the British which the 'massively hostile' vote against Theresa May's deal made necessary. Barnier
said that he made this judgement 'with a certain sadness,
because it is certainly not the goal we have worked towards.
You need a negotiating partner to make a deal rather than
arriving at a no-deal. But, unfortunately, the latter is where
the British context may lead us.'

The grumpy, but so often astute, Elmar Brok summarised
that context: 'If I see the amount of opposition against the deal
as last time, they need an enormous amount of people to change
their position. I do not see that. And then [imagine that they
will] get forty votes off Labour, without talking to Labour.
And then have a majority of ten votes. That is the most risky
counting of votes that I have seen in my political life.'

Not for the first time, Barnier had a grievance about the way
he believed the British were spinning things. 'I heard a minister
saying, "We are nearly there with an agreement. We just need to
change one line – one line, in the Irish protocol – and then we
have a deal," he reported, "'and if the Europeans refuse to change

that line, a no-deal is their fault.'" The problem with this way of representing the position, he said, was that 'that line would mean the beginning of the end for the single market'. It was all too easy to say, 'change a line', he complained, but a change in the way the backstop worked could be the beginning of 'an unravelling of the single market along a border nearly 500 kilometres long'.

And he returned to his conviction that the EU side needed to engage more forcefully than ever in public diplomacy: 'We must explain every day, again and again, what the Irish question is about. The Irish question is a matter of peace, which demands that there is no hard border, and it is a matter of the single market, the protection of consumers and businesses against products which are counterfeit, or which don't live up to the standards required of European firms.' He came back to the principles he and other EU leaders believed were at stake: 'It's not a question of dogmatism, it is not a question of being intransigent. It is our responsibility to future generations – the foundations on which everything else stands.'

That evening, on St Valentine's Day, the British government suffered another defeat in the Commons. MPs voted by 303 to 258 – a majority of forty-five – against a motion endorsing the government's negotiating strategy. The motion was meant to be 'neutral', but members of the European Research Group abstained because they argued it took the possibility of a no-deal Brexit off the table. A number of pro-Remain Tory MPs also abstained, and a few Conservatives – one Remainer and four Brexiteers – joined Labour in the 'no' lobby.

~

Towards the end of February 2019, Michel Barnier sat down with Theresa May again. She was accompanied by Stephen Barclay, her third Brexit secretary – he had taken over from

Dominic Raab — and Geoffrey Cox, whose legal advice had played such a decisive role in torpedoing her deal when it was first presented to the Commons. Barnier reported to the BSG that this was his second meeting that week with the two ministers, and he produced an intriguing titbit of intelligence about Cox. 'It was the first time in forty years he came to Brussels,' he told the group, 'and now twice in one week.'

Cox had now moved centre stage as a player in the Brexit drama. May again said that she was not seeking to extend the Article 50 process because, as Barnier reported her views, 'it would solve nothing'. Instead she was looking for a legal change to the backstop, which would allow her to reassure the Commons that it would only ever be a temporary arrangement. And the attorney general was being deployed as the person who might be able to find a way of getting it over the legal threshold. As Barnier's adviser Stéphanie Riso put it, 'What they say is that the pivotal element is Cox. If Cox can say there is a very minimal legal risk, they can bring back some of the Tories. That's their calculus.'

Attorney generals are not usually high-profile ministers. Cox, a former barrister, had come to public attention at the Conservative Party conference the previous autumn; in his booming courtroom tones — and addressing the conference representatives very much as if they were courtroom jury — he electrified his audience with a magnificent piece of seventeenth-century prose; in the *Areopagitica*, John Milton's defence of a free press, the poet described 'a noble and puissant Nation rousing herself like a strong man after sleep, and shaking her invincible locks: Methinks I see her as an Eagle mewing her mighty youth, and kindling her undazl'd eyes at the full midday beam.' It was just the kind of Brexit rhetoric guaranteed to fire up the Tory membership.

Barnier clearly found him a bit of a puzzle, but he did his best to form a bond. 'He's a strange personage *hein*, the attorney general,' he told the BSG. 'He's a legal man but also very political. So I tried to get a personal link with him that could be useful. I think he understands that we are kind' – and here he corrected himself – 'firm and kind and open. So I think it was a good atmosphere. He clearly said that he wants to explore the possibility of further assurance on the temporariness of the backstop. He understood clearly that we are not ready to open anything. But he wants to explore.'

Stéphanie Riso explained though – and this was something everyone in the room already understood – that any such exploration could only take place within narrow limits:

> What they are looking for is that they say, 'We cannot be in any circumstances trapped forever in the backstop.' So we told them that is our absolute red line: there cannot be a unilateral choice to get out of the back stop, if there is not any other agreed solution. Theoretically, imagine we find others, we have three solutions, they could choose. And then we have no problem for them to choose. But what we cannot accept is that there is no other solution. And then he was exploring whether we could entrust a panel to decide whether in good faith we . . . basically the same story as always. But at least he engaged and he understood our limits.

That 'at least' also had its limits, though, because Barnier ended with, 'The risk of a no-deal is massive now, eh? We are preparing ourselves and everyone has to take responsibility.'

So why was May coming back to Brussels over and over again, for something she knew – or should have known by then – the EU would never give to her? Did she really believe that in the end the EU was going to cave in – as her former Brexit secretary David Davis had predicted? Or was she just 'running down the clock', as Jeremy Corbyn liked to put it – pretending to negotiate, while she drove her MPs closer and closer to the Brexit cliff edge of 29 March, in the hope that in the end *they* would give in? Opinion in the Brexit Steering Group was divided.

Verhofstadt knew that Barnier had more meetings with May and her negotiators planned, and warned, 'They are going to use again the meetings next week to say, "There is no need [to vote again], we are busy," because for the moment this whole thing, also their visits last week, was a joke – they have nothing to say.'

BARNIER: Nothing.

VERHOFSTADT: They have seen every one of us.

BARNIER: They use us.

VERHOFSTADT: They use us. To show that they are busy . . . I don't know in your timing [timetable], what is best to do, but you have to take into account they cannot use the new meetings that they organise with you to say, 'We have not a vote', to delay again. Because we have no interest in a delay. They have to vote now. On something.

Roberto Gualtieri wondered why the EU was having to go back over ground which had so often been covered before: 'Even today we are in the stage of explaining things that they, well, how can they *not* know? They are not stupid. We told them plenty of times. Or are they just really playing?'

Barnier answered: 'They are not really playing. First of all, there are many things we don't know. Between [them] it's so complex. I think they are not playing. They want to win time, probably for the reason mentioned by Guy, to try to avoid a vote next week. I think she tries to push everybody as close as possible to the cliff edge, eh? To push, for all already see the cliff edge.'

Barnier leaned forward, at the table, as if he himself was standing on the cliff edge, looking down at the depths, the rocks, the foam and the deep blue sea beneath. It was one of these images you make documentaries for.

Gualtieri, living up to his reputation as the group's dossier cruncher, wondered whether the British side had offered 'a preparation of a possible text'.

'No, not yet. No text,' Barnier replied. 'They didn't write because they need time. They have lots of discussions between themselves. Today I [told] them, "We are ready to listen to you." [They said,] "Yeah, but we need time."'

Verhofstadt laughed – but it wasn't funny.

2 2

THE BARNIERS ARE TAKING
THE STAIRS TODAY

March 2019

It was not until the second week of March that Theresa May put her deal back to the House of Commons. The vote was set for Tuesday 12 March 2019, seventeen days before the end of the two-year period for the United Kingdom's withdrawal from the European Union laid down by Article 50 of the Lisbon Treaty.

I arrived in Strasbourg late in the evening the previous day and took a cab to where Verhofstadt and his team were having their usual Monday evening working dinner.

The traditional French restaurant Pont des Vosges serves presskopf *(brawn),* tartare de boeuf *(steak tartare) and* rognon de veau entier à la moutarde *(veal kidney with mustard), accompanied by a delicious creamy potato purée — I have tasted it myself. The team would normally stay until close to or even past midnight, discussing the week's speeches and other press conference statements over desserts and then a Poire William.*

But that evening Verhofstadt's driver started the car just before ten— and I was allowed to hop in — because the Brexit coordinator had been summoned to the European Parliament. Theresa May had come over to discuss a unilateral declaration she wanted to make on how the backstop clause in the withdrawal agreement should be interpreted. May believed that an extra interpretative declaration might help her to win a majority in the House of Commons at the second attempt.

But in an international negotiation, such a unilateral declaration is a tricky thing. If it's not challenged by the other party, it acquires legal force. It was a similar problem to the one thrown up by her exchange of letters with Tusk and Juncker two months earlier: if May put something in her declaration with which the EU didn't agree, they would have to react – and that would make the declaration look weaker, and might also open new cans of worms.

Michel Barnier explained this a couple of days later to the BSG:

> I remind you, my dear friends, that in an international nego-
> tiation, if one of the parties makes a unilateral declaration and
> it is not contested by the other party, it becomes enforceable.
> So we looked at this unilateral declaration to make sure that
> it did not create any serious problems for us – and, of course,
> for the Irish government, with whom we had extensive nego-
> tiations and conversation during our meeting with Mrs May.

Theresa May had come to Strasbourg to discuss what Juncker and Barnier would find acceptable in her unilateral declaration, and Verhofstadt was to be part of the choreography. But, hauled out of a restaurant, at ten at night, he was annoyed; he didn't believe the declaration served any purpose, but even more importantly, he wasn't going to be directly involved in the discussions with May. He just had to show up at the official meeting with May afterwards, in the Protocol Room. Until that moment, and who knows when it would come, he would have to sit in his office and wait. So Verhofstadt, in the car on the way to the Parliament, sitting next to his driver, with me and Guillaume McLaughlin in the back, wasn't a happy man.

'We call it not a unilateral declaration,' Verhofstadt complained,

'from now on we call it a shit declaration.' Behind him Guillaume laughed, but then Gaetan Vanderhaegen – his always helpful driver – intervened, saying, 'He's recording everything behind you, eh?'

Verhofstadt looked back at me, and as if I hadn't been following him for over two years by now, told me sternly, 'You have to tell me when you're recording sound, eh, Lode? OK, I'll start with . . .'

I needed to escape the tricky moment, and so used the warning sound that was beeping through the car at that moment to retort, 'Start with putting your seatbelt on.' For two years this had been my biggest challenge, to always be ready with a feisty (but not too feisty) reply when challenged by the sharp-tongued former prime minister of my country, Belgium, who did not care for verbal weaklings.

Verhofstadt complied. 'OK, now you can start,' he said. 'Look, this is Strasbourg by night, and there's the Parliament.'

MCLAUGHLIN: Ten o'clock, and we're going back to the fucking European fucking Parliament.

VERHOFSTADT: Yeah but look, Guillaume.

MCLAUGHLIN: Oh, yes, it's on camera, sorry. It's very unfortunate, we have to go back to the Parliament now, to do a little bit of work, you know, you know what I mean, Lode?

It was a tense moment, more than just bantering – the irritation in the car, with the late hour and the probably useless diplomatic exercise ahead, was tangible. I felt as if I was walking a tight-rope. And Verhofstadt wasn't done yet. Because when we were walking from the garage under the Parliament, to his offices, via a maze of corridors and elevators, he started again.

VERHOFSTADT: I'm tired of your camera, I have to admit. Can't you get another one? Not Sony, but a Hitachi or something?

Guillaume took a picture of me and Verhofstadt, discussing, on his phone.

> ME: You're tired of the camera, but not of being filmed?
> VERHOFSTADT: It's the person behind the camera.
> ME: Well thank you very much. I come here late at night, to follow up on Brexit . . .
> VERHOFSTADT: To record everything . . .
> ME: And then you start reproaching me.
> VERHOFSTADT: For posterity.

A phone call from the Irish ambassador saved me, or us.

Guillaume McLaughlin, in the elevator, answered: 'Good evening, Mr Ambassador . . . I have no idea, eh? I have absolutely no idea at this stage. We're expecting now that the meeting with Juncker and her will be coming shortly to an end. But you know it's a very fluid situation, so we don't know exactly when things are going to be [finished].'

A female voice announced the opening of the doors while Guillaume was hanging up. 'They're going to send us some lines,' he told his boss. 'The Irish — they are going to send me some lines that are OK'd by the Taoiseach.' The big EU communication machine was working overtime.

Up in the office on the sixth floor Guillaume received a text message from Georg Riekeles, Barnier's adviser.

> MCLAUGHLIN: Georg quotes some bullshit. 'Patience is sorrow's salve' [a quotation from the eighteenth-century satirist Charles Churchill].
> DELEN: Team Barnier has gone philosophical.
> VERHOFSTADT: They're making progress or not?
> MCLAUGHLIN: That's my question.
> VERHOFSTADT: Otherwise we are going to sleep.

REIJNEN: So Theresa May has been in a meeting with
Juncker [for] an hour and a quarter?

*A minute later Guillaume received a second message from Riekeles and
read it out: "'Progress? Possibly yes." What the fuck is that supposed to
mean? Possibly yes. Could be possibly no then.' Georg wasn't in the room
with May, Barnier and Juncker, he told Guillaume, so his messages were
not really helpful.*

*But the fact that the meeting took so long was not a good sign,
Guillaume assumed. 'Evidently it wasn't tied up in twenty minutes as was
expected. There we are. Everyone thought that there would be very little
debate, that there really was very little to debate — at least very little fundamental. You don't debate fundamentals in twenty minutes. It ought to
have been prepared — and clearly the ground was not properly prepared.'*

*But Verhofstadt had a more savvy, political explanation: 'Perhaps
because they know it is not the final deal.'*

MCLAUGHLIN: Who?
VERHOFSTADT: Everyone [is saying] that it [the big
moment, when the vote in the House of Commons
finally might pass] is for tomorrow, but [they] know
full well that it's not going to work. So they just give
the impression.
MCLAUGHLIN: Fuck Brexit.
VERHOFSTADT: Fuck Brexit.
MCLAUGHLIN: I want to sleep.
REIJNEN: Sources say there will be a newish thing but it
will be a lot like the old thing.
MCLAUGHLIN: The reason it's not going well is because
it can't go well. Because they're asking for something
which [they] can't get.
DELEN: That's the thing — there's either a backstop or

there isn't a backstop. There's no such thing as half a backstop.

Verhofstadt understood where his speechwriter was going. 'This is not a backstop,' he said, in a reference to the surrealist Belgian painter René Magritte's 'Ceci n'est pas une pipe' — this is not a pipe. 'Yeah, that's the only option,' Bram said, 'the Belgian option: ceci n'est pas un backstop.'

Verhofstadt agreed: 'Ceci n'est pas un backstop.'

More news — or rather another attempt at interpretation of what might be happening in the room with May, Juncker and Barnier — came in via a text message from the deputy secretary general of the European Parliament, Markus Winkler, again to Guillaume McLaughlin, Verhofstadt's antenna to the world: 'Wink says: "Everything delayed, they're also consulting with Dublin." I don't know where he's getting his information from, but he might be getting it from his mate Selmayr [Martin Selmayr, the EU Commission's secretary general].'

MCLAUGHLIN: Wink thinks it's choreography.
VERHOFSTADT: Choreography? To do what?
REIJNEN: [To give the impression] that she fights for it. And that we don't give in. And we do in the end. And she won.

It was after midnight when Verhofstadt was finally called to the Protocol Room to shake hands with Theresa May, have a brief chat, and then wave her out. His chief of staff, meanwhile, had received her unilateral political declaration about the backstop on his mobile. He told his boss, 'I've read it twice, and I still don't understand it, so they have done a fantastic job. It basically says, when it ceases to be temporary, i.e. you used it and it becomes permanent, so it's no longer temporary, then the

UK — and nobody wants it to be permanent, because it's supposed to be temporary — then the situation changes and then therefore in those circumstances, things change. That's how I understand it. Now I don't know what that means, but I think that's part of the point.'

Walking away through the wide middle corridor of the European Parliament, Klaus Welle, the secretary general of the Parliament, told Verhofstadt, 'It was a comedy from the beginning to the end.'

Ceci *was not a backstop. But the next day,* ceci *was not a majority either — because May lost again.*

~

The day of the second vote had, however, begun with hope in the Verhofstadt camp. Guillaume McLaughlin told his boss, who was eating his morning yoghurt in his Strasbourg office, 'The DUP yesterday said they would actually read the text [May's unilateral declaration]. Until now they just chucked it straight away. [So] if Cox [the attorney general] moves, then they can move, and then the 118 Tory MPs [who opposed the government in the first vote on the deal] can move as well, yeah? The important thing today is Cox. He has to give his advice. The point is: does he change his advice?'

The previous week Geoffrey Cox had described his task to the House of Commons with a reference to an item of Tudor-era clothing which had gained currency as Westminster slang. 'It is government policy to achieve the necessary change in the backstop which will cause me to review and change my advice,' he declared from the despatch box. 'That is government policy, and that is the discussion we're having. It's come to be called "Cox's codpiece" — what I am concerned to ensure is what's inside the codpiece is in full working order.'

But the contents of the codpiece failed the test. By the early afternoon of 12 March, *The Guardian* was reporting that the attorney general was advising that 'the legal risk remains that . . . the United Kingdom would have, at least while the fundamental circumstances remained the same, no internationally lawful means of exiting [the backstop].' And with that verdict, *The Guardian* suggested, 'the chances of Theresa May's deal getting through the Commons this evening have receded to almost nothing'.

Verhofstadt and his team had watched the first vote over sushi in his back office. The second vote they followed on Guillaume's mobile, in between the seats of a big meeting room where the liberal ALDE group had just met. But the result took time to come through, and Verhofstadt got restless, so they ended up hearing the result in his car, on their way out and into town for dinner.

'The Ayes to the right, 242. The Nos to the left, 391.'

It was a slightly narrower defeat than the first. *The Guardian* reported: 'Of the Conservatives who rejected the deal in January, when May lost by a record majority of 230, 39 switched sides, including the former Brexit secretary David Davis – with many fearing Brexit would be delayed or reversed if they did not support the agreement.' But seventy-five Conservatives had still rebelled. 'I profoundly regret the decision this House has taken tonight,' was Theresa May's immediate reaction. 'I continue to believe that by far the best outcome is that the UK leaves the EU in an orderly fashion, with a deal – and that the deal we have negotiated is the best and indeed the only deal available.'

At a sombre meeting of the Brexit Steering Group earlier in the day, Michel Barnier had assumed – as everyone by then did – that May was going to lose for a second time, and looked ahead to a possible, forthcoming UK request for an extension of the Article 50 timeframe to allow more time for negotiation. But he wasn't happy with the idea of a prolongation. 'There's no need to prolong the negotiation,' he said. 'The negotiation is finished now. It is finished. So, either it's a technical extension to make it possible [for the UK Parliament] to approve a series of texts necessary to complete the process, or it is a tactical extension, if one can imagine a tactic behind it.' For the first time, Barnier showed clear signs of doubt about his fear that Theresa May was playing a tactical game to extract concessions from the European Union.

There were harsh judgements from the members of the Brexit Steering Group that day. Gabi Zimmer took the view that 'In the House of Commons, they're looking only at their political advantage, and they're [British MPs] coming also in the European Parliament, and [to] our groups, and asking us if we would be ready to pull an extension for a referendum or for that and that. And if you're asking them [the MPs] "What is the majority? Why are you coming to us? Why are you not going to your own political colleagues in your own Parliament?" Nothing. And it's such a burden.'

Guy Verhofstadt reminded the group about his earlier meeting with Theresa May's chief of staff, Gavin Barwell.

VERHOFSTADT: He said, 'No, no, we are going to not change our strategy. We are going to deliver in the second vote; because we are going to buy some Labour votes, we are going to buy some hard Brexiteers, Cox will help us with a positive assessment,' all this was said. He gave, I think now more than a month ago, in detail, what was the strategy to build up a majority. And if you make the analysis, everything failed. There were not these Labour votes, there were not these hard Brexiteers, there was not a positive assessment by Cox.

BARNIER: And [the deal was] not [approved by] the DUP.

VERHOFSTADT [laughing]: And not [by] the DUP, maybe
that's the main element. So nothing was delivered.
This strategy failed completely. So the question is now,
and that's my second point, will they change course
and will they do what is in fact not natural for them?
That is to look to a cross-party [agreement].

Verhofstadt also recalled his meeting with Theresa May, just
after the publication of Jeremy Corbyn's letter suggesting terms
that would allow Labour to support her deal:

May immediately goes, 'The letter of Corbyn, that's party
politics.' Ah, OK. Fine, [but] it's all party politics. Sorry.
And so, I think, [we should make] an appeal to them, in
saying, really, in the interest of the Queen, the Crown and
the country, is it not the moment to do that cross-party
cooperation? There is nothing wrong that one Parliament
says to another Parliament, 'Do like we are doing. Working
together. Defending your interests, like we are defending
our interests, so that we can find a way out of this.' I think
that's not a bad message to give. I think we can give that
better than the negotiator, that's typical for a Parliament.

Elections for the European Parliament were now just over two
months down the road, and from a very early stage Verhofstadt
had been expressing concerns that the campaign would become
embroiled in the Brexit saga. Now that possibility seemed very
real. 'And then my second point, on the extension,' he continued. 'I think that we have to put the interest of the EU first.
We are here to defend the interests of the EU. And the interest
of the EU is not that the elections are hijacked by Brexit. Can

you imagine? European elections hijacked by the whole Brexit discussion, because it's still not solved? We are going to talk only about that, and it is going to give only news airplay to all nationalists and populists, who are not here in this room.'

Michel Barnier then delivered himself of a kind of homily. He liked to describe his role as partly *pédagogique*, educational, and today, as he offered 'a personal view, an overview', he was at his most headmasterly. 'Those of us around this table, men and women, we are all politicians,' he said. 'Most of you will be involved in the European elections – indeed we shall all take part in the debates surrounding those elections, the great political debate about the future of the Union which we have been building for so many years.' But the Brexit crisis, Barnier argued, meant that these elections could not be business as usual: 'I think we have been brought to the heart of our duty as politicians – in a way that is not always the case in the work we do. The discussion we have just been having, which is truly important and serious, touches on the heart of our duty as politicians. If the word politics means anything it is what we are engaged in at this moment. And that matters for all the campaigns we are going to lead – that you are going to lead in the coming days.'

Nothing less than the EU's 'honour' was, in Barnier's view, at stake:

Because the attitude of the EU, which will be directed by the Parliament and the Council, should be serious, worthy and dutiful, to pick up on my earlier use of the word, and that attitude is extremely important for each of you, whichever political party you may belong to. I would even say it is a matter of honour – to keep this emotion in mind, at such a moment. That is why it is important to be – Gabi has raised

428

.this point – extremely calm, responsible and, indeed, somewhat respectful of the British people. We must think of those
on the UK side, and of their feelings for their own country.

The pity that Brok had expressed for Theresa May a year earlier – that
most devastating political emotion – was now extended by Barnier to
the whole of the United Kingdom.

~

The next move in the Westminster game brought to mind Guy
Verhofstadt's jibe about the 'medieval' character of the British
Parliament. Citing a 400-year-old parliamentary precedent, the
Speaker, John Bercow, declared that the government could not
continue to ask parliament to vote on the same question within
one session; if Mrs May wanted to bring her deal back to the
Commons for a third time, it would have to be 'not different in
terms of wording, but different in terms of substance', he declared.

The Speaker gave No.10 no advance notice of his ruling, and so
the government was completely blindsided. The solicitor general,
Robert Buckland, declared a 'constitutional crisis'; there was talk
of 'proroguing' – or suspending – Parliament, and then starting
a new parliamentary session immediately. With little more than
a week before the end of the Article 50 process, however, there
was very little room for manoeuvre. Boxed in, Theresa May
finally applied for an extension to the Article 50 period.

Her 'Dear Donald' letter to the Council president, Mr Tusk,
was sent on 20 March, and laid out the reasons she had found
it impossible to get her deal ratified in time for the United
Kingdom to leave the EU by the scheduled deadline nine days
later. The letter was greeted with derision by the members
of the Brexit Steering Group when they gathered around the
meeting table in Guy Verhofstadt's office that same day.

GUALTIERI: I've never seen a letter as incredible as the
  letter of Theresa May. It's a list of failures. 'We would
  have, but . . . Unfortunately . . .'
VERHOFSTADT [putting on a theatrically teary voice]:
  'And then John Bercow . . .'
GUALTIERI: I almost cried when I read it.
VERHOFSTADT: It's a good summary of everything that
  went wrong.
GUALTIERI: It's a description of a . . . failed politician. 'I
  had the intention to do that, but the bad guy prevented
  [it]. I tried to do this, but I could not do [it]. I wanted
  to do that, but . . .' It's incredible.

*Silence descended over the room while everyone checked their watches,
because Barnier was late that day. Then Guillaume McLaughlin's
mobile vibrated and, in an eloquent reflection of the contrast between
the European and the British side in the Brexit negotiations, he
announced: 'The Barniers are walking, they are taking the stairs
today.' He talked about the Barnier team as if they were a family;
their — and this is obviously me writing — most serious uncle, and his
bespectacled children.*

In her letter, Theresa May asked for a delay of the British
departure date until 30 June 2019. But that had not been her
original plan. In fact, David Lidington, her *de facto* deputy, had
come to see Verhofstadt the day before with a very different
idea. 'Lidington yesterday was completely crazy,' Verhofstadt
told the table. 'Because he was in a totally other mindset. He
explained here, "OK, one year, until the end of the year, no
problem." [European] elections? "There will be a little bit of
UKIP, but less than now." I was shocked. He goes out. [And]
what happened is that in the meanwhile there is a meeting of

the British, of the Cabinet, and there was a revolt against that idea. And then she backtracked [to] 30 June.'

Lidington had also been to see Michel Barnier, and the chief negotiator believed the request for a longer Brexit delay was made because all the big jobs in the European Union were due to change hands in the course of the year. He paraphrased what he believed to be Lidington's thinking: 'We ask for a long prolongation because we think that with a new government, a new Council, a new Commission, a new spirit will be created in the EU, a new spirit about Brexit, on the EU side. Clearly, that was the reason he asked for a long prolongation.'

Roberto Gualtieri thought the switch to requesting a shorter extension than originally envisaged was 'a victory of the hard-liners, because 30 June is a recipe for hard Brexit. Is a sure recipe for hard Brexit. For no-deal.'

Barnier agreed: 'We are [now] facing the huge risk of a no-deal, eh? A huge risk. Even by default. Because there is no more time, eh? If I may, the Plan B of Mrs May is no-deal, eh?'

Two days later, the European Council in Brussels gave Theresa May her extension, but they decided it should be even shorter than what she had asked for (30 June), and they imposed conditions. If the House of Commons approved the deal by Brexit day – now just a week away – the extension would run until 22 May, allowing time for the necessary legislation to be brought through Parliament. But if the Commons failed to ratify the deal by that deadline, the extension would end much earlier, on 12 April. In that event, the UK was required to 'indicate a way forward . . . for consideration by the European Council', and it was warned that if it was still a member of the European Union on 23–26 May, it would have to hold elections to the European Parliament.

~

The following day was a Saturday, and hundreds of thousands of people marched in central London calling for another EU referendum; the organisers of the 'Put It To The People' campaign estimated the total at more than a million. Meanwhile a petition calling for Brexit to be stopped and Article 50 to be revoked was well on its way to attracting 6 million signatures, becoming the best-supported proposal in the history of the House of Commons and government's e-petitions website. But, the Department for Exiting the EU responded, 'It remains the government's firm policy not to revoke Article 50. We will honour the outcome of the 2016 referendum and work to deliver an exit which benefits everyone, whether they voted to Leave or to Remain.'

MPs inflicted another defeat on the government on the evening of Monday 25 March, voting to give themselves control over the parliamentary agenda. The amendment was proposed by the backbench MP Sir Oliver Letwin, a former Cabinet minister and Conservative grandee, and it provided for a series of what were described as 'indicative votes', which, it was hoped, would identify a consensus about the kind of deal Parliament would vote for. Thirty Tory MPs voted against the government, including three ministers. Richard Harrington, Alistair Burt and Steve Brine resigned to join the rebels, with Mr Harrington accusing the government of 'playing roulette with the lives and livelihoods' of Britons. The government opposed the amendment and claimed that it 'upends the balance between our democratic institutions and sets a dangerous, unpredictable precedent for the future'.

In Strasbourg, the news from London was welcomed by

Guy Verhofstadt who told the journalists that he saw it as a sign that British politics might at last be heading in the direction he had hoped for:

> I think that we see for the moment a real Brexit revolt by the people in Britain. The march of this weekend with a million people in London. The petition which has reached more or less 5.7 million signatures. And I'm very pleased that yesterday evening the Letwin amendment has been adopted because it's the first time that there was a vote in favour of something [and] it means it is possible now in Britain to work towards a cross-party proposal that could upgrade fundamentally the political declaration that as you know is linked to the withdrawal agreement.

He was less diplomatic at the Brexit Steering Group, riffing on the theme that British politics had become an entertaining spectator sport. 'We are looking more to the television now to the House of Commons than to the matches in the Premier League,' he said. 'If you ask me, "What is the latest, what has done Manchester City?" I cannot tell you. But if you ask me what was the outcome of the vote yesterday evening, I can give you exactly the outcome. So . . .' He smiled, but then added quickly, 'No, let's stop the joke, [because] it's not a joke. Nevertheless, I think, after yesterday we are in what we call uncharted territories for the UK Parliament.' Michel Barnier, sitting next to him, commented that they had already been in uncharted waters for 'a certain time'. And he also smiled.

And then Barnier made the statement I used to end my documentary:

There is a very serious crisis in the United Kingdom, which in my view is not a crisis linked to the text of the Brexit agreement, and even less the Irish backstop. It is a much deeper crisis, an existential one, which touches on the future of the United Kingdom, the economic model it wants to follow, its relationship with the world, its relationship with the European Union. To put matters simply, the view of the European Union, and I think ours here, is that the United Kingdom must now shoulder its responsibilities. And what I sensed around the table at the European Council last Thursday [when the Council had met to discuss the Article 50 extension] during the afternoon and at dinner, is that there is something more than fatigue – something more than fatigue – including among those countries which are closest to the United Kingdom culturally and economically. The time has now come for the United Kingdom to shoulder its responsibilities. We have done our part.

The forthcoming 'indicative votes' at Westminster were on Guy Verhofstadt's mind as he prepared his monthly Strasbourg speech the next morning, with Bram Delen, Guillaume McLaughlin and Edel Crosse in attendance. He imagined himself already in front of the plenary session of Parliament (and in the recording on his Facebook page) and rehearsed his concluding quote: 'Dear colleagues, I recall the words of Sir Winston Churchill. Success, he said, success is the capability to go from one failure to another with no loss of enthusiasm.' Verhofstadt stopped, for a theatrical moment of silence, even if it was only his staff who were listening for the moment, and then continued: 'He [Churchill] could be talking of the House of Commons and Prime Minister May. Because they will have, if Mr Bercow agrees, naturally, no more than sixteen options [to vote on]. Sixteen options for a Brexit. So there is certainly no loss of enthusiasm.'

But in the plenary session, someone else stole what was usually, or very often, Verhofstadt's moment. The European Council president Donald Tusk made a statement that took everyone by surprise, attacking the Parliament for not being supportive enough of the Remainers in Britain.

The Parliament and the whole EU had always abstained from taking sides, out of respect for British sovereignty. But Tusk, it was known, behind closed doors, did not share that opinion, and that day he said it loudly and clearly: 'You cannot betray the 6 million who signed the petition to revoke Article 50, the 1 million people who marched for a People's Vote, or the increasing majority of people who want to remain in the EU. They may feel they are not sufficiently represented by their UK Parliament but they must feel they are represented by you in this chamber, because they are Europeans.'

Tusk's statement was a reminder that, despite the largely united front Europe had maintained, there were still divisions behind the scenes.

The saga of Oliver Letwin's indicative votes turned out to be something of a shaggy dog story. The veteran MP had struggled long and hard to secure Parliament's right to express a positive view on the kind of Brexit it wanted to see, and he had worked closely with like-minded opposition MPs in a way which would surely have been approved by Guy Verhofstadt. But Parliament declined to say anything positive at all. All eight of the proposals eventually laid before the Commons were rejected; as *The Guardian* headlined its story: 'Parliament finally has its say. No. No. No. No. No. No. No. No.' The two options that got the most votes – more than May's deal on the two occasions that it was voted on, but still not enough for a majority – were proposals for a permanent customs union and a second referendum. Five Cabinet ministers voted for a customs union.

Theresa May made her third attempt to win approval for her Brexit agreement with the EU on what should have been Brexit Day itself, Friday 29 March 2019. To deal with the procedural obstacle to another vote, the government argued that there had been a 'significant development' in yet more reassurances the EU had given about the backstop, and that the date for exiting the European Union, because of the extension she'd been given, had changed. To change the political weather, Mrs May promised that she would leave Downing Street if the deal was voted through the House.

That day I installed my camera in Verhofstadt's office doorway in Brussels. He was alone in the premises, tapping and scrolling away on his mobile, sitting on the red sofas in front of his glass-panelled library. All his staffers were out on half a day of team building – cycling in the centuries-old Sonian Forest on the south side of Brussels.

I knew that May's third and final attempt at finding a majority for her deal was planned for the afternoon. But I also knew Verhofstadt was going out for lunch, so I wanted to capture the moment when he left – because I was pretty sure that he wasn't going to come back. After watching the first vote together with his whole team, over sushi, and the second vote, still together with them, but half out and half in his car, this was the vote too far.

And at 12.30 Verhofstadt got up, put on his scarf and a jacket, picked up his leather satchel, and left.

VERHOFSTADT: Bye.

ME: Bye, are you coming back?

VERHOFSTADT: No. They'll keep me informed. I'm not

going to sit here and watch, what did you think? I have
my phone, eh? We'll know pretty quickly now. At
half past two? And if it's no, on Monday they will vote
again.

ME: What do you think the result will be?

VERHOFSTADT: Who knows? You hear the most
contradictory stuff.

In the film his helplessly raised hands said more than all his words. And then he was off.

Two hours later, Theresa May lost again – this time by 344 to 268 votes.

AFTERWORD

Lode Desmet

One day in the foothills of Umbria, after a long day of filming, I was making some last shots of Guy Verhofstadt sitting under the worn wooden beams of his living room. He was perched over his mobile, waiting for dinner. His wife Dominique had laid the table, and Verhofstadt had put out three bottles of wine to taste – three different vintages of the wine he makes. He was impatient to compare them. So when I kept filming, because the light was nice, he suddenly looked up and asked, 'Are you not finished with your brol *[Dutch for rubbish] yet?' And I replied: 'So that we can start tasting your* brol*?' Verhofstadt smirked and went back to his mobile, while Erik Janda, who was also there, to help with the bottling of that year's wine, raised his thumb to me. I had passed another test.*

Filming Verhofstadt, and his team, for over two years, was a nerve-racking experience. Every day I was afraid of doing or saying something wrong – in the minefield of his offices and the Parliament's corridors.

I often just hung around there – I didn't film the whole time – and then the temptation to engage in the conversations they had, from gossip to a new strain in Brexit strategy, would become irresistible. Or someone, and not only Verhofstadt, would challenge me. I couldn't afford to say something superficial, less than smart, to these utterly demanding

438

and highly competitive people. But I also couldn't be too smart in my replies. It wouldn't have done to tell Verhofstadt something his team should have thought of. Or, worse, to raise a topic or an idea that might lead their boss down a path they'd been careful to avoid, either because it was tricky, politically, or would give them extra work — yet another task on their already long list. Verhofstadt can become very enthusiastic very quickly at times (not to say often) and after midnight in a restaurant — over a glass of wine, yes — the last thing they wanted to hear him say was, 'OK. Find me out more about this, can you prepare a tweet?' Guillaume, Bram, Jeroen, Evan, Erik and Edel got enough nightly messages from him as it was.

But all that stress paled in comparison to my main worry — that at some point someone, Verhofstadt and his team, a member of the Brexit Steering Group, or Michel Barnier, who was always so afraid of leaks, was going to tell me, 'Now that's enough. You've been hearing and filming too much.'

The access they gave me was so exceptional, unusual, that I believed it was never going to last.

But it did — and until today I can't say I understand exactly why.

Part of it was my own doing, surely. I tried to melt into the background as much as I could. My camera was small. I didn't have a sound engineer with me, hovering with a microphone over their heads. And when I filmed, I picked one corner and tried to stay there, quietly — invisibly.

I also always wore a T-shirt and jeans, plus boots, while they were all wearing suits and smart leather shoes — so as to look innocuous, not to be taken very seriously.

I made sure that whenever the BSG met, early in the morning, late at night, I was present — sitting out every single meeting they had from the beginning until the end. Often I was the first in the room, to record their arrivals, and the last to leave, after filming their departures. And, over time, I believe this earned me a degree of respect, because I matched their obsessive commitment to Brexit, stubbornly poring over every detail of every resolution, with an equally compulsive devotion to my film. It created a bond.

In the end, though, I think that all my efforts would have been in vain if, deep down, Verhofstadt, his team, the Brexit Steering Group and Barnier hadn't accepted — against their own, better political judgement that normally controls all communication very strictly — that I was there to play my role in the democracy they believe in, just as much as they were there to play theirs.

I wish it could happen more often.

Even if for me — as a documentary maker who is also his own person — Brexit was a tricky place to travel to.

I was born in 1965 and grew up in a village in Flanders that was almost entirely Catholic, and church-going. It had one inhabitant of African descent, a small Congolese man married to a fortress of a white woman — their seven children ranging in colour from dark chocolate to coffee with a lot of milk. Until the age of twelve I never ate anything foreign, not even Chinese or Italian — while thirty years later my own children of eight and eleven have tasted the whole world already; their favourites are sushi and Ethiopian injera.

It's fair to say that my childhood world was a closed-off place, both culturally and geographically.

Twenty kilometres away from where we lived, policemen at a red and white barrier still checked our IDs when we went shopping across the border in France — the fluctuating exchange rate between the Belgian franc and the French franc at times made that cheaper, and worth the trip with six children to be fed and clothed, but at other times not.

Over the course of my single lifetime, all this changed. The world around me opened up and exploded in a kaleidoscope of colours and tastes. Everything that was distant, came nearer.

My first trip to London, at the age of eighteen, to stay with an

English family for two weeks, took me a whole day — by bus, ferry and train. Today I travel from Brussels to London in two hours. I could almost commute there. Some people, I heard, do the same in England.

I'm sometimes nostalgic for those times when trips took as long as the distance they covered, when queues at the border meant going somewhere was a clear privilege, and when I didn't see the same brands of stores in all the shopping streets in Europe.

But I wouldn't go back there — to the narrow-minded and socially rigid prison of my youth.

As a young adult I was so happy to discover there were institutions out there that did not just defend the interests of a small group of people in a small community — the priest, other notables and the richest local businessmen — but strove to govern rationally, for everyone, everywhere, based on universal values.

The very existence of a European Court of Justice and a European Court of Human Rights meant that I was never going to be shackled again — that I had a place where I could go and fight for what I believed in.

A place where my children could be gay, have an abortion if needed — or be allowed to let me go quietly and decently when I develop Alzheimer's disease like my dad did at the age of sixty-seven. He had to choke on a crust of bread and lose consciousness — which he didn't have much left of anyway at that point — before a hospital would give him enough morphine to make his heart stop beating. It was illegal to do that, but they were being practical.

Brexit, to me, when it happened, was the abnegation of all that has improved in my life over the past forty years. Theresa May told me at the 2016 Tory Party conference in Birmingham, 'If you believe you're a citizen of the world, you're a citizen of nowhere.' I shouldn't take that personally, I guess, but all the same, when I was given the chance to film the Brexit negotiation process behind the scenes, I did so with much apprehension.

There were a number of reasons I got on with it. The most basic one was purely practical: a film means an income. I also realised this was a unique opportunity — politicians of a certain level rarely give that kind of access, and the access, moreover, came at a historical moment. I sensed the chance to shine as a filmmaker.

Most of all, though, I was curious. Because it's all well and good to share your life with 7 billion people, the whole world, instead of just your village, but how do you go about doing that?

Here I was going to witness how twenty-seven or twenty-eight countries, over 700 parliamentarians representing a myriad of ideologies, plus a hoard of civil servants, discussed the future of Europe and Britain, argued about what to do, haggled, reached common decisions, and got stuck again — over principles, but also over personal ambitions. They have a weird bipolar mixture of passion for the world and for themselves, these politicians.

This was democracy in action, in an arena at the highest level, but with a much broader relevance. I remain convinced that what I witnessed probably happens in very similar ways on many levels, in town halls everywhere, in regional and national and other parliaments around the world.

I was given a unique chance, and I felt I had a democratic duty to exploit it to the full.

So I decided: so be it if my case study is about Brexit — an issue that wouldn't have become an issue if 600,000 people had voted the other way around, less than 1 per cent of the UK population (but still a lot more people than the group that decided on Britain's next prime minister). What mattered was the process I was going to be able to observe. Although, when the Brexit Steering Group meetings I filmed became really boring, I often thought to myself: look at me here, so-called in the middle of history in the making, but dealing with a topic that is *een scheet in een fles*, as they say in Dutch [a fart in a bottle].

Luckily, for my own sanity, I was most often able to push back such thoughts to the deepest vaults of my mind — helped not in small measure by the fact that making a film involves so much practical, immediate stuff to deal with, like batteries to charge, tickets to book, and video editors to make plans with, to give just a few examples.

It also helped a great deal that I remained in essence a bystander to Brexit. My life and future, unlike that of my English friends, and Ed's, were not going to be defined by it. For me, even if Verhofstadt and Barnier insisted many times that the future of the European Union was at stake, Brexit always mattered less — and this feeling was only enhanced by the fact that, because of the way the negotiations went, the threats they talked about never materialised. The EU always kept the upper hand.

Both Ed and I spent many, many hours poring over the transcriptions I made, trying to figure out the logic in squabbles — negotiating tactics, who got what wrong and whether anyone was going to be able to do better.

But in my mind those questions only scratched the surface of a much more fundamental issue: where do we want to go from here, as human beings, 60 million Brits, and 7 billion others, all on Facebook, all determined to have our say, but also all in need of a structure that can handle and put into practice our democratic demands?

A structure way bigger than a council of village elders.

For me, the core of my film and this book was always this, an observational study in governance. And as I wrote at one point: what I discovered were human beings, groping along together in a misty swamp, or on a narrow path that skirts perilous mountain ridges, trying to survive together the ordeal they have been landed in. In times of a certain predilection for strong all-knowing leaders, it could be my alternative definition of democracy.

~

Edward Stourton

Early in 2016, some six months before the United Kingdom voted to leave the European Union, I stood on the High Street in Newry, the ancient market town that straddles the Clanrye River in Northern Ireland, brandishing a newspaper cutting from the *Irish Times*. The piece, spotted by a sharp-eyed colleague, began with the arresting sentence, 'If anywhere can claim to be ground zero for the Brexit debate, it's Newry', and we planned to use it to introduce an edition of Radio 4's *Analysis* programme on what Brexit could mean for Northern Ireland.

Newry, which lies just north of Northern Ireland's border with the Irish Republic, has become busy, prosperous and peaceful since the end of the Troubles, and it did not feel like the 'ground zero' of anything. The 'Brexit debate', such as it was at this stage, was focused on London and Brussels, as David Cameron tried to renegotiate the United Kingdom's relationship with the EU before firing the starting gun for his referendum campaign. And when the campaign did begin, Northern Ireland's future ranked very low on the agenda; sovereignty, money, immigration and Britain's place in the world were the big campaign themes.

Yet by 2019 the border question had become so grave that both the United Kingdom and the European Union believed it could threaten their very existence. The two sides had always agreed that the border should remain open, but their efforts to secure that outcome had led them to a perilous stalemate; Brussels was determined it should not come at the cost of unravelling the EU's single market, while a solid body of MPs

444

at Westminster was equally determined that it should not lead to the unravelling of the United Kingdom.

In this book we have traced, from the European perspective, the journey from referendum to diplomatic deadlock. One clear conclusion suggested by the evidence is that both sides tried very hard to make Brexit happen – on time. Suggestions that European negotiators cynically dawdled in the hope that the United Kingdom would change its mind, or that British civil servants deliberately frustrated a project which dismayed them, simply cannot be reconciled with the record of prolonged, intense negotiation by officials on both sides. So why did the stalemate arise?

Looking back over the record, it is also clear that both sides were heavily influenced by – and perhaps misled by – the experience of the United Kingdom's forty-plus years as an EU member. Britain's budget rebate, secured by Margaret Thatcher in the 1980s, and its opts-outs, especially the single currency opt-out which was negotiated by her successor, John Major, taught British diplomats and politicians that, for all the talk of the EU being a rigidly rules-based institution, it was open to pragmatic political compromise.

And EU summits like those at Maastricht (which created the Union in 1992) and Nice (which reformed its institutions in 2000) had also established the pattern of late-night negotiation and last-minute deal-making, which British politicians believed, almost as an article of faith, was the inevitable trajectory for all EU negotiations. The EU message that *this* negotiation was not 'business as usual' seems to have fallen on deaf ears. In the early months of 2019, British politicians still routinely referred to the 'negotiations' in Brussels, long after those negotiations were, as far as Brussels itself was concerned, well and truly over.

Europe's negotiators, for their part, inherited an institutional memory of Britain's diplomatic successes as a member state, which were built on its ability to form coalitions within the EU that served its national interests. That goes some way towards explaining Michel Barnier's constant suspicion about what the British side were up to, and his firm belief, frequently expressed, that the British were being more strategic and cleverer than was in fact the case. It is also worth noting that while Europe's negotiators had had a huge amount of experience in administering the accession process, by which countries become members of the Union, they had never before had to manage a country's departure.

So the device they were using, Article 50 of the Lisbon Treaty – which was, ironically, devised by the British diplomat Lord Kerr – was untested. It proved an extremely effective mechanism for keeping the negotiating focus where the European Union wanted it, forcing the United Kingdom to accept that it must settle its debts and obligations before leaving the club. But the 'sequencing' laid out in the article also made the Northern Ireland issue almost impossible to deal with adequately, because a settlement for the Irish border inevitably involved the United Kingdom's future relationship with the European Union. Only at the very end of the process, when strict sequencing gave way and an element of the future relationship became part of the withdrawal agreement, could a deal be done.

A striking feature of European reaction to the failure of that deal at Westminster has been the charge – made again and again by Guy Verhofstadt and his fellow MEPs – that it represents a broader failure of the British political system.

It is almost a truism to say that Brexit has put a grave strain on the two-party system that has been the settled model of

British politics for most of the past century. The referendum itself created a clash between direct and representative democracy, because the result of a popular vote required the House of Commons to pursue a course that a majority of its members thought misguided.

The referendum was in fact, in formal terms, only 'advisory', but its verdict was taken as an instruction, and as negotiations unfolded the difficulty of following this instruction became more and more apparent; Brexit was not something the United Kingdom could carry out on its own, or at least not without doing what many MPs believed would be terribly damaging to their country's economic stability and international reputation. The tension between the 'will of the people' and the traditional process of parliamentary decision-making became more acute as a result.

Moreover, the leaders of the two main parties during this crisis were, even by the standards of British politics, very tribal. Both have dedicated their entire adult lives to the politics of their respective parties. It is difficult to imagine Theresa May or Jeremy Corbyn forming a coalition government in the way that Mrs May's predecessor, David Cameron, did after the general election of 2010, and that Jeremy Corbyn's predecessor but one, Gordon Brown, tried to do after the same election.

Corbyn's rise to the leadership of the Labour Party was not related to Brexit – it took place the year before the referendum – but it came as a shock to the party's largely pro-European establishment; Mr Corbyn's lack of enthusiasm for the EU is a marked contrast to the views of most of those who served in senior positions in the last Labour government. Mrs May acquired the keys to No. 10 as a direct consequence of the Brexit vote, but because she was crowned in the job without having to fight on the hustings for the support of the wider party (Andrea Leadsom having pulled out of the race at the last moment), she was never tested as a campaigner.

The characters of the two leaders proved decisive when, off the back of the third defeat for her deal in the Commons, Theresa May finally issued a formal invitation to Labour for cross-party talks. Each side suspected the other of putting party before country, and although they kept the talks alive for several weeks (from early April to mid-May 2019), they never came even close to the kind of cross-party consensus which a politician like Guy Verhofstadt would have recognised. In a final attempt to get her deal through Parliament, Mrs May added incentives for Labour MPs to support it, including the offer of a referendum – or at least the offer of a vote on a referendum – but that immediately blew up the unity of her own Cabinet, prompting the resignation of Andrea Leadsom, the woman who had come so close to defeating her for the leadership nearly three years earlier.

Mrs May's tactical mistakes have been well-rehearsed in public commentary on the Brexit process. As soon as she triggered the Article 50 process, she handed a negotiating advantage to the European Union, and she took this highly consequential step before securing a consensus about what the government wanted to achieve. Her negotiating red lines, as Michel Barnier's famous slide so effectively demonstrated, made the direction of negotiations inevitable, and by making her commitments so public and so clear, she greatly reduced her own room for manoeuvre. And while she was unambiguous about what she did *not* want for the United Kingdom's future relationship with the European Union, she maintained a studied ambiguity about what she *did* want right up until the publication of her Chequers plan, a full year after the beginning of negotiations with the EU. The disenchantment and sense of betrayal that followed were also almost inevitable. All of these decisions were dictated by what Mrs May believed to be the demands of managing a party which was, if anything, more divided than ever over Europe.

On 10 April 2019, the European Council agreed to a further extension of the Article 50 process. The new deadline for the United Kingdom's departure was set at 31 October, when the new leaders of the EU's institutions were due to take office – so the timetable was again driven by the EU's requirements, not the United Kingdom's. The Council president, Donald Tusk, sent a message to 'our British friends . . . please do not waste time'. Forced to abandon any hope of securing a majority for her deal, Mrs May accepted that the United Kingdom would have to hold elections to the European Parliament.

The result was widely interpreted as a serious threat to that two-party system which Guy Verhofstadt so often derided. The election was won by Nigel Farage's new Brexit Party, with over 31 per cent of the vote; the traditional third party, the Liberal Democrats, came second with 20 per cent; Labour managed only 14 per cent; and the Green Party came in fourth with 12 per cent. The Tories were consigned to an ignominious fifth place, with a vote share of just over 9 per cent. Even more worryingly for the main parties, opinion polls following the elections suggested this was not just a protest vote; many voters said they would repeat their choice in a general election.

On 24 May, the day after British voters went to the polls, but before the election result was declared, Mrs May bowed to the inevitable and announced she would stand down as Conservative leader on 7 June, remaining as prime minister until her successor was chosen.

The positions adopted by the candidates to replace her suggested that the gap between London and Brussels had grown wider than ever; conversations in the two capitals really were now taking place in parallel realities. Because, with only one exception (the maverick international development secretary Rory Stewart, who doggedly continued to champion Mrs May's deal), all those laying claim to the keys of 10 Downing Street proposed an approach to Brexit that had been explicitly rejected by the EU side in the course of the negotiations.

Matt Hancock, the health secretary, wanted a 'time limit to the backstop', as did the home secretary, Sajid Javid (Mr Javid proposed to negotiate this directly with the Irish government, who had always insisted that they would only work through the EU's negotiators). Andrea Leadsom, the former Leader of the Commons, claimed that her determination that the United Kingdom must leave by 31 October would force the EU to think again, and to agree terms for a 'managed exit' – so essentially a negotiated no deal. The former work and pensions secretary Esther McVey was equally determined that the United Kingdom should leave by the October deadline, suggesting that 'If the EU wants to come back to us, the door is open. If they want to have a better deal, that's fine.' Michael Gove, the environment secretary and a prominent Brexiteer, spoke in general terms of 'a better deal', without specifying what form that might take, saying that he would be willing to delay Brexit for a short period if one were in sight, and the former chief whip Mark Harper promised to 'bust a gut' to get a new deal, but was similarly vague about what kind of deal that might be.

The former Brexit secretary Dominic Raab proposed to 'overhaul the backstop based on Malthouse, the only thing that passed the House of Commons' – a reference to the so-called Malthouse Compromise, which had been brokered by the housing minister Kit Malthouse. The plan proposed either replacing the backstop with a longer transition period, which would provide time to negotiate a free trade agreement, while managing the border with 'advanced customs and trade facilitation measures' (an idea the EU had emphatically dismissed as unworkable), or abandoning the backstop altogether and paying the EU Britain's financial settlement in return for a transition period long enough to allow the two sides time to prepare for the UK's departure without a withdrawal agreement – so effectively another version of that 'managed no deal' the EU had ruled out equally emphatically.

The Malthouse Compromise was one constructed to bridge the gap between different factions of the Tory Party – it was never a realistic basis for a compromise between the United Kingdom and the European Union. The way Conservative politicians continued to advocate it was emblematic of the way the party had approached the negotiations with Europe from the first.

The two candidates who came through the first stage of the leadership election – votes by MPs – both claimed they had the diplomatic skills that would allow them to succeed where Mrs May had failed. Jeremy Hunt argued that as an 'entrepreneur' who had 'negotiated the BBC licence fee and a new doctors' contract', he was best placed to renegotiate the withdrawal agreement with Europe. He spoke of 'conversations with European leaders', who had come to 'understand that the backstop will not get through Parliament, they may not have understood that before'. Europe's leaders and negotiators in fact had a very sophisticated understanding of the arithmetic of Westminster politics, although it is true that Theresa May and her team tried repeatedly to persuade them that the prospects for the deal were better than they actually were.

Boris Johnson declared that he wanted an entirely new withdrawal agreement, and proposed, as a way of putting pressure on the European Union, to withhold the £39 billion divorce settlement Mrs May had signed up to. He committed himself to taking the United Kingdom out of the EU on 31 October, 'do or die', and said that arrangements for the Irish border were something 'we'll negotiate during the implementation period'. The implementation – or transition – period is of course part of the existing withdrawal agreement, and Mr Johnson was later forced to concede that to secure such a period the United Kingdom would need 'some kind of agreement' with the EU.

Jeremy Hunt and Boris Johnson took their case to the Conservative Party's 160,000 members in the country. Towards the end of the campaign, both contenders hardened their Brexit stance, declaring the Irish backstop 'dead' and stating that it must come out of the withdrawal agreement altogether. Johnson, as ever, flagged this red line in extravagant style, saying 'no to time limits or unilateral escape hatches or these kind of elaborate devices, glosses, codicils and so on, which you could apply to the backstop'. He described the backstop as 'an instrument of our own incarceration in the single market and customs union'.

Just after midday on 23 July 2019, the Conservative Party announced that Boris Johnson had won the leadership by a significant margin – 92,153 votes to 46,656. The following day, Michel Barnier and the Brexit Steering Group met to agree a reaction. Afterwards, Guy Verhofstadt condemned Mr Johnson's campaign statements about the possibility of a no-deal Brexit as 'irresponsible'; the BSG statement repeated that the withdrawal agreement was non-negotiable and must include 'the backstop that, in all circumstances, ensures no hardening of the border on the island of Ireland, safeguards the Good Friday Agreement and protects the integrity of the single market'. The group also reminded the new Conservative leader that any withdrawal agreement would 'require the European Parliament's consent'.

That afternoon, Boris Johnson accepted the Queen's invitation to form a government, and, on his return to Downing Street from the palace, he condemned those who questioned his ability to deal with Brexit as 'doubters, doomsters, gloomsters'. Looking ahead to the 31 October deadline, he insisted that, 'in ninety-nine days, we will have cracked it', and added, 'Never mind the backstop, the buck stops here.'

Perhaps the oddest of the many ironies of the Brexit process was exposed in a YouGov poll of Conservative members published in June 2019. Asked whether they would rather avert Brexit if it would lead to Scotland or Northern Ireland leaving the United Kingdom, 63 per cent and 59 per cent said they would be willing to pay for Brexit with the breakup of the union. So Northern Ireland's future, the issue which more than any other led to the defeat of Mrs May's deal in the Commons, had become secondary to Brexit in the minds of most Brexit-supporting Conservatives.

I was back in Newry in the spring of 2019 – to present an edition of *The World at One*. We drove out to Carlingford Lough, the sleeve of silver water that stretches out towards the Irish Sea, to record a report, stopping by the memorial at Warrenpoint; eighteen soldiers were killed there in an IRA ambush in 1979, making it the deadliest single attack on the British Army during the Troubles. At the mouth of the lough we took the ferry from Greencastle to Greenore – crossing the border between Northern Ireland and the Republic somewhere in the choppy waters where the lough meets the Irish Sea, and then drove back to Newry along the lough shore on the Irish Republic side.

The border crossing point was marked by graffiti promising the return of the IRA, and, as we recorded for our report, the driver of a passing van leant out and shouted, 'Fuck Brexit.' Now this really did feel like 'ground zero' in the Brexit debate.

ACKNOWLEDGEMENTS

Edward Stourton

The backbone of this book was provided by Lode's meticulously transcribed and catalogued archive of recordings; it yielded ever richer treasures as the writing progressed.

To build a narrative around the material, we have drawn, for the most part, on published sources. Sarah Harrison's research was invaluable; her work was fast, accurate and comprehensive, and we could not have asked for better support.

Numerous books provided helpful background reading: *Fall Out – a Year of Political Mayhem* (William Collins), the second of Tim Shipman's authoritative Brexit books; *A Short History of Brexit – From Brentry to Backstop* (Pelican), by the Oxford economic historian Kevin O'Rourke; *Understanding the European Union – A Concise Introduction* (Palgrave), John McCormick's widely used guide; *The Passage to Europe* (Yale University Press), Luuk Van Middelaar's celebrated history of the European Union; and Guy Verhofstadt's own critical analysis of the EU, *De Ziekte van Europa* (De Bezige Bij).

The book was a complex project, involving authors in two capitals, a couple of film companies and, of course, a very tight schedule. Our agent at Curtis Brown, Gordon Wise, juggled the sometimes competing interests with great skill and good humour. Ian Marshall, our publisher at Simon & Schuster, understood what we were trying to achieve from the outset; he has been unfailingly supportive throughout, and kept a steady nerve in the face of that frighteningly fast production timetable. We are also grateful to Victoria Godden and Melissa Bond for their scrupulous copy-editing and to Ben Jennings and Matthew Johnson for the striking cover.

Our thanks go to Andrew McKerlie, head of production at Zinc Media, who negotiated the rights to the source material.

My wife Fiona Stourton acts as a kind of backstop editor on all my books – she was the executive producer on Lode's film, so her judgement was even more helpful than usual.

Finally, I would like to thank my co-author, Lode Desmet, for making it such fun.

~

Lode Desmet

I was only able to collect this material because Guy Verhofstadt stood by the promise he made on day one: to give me unfettered access. Whenever he wavered, and sometimes he did, or when his team got tired of my hanging around and prying, it was Bram Delen who climbed the fences and defended the project.

But Guillaume McLaughlin, Jeroen Reijnen, Edel Crosse, Eva Palatova, Erik Janda, Markus Winkler, François Javelle, Nick Petre, Nick Lane, Elmar Brok, Roberto Gualtieri, Gabi Zimmer, Danuta Hübner, Philippe Lamberts, Michel Barnier and Georg Riekeles all deserve appreciation and respect, for boldly allowing me to go where no one behind the scenes of European politics has gone before.

Kris Hoflack and Erwin Provoost should also be thanked for setting the project in motion.

Acknowledgements

I would like to thank Edward Stourton, because what do you do when, after two years of filming behind the scenes of the Brexit negotiations, you sit on a chest full of transcripts detailing the inner workings of high diplomacy? You drag it to Ed Stourton's door, knock, kindly ask whether he can help you map out the crime scene, and write the tale together, like the Brothers Grimm of Brexit.

To my wife Albena Shkodrova, I wish to say: thank you for being my best friend. Your praise and your critical remarks helped me in equal measure to conquer this mountain.

My children Elena-Mie and Artuur every night helped me to forget Brexit, and that was very important as well. I'm only sorry that Atuur's favourite (scatological) scene made neither the film nor the book.